Optimizing UNIX
for Performance

Optimizing UNIX for Performance

Amir H. Majidimehr

For book and bookstore information

http://www.prenhall.com

Prentice Hall PTR
Upper Saddle River, NJ 07458

Library of Congress Cataloging-in-Publication Data

```
Majidimehr, Amir H.
    Optimizing UNIX for performance / Amir H. Majidimehr.
      p.  cm.
    Includes bibliographical references and index.
    ISBN 0-13-111551-0
    1. Operating systems (Computers). 2. UNIX (Computer file).
    I. Title.
    QA76.76.063M344  1995
    005.4'3—dc20                                    95-40312
                                                       CIP
```

Editorial/production supervision: *BooksCraft, Inc., Indianapolis, IN*
Cover design director: *Jerry Votta*
Cover design: *Design Source*
Acquisitions editor: *Mike Meehan*
Manufacturing manager: *Alexis R. Heydt*

© 1996 by Prentice Hall PTR
Prentice-Hall, Inc.
A Simon & Schuster Company
Upper Saddle River, NJ 07458

The publisher offers discounts on this book when ordered in bulk quantities.
For more information, contact:

    Corporate Sales Department
    Prentice Hall PTR
    One Lake Street
    Upper Saddle River, NJ 07458
    Phone: 800-382-3419   FAX: 201-236-7141
    E-mail: corpsales@prenhall.com.

Printed in the United States of America

10 9 8 7 6 5 4 3 2 1

ISBN: 0-13-111551-0

Prentice-Hall International (UK) Limited, *London*
Prentice-Hall of Australia Pty. Limited, *Sydney*
Prentice-Hall Canada Inc., *Toronto*
Prentice-Hall Hispanoamericana, S.A., *Mexico*
Prentice-Hall of India Private Limited, *New Delhi*
Prentice-Hall of Japan, Inc., *Tokyo*
Simon & Schuster Asia Pte. Ltd., *Singapore*
Editora Prentice-Hall do Brasil, Ltda., *Rio de Janeiro*

Table of Contents

To my wife, Lynn, and our children, David, Ryan, and Kamran

Introduction

Optimizing the performance of computer systems has always been an art relegated to a few individuals who happen to have the "right skills." UNIX systems have not escaped this syndrome. It is rare to find anyone who knows how to instrument the system, let alone tune it. This is by no means a fault of the general user community. The problem turns out to be rather complex, requiring good knowledge of computer architecture, UNIX design, and performance-monitoring tools.

Due to a lack of standards in the system performance management area, vendors often take liberties with substituting, enhancing, or altogether removing system-monitoring tools. Even when a familiar command does exist on a system, it may have subtle differences that can easily mislead you. One such example is the unit for some of the fields. In a typical manual page, you see frequent references to units of "blocks" or "pages." Yet there rarely is an indication of how big these things are. As you will see later in this book, a page can be anywhere from 512 bytes to 8 kilobytes, making it very hard to interpret such data correctly.

Beyond the tools, there are also a number of limitations in the UNIX architecture itself. Without knowing about these deficiencies, you could easily chase the wrong problem. A classic example is when people blame the hardware instead of UNIX and vice versa. In the end, we hope that you do not misinterpret our criticisms of one of the best operating systems around. Perhaps our only excuse for pointing out these deficiencies stems from a wise saying that states:

If you cannot criticize something, you do not understand it well enough!

1

I.1 General Style

In this book, we take a *system approach* to performance optimization by covering every-thing from user applications all the way down to the hardware. At the same time, we try not to assume that you have a strong background in either hardware architecture or UNIX internals or, for that matter, extensive experience with UNIX itself. Just in case you have dabbled seriously in any of these areas, we explain each topic in a separate chapter, mak-ing it easy to skip over them.

You will probably also notice that we have dedicated considerably more space to analysis than to simple cookbook procedures. While cookbook procedures do have their place (and we have included a fair number in this text), they do not have any use unless you know when to use them. Armed with an in-depth knowledge of what is going on inside your sys-tem, you will be better able to identify the true nature of performance bottlenecks in your system. As a bonus, you will be in a position to solve a wider set of problems than what is covered here.

In a departure from other texts on this topic, we have taken a very pragmatic view by emphasizing modern techniques for tuning UNIX systems. Had this book been written in the early 1980s, we would have focused heavily on how to modify the operating system parameters to either squeeze the last byte out of it or save a few CPU cycles. The advice would have been sound in that time frame due to the fact that the average machine was well under 5 MIPS and had around 8 megabytes of memory. Any amount of savings would have seemed significant. Current CPUs are orders of magnitude faster with tens or even hundreds of megabytes of memory. The result is that the benefits of many of these optimi-zation techniques are simply "lost in the noise." So, rather than relying on obsolete advice, we focus on higher-level approaches to system optimization. These tacks include optimi-zation of the system hardware, general techniques for resource utilization, and more opti-mal usage of the system and network.

Alas, old habits die hard, and users have a fondness for "poking" values into their system. For this reason, we also cover those parameters and tuning methods that have at least some noticeable impact on the system performance. But we would like to recommend again that you stay away from them if for no other reason than portability. Higher-level techniques work across different UNIX implementations and, for that matter, other operat-ing systems. With their larger impact on system throughput and response time, they are also more rewarding to implement.

I.2 Organization

We start this book by covering the basic principles behind performance monitoring and optimization. They are helpful in forming a strategy for attacking performance problems and steering you clear of potential pitfalls. Although the information presented in this chapter may seem simple in nature, its impact is significant.

Chapter 2 is aimed at giving you a pragmatic overview of the hardware architecture. We are not too worried about the theoretical aspects of this field about which there are many excellent texts. Instead, we cover the major components in a high-performance computer system and show how design decisions made by the system and chip vendors have an impact on the performance of your system. The information should help you determine when a performance problem is a result of the inherent design of the hardware and not UNIX.

Chapter 3 is dedicated to an architectural overview of modern implementations of UNIX *as it relates to system performance*. Our focus is not to teach you the entire operating system (which would occupy a book larger than this one) but to point out those aspects that have an impact on monitoring and optimization of the system. As a result, the topics are presented in fairly terse form, which may be hard to understand. We have made sure, however, that all the necessary facts are highlighted so that complete understanding of the material is not necessary.

Armed with basic knowledge of the hardware and UNIX, you are now ready to start instrumenting your system and to look for performance bottlenecks. We have opted to divide the material into two chapters each dedicated to the traditional implementations of UNIX today, namely System V and BSD. Alas, vendors routinely mix and match BSD and System V tools, so it may be necessary to read both chapters. To make it easier, we have listed the tools available in most common versions of UNIX in Table I.1 along with the relevant chapter in this book.

Because there are still large number of users connected to UNIX systems through serial ports and ASCII terminals, we have dedicated Chapter 6 to UNIX terminal support.

Table I.1 Monitoring Tools Available in Each Version of UNIX

Name	Core OS	BSD Tools (Chapter 4)					System V Tools (Chapter 5)	
		vmstat	iostat	ps	pstat	uptime	sar	ps
SunOS 4.1	BSD	√	√	√	√	√		
Sun Solaris	SVR4	√	√			√	√	√
HP-UX	Sys V	√	√			√		√
SGI IRIX	Sys V					√	√	√
IBM AIX	BSD	√	√	√	√			
DEC ULTRIX	BSD	√	√	√	√	√		
DEC UNIX	OSF/1	√	√	√	√	√		√a
SCO ODT	Sys V	√					√	√
Novell UnixWare	SVR4.2			√	√b	√	√	√
Pyramid DC/OSX	SVR4.2			√	√	√	√	

a. The OSF/1 ps command accepts both System V and BSD options.

b. Incomplete implementation. Does not show load average.

Because the same code deals with modems and sometimes networking, the information should also be useful to those who use workstations and other UNIX systems. Also included is the coverage of tools that let you instrument the terminal subsystem.

Once you find the system bottlenecks by using the monitoring tools, it is time to eliminate or reduce their impact on system performance. Chapter 7 covers the best techniques for dealing with typical shortages such as memory, disk bandwidth, and CPU resources. Again, we cover both high-level techniques for reconfiguration of the system and detailed fine-tuning of each subsystem.

Because it is rare to find UNIX systems that run stand-alone these days, Chapter 8 focuses on basic UNIX networking. This includes the complete suite of TCP/IP along with coverage of various networks and topologies. Because the networking implementation in UNIX is very monolithic with very little room for fine-tuning, we have focused the material on best ways to configure the network and system to avoid performance problems at the start.

Given the widespread usage of NFS, we have dedicated Chapter 9 to its operation and optimization techniques. We point out some major deficiencies in the NFS design and ways to side step them.

The X window system is covered in Chapter 10 starting with an in-depth overview of its architecture. True to our form, we point out its deficiencies as implemented on top of UNIX. Even though X is not generally tunable, we have nevertheless uncovered a few techniques for optimizing it.

Computer marketing is full of buzz words describing the speeds and feeds of various components of the system. Invariably, these terms are derived from some set of benchmarks. To prepare you for your next computer purchase, Chapter 11 covers the most popular industry standard benchmarks. We not only describe what the benchmarks purport to measure but also what the results actually reflect. Because benchmarks are based on pieces of code that are bound to be different than your application, we also attempt to corollate the results to real-life applications.

Chapter 12 is dedicated to the ins and outs of selecting systems and hardware components for best performance. We cover a broad range of systems from PCs to high-end RISC systems. With the information in this chapter, you should be able to select the best hardware for your application so that performance problems do not surface later.

Chapter 13, which covers optimization of the UNIX programs, may seem out of place in such a text. However, these techniques give you an additional and powerful tool in getting the most performance out of your system and applications. We cover the standard UNIX profiling and timing tools, which help you identify what parts of an application can benefit from optimization. This discussion is followed by some common techniques for speeding up typical code sequences and algorithms. The coverage remains brief in this area because of the necessity of keeping from filling the entire text. References are provided, however, for those interested in more detailed information.

I.3 Terminology

Throughout this book, we use the System V and SysV designations in reference to all variants of System V from Release 3.2 to 4.X. Even though these releases share many components, we make sure to point out if a feature is specific to a particular version of System V. A case in point is System V Release 4.X (commonly abbreviated to SVR4), which is quite a departure from older releases of System V. Unless we state otherwise, the SVR4 designation applies only to versions of UNIX that are "pure" implementations of System V Release 4.X.

As of this writing, Sun (with Solaris), SONY, TANDEM, NEC, Pyramid Technology, and Novell (with UnixWare) are some of the vendors that fall in this category.[1] Others, such as SGI, have operating systems that are compatible with SVR4 from a user point of view, but their kernel does not necessarily match the SVR4 sources. Although there is nothing wrong with their approach, the algorithms in these operating systems may not match those used in SVR4.

Being fairly picky about preciseness of units, we use the designation Kbytes, Mbytes, Gbytes, and Tbytes to refer to kilobytes, megabytes, gigabytes, and terabytes, respectively. Likewise, Kbits, Mbits, Gbits, and Tbits refer to kilobits, megabits, gigabits, and terabits. We stay away from terms such as MB and Mb, which are easily confused with each other.

---

1. We are not sure that Sun Solaris is really a pure implementation of SVR4, given the significant work that Sun has done on it.

CHAPTER 1

Performance Fundamentals

Before getting into very specific techniques for optimizing systems, it is important to understanding some of the common-sense principles involved in this field. Despite their generality, these guidelines can be considerably more relevant to your system optimization efforts than many specific techniques. Some severely limit your options in certain areas, whereas others help you avoid costly mistakes and remind you when you are doing too much work for too little reward. As such, it is very important to have a good grasp of these concepts before moving on to the later chapters.

1.1 Why a System Runs Slowly

A system performs poorly because one or more of its resources are being taxed too heavily. When resources cannot keep up with the demand, user applications are forced to wait for them, resulting in longer execution time and a slower system. Finding these bottlenecks is the most important step in performance optimization. Without this information, you are really shooting in the dark if you try to tune your system.

Once you find the (one or more) system bottlenecks, you need to be able to identify *why* the shortages have occurred. As you will see in later chapters, UNIX-monitoring tools are fairly adequate in helping you figure out which resource is being taxed too heavily. But they give you little information as to the cause of overutilization. For example, you can easily determine that the system is disk-bound (i.e., is spending most of its time waiting for disk), but no tool shows you which program is causing the disk traffic! The only solution is to examine how the system is being used and to try to guess what could be happening.

The situation is not as grim as it seems. After some experimentation, you should be able to develop a good "feel" for which user programs or services are responsible for the various types of shortages.

If you cannot identify and eliminate the source of a shortage (the preferred option), you can always take the direct approach of simply adding more hardware to the system until the problem goes away. For example, if you have a memory shortage, adding more memory always helps, even though it physically costs more than lowering the memory usage of the system.

Before rushing to remove system bottlenecks, however, it is important to understand certain theoretical and practical limitations on how fast the system would perform as a result of any optimization. The most restrictive factor is Amdahl's Law, which puts a boundary on the maximum speed-up that can be achieved from any optimization.

1.2 Amdahl's Law

In the 1970s a special class of supercomputers pioneered by CRAY Research began to challenge the role of mainframes in the scientific computing arena. These systems sported special-purpose "vector" hardware along with very fast memories, which dramatically improved the arithmetic computational speed of the CPU. The approach proved very successful because it was easier to speed up just one part of the CPU rather than its entire core. But all was not well. The technique had some major failings that were hard to spot. To see why, let's look at an example.

Assume that you have a program that takes 10 hours to run. Let us further assume that the program spends 2 hours doing arithmetic computations. Now, if you run this program on a machine that has an *infinitely fast arithmetic unit*, the execution time will be reduced to 8 hours. This represents a 20% reduction in execution time, which is far less than what we might intuitively expect from a machine with infinitely fast arithmetic hardware. Because real machines are never infinitely fast, your actual improvement will even be lower than 20%. Now assume that the arithmetic portion was taking 9 hours to execute. This time around, if the arithmetic unit were made infinitely fast, the execution time would drop to 1 hour for a 1000% improvement!

As the example shows, the maximum speed-up that you get for optimizing a portion of a program (or system) is highly dependent on what percentage of the time is spent in that part. Put another way,

> there is a fundamental limit as to how much you can speed up something if you optimize only one portion of it.

This principle has become known as Amdahl's Law after Gene Amdahl (founder of the traditional mainframe maker, Amdahl Corporation), who made this important observation.

Even though Amdahl's Law usually works against you, it does have some positive attributes. By using it in reverse, you can determine when you have reached *the point of diminishing returns*. This is the point after which additional optimization is not going to generate noticeable results. For example, if a program is using 10% of the CPU resources and you reduce its CPU usage by a factor of 2, it speeds up only by 5%—hardly worth the effort.

1.3 Estimating Percentage Speed-Up

In determining whether some optimization is worth the effort, it is useful to be able to estimate how much faster the system would run after the optimization is applied. This is especially important when the improvement comes from hardware upgrades that can cost a considerable amount of money. Fortunately, thanks to Amdahl's Law, you can fairly accurately determine how much improvement can be expected. The key is to look at how much idle time the CPU has (see Chapters 4 and 5 on how to determine this).

> *Because the CPU is the component that ultimately executes user programs, its utilization directly determines how much additional work the system can perform.*

As an example, a busy system that has 50% CPU idle time can potentially run twice as fast. This would be the case if you eliminated all the bottlenecks that were slowing down the CPU. On the other hand, if the idle time is 10%, eliminating other bottlenecks in the system can only result in a maximum of 10% improvement in system throughput. This is the reason behind our advice in later chapters to pay attention to the CPU idle time before looking at any other system shortages.

1.4 The Bubble Effect

In tuning systems, it always seems that as soon as you solve one problem, another one takes its place. The process is similar to pushing air bubbles around under a large surface. The "bubbles" seem to simply move around instead of completely disappearing. Getting rid of one always results in another forming elsewhere. To see how this factor comes into play in computer performance, let's look at another example.

Assume that you have a program that spends 90% of its time in one routine, with the next routine using only 8% and the remaining 2% spread among the rest of the routines in the program. Amdahl's Law forces you to start by optimizing the first routine because it is using the majority of time. There would be no reason to worry about the second routine because even if you eliminate it, the execution time would be reduced by only 8%. Now, if by some means you eliminate the amount of time the first routine uses, the second routine will suddenly account for 80% of the CPU time. This time around, the time spent in the second routine is very significant because eliminating it now can result in a fivefold improvement in CPU time! The CPU usage of the second routine was simply not significant in the presence of the time taken by the first routine. Now you can see why we call this the *Bubble Effect*. Eliminating one bottleneck causes another one to pop up.

A common manifestation of the Bubble Effect is a system that constantly moves from being CPU-bound to I/O-bound and vice versa. When you remove the CPU bottleneck, you wind up waiting for slow I/O devices. As soon as you eliminate the I/O bottleneck, the CPU does not have to wait for anything and becomes the problem. And the process continues forever.

Keep in mind that, in most cases, the initial bubbles are easiest to "pop." The job gets progressively more difficult as you move on to the remaining bottlenecks. Eventually, you have to give up because the amount of work involved is not worth the payoff (you have reached the point of diminishing returns). This is actually a nice side effect because your initial optimizations are the most fruitful and, hence, the most satisfying.

1.5 Response Time Versus Throughput

In looking at improving the system performance, you can opt to improve either the system throughput, the user response time, or both. *Throughput* is the amount of work the system is performing as a whole. *Response time,* on the other hand, is a measure of how long it takes to finish some task.

Although these terms are often used interchangeably, there is a big difference between them. If you have 100 users, increasing the throughput means that all 100 users *collectively* get more work done. It does not indicate that every one of these users experienced faster response. As a matter of fact, the response time could have slowed for some but sped up for others.

Take the situation in which there is only one disk-bound job running on the system and the CPU is constantly idling while it waits for its I/O requests to finish. Now, if you start another job, which only needs the CPU to run, it gets all the CPU cycles it needs without significantly impacting the performance of the I/O-bound process. By adding the second process, you have increased the throughput of the system because it is finishing two jobs at once. In order to improve the response time in the same situation, you would have to speed up the disk subsystem so that the first job finishes faster.

Even though it is usually easier to increase the system throughput, users really like to have faster response time. They do not care about system productivity and, hence, throughput. To improve response time, you need to remove or reduce the impact of bottlenecks faced by user applications. As you have probably guessed, improving response time has the added benefit of increasing throughput because more work can get accomplished in the same amount of time.

1.6 Psychology of the User Response Time

In looking at the response time of a system, you need to look at two parameters: the average response time and the deviations from the average. It turns out that the latter can actually be more important than the former. Specifically,

> *what makes users unhappy the most, is **variations** in response time.*

As an extreme example, it would be preferable to have a program always run for 5 seconds than having it run for 2 seconds most of a time and 10 seconds once in a while.

Of course, once you eliminate the variations, then the only way to achieve additional improvements is through reduction of the response time itself. Even here you must be careful because

> *users cannot usually detect response time improvements of less than 20%.*

Differences smaller than 20% are simply not perceptible by the average user. If the response time shrinks by 30 to 40%, users start to notice the improvement, and the system appears to be more responsive. It is not clear, however, that users would want to *pay* for such improvements unless you achieve a much higher level (e.g., 100%).

Note that these guidelines are most applicable to interactive environments where response time to most commands is a few seconds or less. In cases where a program takes hours to run, any amount of reduction in runtime is sure to be appreciated by the users, especially if the program is used time and time again.

1.7 The Heisenberg Uncertainty Principle

This is a principle coined after the physicist who originally discovered it and states that you distort an event by the mere fact of trying to look at it. The idea is that the monitoring tools used to instrument the system activity can increase the system load leading to distorted data. For example, if you try to look at the memory usage of a system by running a tool that itself uses 5 Mbytes of memory to run, the memory usage of the system displayed by the tool is exaggerated by the same amount. The same is true of any other system resources the tool may use.

The Heisenberg principle is usually cited in performance optimization texts as an important consideration. But we are not sure it deserves the attention it is getting. Witness the BSD's `vmstat` manual page that warns it can consume up to 10% of the CPU cycles. In reality, you will be hard pressed to measure the CPU usage of `vmstat` even on the slowest

UNIX machine you are likely to use, let alone the 100+ MIPS machines that are common-place today. The speed and capabilities of modern systems have made the impact of these tools on the system almost negligible. Advice given in the era of 4-MIPS CPUs with 4 Mbytes of memory is just not valid anymore.

The only exception that we make are the graphical monitoring tools that use a significant amount of memory to run. Care should be taken in using these programs when monitoring system memory usage. Fortunately, they can safely be used to monitor other system activities because their impact on CPU and I/O resources is usually minimal.

1.8 Smoothed Versus Peak Statistics

The key to tuning a system is correct instrumentation. As you will see in later chapters, a number of tools let you identify the usage of various system resources. The tools typically do not show instantaneous statistics but rather data averaged over a user-specified period. This averaging function is actually quite useful and necessary as it smooths out short-term peaks, making it easier to see longer-term trends. To see why this function is useful, let's look at an example.

Suppose that you have a tool that shows the CPU usage. If the tool managed to sample the CPU usage at infinitely small intervals, it would either find the CPU doing something or not. After all, the CPU is either busy or idle. A sample output expressed in percentage busy may look like:

> 100, 100, 0, 0, 100, 100, 0, 0

This kind of output is not very useful because it is very hard to draw any conclusion from it. What you really like to know is how busy the CPU was over a certain period. If you average the eight samples and express them as one number, you get 50%. This tells you that the CPU is only half utilized over this interval and can handle twice as much work. Furthermore, figures like 50, 54, and 60 tell you that the load is increasing, unlike equivalent instantaneous samples alternating between 0 and 100.

Another advantage of using an averaging method is that it reduces the impact of the Heisenberg principle. For example, if a monitoring tool used 0.5 seconds of CPU time to do its work, running it once a second results in a huge amount of error in the reported CPU usage (50%). But if you run the tool every 5 seconds, the error rate drops to an insignificant 10%.

Of course, the scheme can backfire if pushed too far. If you average the CPU usage over 1 hour, you will not see the 5 or 10 minutes that the CPU may have been "maxed out" at 100%. Because users are very sensitive to prolonged resource shortages, ignoring a 10-minute peak is not wise. For this reason we recommend that you average the data for at least 2 to 5 seconds for fast devices such as the CPU and 30 to 60 seconds for much slower devices such as disk drives. These periods are long enough to avoid the previously mentioned problems without ignoring any significant peaks.

1.9 Caches and the Proximity Principle

No discussion of computer performance goes far without including caches. Caches are used to speed access to slow devices. By keeping the most frequently used data in a smaller but much faster device (i.e., the cache), overall access time of a device is reduced.

Caches are rated by how effective they are in holding the required data. A typical figure of merit is the *hit rate* (or ratio), which indicates what percentage of time (on the average) the required data was found in the cache. Hit rates of 95% or better are not unusual in well-designed caches.

Another common specification is the *miss rate*. This is the opposite of the hit rate and specifies how often (on the average) the data were not found in the cache. In our example, the miss rate would be 5%.

Caches are so effective that they are used in just about every subsystem in a modern computer system. They are even used to speed access to other slower caches (in the so-called hierarchial or multilevel caches). For example, database programs use caches to reduce the number of disk requests they have to make. This would be on top of similar caches that UNIX uses to lower the number of disk I/Os.

As a general rule, the slower the device, the more layers of caching that you see on top of it. For example, it is not unusual for a single byte on disk to travel across five or more caches before it gets used by an application!

With hierarchial caches, the question arises as to how to select the best size caches at each level. For example, are you better off with a larger primary CPU cache or should you get a bigger secondary cache? Should you reduce the number of disk I/Os using a disk controller with on-board cache memory or by increasing the size of the UNIX disk I/O cache? The answer lies in what we call the proximity principle. The basic idea is that

> *the closer a cache is to where it is needed, the higher its benefits.*

For example, 1 Mbyte of memory set aside as a cache inside an application to reduce disk traffic is much more effective than enlarging the UNIX disk cache by the same amount, even though they both perform the same function. The reason is that the cached data inside the application are immediately available to it. But the UNIX cache requires that the data first be copied to the user program using a *read system call* (see Chapter 3), which uses many CPU cycles. More important, the application has better knowledge of which disk blocks are likely to be needed again. As a result, the application cache contains more useful data (i.e., has a higher hit rate), increasing its chance of being reused later.

Another important consideration in the use of multilevel caches is the *skimming effect*. A cache speeds an operation because it manages to hold data that can be reused quickly without the need to go to the lower-level device. So, by its very nature, a secondary cache sees only requests for data that are much less likely to be needed in the future. This phenomenon substantially reduces the effectiveness of lower-level caches. As a result,

> *the lower you go in the system, the larger the caches need to be in order to achieve measurable benefits.*

For example, you typically see primary CPU caches of 8 to 32 Kbytes but secondary caches of 256 Kbytes to 4 Mbytes. Even though the primary cache is orders of magnitudes smaller, it usually enjoys a much higher hit rate. So, as a general rule, you should strive to increase the sizes of the caches closest to where they are needed. In this example, doubling the size of the CPU cache from 8 Kbytes to 16 Kbytes usually has a much higher performance benefit than doubling the size of a 256-Kbyte secondary cache to 512 Kbytes.

1.10 Summary

Perhaps the most important concept in this chapter is Amdahl's Law, which sets an upper bound on the potential performance that can be achieved. It can be used to judge whether some optimization is worth the effort involved. On the other hand, the Bubble Effect reminds you that your tuning efforts are not only never done but also keep getting harder as you dive in deeper.

Keep in mind that even though optimizing a system increases its throughput, it does not necessarily improve user response time. Not only that, you need fairly large improvements in response time before the user community acknowledges it (or is willing to pay for it).

The Heisenberg principle advises you to not go overboard with your instrumentation tools in order to keep their impact on the system low. And finally, caches, although useful, need to be placed at the right point, which is always close to where they are needed the most.

CHAPTER 2

Computer Architecture

Even though optimizing UNIX systems does not require for you to be an expert hardware architect, some basic understanding of how a computer system is designed and operates can be quite helpful. The information should also enable you to judge whether a performance problem is caused by the hardware or software. Yet another benefit is the ability to read detailed computer specifications. Take for example the following data for a fictitious computer system:

```
233 MHz, 0.7 Micron, CMOS, superscalar CPU
8+8K I & D L1 cache
256 Kbyte Unified L2 cache
400 MBytes/sec memory system
PCI Localbus I/O
VRAM-based graphics controller with 72 Hz refresh
Caching disk controller with 256 Kbyte on-board memory
1 GByte disk drive with 8 ms seek time
Bus mastering Ethernet Controller
```

Even though some items such as the 233-MHz rating of the CPU in this specification may seem familiar, others may not. In order to be able to evaluate the performance characteristics of a system completely, you should be able to understand all its specifications.

2.1 The Basic Components

Although computer architectures vary, most share some common components. Figure 2.1 on page 17 shows the block diagram of a typical computer system. To understand the impact of each one of these functional blocks on the performance of UNIX and your application, we need to look at how each one is designed and operated.

2.2 The CPU

As you might imagine, the Central Processing Unit or CPU is the most important part of any computer system. It is the single entity that executes instructions and actually performs any work.

In the 1970s and even early 1980s, CPUs occupied many circuit boards and were often housed in large cabinets. Today, they consist of one or more VLSIs (Very Large Scale Integrated circuits) and use only a few square inches of board real estate. Reducing the chip count has helped to speed up the CPU because it eliminates chip-to-chip signal delays. Indeed, the majority of recent CPU designs are of single-chip variety for this reason and are referred to as microprocessors.

Instead of myriads of proprietary architectures that were prevalent in early years, software availability has forced the industry to embrace a small number of CPU architectures. The most common are[1]

- Sun SPARC
- HP PA-RISC
- Intel X86
- SGI MIPS
- DEC Alpha
- IBM Power

All these architectures are based on Reduced Instruction Set Computer (RISC) technology with the exception of the Intel X86, which is a Complex Instruction Set Computer (CISC). As the names imply, RISC CPUs are supposed to have a much more minimalistic instruction set than their CISC counterparts. The theory is that by eliminating unneeded and slow instructions, chip real estate (die area) can be used to speed up other operations such as mathematical computations. This definition is no longer valid because some of the RISC CPUs actually have more instructions than some traditional CISC CPUs.

Opinions now vary as to what constitutes a RISC architecture today. One common distinc-

---

1. For obvious reasons, our list includes only those CPUs used in high-volume UNIX systems.

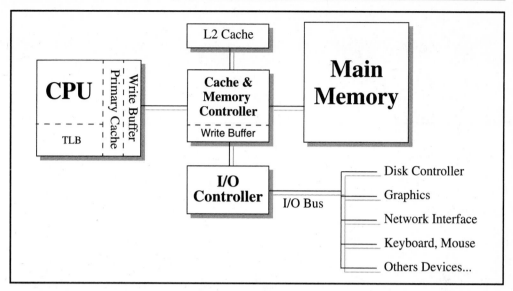

Figure 2.1 Simplified Computer Architecture Diagram

tion is that RISC CPUs do not use microcode to decode and execute instructions.[2] Because the instruction set in a RISC CPU is typically simpler than its CISC counterpart, it can be implemented using hard-wired logic instead of microcode, which can take upwards of 10% of the CPU chip real estate. This makes it possible for RISC CPUs to be smaller (and hence cheaper) or higher performance (by using the extra space for larger but faster logic circuits).

As of this writing, RISC CPUs hold the speed record in some areas such as floating-point arithmetic speed. But devices such as the Intel Pentium and P6 have proven that CISC CPUs can also deliver reasonable performance. So, the choice of processor need not be a "religious" decision but rather one based on the capabilities of the CPU and software availability.

Even though the main goal of the CPU designers is to produce the fastest possible device, there are many other considerations involved such as ease of system design and cost. Even on the performance front, there are many conflicting goals. Let's look at these issues by starting with the most familiar notion, the clock speed.

2.2.1 The Clock Speed

The majority of digital design today is done using sequential circuits that toggle one after the other to perform a complex task such as executing an instruction. The circuits are controlled by a *clock source,* which is a fancy name for a very regular sequence of pulses

---

2. Microcode is a very low-level program that controls the main CPU logic.

(ones and zeros). Every time a clock pulse arrives, the logic circuit advances to the next "state." In the case of a CPU, you may need many such pulses or cycles before even a single instruction is executed.

The clock speed is usually specified in millions of cycles per second or Megahertz (typically abbreviated MHz). CPU clock speeds as of 1995 range from a low of 33 MHz to 300 MHz. These speeds will undoubtedly go up with each newer generation of CPUs resulting in ever increasing performance.

Note that the CPU does not perform all its internal operations sequentially because even with such high clock speeds, the performance will be too low. Instead, the CPU uses a technique called pipelining that lets it execute multiple instructions in parallel with each one being at a different stage of execution. A CPU with a five-stage pipe (short for pipeline) is able to break up an instruction into five separate operations. In each clock cycle, such a CPU can potentially be executing a different portion of up to five instructions in parallel. So, even though each instruction may take five cycles, on the average, over a long sequence of instructions, each one can execute as fast as one per cycle. Of course, this does not work quite as nicely in practice. Conditional branches (if and loop statements) make it difficult for the CPU to determine which instruction needs to be executed next. In addition, data may have to be fetched from main memory, which can take many cycles to arrive causing the pipeline to stall (stop). Note that, in general, the depth of the pipeline (how many stages it has) by itself is not a measure of CPU performance.

It is very important to note that the clock speed of a CPU does not automatically determine the speed with which it can execute user programs. As a matter of fact, a CPU with a lower clock rate may actually outperform one with a higher clock speed. The reason is that the total execution time of a program is determined by the following equation:

$$\mathrm{TotalTime} = \frac{\mathrm{NumberOfInstructions} \bullet \mathrm{AverageCyclesPerInstruction}}{\mathrm{ClockRate}} \qquad (2.1)$$

As you see, the CPU clock rate just gives you one factor in this equation. The other factor, Average Cycles Per Instruction, depends on the program being executed, the CPU architecture, and other system issues such as memory and cache speeds (described later in this chapter). By applying this formula, it is easy to see why a 100-MHz CPU with an average instruction time of 1.5 cycles will be *slower* than a 80-MHz CPU that averages 1.0 cycles per instruction. As an example, if there are 100 million instructions to be executed, the 100-MHz CPU will take 1.5 seconds to run the program, whereas the 80-MHz CPU will take 1.25 seconds to do the same. By now, it should be clear that

you should never use the clock speed of a CPU to judge its performance.

The only exception to this rule is when you are comparing identical systems with varying clock rates. In this case, the only variable in Equation 2.1 is the clock speed, and the comparison is valid. This means that the rampant clock-speed marketing in the PC arena is not totally flawed. Of course, when vendors compare clock speeds of machines with different

CPU architectures (and hence differing Average Cycles Per Instruction), they are violating Equation 2.1 and their claims should be ignored.

Note that we are not saying that higher clock speed is bad. Quite the contrary. Given a CPU design, you want to clock it as fast as possible. After all, if you have two CPUs with identical architectures, the one with the faster clock rate will have higher performance.

As nice as Equation 2.1 seems, it is hard to use in practice. The reason is that it is very difficult to figure out the total number of instructions and the average cycles to execute each one for every application that you are bound to run. Programs vary greatly in their instruction mixes and execution profile, making their average instruction times vary wildly. The average instruction time for a compiler will not be the same as the UNIX operating system nor will it resemble the time for a scientific application. The CPU designers resort to special simulator programs that can generate this kind of information, but you are not likely to get access to them.

2.2.2 Semiconductor Technology

Looking at the common processor today, you find a wide variation in clock speeds. Although many factors have an impact on the ultimate clock speed of a processor, the most fundamental is the choice of semiconductor technology.

All integrated circuits are manufactured from semiconductor dies or wafers that hold the individual transistors that make up a device such as a CPU. The most common figure of merit for a chip technology is the *channel* length (also called the geometry). The units for this measure are in microns (one millionth of a meter). As a general rule,

> *the narrower the channel length, the faster the circuits using it.*

The higher speed is the result of shorter distances between circuits and improved electrical characteristics of the device. By applying this rule, a given CPU design runs faster at smaller geometries. Indeed, a common technique for speeding up a CPU involves shrinking it to a finer geometry (e.g., from 0.8 to 0.6 micron). The technique allows vendors to buy time while they get their next generation CPU working with a more advanced design. Witness the Intel 486 CPU, which has climbed from 25 MHz to 100 MHz over its lifetime.

Finer geometries usually result in smaller dies but not always cheaper CPUs because newer semiconductor processes initially come at a premium price. This has to do with the fact that the *yield*, or what percentage of devices are operational out of a manufacturing run, can be lower on a new chip process. As the designers and chip developers climb the learning curve, the yields improve and prices drop. Another contributing factor is, of course, competition. The cost is bound to remain high where there are only one or two vendors offering a new chip process. As the technology matures, other players get in the market, and the prices come down. The CPU and system vendors often play the same game by charging premiums for their newer designs to recoup their development costs.

These factors all work to make the prices of new CPUs double or triple of the ones using mature technologies.

Another important characteristic of an IC technology is the number of interconnect layers. Even though the base die of an IC simply holds the individual transistors, they need to be interconnected to perform useful functions. This is done by laying down additional "metal" layers, which act as wires between the circuits. Given the large number of interconnects involved in a multimillion transistor CPU, most designs are limited by how densely they can be routed (i.e., interconnected) as opposed to how many transistors they use. As a result,

the higher the number of the metal layers, the faster and denser the chip.

As of 1995, two-layer metal IC processes are very mature and represent the lowest cost level. The utilization in two-layer metal, however, can be as low as 35%. That is, in a die that is 100 mm^2, only 35 mm^2 contains useful circuits and the rest of the base die is wasted by the interconnect traces.

Three-layer metal is being used on many CPU designs and commands only a slight premium. The added layer in three-layer metal designs allows much better utilization of the base die (up to 65% or better). Unfortunately, the savings in die area is partially offset by the additional cost of the extra step to lay down the third metal layer. In practice, the motivation to use a higher number of metal layers is often not cost but performance. Additional routing layers make it possible to minimize the length of the interconnects and hence the amount of time it takes for a signal to travel from one circuit to another. So, adding more layers can indirectly contribute to higher clock speeds. As you can see in Table 2.1, many current designs use three-layer metals, with some sporting four layers to meet chip density and required performance targets.

Table 2.1 Chip Technologies Used by a Sample of Popular CPUs (as of Q1, 1995)

CPU	Clock Freq (MHz)	Process	Geometry (micron)	Metal Layers	Transistors (millions)	Chip Area (mm^2)
Intel 486DX4	100	BiCMOS	0.6		1.6	77
Intel Pentium[a]	100	BiCMOS	.6	4	3.3	164
MIPS R4400	150	CMOS	.6	3	2.3	184
Sun/TI SuperSPARC+ (2 chips)	75	BiCMOS	.72	3	3.1	256
HP PA 7150	125	CMOS	.8	3	0.85	196
IBM PowerPC 601[b]	100	CMOS	.5	4	2.8	N/A
Digital 21064	275	CMOS	.5	4	2.8	164

a. Older 60-MHz Pentiums use 0.8 micron, four-layer design with die area of 294 mm^2.

b. 60-, 70-, and 80-MHz parts use 0.65-micron process.

Perhaps the most fundamental choice in the CPU designs is the type of semiconductor technology itself. The most common is CMOS, which has the advantage of high density and low power consumption (a key when a CPU has millions of transistors). The drawback to CMOS is its slower speed compared to other technologies such as BiPolar and Gallium Arsenide (GaAs). Although faster, these other technologies are much less dense than CMOS, making them inappropriate for most transistor-hungry CPU designs. Some designs use a mixture of CMOS and Bipolar called BiCMOS, which takes advantage of high density of CMOS and the speed of BiPolar where needed. Unfortunately, as with most things, there is a price to be paid for this technology both in terms of higher manufacturing costs and greater power consumption. It also seems that most of the BiCMOS vendors are switching to CMOS as evidenced by Sun's choice for UltraSPARC.

2.2.3 Performance Characteristics

Despite popular misconceptions, the performance of a CPU is highly application specific and cannot be described using one or two numbers. Specifically, the types and frequency of instructions used in a program determine the performance that you can get out of a CPU.

Generally, the CPU instructions fall into two distinct categories: floating-point (FP) and integer. Floating-point instructions manipulate fractional numbers and hence are heavily used in some scientific and engineering applications. By contrast, there is no good definition for integer instructions and the term generally refers to all non-floating-point instructions.

CPUs vary as to the degree with which they are optimized to execute floating-point or integer instructions. To see what makes a CPU fast in one area or the other, let's take a look at what makes a good integer or floating-point CPU.

2.2.4 Integer Performance

Anytime you load a value into a register, compute the index of an array or add a value to an integer variable (e.g., int type in C), you are using integer instructions. There are many examples of integer applications including databases and word processors, but perhaps the best example is the UNIX operating system itself:

the entire UNIX operating system and its utilities are pure integer codes.[3]

Therefore, if you care about the performance of the UNIX system and utilities, you need to pay special attention to the integer performance of the CPU.

Optimizing integer performance presents a difficult challenge to the CPU designers because there are less opportunities for parallelism in integer code (i.e., it must be executed sequentially most of the time). The most obvious method for speeding up integer

---

3. We use the term *pure* rather loosely here. While there are floating-point operations in some commands and the kernel, they do not account for a significant amount of CPU cycles used.

code is increasing the clock speed. This is usually possible with shrinks to smaller geometry as discussed before. Another solution is known as *superpipelining*, which increases the number of pipeline stages by breaking each instruction into much smaller operations. The resulting CPU can run at higher clock speeds because the individual pipeline stages do not take as much time to execute. The SGI MIPS R4400 processor is an example of a super-pipelined architecture as is the Intel P6.

A more popular scheme for speeding up not only integer but also other types of instructions is superscalar execution.

2.2.5 Superscalar Execution

The majority of high-performance CPUs today use a superscalar design, which simply means that the CPU can execute multiple instructions in each cycle. Examples are the Intel Pentium and P6, IBM Power series and PowerPC, HP PA-RISC and Sun SuperSPARC. The only major holdout is the previously mentioned SGI MIPS R4400, but its next generation chip, the R10000, is also superscalar.

A superscalar CPU is able to detect parallel paths of execution within a program and execute multiple instructions in parallel. A crude figure of merit is the level of parallelism, which is specified as n-way superscalar. For example, the Intel Pentium is a two-way superscalar, meaning that it can execute up to two instructions in parallel. Note that we said *up to* two instructions meaning that this happens only if all the conditions are right. The two instructions will execute in parallel if they do not rely on each other's results (i.e., do not have any dependencies) and their data are immediately available to them. Some high-end RISC processors are four-way superscalars, which means that under ideal conditions, they can run up to four times as fast. Of course, ideal conditions rarely occur in real-life applications (but, interestingly enough, they do occur in computer benchmarks!). This means that the performance of a superscalar CPU can vary wildly depending on the type of application being run. As a general rule, most integer applications lack the parallelism required to get very high utilization out of a superscalar CPU. Going beyond two instructions per cycle is considered difficult in most integer codes.

You may have noticed that some vendors recommend that you recompile your applications for their new superscalar CPUs. The compiler optimizers in these systems have been enhanced to rearrange application code to make it more likely for the CPU to find instructions to run in parallel.

To increase the likelihood of finding work for the CPU, newer "aggressive" superscalar designs use *speculative* execution. This technique allows the CPU to follow multiple execution paths in the program. Then, depending on which path the program actually takes, it will undo the changes made by the alternate thread. While this method is rather complex, it does yield higher efficiency and is almost a necessity for highly parallel, superscalar designs. The SGI MIPS R10000 and HP-PA 8000 are prime examples of very aggressive superscalar designs.

2.2.6 Floating-Point Performance

As we mentioned, floating-point operations involve arithmetic computations that use fractional numbers (e.g., 1.032, 4.0E12). Any time you declare a variable as `float` or `double` in C, or REAL, REAL*8 in Fortran, you are instructing the compiler to generate code that uses floating-point instructions.

The floating-point instructions are completely separate from the integer unit and operate on a set of dedicated registers that hold "normalized' floating-point numbers in scientific notation (fraction and mantissa). Floating-point values can either be single precision (4 bytes each) or double precision (8 bytes each). As the name implies, double precision provides much better accuracy and range and hence is used more commonly.

Floating-point usage is high in scientific and some engineering applications such as analog electronic circuit simulation (e.g., spice), mechanical CAD, and computational physics (e.g., stress and heat analysis). As mentioned before, the UNIX kernel and utilities rarely use floating point so the floating-point speed of the CPU does not have any bearing on how fast the system operates unless you are running a floating-point intensive application.

Older CPUs did not have built-in floating-point units and required separate chips to perform these instructions. A case in point is the Intel 386 CPU, which required the 387 numeric coprocessor. Without this extra chip, the compiler would use integer libraries that emulated the floating-point operations. The result was excruciatingly slow execution of floating-point instructions. The denser chip geometries available today have made it possible for the majority of modern CPUs to have built-in floating-point units (FPUs). This does not mean, however, that they all have similar performance. On the contrary, there is a wide variation in the floating-point performance of various CPUs due to cost and chip space trade-offs made by the designers.

The most basic approach to speeding up FPU performance is the reduction of the number of cycles for each floating-point instruction. Being fairly complex, floating-point instructions can use tens of CPU cycles. The number of cycles can be reduced by using more sophisticated arithmetic units that can overlap the different operations required to perform a floating-point computation.

Of course, given a certain chip area and process, there is a limit to how fast an FPU engine can run. Well-designed CPUs allow multiple FP operations to be pipelined so that after an initial delay, results are generated in a shorter number of cycles than if you executed just one operation.

Because floating-point operations are very repetitive in nature (e.g., summing all the values in a large array), they can also be sped up by using multiple functional units that can run in parallel. A common technique is to have separate units for add/subtract and multiply instead of a combined unit. This allows operations such as

```
for(i =0; i < N; ++i)
        s += a[i] * b[i];
```

to be performed in half the time because the multiplication of the i'th element can be overlapped with the addition of the i − 1 results. Even though this technique is very effective, it is not new and used to be called chaining in supercomputers with vector instructions.[4] This method can be extended by using twice as many functional units of each type so that you can perform two similar operations simultaneously. A more generic solution is to use the previously mentioned superscalar architecture, which would allow overlapped execution of two or more floating-point (and possibly integer) instructions in parallel. In our previous example, a superscalar CPU would generate the results for both the i'th and i + 1 elements simultaneously with a little help from the compiler.

Although the CPU designers have more options in the floating-point area than in integer, nothing is for free. Increasing the number of functional units, for example, enlarges the CPU die, making it more expensive. So, a cost trade-off needs to be made. Even if a faster floating-point unit does not result in higher manufacturing cost, the chip vendors will more likely charge a premium for the higher performance. So you wind up paying more for it either way.

2.2.7 Impact of Memory Speed on FP Operations

Floating-point performance only matters if you have large numbers of floating-point computations to make. With this also comes the need to access large amounts of data. This means that the performance of the CPU floating-point unit is highly dependent on how fast it can be "fed" by the caches and the memory controller.[5] Let's look at an example to see the dependency of floating-point operations on main memory speed.

Assume that you have a 1000 by 1000 matrix of double-precision floating-point numbers. The amount of storage you need for the entire matrix is 8 Mbytes because each element is 8 bytes long. This matrix is considerably larger than most (primary or even secondary) CPU caches, which means that, unless a clever algorithm is used, the hit rate will be very low. The resulting thrashing of the cache means that the effective access time of the cache will actually be higher than not having one at all!

Keep in mind that if the cache hit ratio drops too low, the memory-speed requirements can be astronomical. A case in point is a CPU that can (in pipeline mode) perform a floating-point multiply in one cycle and runs at 75 MHz. If two values have to be fetched to be multiplied and the results stored in yet another location, the CPU needs to access three 8-byte values in each cycle (24 bytes total). Put another way, to keep the CPU busy all the time, the memory speed needs to be 1.8 Gbytes/sec (i.e., 24 times 75 million)! Of course, the hit

---

4. Vector instructions can apply an arithmetic operation to a row of array elements stored in vector registers that are typically 32 to 128 elements long. This increases the computational performance because the CPU does not need to decode new instructions constantly to do the same operation.

5. Although integer code can also benefit from faster memory and cache subsystems, its data sets are typically much smaller and easier to fit in a cache.

ratio of the cache(s) is not usually zero as in this case. Even so, the problem cannot totally be eliminated because there are few caches that can hold the entire data set of large floating-point applications.

There are a number of solutions to this problem. One is to use a blocking algorithm where the matrix is divided into many smaller matrices (i.e., blocks) in a way that each one fits in the cache. The operation is then performed on the smaller matrices resulting in higher hit rates and much better performance. Another solution used in supercomputers is to bypass the cache and simply employ a very high bandwidth memory. HP PA RISC uses a modified version of this scheme with a very large primary cache without a secondary cache. This reduces the "the double miss penalty" of the two caches when you do have to go to main memory.

In summary, you should not evaluate the floating point of a CPU outside a system. Both the memory and cache speeds heavily impact the actual achieved performance in user programs.

2.2.8 The Bus Interface

It is one thing to transfer signals a few millimeters inside a CPU die, but an entirely different matter to transfer the same signal to another chip. Electrical signals slow down when either the distance or the load that is being driven is increased. This usually means that the CPU interface (or bus) usually runs much slower than the internal clock speed of the CPU.

Ignoring the loading and distance issues, designing a *system* that can keep up with the CPU at its internal clock rate is still a difficult task. The problem has to do with the response time of devices outside the CPU. Unlike the CPU, external interface chips are designed with less exotic technology and must be cheap (10-20% of the CPU price is typical). As a result, most will struggle to keep up with a 33-MHz bus clock let alone the greater than 100-MHz speeds that are common in modern CPUs. One solution to this problem is to allow the external device to use two cycles to transfer data instead of one. In case of a 66-MHz CPU bus, this gives the device 30 nanoseconds instead of 15 to respond. This is commonly referred to as adding wait states to the CPU. In this example, the CPU is running with one wait state.

Another solution to the interface response time problem is to run the CPU bus at a lower speed than its core logic. This scheme has been made popular by Intel with its "DX2" parts in which the external bus runs at half the CPU clock rate. For example, in the case of the Intel 66-MHz 486DX2, the bus runs at a comfortable rate of 33 MHz instead of 66. For obvious reasons, these devices are known as "clock doublers or triplers" depending on the speed ratio of the bus to internal clock. A more flexible scheme used in the MIPS R4400 CPUs and some other RISC CPUs allows odd ratios such as two thirds. This makes it possible to fine-tune the bus speed to a higher degree. For example, you can run the external bus of a 75-MHz CPU at 50 MHz instead of 37.5.

Note that even though all these solutions make the job of the system designer easier (and result in lower cost systems), they do degrade the CPU performance. A bus that runs at half speed also reduces the CPU data throughput by a factor of two. For example, with a bus clock of 33 MHz, the 32-bit bus on a 66-MHz CPU will be limited to a maximum peak bandwidth of 132 Mbytes/sec instead of 264 Mbytes/sec. As a result, floating-point intensive applications that have a ferocious appetite for data tend to suffer. Reducing the bus speed by half can degrade the floating-point performance of a high-performance processor by as much as 30% or more on real applications. The drop in performance is smaller for processors with slow floating-point performance such as the 486 (and hence the popularity of 486DX2 processors).[6] In these processors, the performance of the application is dominated by how long it takes to actually do the arithmetic operations and not the data access time.

A worrying trend in the industry is the ever-widening gap between the bus and internal clock speeds. Before processor clocks passed the 33-MHz point, the bus speeds matched the CPU clock. As the speed climbed, so did the ratio between the bus and the CPU clock. Take the Intel parts for example. The 33-MHz 486 clocks the CPU and the bus at the same speed. But the 66-MHz part runs the bus at half the speed. The 100-MHz Intel DX4 CPU widens the gap further by running the bus at the same 33-MHz speed for a ratio of 3:1. The situation is worse in higher-performance processors where the bus speed runs four to six times slower than the CPU in some designs. Vendors are dealing with these problems by increasing the CPU caches (e.g., the DX4 cache is double the size of INTEL DX2 parts), which seems to be an adequate solution given the ever-increasing CPU densities.

2.2.9 Manufacturing and Cost Factors

One of the biggest constraints in designing a new CPU is the final chip cost. As we have discussed, most performance increases are a function of how large a logic circuit is dedicated to a specific unit. For example, doubling the number of FPUs or the cache size almost always results in a faster CPU. The drawback is that chip size also increases resulting in higher per-chip cost. What is worse, the cost rises exponentially relative to the chip size. A chip that is twice as big often costs four times as much to manufacture. To see why the chip cost climbs so rapidly, we need to first look at how ICs are manufactured.

When an IC design is finished, it is turned over to a foundry (commonly called a fab). The foundry's job is to turn the design into an actual device. The IC is laid out on 6- to 8-inch silicon wafers which are divided into square pieces large enough to hold the individual ICs. Once the wafer is processed (which may require many steps), the individual dies are separated and mounted in packages. Each chip is then tested and verified before being shipped to the customer.

---

6. The slow-down is also felt much less in PC applications that have traditionally been mostly integer-intensive codes.

Because the processing cost of a wafer on a specific process is more or less fixed, the larger the die, the smaller the number of chips that can be produced. This means that a chip that is twice as large yields half as many chips, resulting in a die that is at least twice as expensive. But the cost increase does not stop there. Because no manufacturing process is perfect, some portions of a wafer are bound to have contaminations or process variations that will render the devices in that area useless. As a result, the yield for a wafer run is almost always less than 100%. In general,

> *the yield is a function of the chip size and drops off very rapidly (i.e., exponentially) as the chip area increases.*

As an extreme example, a chip that takes the entire wafer tends to have almost zero yield because chances of having a perfect wafer that is 6 to 8 inches is almost nil. Obviously, current chips do not approach these sizes, but to get good yields the designers must stay far below certain "sweet spots" on the yield curve.

Because the IC process has slight variations in it where some circuits may run slower or faster, some chips may fail to run "at speed" (i.e., the required clock frequency) in the final testing. The CPU designers work hard to minimize the chances of this occurring by speeding portions of the CPU logic that are susceptible to such variations (i.e., do not have enough timing margin). For this reason, supplies of new CPUs are initially very low, often averaging a handful of working devices from a wafer instead of the typical range of 40 to a few hundred. The situation improves as the CPU designers and the foundry "climb the learning curve" and improve yields.

Keeping the chip size down without sacrificing performance is one of the CPU designer's biggest challenges.

2.3 The Memory Controller

The memory controller handles memory transfer requests from the CPU and, in most cases, the I/O devices. Even though a few CPUs such as Sun's MicroSPARC and the DEC 21066 CPUs have built-in memory controllers, most do not. Instead, each CPU has its own proprietary bus that needs to be interfaced to the memory subsystem. The rational is that this allows a much wider range of designs. We are not sure if we agree with this line of reasoning because the chip-to-chip delays and any mismatch between the CPU bus and the memory controller can add considerable latency to data transfers.

2.3.1 DRAMs

The heart of any memory system is the memory chips themselves, which almost universally are of the DRAM (Dynamic Random Access Memory) variety. Although most people have heard of DRAMs, few are aware of their intricacies and the impact they have on the performance and cost of the system.

The keyword here is *dynamic*, which relates to the data retention ability of DRAMs. A bit stored in a DRAM cell is in the form of a small electrical charger (a capacitor in electronic terms). Because it is impossible to build a perfect charge container, the stored charge gradually drains resulting in the data getting lost. Typical DRAMs keep their contents alive for only a few milliseconds. In addition, reading the contents of a cell requires that its capacitor be discharged first, which obviously leads to another source of data loss.

The solution to the gradual discharge is to read the contents of each cell and rewrite it back into the same location on regular intervals (e.g., every 8 to 16 milliseconds). During the refresh cycle as this is called, the DRAM chip (or chips, since DRAMs are ganged together to make wider devices) cannot be accessed. This causes more or less random delays in accessing main memory and, on the average, drops the throughput of the memory subsystem by a few percentage points.

The second data loss problem is more severe from a performance point of view. When a memory location is read, its contents need to be written back to the same location or its data will be lost. During this write-back procedure (or *cycle*) the DRAM cannot be accessed. Unlike the refresh cycle, which occurs rather infrequently, reading data from memory occurs very often specially in memory intensive, floating-point applications.

Due to these considerations, DRAMs are rated by their *access time* and *cycle times* with the former being the most often noted number. The *access time* determines how long it takes to read a random piece of data and the *cycle time* indicates how long you have to wait before the DRAM can produce new data (which includes the write-back cycle). Typical DRAM *access times* are in the 60- to 80-nanosecond range, with *cycle times* being twice as long.

To increase the performance of DRAMs, vendors have added a page mode scheme, which allows sequential access to a block of data (i.e., a page) to be done in almost half the time (25 to 55 nanoseconds are typical). This is possible because DRAMs read an entire row at a time from the chip instead of just a single location. The row is stored in an on-chip buffer that can be accessed without all the latencies associated with the initial access. The result is a significant boost in performance because the majority of memory accesses in typical programs are sequential. This stems from the fact that the CPU fills its caches with multiple bytes at a time regardless of the specific location the user has requested (see caches in the next section). With typical page sizes of 4 to 16 Kbytes, page mode DRAMs substantially increase system performance. This is the reason for their ubiquitous use in just about every computer sold today.

Despite its advantages, the access time of a paged mode DRAM is still too slow to satisfy the needs of a modern CPU. For example, an 8-bit-wide DRAM with a page mode access time of 40 nanoseconds only has a peak transfer rate of 25 Mbytes/sec. A low-end CPU with a 32-bit bus running at a speed of 50 MHz would theoretically need 200 Mbytes/sec (4 times 50 million) to run at peak speed. To achieve these high rates, multiple DRAMs must be used in parallel. For example, you can use eight 4-bit-wide DRAMs to effectively get 32 times the bandwidth of one device. The drawback to this scheme is that the minimum memory increment that you can add to the system becomes large. In the case of eight 4-bit-wide, 16-Mbit memory chips, the minimum memory size and the amount that can be added is 16 Mbytes. Although wider parts are available to mitigate this problem, they cost more since they have much lower yields.

In addition to page mode access, designers also resort to interleaving to increase memory bandwidth. By using two or more separate banks of memory modules and alternating memory addresses between them, performance can be increased because one bank is ready when another is being cycled. However, the cost of such a system can become very high as the interleaving rate increases. For this reason, most systems stay with two- to four-way interleaving with the former being by far the most common.

2.3.2 DRAM Alternatives

By now it should be clear that DRAMs are not good solutions for modern, bandwidth-hungry CPUs. As a result a number of alternatives have appeared on the market lately in an effort to squeeze more bandwidth out of the standard DRAM cell. So-called Synchronous DRAM (SDRAM), Window RAM (WRAM), and devices using the Rambus interface attempt to transfer the data inside the row buffer at much higher speeds than standard page mode DRAMs. For example, a Rambus DRAM can supply a byte every 2 nanoseconds, which produces a high transfer rate of 500 Mbytes/sec from *a single memory chip*. These devices are finding use in graphics frame buffer applications where the need for bandwidth is even higher than most CPUs.

The EDO (Extended Data Out) DRAMs are a recent entry and offer an attractive proposition: faster access time with very little premium in cost. EDO DRAMs are essentially standard DRAM chips modified to have slightly better access times. The additional speed is just enough to allow the CPU bus to run at higher clock speed resulting in higher bandwidth. Since they have no cost premium over standard DRAMs, we expect EDO DRAMs to fairly quickly displace most of the standard page mode DRAMs over the next few years.

2.3.3 Memory Subsystem Speed Specification

Because the CPU must go through the memory controller to access the memory devices, you should also pay attention to its performance. Poorly designed DRAM controllers can add significantly to the overall access time of the memory device. For this reason, we recommend that you look at the memory *subsystem* (memory and controller) performance as a whole.

Memory (and cache) subsystems are typically rated by their peak transfer rate expressed in megabytes per second (numbers from 80 to 400 Mbytes/sec are typical). We find this specification rather vague and misleading. Although the rating does show the peak transfer rate of the memory subsystem, it fails to state the initial latency (i.e., delay) incurred during the initial access. For example, it is not unusual for the first word transferred from memory to take two to three times as long as all the subsequent words.

Another problem with peak memory specifications is that it has little meaning without the specification for the burst rate of the CPU bus. For example, if the CPU runs at a peak rate of 400 Mbytes/sec and you have a 200-Mbytes/sec memory speed, you clearly have an imbalance. But in absence of the 400-Mbytes/sec CPU bus rating, the 200 Mbytes/sec seems impressive when in reality it is not.

A better memory specification than the peak bandwidth is latencies for each word being fetched. This is usually specified as the number of CPU bus cycles for each word in the form of X-Y-Y-Y (e.g., 4-2-2-2)[7]. The X value indicates the number of CPU bus cycles to fetch the first word (which could be from 4 to 32 bytes depending on how wide the CPU bus is). The Y values, which are usually the same, indicate the transfer time for subsequent words.

The Y figure is usually smaller than X due to page mode hits and the fact that memory controller delays are pipelined and, hence, are hidden in the rest of the transfers. By inverting the Y value and multiplying by the bus width and clock frequency, you arrive at the peak bandwidth rating explained before. For example, if Y is two cycles at 50 MHz and the memory bus is 4 bytes wide, the peak or bust speed is 100 Mbytes/sec. For historical reasons, a machine with Y and X values of 1 is sometimes referred to as having a zero wait state memory.

Assuming that you can get your hands on the memory specifications (which is not always easy), you should select a system with the smallest initial latency (2 to 7 cycles are typical) with 1 to 2 cycles per word after that (e.g., 5-1-1-1). Note that similar specifications exist for the external CPU caches. In that case, you should insist on a system with single-cycle latency (e.g., 1-1-1-1).

2.3.4 SRAMs

Static Random Access Memories or SRAMs are made out of either CMOS or bipolar technology and can hold their data indefinitely assuming that you keep them powered. In addition, there is no data loss after a read request. These features make SRAMs much faster than DRAMs with access times ranging from a few nanoseconds for exotic (and expensive) chips to garden-variety low-cost, 12- to 20-nanosecond types used in mass market PCs.

As usual, there is a price to be paid for the convenience and speed of SRAMs. The individual cells in an SRAM are four to six times larger than DRAMs, which means that, given the same die area, an SRAM holds much less data. As a result the price per bit for SRAMs

---

7. The number of Xs and Ys depends on the number of words the CPU fetches at a time. In our example, it is four.

is from 4 to 8 times higher than DRAMs. Needless to say, despite some special cases (e.g., in supercomputers and small-memory embedded systems), SRAMs are not suitable for general-purpose memory storage. The most common application for SRAMs is in caches.

2.4 Virtual Memory Management

Modern CPUs support multiple memory addressing modes with the simplest being real or physical. In this mode, program addresses are simply passed by the CPU to the memory subsystem unchanged. Naturally, the possible range of addresses in physical mode is from zero to the maximum amount of physical memory available in the system.

Despite its simplicity, the physical mode is not very suitable to running modern operating systems such as UNIX. To use this mode, programs must be loaded into memory contiguously. This practice quickly leads to fragmentation of system memory as programs run and exit. One solution used in segment-oriented operating systems is to constantly copy programs around to make room for new ones. Needless to say, this is very inefficient. The right solution, known as virtual memory management, allows pieces of a program to be freely spread around the memory systems without the user program knowing it.

In virtual mode, each memory address in the user program (for either instructions or data) is first translated by the CPU Memory Management Unit (MMU) to a different address before being passed on to the memory system. The translation is performed on a page-by-page basis with each page being a fixed number of bytes. Page sizes range from a low of 512 bytes (on the old DEC VAX system) to 1 Mbyte or more. But by far, the most common page size is 4 Kbytes.

Virtual mode works by mapping (translating) each page in the user address space to an alternate page in physical memory. So, page 0 in user program could be mapped to page 501 in memory and page 1 to 312 and so on. Note that all the addresses within a page (e.g., from 0 to 4095 on a system with 4-Kbyte pages) are translated to the same alternative page (2,052,096 [501*4096] to 2,056,191 [501*4096 + 4095] in our example).

Note that the translation is handled completely by the hardware with no software intervention. The operating system is responsible only for filling the page descriptor table, which lists all the alternate page numbers in sequence. In our example, the first entry in the page descriptor table would have 501 and the next, 312. As the user program accesses various locations in its logical or virtual address space, the MMU continuously maps the logical page numbers to physical to find the actual page and byte number to access. *Because page descriptor tables can get very large and one is required per running program, they are stored in main memory and not inside the CPU.*

One of the nice advantages of memory management is that user programs can have arbitrary addresses that bear no relationship to physical memory. An interesting benefit is that *user program addresses can go beyond the physical size of main memory because the hardware can be told to map them to lower, real addresses in main memory.* Another advantage is that user programs can share the same logical addresses without interfering with each other. By setting up the page descriptors appropriately, identical user addresses would map to different physical memory locations giving both privacy and protection to user programs.

The memory protection feature comes as a result of protection bits in the page descriptors. Architectures vary as to the number and functions of each bit, but most share a common subset. All systems have a Valid bit, which, if clear, causes the CPU to stop the execution of the currently running program and branch into the operating system (this sort of "exception" is referred to as a *trap*). This is the key mechanism behind *demand paging*, which allows the operating system to run programs that are larger than the physical memory. In addition, the protection bits allow specific pages to be marked as read-only, which is useful in stopping errant programs from corrupting their instruction space. See Chapter 3 for a more complete description of how UNIX uses the MMU to implement these and other similar services.

2.4.1 The Translation Lookaside Buffer

Designing an efficient MMU can be rather difficult because at least two address translations are required for each instruction executed: one to figure out the physical address of the instruction to be fetched and one (or more) for any data references performed by the instruction itself. For example, if the next CPU instruction is at logical address 1020, and the instruction at that location wants to load the content of location 92040 into a register, the CPU must map both addresses into their corresponding physical locations before it can finish the execution of that instruction.

Even though the arithmetic operations needed to translate the addresses (shift and add) can be performed very quickly, fetching the page table entries from main memory cannot. As a minimum, there would be a one-cycle penalty (if it comes out of primary cache) and, at worst, many cycles to fetch it from main memory.[8]

The solution to this performance bottleneck is a special cache known as the Translation Lookaside Buffer or TLB. This is a fully set associative cache (see the next section) that resides inside the CPU and holds the most commonly accessed page table entries. The TLB is either filled by the operating system (in the case of most RISC architectures) or automatically by the CPU when it encounters a page table entry that is not in the TLB. Although it takes many cycles to load a value into the TLB when a page is first accessed, it can be used in a fraction of a cycle thereafter.

Because of its high degree of associativity, the TLB tends to require a large amount of CPU real estate. As a result, the total number of TLB entries is usually very small. Typical sizes range from 16 to 128. Note that unlike page descriptors, *the TLB is shared among all*

---

8. The delay out of the primary cache can be hidden by pipelining, but the latency of the external caches and main memory is just too high to hide.

programs in the system including the operating system. Because the allocation is done on demand, it is possible for one program to hog (grab) all the TLB entries, although some architectures (e.g., MIPS) allow the operating system to wire in (reserve) some entries for itself.

As with any cache, an entry in the TLB must be freed to make room for new items. Even though it is desirable to use a Least Recently Used (LRU) algorithm to reduce the chances of throwing out an entry that is going to be needed soon, most architectures simply use a random replacement policy. The reason for the crude selection process is that it is fast and does not require extensive logic to implement.

Just like any other cache, it is possible to thrash the TLB by constantly accessing more pages than can be held inside it. For example, your performance slows significantly if you try to access 100 pages randomly on a machine with 16 TLB entries. There is simply no room to hold all the page table entries necessary to run the program. Luckily, most programs are better behaved than this example and tend to access a smaller set of pages at a time.

Another troubling situation is trying to run hundreds of jobs (or users) on a system with a small TLB. Because the minimum number of TLB entries needed per job in UNIX is three (one for instructions, another for data, and a third for stack—see Chapter 3) you would run out of TLB entries very quickly, and thrashing ensues. The situation would be as bleak even in a CPU with a 128-entry TLB. A common solution is to use more than one CPU in such systems, which results in a correspondingly larger effective TLB size.

2.5 Caches

The slow speed of main memory is a major problem for a fast CPU. If it takes two or more cycles just to fetch a word from a DRAM, how can you execute an instruction in one cycle or less? The answer is to use a mixture of faster memory (usually in the form of SRAMs) and DRAMs. By keeping the most frequently used data in the faster memory (i.e., the cache), system performance improves substantially without a huge cost increase.

There can be many levels of caching but most systems stop at two. The first level, called the primary or L1 (level 1) cache, is usually inside the CPU. With the notable exception of HP PA RISC, all modern CPUs today include some amount of on-chip primary cache. Typical sizes range from 8 Kbytes (e.g., on Intel 486DX2) to 36 Kbytes (Sun/TI Super-SPARC). These sizes are bound to get bigger as the geometries shrink and designers have more transistors to use for larger caches.

In addition to the primary cache, most systems use a secondary or L2 (level 2) cache outside the CPU to further lower the effective access time of main memory. L2 caches are typically quite large ranging from 128 Kbytes on low-end PCs to 4 Mbytes on high-performance workstations and servers. As we mentioned in Chapter 1, due to the skimming effect, secondary caches need to be rather large to give good performance. Although hit rates as high as 98% are common for primary caches, secondary caches usually struggle to achieve anything above 90% despite their larger size.

The effectiveness of a cache depends on its size, organization, and line size. Even though it is intuitive that a larger cache has a better hit ratio, the other factors need further explanation. As you recall, there is a high penalty for the first word fetched from a DRAM, but page-mode access allows subsequent words to be read rather quickly. Designers take advantage of this fact by making caches that fetch multiple words at a time. Instead of just freeing a single word, *the cache controller replaces a group of sequential words known as a line*. The line size can be as small as 4 and as wide as 256 bytes with the most common sizes being from 8 to 16 bytes. As a general rule,

the larger the line size, the higher the hit rate of the cache in typical applications.

The reason for this rule is that the larger line size tends to better match the sequential access pattern in user programs because most applications tend to access adjacent instructions and data. Of course, if a program accesses random bytes in memory, then the longer line can be a hinderance.

Beyond the line size, caches are also classified by the algorithm used in replacing a new line with an old one (i.e., figuring out which line is not going to be needed as often). Because caches are much smaller than main memory, their replacement policies can make a large impact on their performance. There are a number of possible choices in this area. Let's look at a few.

2.5.1 Direct Mapped Caches

This scheme is the simplest and involves a direct translation of the memory addresses to the cache location. The cache controller uses the lower address bits as a simple index into the cache. Because no search is required, the replacement logic in direct map caches is simple (hence cheap) and very fast.

All is not well, however. Because caches are much smaller than main memory, many memory addresses map to the same location in the cache. For example, in an 8-Kbyte cache, the memory addresses 0, 8192 (8K), 16384 (16K), and 32768 (32K) would all map to the same location in the cache (i.e., their lower 13 bits are the same). So, if your program constantly accesses memory locations that are separated exactly by the cache size, you get no advantage from the cache. The same line in the cache keeps getting replaced with no reusability.

The poor replacement policy of direct map caches does not make them bad, however. Because the data in the cache can be found very quickly, direct mapped caches often have faster access times. Also because they require little logic to implement, they are usually the first choice in external (L2) caches.

2.5.2 Set Associative Caches

The thrashing problem in direct mapped caches can be somewhat mitigated if multiple words with identical lower address bits could simultaneously be held in the cache. In case of a conflict (i.e., more than one memory address mapping to the same cache line), the cache controller could simply use an alternative line. This is exactly what is done in a two-way set associative cache where a memory address can map into two possible cache lines. Likewise in a four-way associative cache, a line of memory data can be stored in one of four different cache lines.

As an example, in a two-way set associative, 8-Kbyte cache, the memory location 0 can be stored in either cache location 0 or 4K. The choice of which one depends on the implementation. The most common scheme is a random algorithm where the cache line is picked at random. Even though it is desirable to use an LRU algorithm, its overhead and cost to implement are not typically justified because the performance advantage can be small.

> *Because of the fact that set associative caches can handle conflicts better, they can have better performance than direct mapped caches.*

Set associative caches do have some disadvantages though. They are more expensive to implement and, interestingly enough, can actually have lower performance than direct mapped caches if not designed carefully. The reason is that on a read request, the memory address bits do not provide sufficient information to find the needed cache line. Therefore, the cache controller must search all the possible lines to find the right address. This is done by searching the contents of a special, high-speed tag RAM that holds the upper bits of the memory address. The search time and associated logic can add delays that lead to slower cache access time. This can easily outweigh the benefits of slightly higher hit rates.

Of course, we hope that a cache designer does not resort to a more complex, two- to eight-way set associative cache just to wind up with a slower access time. Just to be sure, check the system as a whole using your own applications or benchmark data to see if the more complex cache is indeed providing better performance.

2.5.3 Cache Write Policies

The write policy of a cache can be one of two types: write-through or write-back. In the former case, any data written by the CPU gets stored in the cache and then immediately goes to main memory. This policy simplifies access by other devices besides the CPU (e.g., I/O controllers), which need access to main memory. Because the cache data and memory are always kept consistent, these devices can just read their data from memory without first searching the cache. The drawback to this scheme is that frequent CPU writes can generate large amounts of bus and memory traffic that can slow down the system.

Write-back caches hold on to the CPU data until they need to free a line. At that time, if the line to be freed is dirty (i.e., was written to by the CPU), its contents are written to main memory before being released. A nice feature of these caches is that frequent writes to the same cache line do not cause multiple writes to main memory. As a result, this scheme substantially reduces memory traffic and can have a large impact on the system performance. The drawback is that the contents of main memory are no longer fully valid. In most modern systems, it is the responsibility of the operating system to flush the cache (write out its contents) to main memory before starting any outgoing I/O transfers.

Write-back caches are especially popular in shared-memory, multiprocessor systems. By using a write-back policy, the amount of traffic generated by each CPU is reduced, allowing the memory subsystem to serve more CPUs efficiently.

2.6 Write Buffers and FIFOs

To reduce the impact of write traffic especially in systems with write-through caches, some memory controllers (and CPUs) implement write buffers. These are simply intermediate registers that accept data quickly but let it drain in the background to main memory (or whatever device they are buffering). Smarter write buffers allow read requests to get processed ahead of the write buffer traffic, which further improves the system performance. You will find write buffers inside the CPUs, memory controllers, and I/O devices (including graphics controllers). In case of later applications, they are referred to as FIFOs (First In, First Out), but the function remains the same. As with caches, the deeper the write buffer, the better.

Unfortunately, it is not always easy to determine whether a system component uses write buffers and, if so, how deep they are. The only way is to examine the specification for the chip itself.

2.7 The I/O Subsystem

An often-overlooked area, the I/O subsystem of a machine, can play an important part in the performance of the system in many applications. Complications arise from the fact that there are very few performance metrics for the I/O subsystems, and its efficiency or lack thereof, is often obscured by the rest of the system. By understanding how each class of I/O device is interfaced to the system, you should have an easier time analyzing its performance.

2.7.1 Polling

The main job of an I/O device is to transfer out some piece of data from main memory (a write) or to fetch data from an outside device and store it in main memory (a read). The polling method is the simplest way to do this. It works by letting the CPU do all the work. After all, the CPU already knows how to access memory. On a read, the CPU loads the piece of data from the I/O device into a register after which it stores data in main memory.

On output, the CPU passes the data to the I/O device and waits for it to accept the data. The CPU must check the readiness of the device by constantly examining a status register in a tight loop. As a result, the CPU cannot get any other work done while it is waiting for the I/O device. So, even though polling costs very little to implement, its performance characteristics leave something to be desired.

The best use of polling is for very slow devices. A prime example is the keyboard. When the user types on the keyboard, an interrupt is generated which stops the CPU from executing the current program and forces it to branch into the operating system. The appropriate code in the operating system (known as the interrupt handler) then fetches the keyboard data and stores it in memory after which it resumes execution of whatever it was doing. Because the maximum data rate of the keyboard is very low (a few characters per second), polling is an adequate solution. Of course, the same cannot be said of many other devices such as disk and network controllers where the high data rates could totally stop the CPU from doing any useful work if polling were used. Nevertheless, some borderline devices such as the PC printer port inappropriately use polling, which causes simple operations such as printing a file to slow down the system substantially.

2.7.2 DMA Devices

An effective way to increase the efficiency of the I/O subsystem is to allow direct transfer of data to and from main memory without the CPU intervention. This can be done with general-purpose memory transfer devices known as DMA (Direct Memory Access) controllers. The DMA logic works in tandem with the I/O controller to automate the entire I/O process. To start an I/O, the CPU programs the I/O controller with the request in addition to setting up the starting memory address and byte count in the DMA controller. The DMA logic then takes over and handles the entire memory transfer without any help from the CPU. When the I/O is finished, the CPU is interrupted, at which point it simply checks to see if the I/O was successful.

Needless to say, using DMA is a major improvement over polling. The CPU can run unhampered assuming it does not collide with the DMA devices when accessing memory. And given today's large CPU caches, this is not much of an issue. DMA controllers (which have multiple channels) are standard in the PC architecture and are used for many functions from floppy to hard disk accesses.

2.7.3 Bus Mastering

One problem with the DMA solution is that you are stuck with their limited number of channels and performance characteristics. This means that even if you upgrade your I/O controller, you may not experience any improvement in speed because of bottlenecks in the DMA controller (which lives on the main system logic). A solution to this problem is bus mastering. In these controllers, the I/O device itself has the intelligence to access memory and does not need help from the system DMA controller. A bus-mastering controller acquires the memory bus when it needs to access main memory and releases it when done. Because the bus-mastering logic is part of the I/O controller itself, it can be optimized for the kind of operations that are needed for the specific device.

Bus mastering has all the advantages of DMA devices and none of its disadvantages. Although a bit more complex than simple DMA solutions, availability of dense ASICs (Application Specific Integrated Circuits) has made bus-mastering implementations very feasible even in low-cost PCs. Bus-mastering controllers are common in many workstations and new PC peripherals such as Ethernet, SCSI, and graphics controllers.

2.8 Expansion I/O Buses

Almost every system that you buy today includes some kind of I/O expansion bus, and some systems rely solely on them for their entire I/O subsystem. A prime example is the PC architecture with its ubiquitous AT expansion bus (now called ISA—see below). Others use proprietary data transfer buses internally and provide an I/O bus only for expansion. An example is the HP 700 workstation line, which has a private I/O bus internally in addition to an EISA expansion bus.

The I/O bus can either be open or of a proprietary design. Needless to say, an open design is preferable due to the potential availability of a wider range of devices and lower costs. At the same time, some open designs are of very low performance and should be avoided if possible.

The most popular open buses today are

- Sun's SBUS
- PC ISA
- PC EISA
- IBM MicroChannel
- VESA VL local bus
- PCI local bus

In considering these buses, you need to keep in mind that the typical speed specifications are for peak or burst rates. In other words, this is the speed that you can expect to see on large transfers after an unknown initial latency. In addition, just because a bus has a high rating, it does not mean that all the devices sitting on it can utilize it at its peak rate. Although having the full performance specification is best, the burst rates are fairly good figures of merit and, in any case, are all that you have to go by.

2.8.1 Sun SBUS

SBUS has enjoyed widespread usage due to the fact that it has been available as a standard expansion bus on Sun systems for a number of years. It is 32 bits wide and has a respectable burst (peak) transfer rate of 80 Mbytes/sec. Because SBUS is usually synchronized to the CPU bus clock with some kind of divisor, the actual burst speed varies considerably from system to system. Some high-end Sun workstations, for example, have slower SBUS speeds than lower-cost systems.

The main drawback to SBUS is its very small form factor. This makes it difficult to build large and complex cards that fit in one slot. As a result, some of the I/O expansion cards occupy two slots.

Despite its popularity on Sun platforms and decent performance, we expect SBUS to eventually give way to newer, multiplatform buses such as PCI.

2.8.2 ISA

The ISA (Industry Standard Architecture) bus has been the lifeline of the PC systems since IBM introduced it in the original model of the PC in 1980. Initially called the PC XT bus, the 8-bits-wide bus was renamed later to ISA. The width of the ISA bus was later changed to 16 bits with the introduction of the PC AT system (which had a 16-bit CPU and used the ISA bus for memory in addition to I/O).

Despite its immense popularity, the ISA bus suffers from a very slow clock speed (8 MHz) and narrow width. It struggles to achieve data transfer rates in excess of 4 Mbyte/sec, with most devices faring much worse than this limit. As a result, the ISA bus is a severe bottleneck in PCs that use it as their sole form of I/O channel. Of special concern is the graphics controller that needs very high bandwidth to the CPU in addition to main memory. *If you care at all about good display performance, stay away from ISA-based graphics cards.* Devices such as disk and network cards do not belong on the ISA bus either, although the case is not as strong as graphics.

Even though the ISA bus is not ideal, it is adequate for the typical complement of devices connected to it in a standard PC such as keyboard, serial port, parallel printer port, floppy disk, and real-time clock. The data transfer rates for these devices is in hundreds of kilobytes or less, and the ISA bus provides access to them at an extremely low cost.

The performance limitations and the wide availability of much faster buses such as VL and PCI mean that the lifetime of ISA is rather short. We expect the ISA bus to be gradually phased out over the next few years.

2.8.3 MicroChannel

The first bus proposed to address the performance (and configuration) problems of the ISA bus was from IBM. The MicroChannel bus, in addition to being faster, includes an autoconfiguration feature that eliminates DIP switches and jumpers (a very welcome enhancement over the ISA bus). As for speed, MicroChannel allows different bus configurations that range in speed from 40 (32-bits) to 80 (64-bits) Mbytes/sec. The version implemented in PCs runs at the lower end of the spectrum with the IBM RS/6000 work-stations using a mix of these configurations. For example, model 580 runs in 32-bit mode whereas the 970 uses an XIO bus that supports the 64-bit mode (by using the address lines to carry data).

Despite its reasonable performance, MicroChannel has garnered only limited support in the industry and, for the most part, is available only on the IBM-manufactured hardware.

2.8.4 EISA

One of the problems with MicroChannel is that it is not backward compatible with the ISA bus. The IBM designers felt that in order to fix the deficiencies of the ISA bus, they had to design a totally new interface. A number of major PC vendors disagreed and formed a consortium to standardize the Extended ISA bus or EISA. The resulting bus widens the data path to 32 bits but keeps the clock speed the same. Also new are higher-performance streaming (i.e., burst) modes that allow the bus to reach a peak speed of 33 Mbytes/sec (8 MHz times 4 bytes per transfer). Like MicroChannel, EISA systems include dynamic configuration through a standard utility program.

Even though EISA did improve the performance of the ISA bus substantially, it did so at the cost of increased hardware complexity. As a result, EISA-based systems have always been much more pricey than their ISA counterparts. Even 5 years after its introduction, the EISA controller chips cost over $100, which usually added $300 or more to the price of a typical PC. The higher cost kept the EISA bus from capturing as large a market share as was originally hoped. The newer local buses (PCI and VL) have practically wiped out the EISA bus in the PC market.

2.8.5 High-Performance Local Buses

The ever-increasing desire for a low-cost but high-speed bus has led to two new I/O buses: VL and PCI. Both buses are referred to as local buses. The name stems from the fact that these buses (especially VL) are similar to the private (i.e., local) bus of the CPU, which used to handle only memory transfers and not I/O traffic. By tailoring these buses to accept external I/O devices, very high performance can be achieved. Both VL and PCI have become quite popular especially in the PC market. As to which one is winning, we have to give the nod to PCI because of its availability on non-Intel platforms such as DEC Alpha and Apple Power Macintosh.

2.8.6 VESA VL

The VESA Localbus or VL was the first local bus to become popular and has been standardized by the VESA committee (a group of PC graphics and peripherals card manufacturers). The bus is fashioned after the Intel 486 CPU bus (and hence the name local, i.e., private CPU bus) being 32 bits wide and running at 33 MHz. This pegs its peak rate at 132

Mbytes/sec[9]. Unfortunately, this rate is achievable only for reads. The bus does not support burst writes to any extent, so the theoretical rate here would be closer to 66 Mbytes/ sec.

These numbers do not tell the whole story as the current VL chip sets struggle to achieve actual throughput rates over 30 Mbytes/sec in either read or write mode. This is both a function of the VL bus controller on the system motherboard and the interface chips on the I/O cards. Given time, both should improve as should peak throughput (assuming that the VL bus stays around—see the next section on PCI).

A drawback of the VL bus is that it relies on the older ISA (or EISA, although this configuration is less common) for control information. The VL connector is used only for data transfers. This means that the VL bus boards are also saddled with jumpers and switches for device configuration. A new addition to the specification calls for autoconfiguration, but as of 1995, there are no boards complying with this option. On the plus side, the VL bus is almost free to implement because it is simply a buffered version of the 486 CPU bus to memory, which already exists in all 486 PCs. As a result, since its introduction in 1992, VL bus has gained a substantial following. Its cost advantage, however, is not clear in a Pentium-based system leading to widespread competition from PCI.

2.8.7 PCI

The major competition to VL is the PCI (Peripheral Component Interconnect) bus designed by Intel (and now under the direction of the PCI Special Interest Group). PCI cards can be configured through software and do not require any switches or jumpers (although, as of this writing, many of the PCI cards lack this feature). This so-called plug & play (PnP) technology is a godsend to anyone who has ever tried to configure a PC using the jumpers on ISA cards.

Like VL, PCI is a 33-MHz, 32-bit bus so, in theory, it can be driven to a theoretical limit of 132 Mbytes/sec. Not having to be compatible with the 486 CPU bus means that the PCI bus can handle burst reads *and* writes. But this has not helped the first two generations of PCI bus controllers (in PC platforms) to achieve anything better than 30 Mbytes/sec. Fortunately, newer chip sets such as the Intel Triton boast zero wait state on PCI transfers, making it possible to achieve actual data transfers in excess of 100 Mbytes/sec.

Note that even with the older chip sets, the performance of PCI (and VL) far surpasses that of ISA. In addition, we expect many workstation vendors to adopt PCI as the I/O bus of choice. Some, like DEC, have already made the switch. So, without sounding too much like an advertisement, we expect PCI to be an extremely successful I/O bus for years to come.

---

9. The clock speed is a bit higher than 33 MHz leading some people to spec the bus at 133 Mbyte/sec instead of 132.

2.8.8 Other Buses

Two other buses are worth mentioning here. One is the DEC TURBOchannel, which has enjoyed limited success due to availability on most of DEC's pre-1995 RISC-based systems. The bus is fairly simple to interface to and provides very respectable performance of 100 Mbytes/sec using a 32-bit-wide bus. DEC has started to phase out TURBOchannel in favor of PCI, which is just as well because PCI provides similar performance but with much wider appeal.

Another older bus, which still has some (minor) following, is the VME bus. Once the main I/O and memory interface for a large number of (mostly 68XXX-based) systems, VME has fallen out of favor as of late. Being a rather dated standard, its throughput is rather lackluster ranging from 10 to 40 Mbytes/sec.

VME is no longer being designed into new mass-market UNIX systems due to large form factor and cost. It is currently in use in some SGI systems in addition to the AUSPEX file servers where it has been enhanced to run at the top end of its speed range.

2.9 Disk Controllers

The most fundamental device typically connected to an I/O bus is the disk controller. Generally, disk controllers fall into two categories. The so-called dumb controllers, which are the most common, and the intelligent caching controllers. Let's look at what sets each one apart.

2.9.1 Caching Disk Controllers

Even though we do like the idea of a well-designed disk controller, we are not great fans of the so-called intelligent or caching controllers. These devices employ a CPU and some local memory that is used to cache requested blocks from the drives connected to the controller. The cache size typically ranges from 256 Kbytes to as large as a few megabytes. Needless to say, the added memory and additional logic makes these controllers more expensive, which presumably is offset by their higher performance.

If we seem cynical, it is because we do not think caching controllers are worth their additional cost. The problem is not that the added caching does not help system performance. It does. The question is whether the money is best spent on adding memory to a disk controller or to the base systems. As you will see in Chapter 3, the UNIX operating system has its own disk cache, which is much more effective at this job. There are many reasons for this. For one, a disk block in the UNIX cache is immediately available to the system, whereas a disk block sitting in the disk controller cache needs to first be transferred into the UNIX cache across a potentially slow I/O bus. In addition, the skimming effect severely limits the hit rate of the disk controller cache. The result is that the UNIX buffer cache will have a much higher hit rate than an equivalent size cache on the controller.

Alas, there are two situations in which caching disk controllers might be beneficial. One is when you are not able to increase the size of your system memory. In this case, it is not possible to enlarge the UNIX cache, and your only option for higher disk performance is a caching disk controller. The other situation is an NFS server whose synchronous writes can be delayed to boost performance (see Chapter 9).

2.9.2 Dumb Disk Controllers

A controller is termed *dumb* if it does not have a CPU on it. The CPU is not necessary if all that is required is a translation of the I/O request from the internal I/O bus to the disk drive interface (e.g., SCSI and IDE—Section 2.11). Requests from the operating systems are simply passed on to the disk drive, and no data are kept in the controller.

From a performance point of view, dumb controllers work much better than their name may indicate. The main reason is that the UNIX file system code likes to have as close an interface to the disk drive as possible. Specifically, a common UNIX file system such as FFS (see Chapter 3) wants to know exactly when and where the data get transferred to and from the device. Having a second CPU on the controller board second guessing it is not usually productive. As a result, extremely good performance can be gained from well-designed dumb controllers, which is the reason for their popularity.

We should note that there is now a new class of (SCSI) disk controllers that handles some of the low-level protocols internally. These devices can reduce the number of interrupts required for each I/O, which can off-load the CPU of this burden. Even so, we still consider these controllers as dumb.

Yet another feature on some controllers allows *scatter-gather I/O*. This means that the disk controller can handle transfers from disjointed memory locations. This is useful when the request spans more than one page. Take for example a situation where 8 Kbytes of memory need to be transferred to disk. Virtually, this memory looks contiguous, but in reality it is stored in two different memory pages on a system with 4-Kbyte pages. It is very desirable to be able to issue a single write request to the disk controller that would transfer the entire 8 Kbytes in one I/O. Without any kind of extra hardware, you would have to issue two separate I/O requests to the controller (one for each page). Now, if the system supports scatter-gather I/O (as is the case in most workstations and higher-end systems), a list of I/O requests could be built. In our case, this list would include two memory addresses and byte counts. This scatter-gather logic (which can either live in the disk controller or on the system logic board) would handle the disjointed memory transfer, and the CPU would be interrupted only once at the end. Needless to say, scatter-gather I/O is a very useful feature to have.

2.9.3 RAID Controllers

Yet another type of "intelligent" disk controller is RAID (Redundant Array of Inexpensive Disks). These controllers turn a cluster of disk drivers into one logical drive in order to reduce overall latency and increase throughput. The concept is nothing new and has been used successfully on supercomputers for years to get higher data rates than is possible with a single drive. The recent publicity is the result of an interesting RAID paper that described various techniques for replacing expensive and large mainframe disk drives with a number of lower-performance but much cheaper drives. The premise was that a number of inexpensive disks could be grouped in various configurations to achieve high throughput, reliability, or both. Ironically, RAID systems often cost more, not less, than the systems that they replace (due to the cost of the much more complex controller). Today, the motivation has changed from trying to reduce cost to increasing performance.

The basic concept behind RAID technology is to spread (or stripe) the I/O requests among a cluster of disk drives using a technique similar to memory interleaving. In theory, the throughput of a RAID system can grow linearly as the number of drives increases. But for this to happen, the disk traffic must be spread equally among all the disk drives—a situation that is hard to achieve in general-purpose systems. To understand why, we need to first look at various algorithms for spreading the I/O traffic.

The RAID paper outlined five levels (which have now expanded to six) with each having varying levels of throughput, latency, storage efficiency, and reliability (see Table 2.2). The two schemes for spreading disk traffic are bit and block striping. In bit striping, a single data block is split among all the drives, and each handles a few bits of each data byte. For example, in a four-drive system, each drive would get 2 bits of every data byte. In contrast, block striping involves giving each drive a complete block to handle. For example, if you had 16 Kbytes to transfer on a two-drive system, the first drive would get the first 8 Kbytes and the other, the last 8 Kbytes.

Table 2.2 RAID Levels

Level	Description
0	Block striping without redundancy. Provides high performance but is susceptible to huge data losses if any drive goes down. Is usually implemented as an extension to the operating system (as part of "disk suites" or logical volume handlers).
1	Disk mirroring. Data are written to two sets of drivers simultaneously. If one goes down, the other can take over. Hence, the redundancy overhead is 50%. Provides a slight increase in performance because the system can alternate between the drives on reads since they both contain identical data.
2	Bit striping. Data bytes are broken into bit groups and spread across multiple drives. Provides good performance but very hard to expand the drive configuration.
3	Full striping (level 0) plus a fixed redundant drive. On a four-drive system, the extra drive for redundancy means a 20% overhead in storage cost (12.5% on an eight-drive system). The redundant drive can cause a bottleneck in write-intensive applications (it needs to be updated regardless of which drive has changed).
4	Similar to level 3 but with block striping instead of byte.
5	Similar to level 3 but the parity drive rotates between the drives lowering the write overhead. Provides excellent performance and scalability. It is by far the most popular solution in the hardware RAID systems.

Note that for block striping to work well, the transfer size needs to be rather large. This requirement is due to the fact that, to get maximum throughput from a drive, you need to transfer a minimum amount of data per transfer (in the order of 32 to 64 Kbytes).

To make matters worse, the best block size for a block-striped system is this number multiplied by the number of disk drives. This means that on a subsystem with eight disk drives, maximum transfer rate can be reached only if you transfer 256 Kbytes or more in each request. This is, of course, not possible in all environments and applications.

Even though RAID vendors are quick to multiply the data rates of individual drives by the number of drives for their performance figures, their claims should be taken with a grain of salt if your application cannot generate large transfers. That is not to say that RAID systems are not beneficial. They are. But their effective throughput is going to be far below the maximum on the average.

While striping data across multiple drives can result in higher throughout, it also creates a reliability problem. Specifically, if a single drive fails, the data on the remaining ones become useless because there is now a giant hole in the data set. The solution is to add parity to the system in the form of an additional drive. In this scheme, every time a block of data is written to a disk cluster, a parity block (or bit) is computed and is written to the parity drive. If any one drive fails, the data in the parity drive can be used to reconstruct the contents of the broken drive. The resulting system has a reliability figure that far exceeds the rate for any one drive. Note that depending on the RAID level used, the parity drive can be fixed or rotating among all the drives (as in RAID 5).

The drawback of the parity scheme is that it increases the storage cost of the system. On a four-drive system, the additional parity drive results in a storage penalty of 25%. So, the higher performance of striping does come at a rather substantial increase in cost even at media level.

Among the various levels, RAID 5 has gained the most popularity given its good compromise between speed and reliability. Others such as level 4 are also becoming popular in throughput-intensive applications like video servers.

As mentioned, RAID controllers cost considerably more than standard devices. As of this writing, high-performance PC-based controllers cost close to $1000, whereas a typical SCSI controller can be had for less than $200. The higher cost stems from the fact that the controller must handle transfers from multiple drives simultaneously, which usually involves on-board CPUs, memory, I/O buffer space, and other control logic.

Whether a RAID system is right for you depends on your hard disk usage pattern. If you require high bandwidth sequential access (e.g., in a video server or data acquisition), RAID makes a lot of sense. Similarly, if you like good (but not necessarily optimal) disk balancing, RAID can be a good solution. The benefits, of course, need to be weighed against the higher cost. You need to ask yourself whether the extra money can be better spent on other parts of the system (e.g., increasing memory size or buying faster disk drives). Of course, if you need five times higher performance than you can get from the fastest drive on the market, then you have no choice but to use a RAID system.

To get additional information on RAID, you may want to contact the RAID Advisory Board (RAB), which is made up of a group of companies that are interested in promotion of RAID technology and products. The group has published perhaps one of the best documents on the subject (*The RAID Book*). To get more information on RAB, contact

> RAID Advisory Board
> Technology Forums
> 13 Marie Lane
> St. Peter, Minnesota 56082
> Phone: (507) 931-0967
> Fax: (507) 931-0976

2.9.4 Software Disk Striping

Many vendors offer software-based disk-striping solutions that can give you similar performance to RAID subsystems but without the reliability features (i.e., RAID level 0). It takes little work for the operating system to spread the disk traffic across multiple controllers the same way a RAID controller would do. The only issue is that it would be too time-consuming to compute the parity in software, which is the reason for its absence. So, if reliability is not an issue, these packages make an adequate substitute.

Unfortunately, some UNIX vendors have unbundled these packages and charge a fair amount of money for them. So, again, you have to weigh the cost against the potential advantages.

2.10 Disk Drives

As you will learn in later chapters, disk drives are one of the worst enemies of your system performance. These mechanical devices have not enjoyed the same level of performance improvements as the CPU and can quickly become major bottlenecks. The problem is exacerbated by the fact that too often the only criteria for purchasing a disk drive are its size and cost. This is not wise because disk drives vary considerably in their performance characteristics due to the wide variety of factors involved in their design. The key is to understand the specifications published by the disk drive vendor.

2.10.1 Disk Drive Performance Metrics

A disk drive consists of one or more platters spinning at a constant speed commonly specified in revolutions per minute or RPM. Each platter usually has two surfaces where the data are stored and then accessed using a dedicated read/write head. The surfaces themselves are broken into concentric tracks, which are yet again subdivided into a number of (usually 512-byte) blocks or sectors.

To access a specific piece of data, the drive first has to seek out the right track and then wait for the desired sector to spin under it, at which time the data transfer begins. The amount of time it takes to get to the specified track is called the *seek time*. The amount of time it takes for the right sector to arrive under the head is called the *rotational latency*.

The number of sectors per track is fixed in the older drives. But in newer devices, the outer tracks have a larger number of sectors. In these so-called Zone Bit Recording (ZBR) devices, the drive electronics is smarter and varies the data rate depending on which track it is accessing. It is not unusual for the outer tracks to have almost twice as many sectors as the inner ones. As a result,

> *any data stored in the outer tracks (i.e., the beginning of the drive) in ZBR drives will be transferred much faster than inner tracks.*

What this means is that you should place your most often used data at the beginning of the drive rather than at the end, as is often the case.

The most popular specification for a disk drive is its average seek time even though it is often incorrectly stated as *access time*. The latter is the sum of seek time plus rotational latency. Because there are no standards for seek time measurements, the numbers that you see advertised are usually 40 to 50% of the maximum seek time (the amount of time it takes to go from track zero to the last track on the drive). Needless to say, you should get a drive with the fastest average seek time.

Keep in mind that small variations in seek time specifications have little meaning. We have a hard time judging a drive superior when it has a 0.5 milliseconds faster seek time than another drive.

Commodity drives as of this writing have a 12- to 20-millisecond seek time with faster ones at around 10 to 13 and state-of-the-art in the 8-millisecond range.

The latency figure specified for the disk drive is also an average number. It is calculated by dividing by two the time it takes for the drive to complete one revolution. As such, *rotational latency* is a direct function of how fast the drive spins. As an example, a 3600-RPM disk drive spins at 60 times a second or once every 16 milliseconds. Therefore, its average rotational latency would be 8 milliseconds. Because rotational latency can become a significant part of the total access time of a drive,

> *you should buy a disk drive with the highest RPM possible.*

It turns out that designing a drive to spin fast is fairly challenging, which is the reason behind the slow pace of increase in drive speeds. Because the start-up current (i.e., power) requirements for high RPM (e.g., 7200) drives are higher than ordinary drives, be sure to check the power supply rating of your system before installing these drives in your machine. You should also make sure there is ample air flow in your system to keep the drive below its maximum temperature rating. Fortunately, this problem is going away due to the fact that the number of disk platters is shrinking and, hence, the total energy/heat required to spin the drive fast.

As of this writing, disk drives running at 4500 RPM are gradually being phased out in favor of 5400 RPM. The state-of-the-art drives currently run in the neighborhood of 7200 RPM, which gives them significantly higher performance but at a premium price.

Most drive vendors are quick to publish their interface (e.g., SCSI) data rates but not the actual transfer rate that can be achieved. Fortunately, this information is readily available from the detailed drive specification brochure under the "internal data rate" heading. Typical ratings will be in megahertz, specified as a single number for the older drives with fixed sectoring, and a range for ZBR drives. To get the effective data rate of the drive, simply divide these numbers by 8 (they are in bits per second rather than bytes per second) and then multiply the result by 80%. The derating by 20% is needed because there are gaps between sectors where no data are stored. Because the exact length of the gap is hard to come by, you are stuck with this estimate. As an example, a drive rated at an internal transfer rate of 40 MHz will have a maximum transfer rate of 4 Mbyte/sec. A faster ZBR drive with a range of 49- to 83-MHz internal rate will have a maximum data transfer rate of 8.3 Mbytes/sec on the outer tracks but will slow down to 4.9 Mbyte/sec on the inner tracks.

Note that *the maximum data rate computed previously is the highest read/write rate you could ever achieve with this kind of drive on a sustained basis (i.e., more than a few kilobytes).* So even if a drive has a 20-Mbyte/sec interface, you are still bound by its slower maximum internal transfer rate, which in most cases will be less than half this rate.

On-board caches are a standard feature on all disk drives today. The algorithms used in these caches are somewhat guarded secrets so it is hard to make general statements about their effectiveness. But most drives implement one or more of these policies[10]:

- **Multisegmented reads** where the cache can hold different sectors and hence ˚speed frequent read requests to the same blocks. Nonsegmented caching was used in older drives and could only handle caching of contiguous sectors (and hence was very ineffective in a UNIX environment).

- **Write caching** means that the drive quickly copies write data to its buffer and acknowledges the completion of the request. It then asynchronously (in the background) writes the data to the drive. This lowers the write latency because the system can go about its business while the controller waits for the drive to seek and write the data. The drawback is that, if a write error occurs, it will be hard to trace it back to the I/O request that caused it. This is not much of a disadvantage because UNIX performs the same optimization and has the same problem regardless of whether the drive does this or not (see Chapter 3 on how the buffer cache works).

10. These are on common SCSI drives. The descriptions are based on a MICROPOLIS TAURUS drive brochure.

One place where this optimization helps is in NFS servers where UNIX disables its own write caching.

- **Write Combining** concatenates multiple write requests into a single request for a given track. This allows back-to-back write requests to be written to the same track without missing a revolution (having to wait for the drive to make a complete spin to write each block).

- **Tagged Command Queuing** means that the drive can sort requests in the most optimal manner and handle back-to-back sequential transfers. The latter feature is extremely important because it allows the drive to combine requests for consecutive sectors even though they are issued as separate I/O requests. This is needed because UNIX does not issue contiguous requests for more than one page (4 to 8 Kbytes) at a time. Instead, enhanced implementations of UNIX such as SunOS 4.1 issue read requests for multiple sequential blocks. Without command queuing, the drive would not be able to process the requests fast enough even if they are for adjacent blocks.

As with caching disk controllers, the effectiveness of the drive read/write caching is rather limited. Nevertheless, the larger the cache, the better its performance. Most drives today have cache sizes of 256 Kbytes, but some high-performance drives include as much as 1 Mbyte on board. As memories continue to become denser and cheaper, disk drive caches will invariably grow in size.

An almost unknown feature of modern drives known as thermal recalibration has gained some notoriety of late due to its impact on real-time response of the drive. To compensate for physical change in the media due to temperature variations, disk drives internally perform seeks on a regular basis (usually every 5 to 6 minutes) to calibrate their internal parameters. The performance lost due to this rather long seek in normal usage is too small to worry about. However, its almost random nature can be rather catastrophic in real-time applications such as video servers where data rates must be guaranteed. For this reason, drives developed for these new applications let the operating system disable thermal calibration and perform it on demand when the drive is idle.

2.11 Disk Drive Interfaces

Once the data are read from the media, they need to be transferred to the system. To ease this job, the industry has standardized a number of interfaces. The most common are Intelligent Drive Electronics (IDE) and Small Computer Systems Interface (SCSI).

2.11.1 The IDE Interface

The IDE (or more correctly ATA for AT Attachment) interface originated from the IBM PC. It is simply an extension of the PC ISA bus and, hence, requires very little in the form of control logic on the main system board. As a result, it costs next to nothing to implement in a PC (typical wholesale prices for an IDE controller are in the $5 range). This is the reason behind the immense popularity of IDE in the PC market.

Being based on the ISA bus, IDE drives are limited in transfer rates to roughly 2 Mbytes/ sec. As a result, most IDE drives are of low-performance designs. They tend to spin on the slower side (none above 5400 RPM as of this writing) and have long seek times (12 to 20 milliseconds is typical).

As of this writing, a new "enhanced" IDE standard has been adopted by the PC industry, which significantly changes this situation. The new standard substantially increases the transfer rate (to over 16 Mbytes/sec), expands the maximum storage size, and allows for other devices such as CD-ROMs to be connected to the same controller. But until the fastest drives become available with this interface, we recommend that you base your disk subsystem on the SCSI solution described next.

2.11.2 The SCSI Interface

SCSI owes its popularity to widespread usage on workstations and the Apple Macintosh computers. Being a high-level interface, SCSI hides the specific details of the drive (e.g., defect management) from the system. Another advantage is that SCSI allows up to eight devices (really seven because the SCSI controller is counted as one of the devices) to be connected on the same cable. Note that this does not mean that all the SCSI devices can communicate at once. Because they all share the same bus, only two devices (usually the controller and one other device) can communicate at any one time. Although it is possible for more than one device to be doing some work (e.g., two drives seeking simultaneously), only a single data transfer can occur at any one time.

SCSI support is not limited to disk drives. Other peripherals such as CD-ROMs, Magneto Optical (MO) drives, 8mm and 4mm tape backups and scanners are also available with SCSI interfaces.

The original SCSI specification (finalized in 1986) was fairly broad so disk drive vendors picked their own subset to implement. The resulting incompatibility gave SCSI a bad reputation as far as compatibility was concerned. To deal with this issue, the latter SCSI-2 specification outlined a minimum command subset (called a CCS), which every conforming device had to support. This has made it much easier to mix and match various disk drives and controllers.

The SCSI-2 specification allows devices to run at higher transfer speeds ranging from 10 to 20 Mbytes/sec (the original specification only allowed peak rates of 4 Mbyte/sec in asynchronous mode and 5 Mbyte/sec in synchronous mode). These higher speeds are achieved by allowing the bus to run at higher clock speeds and wider widths. You can start with a 5-MHz clock frequency, which at 8 bits results in a speed of 5 Mbytes/sec. Double the clock speed to 10 MHz, and you get Fast SCSI at 10 Mbytes/sec. Widen the bus to 16 bits and you now have Wide SCSI and the same rate. Make the clock frequency 10 MHz, and you get Fast & Wide SCSI with a peak transfer rate of 20 Mbytes/sec.

Note that all these speed ratings are peak transfer rates. The command and bus acquisition overheads result in a 20% loss on the average. As a result, a Fast SCSI cannot sustain more than 7.5 to 8 Mbytes/sec on real-life transfers. Likewise, you will be hard pressed to get more than 16 to 17 Mbytes/sec on Fast and Wide SCSI.

Do not make the mistake of assuming that using Fast and Wide SCSI actually doubles the transfer rate of a disk drive. It does not. Because the media transfer rate of most drives is less than 10 Mbytes/sec, the faster interface is not going to speed up the transfer rate unless the requested sector is in the disk drive's cache. Typical improvements are about 15%. Of course, having the faster bus allows multiple drives to run more efficiently on the same bus.

Beware of another misconception that SCSI-2 is twice as fast as SCSI-1. This is not true. To be faster, a drive (and controller) need to support either the Fast or Wide interface, neither of which is mandatory in SCSI-2.

Fast SCSI interfaces have become fairly common these days as the additional cost to produce them is minimal. Wide SCSI, however, is more elusive because its interface is different (due to the wider bus) and the cost to support it is also higher.

Note that to really see the benefits of faster SCSI modes, you need to be using a high-performance controller. An ISA-based controller on a PC cannot transfer data faster than 2-4 Mbytes/sec to the system memory so the extra bandwidth between it and the drive is of little value. This is typically not an issue on workstations and larger systems where the SCSI controllers sit on fast high-performance buses.

2.12 Other Storage Peripherals

In addition to disk drives, many systems have other peripherals in the form of tape backups, CD-ROM, etc. You should keep in mind that these devices run considerably slower than hard disks and can easily create I/O bottlenecks of their own.

Table 2.3 shows a list of common peripherals that you are likely to run into along with their performance characteristics. As you can see, some devices such as CD-ROMs have quite a way to go before they catch up with hard disks. With a transfer rate at 10% of a modern hard disk and access times that are 10 times slower, they are unlikely to provide a snappy response. Of course, the final choice of a peripheral depends on factors other than performance (e.g., cost/Mbyte). But if you do have a choice, pick the fastest device in each category.

Table 2.3 Performance Characteristics of Common Peripherals

Device	Max. Capacity (MB)	Access Time (ms)	Transfer Rate (KB/sec)	Comments
3.5" Floppy	1.44		128	
3.5" Floppy	2.88		256	
Single-speed CD-ROM	550-680	600+	150	
Double-speed CD-ROM	550-680	220-400	300	Make sure to check cache size, which varies from 64 to 256 Kbytes
Triple-speed CD-ROM	550-680	200-300	450	Make sure to check cache size, which varies from 64 to 256 Kbytes
Quad-speed CD-ROM	550-680	160-220	600	Make sure to check cache size, which varies from 64 to 256 Kbytes
3.5" Magneto-Optical (MO)	128/side	16	375	Requires track to be erased before write
5.25" Magneto-Optical (MO)	1300/side	30-50	2000 (read) 1000 (write)	Some require tracks to be erased before write
Floptical	20	130		
3.5" SCSI Hard Disk	4000+	8-15	2000-8000	
4mm (DAT) Tape	2000-8000	N/A	183-1024	Uses compression to increase capacity and throughput
8mm (Exabyte) Tape	2300-8000	N/A	245-2000	Uses compression to increase capacity and throughput

2.13 The Graphics Subsystem

With the exception of servers and multiuser machines, most UNIX systems include a bit-mapped graphical interface. Together with appropriate software (e.g., X Window), users can take advantage of multiple virtual terminals and easier to use graphical applications.

Unlike traditional terminals where each piece of data was a single byte, graphical systems must handle a large amount of screen data (pixels). This can put a very heavy burden on the system performance. To see why, we need to look at how a typical graphics controller works.

2.13.1 Video Update and Refresh

Any data sent to a computer monitor are visible only for a very short amount of time, after which they fade to black. The stable display that you see is the result of constant refresh (repaint) of the screen contents. This repainting literally requires that the screen pixels be read one by one and output to the monitor on a regular basis. If the interval is high enough, the eye perceives the data to always be on the display.

To get a flicker-free display, the refresh rate (number of times the entire screen is output) must be a minimum of 60 Hz (i.e., 60 times per second) or higher. The preferred rate is 72 Hz or higher, which not only reduces flicker but also eliminates "beating" with other light sources that run at the AC line frequency of 50 or 60 Hz (e.g., fluorescent lights).

It is unreasonable to require that the application programs or the operating system constantly rewrite the screen contents. This job is left to the graphics controllers, which employs a frame buffer (a piece of memory) where the screen contents are stored. On every refresh interval, the controller reads the pixels one at a time and outputs them to the monitor (through a digital-to-analog converter device known as a RAMDAC).

The type of memory system used for the frame buffer can have a large impact on the performance of the graphics controller. The frame buffer must support all the refresh traffic in addition to providing adequate bandwidth for the CPU to store data in. The lowest cost solution involves using DRAMs, but a quick computation shows that the DRAM performance is not adequate for high-resolution, high-refresh-rate applications. A graphics controller that supports a standard resolution of 1024 by 768 with 256 colors (8 bits) requires that 0.75 Mbytes of data to be read in each refresh cycle. At 72 Hz, the required data rate for refresh alone will be 54 Mbytes/sec. An 8-bit DRAM with a page mode access time of 50 nanoseconds will have a peak bandwidth of only 20 Mbytes/sec. A typical, 32-bit-wide frame buffer will then have a peak bandwidth of 80 Mbytes/sec of which 68% is used for refresh traffic alone. Such a controller would not be able to support higher resolutions or depth (colors). A 24-bit ("true color") display would significantly worsen this situation by requiring more than 150 Mbytes/sec just for refresh!

Now you see why some graphics controllers are limited in resolution as well as refresh rates. Often a graphics card is rated to support a high resolution of 1280 by 1024, but the fine print shows that it supports only a 60-Hz or lower refresh rate. Some boards even resort to interlace mode where only every other line is refreshed in each cycle. This effectively results in a 30-Hz refresh rate with a very annoying flicker.

Needless to say, DRAMs do not make high-performance frame buffers. Their main advantage is low cost and hence their popularity in the PC graphics world. A solution to the bandwidth problem of DRAMs is to use a special type of memory chip called a Video RAM or VRAM. These devices have two data ports with one optimized for sequential access (used for refresh) and the other for random access (used by the CPU and graphics controller to access the frame buffer). The two ports can be active at the same time, which almost doubles the effective frame buffer bandwidth.

As with most things in life, the added performance comes at a cost that is 50 to 100% higher than DRAMs. The additional cost adds up quickly as the frame buffer becomes larger (due to higher depth or resolution). As you would suspect, workstations that are not as price-sensitive as PCs come standard with VRAM-based frame buffers.

2.13.2 Graphics Operations

While refresh is a heavy burden on the graphics controller, it is the speed of various graphics operations that determines the ultimate performance of the device. These operations include outputting text and drawing and filling various shapes (lines, boxes, circles, etc.). In the simplest scheme (in so-called dumb frame buffers), the CPU computes the actual pixels and writes them into the graphics frame buffer. Most controllers, however, have a graphics coprocessor that is optimized for these operations.

Performance of a graphics controller varies depending on whether the operation is compute- or bandwidth-intensive. Filling operations (e.g., drawing a box filled with a specific color) are very bandwidth-limited. Other operations such as line drawing do not involve accessing many pixels but require smart hardware to compute the location of each pixel.

It turns out that the required bandwidth for good graphics performance can be surprisingly high. Take the simple case of clearing the screen and filling it with data. In our example of a 32-bit, DRAM-based frame buffer, only 26 Mbyte/sec is available to the CPU for read and write out of a total bandwidth of 80 Mbytes/sec. Assuming 100% efficiency, it would take 0.03 seconds (0.75/26) for the CPU to clear (i.e., zero) the frame screen and another 0.03 seconds to fill it with data. Put another way, you can do this operation only 16 times a second. In reality, the rate will be closer to 8 to 10 times per second; the page-mode access in the DRAMs would fall apart because it is unlikely that the CPU would want to access the same row that is being refreshed. Such low rates are far from instantaneous, which is what the user expects.

Besides using VRAMs, the bandwidth can also be increased by using more chips in parallel. While most designs use 32-bit frame buffers, some high-end controllers have 64-bit-wide memories (which is what is typically meant by "64-bit graphics controller" often seen in the vendor advertisement). By using multiple memory chips in parallel, the bandwidth can be increased linearly resulting in proportionally faster drawing rate by the CPU or the graphics controller. Of course, wider interfaces cost more because they may require more chips to drive them. In addition, the minimum frame buffer size can grow due to the large number of memory chips required. Very wide memory subsystems are used in 3-D graphics controllers in which the appetite for bandwidth is far greater than the standard 2-D graphics cards.

The last important consideration in the design of the graphics hardware is its interface with the CPU. Even with an "intelligent" graphics controller, the CPU needs to transfer large amounts of data to the frame buffer. Fast and wide I/O buses such as VL and the PCI bus in the PC world are quite effective in maximizing the graphics performance. Workstations have traditionally used 32-bit or 64-bit interfaces, which also do a good job of keeping the bandwidth to the CPU high.

2.14 Additional Information

To learn more about computer architecture in general (e.g., the CPU, caches and memories), you may want to get a copy of

> Patterson, D. A., and Hennessy, J. L. [1990]. *Computer Architecture: A Quantitative Approach*, Morgan Kaufmann Publishers, San Mateo, CA

As excellent as this text is, it does not cover some of the newer architectures that have come out in recent years. For this and many other excellent topics, we highly recommend that you get a subscription to the *Microprocessor Report: The Insiders' Guide to Microprocessor Hardware*. As of this writing, the report comes out 17 times a year and costs $445. To get more information, contact

> MicroDesign Resources
> 874 Gravenstein Hwy. So., Suite 14
> Sebastopol, CA 95472
> Phone: (707) 824-4004 or (800) 527-0288
> Fax: (707) 823-0504

2.15 Summary

There is more to computer system performance than simple specifications published by vendors. Some systems are designed with high integer performance, which makes UNIX run well, whereas others have excellent floating-point performance for running compute-intensive engineering and technical applications. Little-known aspects of the system design such as the memory and cache controller have a large impact on the performance of the system in floating-point-intensive applications. Even familiar topics such as virtual memory have performance limitations depending on the design of the TLB. Understanding these factors makes it possible to determine when a performance problem is caused by hardware limitations and not UNIX. Moreover, better knowledge about what makes a good system should enable you to make a more informed purchase decision in the future.

CHAPTER 3

Performance Characteristics of the UNIX Design

While this is not a text on UNIX internals, the analysis of system performance becomes much easier with a good understanding of how UNIX operates. For the sake of brevity, we concentrate only on those aspects of the UNIX design that have a significant impact on the performance of the system. For a more complete coverage of these topics, see the list of references at the end of this text.

3.1 The Basics

A UNIX system consists of a set of user programs and the operating system. The programs are typically referred to as processes or jobs, and the core operating system is called the kernel. The kernel is the main controlling program that gets loaded in memory when the system initially boots and stays resident at all times. It usually lives in /unix or /vmunix in BSD-derived systems (e.g., SunOS 4.1), and /stand/unix in many System V derivatives. However, there is no real standardization in this area, and some vendors have either moved or renamed their kernel. Two examples are the HP-UX kernel, which lives in /hp-ux, and Solaris, which uses /kernel/unix.

3.2 Determining the Kernel Size

The first thing to note about the kernel is that it is one of the largest users of system memory. Surprisingly, there is no accurate method for determining its size. All is not lost, however. With a little bit of trial and error, you should be able to find its approximate size.

Even though your first inclination may be to use `ls -l`, the size shown by it can be quite incorrect. What `ls` shows is the number of bytes the kernel image occupies on disk and not the amount used in memory. The kernel image on disk has many other pieces of information in it such as the symbol table (used by debuggers to identify the program variable address), which never gets loaded into memory. Furthermore, the kernel allocates a fair amount of memory for its internal data structures when it first starts execution (at boot-up time) and as it runs. It is impossible to get this information from the static listing that you get from `ls`.

The most foolproof way to estimate the kernel size is to look at the console output generated as the system boots. The kernel reports all the available memory that it finds after the **mem =** label and how much remains after taking what it needs on a line that starts with **avail mem =** .[1] To determine the initial kernel size, simply subtract the two numbers.

Rebooting the system to see the start-up memory usage message is rather inconvenient. Fortunately, BSD systems and some System V derivatives such as HP-UX include a `dmesg` utility that displays the previously printed console messages. Note that you must have root privileges to run `dmesg` on some systems like HP-UX:

```
SunOS4.1% /etc/dmesg |grep mem
mem = 32768K (0x2000000)
avail mem = 30494720
```

`dmesg` reads console messages from a circular buffer inside the kernel, which wraps around when it fills up. Therefore, if the kernel has printed more than a certain amount of console messages (usually 4-8 Kbytes) Since the system was booted, the kernel size information cannot be displayed with `dmesg`. Fortunately, the console message are periodically saved in `/usr/adm/messages`[2] so you may want to `grep` in there before resorting to a reboot.

Note that you can see only the start-up size of the kernel using these methods. With the exception of DEC UNIX, we know of no standard method to display the actual kernel size at runtime. This is a shame because the kernel maintains this size internally and it would have required little effort to have one of the system utilities display it.

---

1. The actual wording of the memory-usage message may vary from system to system. Just browse through the boot-up messages, and you should be able to spot it.

2. dmesg is run with -a option frequently by `cron` to save console messages in `/usr/adm/messages`.

3.3 User Processes

Each user process consists of at least four memory segments. The text segment holds the CPU instructions; the data segment contains all global variables that are initialized to certain value (e.g., int MaxSize = 5); the BSS segment is used for uninitialized global variables (e.g., char data[1000]); and the stack holds all the local and temporary variables. You can display the *initial* size of the text, data, and BSS segments by using the size command[3]:

```
% size /bin/cp
text    data    bss     dec     hex
5632    1488    24      7144    1be8
```

Again, this is the initial size of a program because its actual memory usage can grow as it executes. Because programs are free to enlarge their BSS segment by calling the malloc library routine, it would be impossible to determine the true size of a process from its copy on disk. In addition, the stack segment, while small at the beginning (usually 16-32 Kbytes), is grown automatically by the kernel. Because the memory allocated for stack depends on the actual runtime behavior of the program, size has no way of determining its size. The ps command, as described in later chapters, can be used to display the true size of a running program.

3.4 System Calls

User programs can take advantage of functions built into the system by using libraries and system calls. The standard C library (libc) contains many useful functions such as printf, strcpy, and qsort that can be called by user programs. Some of these functions are implemented using standard-user-level code and do not need any help from the kernel (e.g., strcpy). Others such as printf have to ask the operating system to perform certain services (in this case, output to user terminal). The reason for the distinction is that accessing the I/O subsystem is a "privileged" operation from the hardware point of view and normal user programs are not allowed to perform them. The requests to the kernel are made in the form of system calls.

To user programs, system calls appear as normal procedures and are called just like any other function. The distinction is that the code for the system call is not contained in the user program but actually lives inside the kernel. Examples of UNIX system calls are

- open, read, write, and close to access disk files,
- sbrk (used by the malloc C library routine) to allocate memory, and
- fork/exec to create/execute programs.

---

3. Run under SunOS 4.1 on a SPARCstation 2.

System calls are implemented using special hardware instructions that suspend a process upon execution (i.e., generate a hardware trap) causing the CPU to branch to a special kernel routine called the system call trap handler. The trap handler then calls the relevant routine inside the kernel, which knows how to provide the requested service.

The kernel routines can be as simple as a few lines of code (e.g., as in the case of the `get-pid` system call, which just returns the current process id) or thousands of lines of code (in case of network access). Regardless of the size, these routines eventually return to the user program and allow it to execute again. So, in essence, system calls are indirect function calls into the kernel. The main reason for this elaborate mechanism is to make sure that there is only one (secure) entry point into the kernel.

The many steps involved in making a system call means a very long execution time compared to normal, user-level function calls. Even simple systems calls such as `getpid` are hundreds of times more time-consuming to execute than ordinary functions. So, take care to use them judiciously. For example, it is considerably more efficient to make one `write` system call to output 80 bytes than to make 80 system calls each with 1 byte to output.

Even though the kernel supports over 200 system calls, studies show that the most heavily used system call is `read` followed far behind by `write`. The reason is that UNIX treats all I/O devices as files so that almost all interactions with the system are in the form of `read` and `write` system calls. Heavy reliance on shell scripts and temporary files (mainly used by compilers and editors) also points to large usage of `read` and `write` system calls. The efficiency of these services has a direct bearing on the performance of the system as a whole. One of the most important optimizations in this area is the buffer cache subsystem, which significantly boosts file I/O speed.

3.5 The Buffer Cache

When a process requests a block of data to be read from a file, the kernel first reads the corresponding disk block into a special buffer in memory and then copies it from there to the user program. This intermediate buffer is preserved in case another request for the same piece of data is made. In this case, the system simply fetches from memory avoiding a slow disk read operation. The memory pool used to hold these temporary buffers is called the buffer cache.[4]

To see how effective the buffer cache can be in practice, let's look at a simple example. Assume that you execute these commands quickly one after the other:

```
% cat foo
% vi foo
```

---

4. Do not confuse this with the cache memory used by the CPU. Buffer cache uses main memory to speed disk accesses, whereas the CPU cache uses very fast memory to speed main memory accesses.

When `cat` starts running, it opens the file `foo`, then makes read requests and displays the data until it reaches the end of the file. With every read request, the kernel allocates a buffer (a chunk of memory) large enough to hold the individual blocks in the file. It then issues a read request to the disk drive to fetch the data. Once the transfer is complete, the data are copied from the buffer to `cat`'s program space. Assuming that the buffer cache is larger than the size of the file `foo`, a complete copy of `foo` remains in the buffer cache after `cat` is finished reading it block by block. Because the kernel always looks in the buffer cache before going to the disk drive (or the network in the case of NFS), when `vi` requests the same set of blocks out of `foo`, it gets the copies already in the buffer cache. By avoiding costly disk or network reads, the buffer cache reduces file access time substantially.

Note that the buffer cache is a universal resource in the sense that the data blocks that it holds do not belong to any specific program. They live long after the program has finished execution, as is evident in our example.

In addition to read cache, the kernel also implements a write optimization policy called write-back or delayed-write. When a process issues a `write` system call to transfer a block of data to a disk file, the kernel simply copies the data from the user process into a block in the buffer cache and immediately returns to the process *without writing the data to the disk drive*. The buffer containing the data is simply marked as "dirty" and is kept in the buffer cache. These dirty buffers are flushed (written) to disk if the kernel needs a buffer and no free ones are available. In addition, the system writes out *all dirty buffers* when the `sync` system call is executed.

In BSD UNIX, the `update` program executes a `sync` system call every 30 seconds.[5] User programs can also call the `fsync` system call to flush dirty buffers associated with a specific file. (`fsync` is a very slow system call as it has to search the entire buffer cache to find the buffers that need to be flushed. You should avoid the temptation to use it.)

The System V kernel uses a somewhat more sophisticated mechanism for flushing the buffer cache. Instead of an external program, the kernel internally flushes the dirty buffers on a regular interval. SVR4 uses a more complex formula, which writes out the dirty blocks one batch at a time. This algorithm has the benefit of not causing an avalanche of write requests on systems with large buffer caches.

The write-back policy increases the performance of the system substantially but for a price. What if the system loses power before the dirty buffers are flushed to disk? *The simple answer is that all data that are not written to the disk drive will be lost!* You should keep this in mind when determining the right size for the buffer cache. The bigger it is, the higher the performance, and the larger the amount of data that can get lost.

---

5. The AIX equivalent is `syncd`, which executes every 60 seconds.

3.5.1 Buffer Cache Memory Allocation

Traditional implementations of UNIX preallocated space for the buffer cache when the system was booted. Today, with the major exception of SCO UNIX, no other implementation does this. Instead, they have integrated the buffer cache memory allocation with the scheme used for paging programs into memory page. Briefly, the kernel allocates memory for a block of file data from any available memory. As such, the buffer cache can grow up to the size of the available memory. The advantage of this scheme is that the buffer cache can start with a size of 0 and grow to a very large size. In the older scheme, if you wanted to enlarge the buffer cache, you had to reconfigure your kernel. With these so-called dynamic or paged buffer caches, there is no need to do anything.

As with most things in life, the dynamic or paged buffer cache comes at a cost. The problem is that no matter how large your main memory is, it will not take long for the buffer cache to fill it. So, the kernel must have an efficient algorithm to free memory on a regular basis. It turns out that this is a rather complicated problem and the reason for the poor performance in some early implementations (e.g., SunOS 4.0 and HP-UX 9.0). For a more detailed look at these problems, refer to Section 3.14.4.

3.6 The File System Layer

The file system layer sits above the buffer cache and is primarily responsible for management of the storage blocks and directory structure. Disk partitions (which are logical drives within physical drives) must be mounted first before UNIX can use them. The aptly named `mount` command associates a disk partition (e.g., `/dev/sd0d`) with a path name (e.g., `/usr`). Let's start by looking at the key structures in a UNIX file system, namely, directories and inodes.

3.6.1 The UNIX Directory Structure

Each file in UNIX is connected to a directory. The directory itself is just a special type of file that has for its contents a list of file names and inode numbers. The file names are what the user would specify in an `open` or `creat` system call. The inode is a data structure that contains all the information that describes a file or directory (see the next section).

The file names in older implementations of UNIX are limited to 14 bytes (with the 2-byte inode number, the total size for each entry was a nice round number of 16). All new implementations (see Section 3.6.5 on FFS) allow variable-sized file names with up to 255 characters. This has made the directory structure a bit more complex because it must maintain a size field for each file name entry.

3.6.2 The Inode Structure

Every file and directory in a UNIX file system has an inode associated with it. The inode includes such essential information as the disk block numbers allocated to the file, its size, owner, permissions, and access time. Before the kernel can open a file, it must first fetch its inode (from the disk drive) and check the user permissions against what is included in the inode.

The number of disk inodes (also called `dinodes`) in a fresh file system is determined automatically by the `mkfs` utility, which is responsible for making file systems. With the exception of some newer file systems such as the IBM LVS, the number of inodes on disk cannot be changed once the file system is created. To find out the number of inodes in your existing file systems, use the `-i` option of the `df` command:

```
% df -i
Filesystem          iused   ifree  %iused  Mounted on
/dev/sd0a            1572    13916    10%   /
/dev/sd0g           10604  175252     6%   /usr
/dev/sd0d           31812   53372    37%   /export
```

Unused inode entries simply waste disk space (each disk inode is about 256 bytes). On the other hand, if you run out of inodes, you will not be able to create new files or directories regardless of the amount of free disk blocks that you have. Either way, there is no performance impact.

Because there are too many inodes in each file system to be read all at once, the kernel reads inodes into memory on an as-needed basis. Each entry is put in a table called, appropriately, the *inode* table. This table acts as a cache to speed frequent accesses to the same file or directory by avoiding the constant update to the inode on disk. In addition, the inode entry remains in memory even after a file is closed. This means that the kernel can reuse the same inode entry if the file is reopened before its inode is used for another file. Of course, the entries in the inode tables eventually are reassigned to other files. How fast this occurs is a function of the size of the inode table and how many different files and directories are being accessed at one time.

The number of entries in the in-memory inode table is a parameter that is configured into the kernel. You must have at least one in-memory inode for each open file in the system along with one for the current directory of each user. So, you should make sure that you have an ample number of inodes. Otherwise, not only will you suffer from performance problems, you may also encounter application failures as their `open` requests are denied. As you will see in the next two chapters, the BSD `pstat` and the System V `sar` utilities let you display how big the inode table is and how many entries are in use.

Once an inode is fetched from the file system, the kernel uses it to figure out which disk blocks correspond to the logical blocks in the file. In case of an existing file, the first 12 ("direct") block numbers are stored in the inode structure itself. In the case of a file system with an 8-Kbyte block, quick access can be made to the first 96 Kbytes of the file.

In addition to the first 12 direct disk block numbers, the inode contains three other "indirect" block numbers. Instead of being the actual block numbers for the file, these entries point to disk blocks that contain additional block numbers for the file. So, to access the 13th block in the file, the kernel would have to read the first indirect block and then read whatever block number it finds at the beginning of it. Because block numbers are usually 4 bytes wide, a single indirect block would let you access files as large as 16 Mbytes (2048 entries times 8 Kbytes each) in our example. The next entry in the inode is a double indirect meaning that it points to a disk block, which itself contains nothing but single indirect blocks. In our example, this would let you access up to 32 Gbytes. The last entry in the inode is a triple indirect block meaning that it points to a double indirect block, which itself points to an indirect block. Following our scheme, this allows access to files as large as 64 Tbytes.

Despite the potential to access very large files, most UNIX systems cannot actually read or write files that are more than 2 Gbytes. This stems from the so-called seek pointers, which are 32-bit signed variables meaning that the largest range of positive numbers that you can represent is from 0 to 2 Gbytes. Some newer implementations of UNIX such as DEC's OSF/1 use 64-bit integers to represent file positions and hence can access much larger files.

Needless to say, it is very unlikely that your files will ever need more than double indirect blocks to access. On the other hand, you would do well to keep your files small so that they can be accessed with no indirection or just one indirect block.

3.6.3 The Name Lookup Cache

Looking up the inode for a file can be a very CPU-intensive process. The kernel must search each directory in the file path name before it can find its inode. For example, if you try to open the file /usr/tmp/foo, the kernel must search the root, /tmp and /usr/tmp directories in sequence before it can find foo's inode number.

A quick look at typical file names in UNIX shows that the majority of them start with the same set of path names (e.g., /, /usr, /tmp). Searching these directories time after time is simply wasteful. Indeed, studies in the early 1980s showed that the kernel namei routine, which was responsible for decoding file names and returning inodes, used up to 20% of the CPU cycles.[6] So, all versions of UNIX today implement a name-caching scheme for file name and inode pairs. Given a file name, the look-up or directory cache can quickly return its inode number eliminating the need to search each byte in the directory for the same information. To limit the amount of memory used for each cache entry,

> only path name components (e.g., tmp in /usr/tmp/foo) that are 14 bytes (32 bytes in Solaris) or less are cached.

So, you should use short file or directory names if at all possible. Another benefit of using short file names is that the fragmentation in the directory file will be less. Because the kernel does not compact directories, if you keep creating and deleting files, you wind up with a rather larger directory.

---

6. This, of course, was on a 1-MIP CPU, but the impact is still felt even on today's much faster CPUs.

3.6.4 Traditional UNIX File System

So far, we have ignored the issue of how inodes and directories are allocated on disk. From a performance point of view, the algorithm for placement of this data on disk can make a profound impact on the effective throughput of the file system.

The original UNIX file system (sometimes called s5) was designed with much flexibility and sported nice features such as 14-character file names[7] and the ability to access very large files and disk partitions. But good performance was not one of its strong traits.

As is evident in Figure 3.1, the s5 file system places inodes at the beginning of the partition after the superblock. The superblock is a fancy name for the data structure that describes the global properties of the file system. The most important information in the superblock is the list of free inodes and blocks. The kernel reads the superblock into memory when the file system is first mounted and only writes it out when a sync operation is performed or the file system is unmounted.

The first problem with the s5 file system is that it is very fragile in practice. The robustness problem stems from the fact that when the s5 file system wants to write out directory information, it uses the delayed write mechanism of the buffer cache. This means that if the system crashes and the buffer cache data are lost, you not only lose the contents of files but also any directory manipulations that you may have performed. The problem is worse than it seems because the buffer cache writes out blocks in more or less random fashion. This means that it is possible for the contents of a file to be written to disk before its inode entry. The result is that you can get "orphan" disk blocks and inodes that have to be removed because it is impossible to figure out where they belong (the file system check program, fsck, puts these files in the lost+found directory).

As for performance, there are a number of deficiencies in the s5 file system. The most important one (and perhaps the easiest to fix) is the small block size. The original implementation of s5 used a 512-byte block size (hence the reason for many file system utilities such as df using this as their unit of measurement). Later implementations increased the

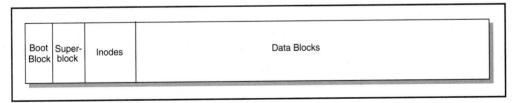

Figure 3.1 Traditional UNIX File System Layout (not to scale)

---

7. We know that 14 bytes no longer is considered a long file name, but recall that this feature was included in a file system in 1969 and today we are still using 8-character file names in PC DOS operating systems.

block size to 1 Kbyte and eventually to 2 Kbytes. But these are still too small to get good file I/O performance. To see why, we need to look at how a disk drive operates.

When you ask a drive to read a block, the disk drive head has to first seek to the right track where the block is located. Once there, it has to wait for the platter to rotate until the block that you are interested in reaches the head. At that point, the drive starts to read the data until it reaches the last sector in the block. Once the data have been read, the drive continues to turn as it always does. Because the rotational position of the drive is unknown, statistically, you have to wait for half a revolution before you can read your data block. On a drive that is rotating at 3600 RPM, it takes 16 milliseconds for an entire rotation or 8 milliseconds for half a rotation. Using this figure, you would be able to read at most 125 blocks in 1 second (i.e., one over 0.008). If the block size is 1 Kbyte, this would add up to a throughput figure of only 125 Kbytes/sec. This is less than 10% of the throughput of a modern disk drive and far lower than what could reasonably be achieved.

We have portrayed perhaps a rather pessimistic view of what can occur. Surely the system can read more than one block from a track (which can hold 32 to 64 Kbytes typically) once it gets to the right sector. Indeed, the s5 file system attempts to do that. The problem is that as data blocks are allocated and deleted, the free block list becomes totally random. This means that after some usage of the file system, it is unlikely that the blocks allocated to a new file are in the same vicinity let alone the same track. So, not only do you incur a rotational latency, you also have to pay a seek penalty to get to each block. The resulting throughput can actually be lower than the preceding computations if the file system is very fragmented. This is the reason for the old advice of backing up your s5 file system, remaking it and restoring its contents on a regular basis to avoid the performance degradation due to fragmentation of the file system.

A quick and dirty solution to this problem is to enlarge the file system block and hence the reason for the growth of the block size over the years. Although this increases the performance dramatically, it has the side effect of increasing file system waste. The reason is that the kernel allocates a minimum of one block to a file. Because the majority of files in a typical UNIX system are small, using a large block size can waste considerable space (half a block per file on the average).

Another serious performance problem is the placement of inodes on disk. The inodes sit at the beginning of the drive and usually occupy less than 5% of it. This means that every time you want to open a file that has not been accessed lately (i.e., is not in the inode cache), the drive must seek all the way back to the beginning the drive to read the inode and then seek back out to access the data blocks. Even with fast disk drives that sport seek times of 8 to 10 milliseconds, this is a very slow operation.

These problems, along with some finer ones that we did not mention, led to the development of a new file system by Kirk McKusick at UC Berkeley, which first appeared in the BSD 4.1C release in the early 1980s.

3.6.5 The BSD Fast File System

The BSD file system, which is typically referred to as FFS (also known as ufs in the SVR4 quarters), attempts to fix most of the shortcomings of s5. The key to its success is intelligent allocation of inodes and blocks to minimize disk latencies. The resulting performance can reach hardware speeds on good implementations, which has resulted in its widespread use even on System V machines (e.g., HP-UX).

To deal with the reliability issues, FFS writes out any information that changes the structure of the file system synchronously and waits for the I/O to finish. This means that if the system crashes, the chances of losing file names, directories, and inodes is sharply minimized.[8] FFS is also careful in how it performs certain risky, nonatomic operations (e.g., renaming a file) so that its companion program, fsck, is able to fix any problems that may arise should the system crash in the middle of the operation. This sharply reduces the chances of mangling the file system due to a sudden system crash. As an added measure, the super block is replicated multiple times so that if one copy is lost, the alternates can be used in its place (by fsck). So, there is no single block that can completely invalidate the file system as there is in the case of s5.

A side effect of this file system hardening is slower performance in certain applications. Specifically, directory- and inode-intensive operations such as rm -rf are painfully slow because each directory and inode change requires a disk access. Although the older implementations could handle thousands of directory deletions per second, FFS averages 50 to 100 depending on the average access time of your disk drive.

To increase performance, FFS enlarges the default block size to 4 Kbytes with many implementations (e.g., SunOS 4.1) using 8 Kbytes. This alone causes the throughput to go up by a factor of four to eight over an equivalent s5 file system. Even though FFS sports many other optimizations, they pale in comparison to the performance boost from the larger block size.

To deal with the file system waste due to the larger block size, FFS invents the notion of a fragment that can range in size from one eighth of a full block all the way up to the block size itself. For example, if the block size is 8 Kbytes, the fragment size can range from the default value of 1 Kbyte to a maximum of 8 Kbytes. Because fragments are the minimum unit of file allocation, the storage efficiency of FFS is as good as or even better than an s5 file system. But note that, like the block size, the minimum fragment size can be set only when the file system is first created with mkfs.

To understand the remaining optimizations in FFS, we need to look at how the file system is laid out (see Figure 3.2). The file system is divided into what are called cylinder groups. To minimize the long seek to fetch the inode for a file before accessing its blocks, FFS

---

8. You cannot eliminate this risk altogether because on a system crash the hardware can still corrupt disk blocks that may contain inodes or directories.

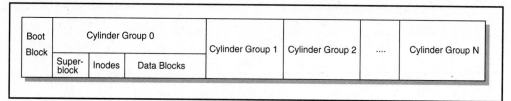

Figure 3.2 BSD Fast File System (FFS) Layout (not to scale)

attempts to keep all the relevant information for a file (i.e., directory, inode, and data blocks) in the same cylinder group. Because cylinder groups are fairly small compared to the overall size of the disk partition, the technique reduces seek times substantially.

For these algorithms to work well, the cylinder groups need to have ample free space. Otherwise, FFS would be forced into selecting a less optimal cylinder group for the file. Therefore, to increase the chances of optimal placement,

> *by default, the last 10% of the file system space cannot be used by normal (nonroot) users.*

The system goes one step farther by having the df command show that the file system is 100% full when it has really reached 90% capacity. The deception works so well that most users are not aware that there is so much space being wasted on each one of their disk drives (and they get very puzzled when df reports a file system that is over 100% full!). When this "feature" was first implemented, a 300-Mbyte disk drive was considered "large" and setting aside 30 Mbytes seemed reasonable. But on today's multigigabyte drives, leaving 10% of space (e.g., 200 MBytes on a 2-Gbyte drive) seems rather excessive.

Even though all advice in this text is geared toward performance, we are going to be pragmatic and recommend that you reduce the amount of space that FFS sets aside. You can safely ignore the warning given in typical documentation that going beyond 90% substantially lowers the file system performance. Our experience is that any sort of performance loss is not noticeable, and, in any case, the added disk capacity typically makes users more happy than a minor performance improvement. Furthermore, any loss of performance will be limited to files created *after* the file system has reached 90% capacity. Files created earlier would not have been affected. As a compromise, you may want to let the file system grow to 95%.

To make any changes, you need to modify the file system parameter, **minfree**, using the tunefs command (or mkfs when you are initially building the file system). Refer to Chapter 7 on how to do this.

3.6.6 Symbolic Links

One added feature of FFS is symbolic links that allow a file to be referenced with more than one name (or path). UNIX has always had a similar hard link feature that is implemented by having multiple directory entries point to the same inode. Because inodes are only unique within individual file systems, you cannot create hard links that point to files outside the same file system. Symbolic links, on the other hand, are special files whose contents are a path to another file name. This mechanism allows symbolic names to point to any file regardless of its location. For that matter, symbolic links can point to files that do not even exist.

Because accessing a file using its symbolic link requires that the kernel perform an additional disk read to fetch the actual path, many texts warn against using symbolic links frequently. Although they are correct in suggesting this, in most cases, heavily used symbolic links will be cached by the buffer cache. So, there is typically little additional I/O overhead. In addition, some implementations such as SunOS embed the alternate file name in the inode of the symbolic link file. This eliminates the need to do any other I/O operation to read the link—the data are already there (but only if the symbolic link name is less than 50 bytes or so).

The advice is still well taken though but for a different reason. Symbolic links are to the file system what `gotos` are to C programs. If used too frequently, it becomes very hard to decipher what really happens when you access a file. Because symbolic links can cross file systems and hence disk drives, they make it hard to analyze why a certain disk drive is being used heavily. So, use them judiciously.

3.6.7 Journalled File Systems

Despite its major improvements over the older system V file systems, FFS is not perfect. It still requires a lengthy file system check (by running the `fsck` program) after a system crash, which can be very time-consuming on large file servers. In addition, the synchronous nature of FFS when it comes to file system "meta data" (inodes, directories, cylinder group data, etc.) means that its performance can slow to a crawl in certain situations.

These problems have led to development of log structured and journalling file systems. These file systems differ from FFS in that, when the file system is being modified, the data are written sequentially to a log file (which is usually placed on a separate drive). The log changes are then applied gradually to the file system. If there is a system crash, recovery is quick because only the entries in the log file need to be reapplied. The process takes a few seconds compared to minutes for `fsck`.

Log-structured file system implementations include the AIX Journalled File System (JFS), the DEC Advanced File System (AdvFS), and the Sun UFS with Transaction Logging in Solaris DiskSuite. Some file systems such as JFS have additional bonus features, which include dynamic file system growth by simple addition of more partitions. In these systems, the inodes are kept as special files (much like directories are) and, hence, allow the disk inodes to grow indefinitely. In addition, this allows the inodes to be placed very close to where the files are located, further minimizing seeks.

On the performance front, log-structured file systems can perform better than FFS in environments where many files are created, deleted, and modified. All these operations slow down FFS but have little impact on a log-based file system because they simply append the required changes to the end of a sequential file. Because no random access I/O is required to the disk (as would be the case in FFS), performance is improved. Note that the assumption here is that the log file is placed on a separate disk. If this is not the case, it is debatable how much better a log-based file system performs. In systems such as DEC UNIX and Sun Solaris where you have a choice of file systems, you may want to experiment with each file system in your environment to see which one performs better.

3.6.8 Raw Partitions

Even though the UNIX file system code is very efficient, in certain environments you may want to bypass it. For example, databases routinely access random, 2- or 4-Kbyte blocks in very large files. This means that the blocks are not only too small for good file system throughput but also require indirect blocks to access. Another reason to avoid the file system is that there is considerable CPU overhead to access data through the buffer cache because it reads the data into its own data segments and then *copies* the data to the user buffer.

To deal with these issues, UNIX provides a back door into the disk subsystem called the raw or character interface. This interface bypasses both the buffer cache and the file system code. By opening the disk drive partition (e.g., /dev/rsd0a) directly, a user application can read or write any block it chooses. The data transfers from the device then occur directly into the user address space, eliminating the expensive copy operation. Because the file system is not used, the data on the disk partition look like a simple sequence of bytes with no structure whatsoever. It is the responsibility of the application to keep track of what it has stored on disk and how to retrieve it.

Because database servers already know how to manage data blocks, they are a good fit for raw partitions. The performance increase can be up to 20% compared to using the standard file system. While tuned file system implementations can close this gap, raw partitions do the job with less work.

Note that using the raw partition means that there is no write-behind, read caching, or read ahead of data. This means very slow performance for most applications aside from databases. So using raw partitions by no means is a generic optimization technique.

3.7 Process Creation

UNIX is a multitasking operating system, which means that it can create an arbitrary number of processes and make them appear to run simultaneously. Strangely enough, to run a new program, you must first create a new process by making a copy of an existing one. The copy of the process then overwrites itself with the new program to be run. The reason for this odd mechanism is the fact that when UNIX was first designed, it was easier to implement process creation using this two-step model.

The system call to copy or clone a process is called `fork`. Upon execution, `fork` results in two copies of the calling program running in the system. The program executing `fork` is called the parent, and the new process is referred to as the child. As a result of this bit-by-bit copy, both the parent and the child share and execute the same set of instructions.

To make it possible for each process to tell whether it is the child or the parent, the return code of the `fork` system call is different in the parent from the child. This allows the code to be structured in a way that separate pieces of code get executed on behalf of the parent and the child.

`fork` is only half the equation because the user typically is not interested in duplicating the current program but rather wants to run something else. The solution is the `exec` system call that overlays the calling program (usually the child) with a new one. The calling program is destroyed in the process and never regains control.

The shells are the heaviest users of `fork` and `exec` system calls. Anytime you type in the name of a program at the shell prompt, the shell executes a `fork`, and its child calls `exec` to run it. For example, when you type `ls` at the shell prompt, for a short period of time, there are two copies of the shell in the system (as a result of `fork`). The child shell, however, quickly calls `exec` with `/bin/ls` as its argument, which results in `ls` running in its place. The parent shell usually calls the `wait` system call, which suspends its execution until its ultimate child (`ls` in our example) finishes execution. If you type an ampersand (`&`) at the end of the command line, the parent shell simply skips the `wait` system call and continues execution by giving you its prompt.

As you might imagine, this two-step process can be rather inefficient. Indeed, making a copy of a process and then throwing it away by loading a new one on top of it can be very slow. This fact has not escaped UNIX developers who have tried many approaches to solve this inefficiency. There is great motivation for such efforts because `fork` and `exec` remain two of the most "expensive" system calls in terms of CPU cycles.

One optimization is to take advantage of the fact that user programs by default have read-only text (instruction) segments. Therefore, both the parent and child processes can safely share the same physical text memory, and no copying is necessary. This is fairly easy to do because there is direct hardware support for sharing memory between processes (see Section 3.13). Unlike text, however, the child needs to be able to modify the segments that it has write access to without corrupting the parent's data. This means that the kernel must make private copies of the data (including heap) and stack segments for the child.[9] This is inefficient, however, as the child typically does not access the entire contents of its data segment and, in any case, throws it away by calling `exec` to run a new program. Additional optimizations are performed to deal with this problem. Two common solutions are `vfork` and copy-on-write.

---

9. Heap is memory allocated by user programs at runtime (e.g., by calling `malloc`). Stack is a memory segment used to hold temporary variables such as function call arguments.

3.7.1 BSD's vfork

In BSD UNIX, a new version of fork called vfork was invented that does not copy any portion of the parent process. Instead, it "borrows" the physical memory of the parent process long enough for the child to run and call exec, during which time the parent process is suspended. Once the child copy goes away by calling exec, the parent is allowed to execute again. This makes vfork considerably faster than fork. The major drawback is that the child code needs to be written carefully so that it does not modify anything in its data or stack segments because doing so corrupts the parent's data. Therefore, vfork is not a direct replacement for fork. In BSD UNIX,

> *the C shell (csh) and make programs use vfork, but the Bourne shell does not.*

This means that C shell scripts may execute a bit faster than Bourne shell, all else being equal. The speed differential (up to 20%) is visible only when many quickly executing programs are used. Note that some implementations of csh in System V-derived kernels (e.g., HP-UX) do not use vfork. The result is that C shell scripts may actually run slower depending on how the vfork code is implemented. Timing the execution of a shell script with a few hundred lines of /bin/echo >/dev/null can tell you if there is any advantage to using csh. [10]

3.7.2 System V's Copy-on-Write Optimization

In System V-derived kernels, the fork implementation itself is modified to be more efficient. In a similar manner to vfork, both the parent and child processes are allowed to execute from the same shared physical memory for *both text and data*. But each process gets only read access to this memory so that they cannot corrupt each other's data.

If either the child or the parent attempts to modify a part of the shared memory, the hardware generates a write protection fault (a trap) that gives control to the kernel. The kernel then makes a new and distinct copy of the offending memory page for the process. This involves allocating a new page and copying the contents of the corresponding shared data page to it. This mechanism of waiting to copy something until it is written to is known as copy-on-write.

Copy-on-write is more efficient than the older implementation of fork because it potentially avoids copying all the data segment. But in practice, it does not work as well as its designers had hoped. The reason has to do with the way the shell uses fork and exec. Between the time that the shell calls fork and when exec is involved, the child shell modifies so many of its global variables that the kernel is forced to make new copies of most of the parent's data segment. Because each write protection fault represents additional overhead that did not exist in straight copying of the data segment, the CPU usage

---

10. We use this simple script because its syntax is compatible with all three shells (sh, csh and ksh) and the size of the echo program is smaller than the shells which makes the fork overhead versus vfork more visible.

actually can go up compared to a simple `fork` even if some of the pages are not copied. For this reason,

> *some vendors have disabled copy-on-write for small processes such as the Bourne shell.*

Ironically, the main motivation behind creation of the copy-on-write mechanism was to speed up the shell, which is the heaviest user of `fork` and `exec`.

3.8 Process Termination

Once a process has finished running, the system needs to free all its resources. This is done through the `exit` system call. `exit` can be called explicitly by the user application or on return from `main`.

The main purpose of `exit` is to free any memory allocated to the process in addition to kernel data structures. `exit` also attempts to return a status value to its parent (called the exit code) and close any open files.

While the process is in the `exit` system call, the kernel marks it as a zombie and programs such as `ps` display this status as defunct. Some processes can get stuck in this mode indefinitely if they are not able to close their open files. This situation occurs if as part of closing the file, some I/O operation hangs (e.g., a tape drive that breaks and does not respond to a rewind command). Because the kernel frees most of the resources used by the process at the entrance to the `exit` system call, zombie processes present little burden to the system and can be safely ignored.

3.9 Process Scheduling

Because UNIX allows many jobs to be runnable at once, it needs to have a mechanism to share the CPU among them. After all, the CPU is a single resource and can run only one program at a time. The simplest solution is to put each process in a queue (appropriately called the run queue) while it is waiting to be run by the CPU. When the CPU finishes running the current process, it picks up the next process in the queue and runs it.

The actual organization of the run queue varies from system to system. Figure 3.3 shows the implementation in BSD UNIX[11].

The priority assigned to a process is a function of the scheduler in your UNIX implementation. The scheduler assigns default priorities to processes when they start. The priority is

---

11. The actual organization is a doubly linked list for ease of insertion and deletion. For simplicity, we have omitted the reverse links.

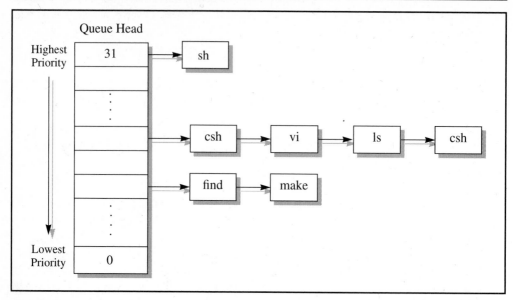

Figure 3.3 BSD Run Queue Organization

then varied based on the activities of the process (see the following sections on how this occurs in BSD and SVR4 versions of UNIX). Because the kernel searches for a process to run by looking at the queues from top to bottom, a process with a high priority runs ahead of one with a lower priority. If there is more than one job in any queue, the kernel runs each one for a maximum of one time quantum or slice (one tenth of a second in BSD UNIX). This scheme is commonly called round robin scheduling because jobs with the same priority are treated equally. The kernel will not go down to a lower queue unless all the upper ones are empty. Therefore, higher priority jobs run until either they give up the CPU or their priority lowers because of their high CPU usage.

Note that the run queue may have a smaller number of rows or slots than the range of priorities in the specific scheduler. An example is the BSD system, which has 256 priority levels but only 32 queues. In this case, the kernel divides the priority of each process by eight to arrive at the right queue number. Due to this scaling and the resulting loss of precision, small changes in priority (e.g., from 4 to 7 in the BSD scheme) may not make a process more or less likely to run because it does not result in a change in its position in the run queue.

3.9.1 The Idle Loop

When the run queue is empty, the kernel executes a "do nothing" loop waiting for some outside event. This could be an interrupt telling the system some I/O operation has finished potentially waking up a user process. The kernel then exits the idle loop and searches the run queue to find a process to run. The amount of time spent in the idle loop is extremely significant in system tuning because it indicates how busy the CPU is. See the next two chapters on how to display the idle time in your respective version of UNIX.

3.9.2 Process Suspension and Restart

The kernel often has to deal with events that can take a long time to finish. For example, an I/O request to a hard disk may take up to 20 milliseconds to complete. Although this may not seem long, modern CPUs can execute millions of instructions in the same amount of time. Therefore, for best efficiency, it is important to run another process rather than simply to wait for the I/O request to finish. To do this, we need to have a mechanism for temporary suspension of program execution and the ability to restart it when the event it is waiting for completes.

The kernel suspends the execution of a process by putting it to sleep. This operation requires only that the sleeping processes be left out of the run queue. The situation is simplified by the fact that the currently running job is not in the run queue (it is taken out of the queue before execution). So, when a process wants to go to sleep, the kernel simply abandons it and goes searching in the run queue for the next process to run.

When the request that the process is waiting for completes, the system wakes up the process by putting it back in the run queue. This allows the process to run again the next time the kernel searches the run queue.

The most common users of sleep and wake up are processes making I/O requests. In a typical system, most processes are waiting for keyboard input. These processes are in the sleep state *using no CPU time*. The next common occurrence is disk or network I/O. In all cases, a process is awakened when an interrupt occurs indicating the termination of the I/O request.

3.10 The BSD Scheduler

In BSD UNIX, process priorities range from -128 (highest) to +127 (lowest). Note that processes with a numerically lower priority run ahead of processes with numerically higher priorities, even though this may seem reversed. That is, a process with a priority of 0 runs ahead of one with a priority of +100. Just to keep things clear in this text, when we refer to a process as having a higher priority, we mean that it has a better chance of getting CPU time even though the numerical value of the priority may actually be smaller (or even negative) as is the case in the BSD scheduler.

In UNIX, you cannot manipulate the process priority directly. Instead, you give the system a hint as to what the value should be by specifying its nice value. The nice value of a new process is the same as its parent (which is usually zero). You can change the nice value in order to increase or decrease your chances of getting CPU time. We use the word *chances* because the actual priority of a process depends on a scheme called priority migration.

3.10.1 Priority Migration

UNIX scheduling is designed more for "fairness" than for keeping any one user happy. Specifically, the system wants to make sure no process ever starves for CPU regardless of its priority. So, instead of allowing a process with the best nice value (-20) to have the system to itself, the kernel uses the nice value as one of the (important) parameters to determine the actual priority of a process. The factors used to calculate the ultimate priority of a process in BSD are

- the amount of CPU time the process has used,
- the nice value, and
- the amount of free memory.

The system lowers the priority of a process if it uses too much CPU (and by a small amount if there is a memory shortage). The priority is raised if it has been waiting too long for the CPU. This algorithm is applied to the priority of every process in the system once a second. The exception is the priority of the currently running job, which is lowered every four clock ticks (each tick is typically 0.01 seconds). The technical term for this process is priority migration. To see this process in action, use the `ps` utility to display the priorities of the processes as they run (see the next two chapters).

Note that there are no user tunable parameters in the computation of priority outside of the nice value. However, there may not be much need for tuning as this mechanism works fairly well for general time-sharing use.

3.10.2 System Level Priorities

When a process goes to sleep inside the kernel (as a result of a system call), it gives up the CPU. But before doing so, it notifies the kernel that it should wake up at a much higher priority. These so-called system priorities are above the best values that normal processes can achieve. This means that once a process wakes up (e.g., when its disk I/O finishes), the kernel makes it runnable ahead of any normally executing job and regardless of the original priority or nice value of the process.

The reason for this temporary boost in user priority is to allow the process to finish execution inside the kernel and exit as quickly as possible. The thinking is that a sleeping process is potentially holding on to kernel resources (i.e., data structures) that it can free once it wakes up. Note that once the process starts execution, its priority reverts back to normal.

There are a range of system priorities that the process can choose before going to sleep. The lowest level is for user-requested sleeps (e.g., when you type `sleep 20` at the shell prompt) or the `wait` system call (which the shell uses to wait for the user commands to finish execution). The highest priority is reserved for memory waits with disk I/O falling somewhere in between.

Just in case you are wondering, there is no mechanism for a user to assign system priorities to a process. The selection is done on behalf of the process when it is executing inside the kernel.

The problem with system priorities is that they reduce the fairness of the scheduler because some processes get system priorities more often than others. For example, if a low-priority process constantly issues systems calls that cause sleeps (e.g., disk I/O), it may run ahead of many higher-priority processes. This is the reason that niceing I/O bound jobs usually has little effect.

3.11 The SVR4 Schedulers

Traditional UNIX schedulers have been hard-coded in a sense that unless you had access to the kernel sources, you could not modify them. Although these schedulers work fairly well in a time-sharing environment, users of other applications and those familiar with other operating systems have been asking for a more flexible system. To this end, SVR4 has a modular scheduler system where you can plug in different schedulers in the kernel, on a per-process basis.

The standard SVR4 implementation includes three schedulers: Time Sharing (TS), Real Time (RT), and System (SYS). In addition, it is possible to add other schedulers to the system, but, as of this writing, the job requires access to the kernel sources. The TS and RT schedulers are highly tunable, and their parameters can be modified using the dispadmin (dispatcher administration) utility.

The various schedulers can be configured in or out of the kernel (which as a minimum requires changing a configuration file and rebooting the system as with Solaris 2.X, or rebuilding a new kernel as with some other SVR4 implementations). To see which ones are configured in your system, use the dispadmin command with the -l option:

```
Solaris# dispadmin -l
CONFIGURED CLASSES
==================

SYS     (System Class)
TS      (Time Sharing)
RT      (Real Time)
```

As the names imply, TS is for general time-sharing use and RT is for real-time processes. The SYS class accommodates the system priorities already discussed for processes that are sleeping in the kernel.

3.11.1 Global Priorities in SVR4

The RT class has control of the highest range of global priorities with the SYS and TS class schedulers owning the lower two segments, respectively (see Figure 3.4 on page 80). This means a real-time process has a higher priority than any TS process whether that process is running in the kernel or not.

Even though the scheduler in SVR4 has its own range of priorities, there is only one set of global priorities that the kernel uses to decide which process to run next. The individual schedulers are responsible for translating the user priority into the global priority.

Because the scheduler class of a process is inherited across a `fork` system call, all the children of a process have the same scheduler. For example, if you change the scheduler class of your shell script to RT, all the processes started from it also have real-time priorities. This is the key to providing backward compatibility with older versions of UNIX. The `/etc/init` program, which is the first user process ever started in the system (and hence is the parent of all the processes in the system), uses TS as its scheduler. As a result, every process by default becomes a TS process without making a specific selection.

3.11.2 The Time-Sharing Scheduler

The TS scheduler has been designed to work similarly in behavior to the traditional scheduler in UNIX. However, appearances can be misleading. The actual behavior of TS is markedly different from older schedulers. Instead of a fixed time slice of 0.1 second, the default time slice is variable and becomes smaller as the priority of the process goes up. In another departure, numerically higher values actually mean a higher probability of getting CPU time (but to make it even more confusing, the interface provided to the users is the traditional inverse sequence).

The TS, like the other schedulers in SVR4, is highly tunable. To see all its parameters, use the `dispadmin` command. This is an example from Sun Solaris:

```
sunshine# dispadmin -c TS -g
# Time Sharing Dispatcher Configuration
RES=1000
```

# ts_quantum	ts_tqexp	ts_slpret	ts_maxwait	ts_lwait	PRIORITY	LEVEL
200	0	59	0	50	#	0
200	0	59	0	50	#	1
200	0	59	0	50	#	2
200	0	59	0	50	#	3
200	0	59	0	50	#	4
200	0	59	0	50	#	5
200	0	59	0	50	#	6
200	0	59	0	50	#	7
200	0	59	0	50	#	8
200	0	59	0	50	#	9
160	0	59	0	51	#	10
160	1	59	0	51	#	11
160	2	59	0	51	#	12
160	3	59	0	51	#	13
160	4	59	0	51	#	14
160	5	59	0	51	#	15
160	6	59	0	51	#	16
160	7	59	0	51	#	17
160	8	59	0	51	#	18
160	9	59	0	51	#	19
120	10	59	0	52	#	20
120	11	59	0	52	#	21
120	12	59	0	52	#	22
120	13	59	0	52	#	23
120	14	59	0	52	#	24

120	15	59	0	52	#	25
120	16	59	0	52	#	26
120	17	59	0	52	#	27
120	18	59	0	52	#	28
120	19	59	0	52	#	29
80	20	59	0	53	#	30
80	21	59	0	53	#	31
80	22	59	0	53	#	32
80	23	59	0	53	#	33
80	24	59	0	53	#	34
80	25	59	0	54	#	35
80	26	59	0	54	#	36
80	27	59	0	54	#	37
80	28	59	0	54	#	38
80	29	59	0	54	#	39
40	30	59	0	55	#	40
40	31	59	0	55	#	41
40	32	59	0	55	#	42
40	33	59	0	55	#	43
40	34	59	0	55	#	44
40	35	59	0	56	#	45
40	36	59	0	57	#	46
40	37	59	0	58	#	47
40	38	59	0	58	#	48
40	39	59	0	58	#	49
40	40	59	0	59	#	50
40	41	59	0	59	#	51
40	42	59	0	59	#	52
40	43	59	0	59	#	53
40	44	59	0	59	#	54
40	45	59	0	59	#	55
40	46	59	0	59	#	56
40	47	59	0	59	#	57
40	48	59	0	59	#	58
40	49	59	0	59	#	59

As shown under the **PRIORITY LEVEL** column, the range of priorities is from a low of 0 to a high of 59. The time slice (under **ts_quantum**) for the highest-priority process is 0.04 second and 0.2 second for the lowest-priority process. The **RES=1000** heading indicates that the values are (by default) in 1/1000 of a second or one millisecond. But note that despite the high resolution of the kernel scheduling tables, the system eventually uses clock ticks to schedule jobs. Because clock ticks typically occur 100 times a second, the actual resolution is limited to 10 milliseconds.

The time slice scheme in the TS scheduler may seem backward at first glance. After all, it would seem intuitive that processes with the highest priority also deserve longer time slices. But careful analysis shows that high-priority jobs get plenty of CPU time anyway so longer time slices are of little value to them. Where the time slice makes a lot of difference is for low-priority processes. In such cases, the throughput of low-priority processes can be increased by giving them longer time slices. To see why, let us look at an example.

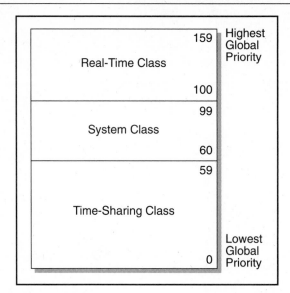

Figure 3.4 Relative Position of the SVR4 Schedulers

Imagine having a few low-priority processes running in the background. These processes only run if there are no other "normal" or high-priority jobs for the CPU to run. Because the low-priority jobs run infrequently, it is unlikely that any of the system caches (CPU, buffer cache, etc.) can retain any data that belong to them. As a result, when one of these jobs eventually starts to run, it encounters many cache misses. It takes a fair amount of time for all the caches to fill up (or warm up as it is commonly called) with the right data for these processes. It would be inefficient to let a process go through all the work of updating the system caches and then taking the CPU away from it just before it can reuse its data. High-priority jobs do not require this sort of assistance because they run more frequently and, hence, have a better chance of finding their data in the caches.

Another benefit of long time slices is that they reduce the context switch rate of the system. With a time slice of 0.04 second, two processes at the same priority will cause 25 context switches per second. Increase the time slice to 0.2 second, and the rate drops to five.

Note that the virtues of longer time slices do not apply to higher-priority interactive processes. Enlarging their time slice slows down interactive response as the system takes longer to switch from one process to another. The effect is the same as running a movie at one or two frames a second instead of 16 to 24—the illusion of having a CPU for each process is lost. Low-priority processes are somewhat immune to this problem because they are less likely to have someone looking at their output.

3.11.3 Priority Migration Under the TS Scheduler

As a process uses up its time quantum (**ts_quantum**), the kernel changes its priority from its current value shown under **PRIORITY LEVEL** to a new value listed under **ts_tqexp**.

As you see in the sample output, the default scheme is to penalize a running process by lowering its priority by 10 every time it uses its full time slice. For example, a process running with a default priority of 30 will have its priority reduced to 20 if it uses 0.08 second of CPU continuously. At the same time, its maximum time slice increases to 0.12 second. If it continues running, its priority eventually drops to the lowest level, which is zero.

3.11.4 The Impact of the nice Parameter

All TS processes start with a priority equal to one half of the maximum possible TS priority. Using the default maximum of 59, the initial priority becomes 30. The midpoint selection allows the widest dynamic range for the process priority.

The default nice value for each process in SVR4 is 20. The nice command can be used to change the nice value from 0 to +39 (a variation of -20 to +19). The effect of the nice value on the process priority is much simpler than BSD. Its value is simply added to the priority of the process with the sign reversed. For example, if you run a program using nice -10, its priority will start at around 40, which is simply 10 points above the initial value of 30. This results in the process getting more CPU time. Likewise, if you start a process with a nice value of +19, its initial priority will be 11, which causes it to get much less CPU time. Note that like all versions of UNIX, the nice command does not let you use negative values unless you have superuser privileges.

As you have probably noticed, the sense of nice values is reversed from priorities within the TS class. This reversal is due to historic reasons and backward compatibility because lower (and negative) numbers have always been associated with higher priority in UNIX.

The nice interface, while familiar, is a poor way of dealing with the TS scheduler due to its wider range of priorities. A new and more flexible method for affecting the priority of a process is priocntl.

3.11.5 The priocntl Interface

This new interface replaces the older nice scheme, although its behavior is fairly similar. The range of possible values for the user specified priority bias (i.e., nice value) can be retrieved using the -l option of the priocntl command:

```
sunshine% priocntl -l
CONFIGURED CLASSES
==================

SYS (System Class)

TS (Time Sharing)
        Configured TS User Priority Range: -20 through 20

RT (Real Time)
        Maximum Configured RT Priority: 59
```

The output shows that the possible range of user values for the TS scheduler by default is from -20 to +20 (on Solaris 2.3). The range can be modified by changing the kernel tunable parameter, **ts_maxupri**. Because this is a single value, the actual range is from **-ts_maxupri** to **+ts_maxupri**. Note that if you make the range smaller than -20 to +20, the nice values also become compressed which can cause compatibility problems with existing shell scripts and programs. Increasing the range makes it possible to affect the priority of a process by a larger margin, although this increase leaves less room for the kernel to manipulate process priorities.

To run a process with a different user priority, use the `-p` option of `priocntl`. The following is roughly equal to running `nice +19 ls`[12]:

```
Solaris% priocntl -e -c TS -p 20 ls
```

In a manner similar to the `nice` command, the sign of the specified value to `priocntl` is reversed and then added to the current priority of the process. Just the same, smaller (and negative) values boost the process priority.

The `priocntl` facility that exists both as a command and a system call by the same name has built-in protection against ordinary users trying to boost their priority. Normal users are allowed only to decrease their priority. Increasing the priority requires superuser privileges. In a departure from the `nice` facility, you can change the threshold from 0 to anything you like. A special parameter called **ts_uprilim** (user priority limit) establishes the lower bound that only the superuser can cross. By default, **ts_uprilim** is set to 0, which makes the priocntl behavior similar to `nice`. You can use the `priocntl` command to display the **ts_uprilim** parameter for any process. For example, to look at the scheduling parameters for the current shell use ($$ is the pid of the shell)

```
Solaris% priocntl -d $$
TIME SHARING PROCESSES:
    PID     TSUPRILIM     TSUPRI
  12449         0            0
```

In this output, **TSUPRILIM** is the priority threshold for which you need superuser privileges to go beyond. **TSUPRI** shows the current user priority bias, which is the same value specified with the -p option of `priocntl` or with `nice`.

3.11.6 The Real-Time Scheduler

Even though UNIX has never pretended to be a real-time system where the response to external events must occur within a fixed amount of time, its popularity has prompted people to try to use it in these environments. The most obvious problem with using UNIX in a real-time application is the priority migration scheme. Real-time users would like to be *guaranteed* that high priority jobs run ahead of lower-priority ones. As you know by now,

---

12. Even though `priocntl` is more flexible than `nice`, we doubt that the syntax shown in the example is going to win followers anytime soon.

priority migration in UNIX can result in the priority of a higher-priority process to drop below that of a lower-priority one if it uses too much CPU time. Fixing this is really not difficult; indeed, many vendors have added real-time priorities to their standard schedulers, which are not subject to priority migration. Likewise, SVR4 adds a real-time scheduler in the form of the RT class.

Processes in the RT class have fixed priorities and always run ahead of not only TS processes but also the system processes (see Figure 3.4 on page 80). As such, even the lowest-priority RT process gets the CPU before the highest-priority TS process.

Within the RT class, processes run according to their fixed priority. Because by default all processes run in the TS class, you need to specifically change the scheduling class of a process for it to run in the RT class. To do this, use the `priocntl` program or system call. For example, to run `ls` as a real-time process, use

```
# priocntl -e -c RT ls
bin          etc          kadb          mnt          sbin          var
cdrom        export       kernel        net          tmp           vol
dev          home         lib           opt          ufsboot
devices      hsfsboot     lost+found    proc         usr
```

 Before going farther, here is a word of caution:

> *Because RT processes run ahead of all TS processes, you can hang the entire system if the RT process gets stuck in an infinite loop.*

This situation can easily occur due to the fact that your shell runs as a TS process and, hence, cannot preempt a runaway RT process. That is, any commands typed at the shell prompt will not take effect because the shell is not able to get any CPU time to run. The situation is worse in workstations where none of the windowing applications can run. In this case, even character echoes will be lost if the RT process does not give up the CPU. Because of these potential problems, the RT scheduler is reserved for processes with superuser privileges.

A partial solution to this problem (in nonwindowing environments) is to change the scheduler class of your shell to RT with a higher priority than whatever RT process you are running. But this scheme can backfire if the shell itself gets stuck in an infinite loop either because of what you tell it to do or due to any bugs in the shell. So, the best advice is to run processes as real-time only if they are designed for this purpose and only on a test system where hangs do not cause data or productivity losses.

We should note that an RT scheduler by itself does not make a real-time system. The problem is that the kernel does not schedule a higher-priority process if another process is in the middle of executing a system call.[13] Put another way, UNIX has a preemptive sched-

---

13. Some systems such as the IBM AIX do preempt system calls and can, therefore, provide a much better real-time response.

uler that works only on processes that are running in their own address space. SVR4 partially solves this problem by allowing system calls to be interrupted in certain sections. System calls that take a particularly long time have been enhanced with these preemption points, which help to lower the maximum scheduling latency substantially.

The preemption points, however, may be too much of a good thing for some other subsystems such as X window. The faster preemptions cause the context switch rate between the client and the server to increase, which in turn substantially raises the CPU overhead. The problem also manifests itself in other client-server applications such as databases. Fortunately, most SVR4 vendors have enhanced their systems to deal with these problems, but the negative side effect is nevertheless unfortunate.

3.12 The IBM AIX Scheduler

The scheduler in AIX 4.1 does away with the esoteric parameters in BSD and uses a fairly straightforward scheme. The priority of a process starts at a base value of 40 plus whatever the nice value is. Because the default nice value is 20, the starting priority of a process is 60. Priority migration takes the form of adding 0.5 to the user priority for every 10-msec time of CPU usage. So, if a process runs for 0.1 second, its priority degrades from 60 to 65. As usual, lower numbers are better, meaning that the process will have higher chances of getting CPU time.

To accommodate real-time processes, the system call `setpri` can be used to set the priority of a process to an absolute value. But unlike the RT scheduler in SVR4, the fixed priorities of real-time processes overlap the priority range for the normal processes. Given the fact that the best nice value is -20, the true range for real-time processes is really from 0 to 19. Any value higher than this potentially causes a real-time process to compete with a time-sharing process.

To tune the scheduler parameters in AIX, use the `schedtune` facility. See Chapter 8 for some possible suggestions.

3.13 Memory Management

Managing memory is quite a complex task for the UNIX kernel. This stems from the fact that the system must create the illusion that every program "owns the entire computer." Specifically, all processes in the system are given identical memory addresses to use, and yet the contents of these memory locations must remain private to every process. As an example, when one process modifies location 0, it must not wipe out the same location in all the other processes.

The key to providing this "magic" is the page descriptor table. UNIX allocates a separate page descriptor table for each process in the system. The page tables are filled with unique physical page numbers allowing the hardware to map identical logical addresses in multiple processes automatically to distinct locations in the system memory. As an example of how this occurs, let us look at the demand loading and the shared memory facilities.

3.13.1 Demand Loading of User Programs

Before the advent of virtual memory management, UNIX systems loaded the entire image of a program from disk into memory before executing it. The problem with this scheme is that it can take a long time for large programs to start running. In addition, the process is very inefficient because most programs do not need all their data and instructions (e.g., error-checking routines, which may never get called). Loading these sections into memory is not necessary and can only increase the memory requirements of a process in addition to slowing down its start-up time. As a result,

> *all implementations of UNIX support demand paging, which allows programs to be loaded into memory one page at a time on an as-needed basis.*

This feature allows a user program to start executing as soon as its first few pages are loaded into memory. What makes this mechanism possible is the valid bit contained in the page descriptor. When you `exec` a process, the kernel figures out the size of the process (which is stored at the beginning of the executable image on disk) and allocates enough page descriptors to map the entire process (i.e., one per page). The page descriptors are initially left blank with no physical memory allocated to the process. The kernel then simply branches to the address of the first executable instruction in the program.

Recall that the CPU always attempts to translate a logical address to physical before using it. So, before taking the branch to the first instruction, the CPU fetches the page descriptor that corresponds with that address. It then checks the valid bit and notices that it is not set. The CPU considers this an error condition and causes an immediate page fault trap and a branch back into the kernel. A special kernel routine, aptly called the page fault trap handler, is invoked to deal with this situation. After certain amount of error checking, the page fault handler allocates a physical page of memory, stores its page number in the page descriptor table, and sets the valid bit. Because this is an instruction page, the kernel also fetches the relevant page of the program from its image in the file system (e.g., block 1 of the file `/bin/ls` if `ls` is the program being run). The process is put to sleep while this happens. Once the disk read finishes, the kernel instructs the CPU to reexecute the first instruction. This time the CPU sees that the valid bit is on and goes ahead and translates the user address to the physical page just allocated. Once the translation is finished, the CPU fetches the instruction from that page and executes it.

So far, we have loaded only one page of the process into memory and have allowed it to execute from there. Soon, the program tries to access an address in another logical page (either data or instruction). The CPU yet again notices that the page descriptor for that page does not have the valid bit set and the preceding scenario repeats.

By now it should be obvious why this mechanism is often called demand loading. Because pages that are not touched by the process are never allocated or loaded into memory, the system can manage to run a process in less memory than would otherwise be needed.

Figure 3.5 shows the relationship between the process image, page descriptors, main memory, and disk blocks for one process. In this example, the process has accessed four out of nine pages of its address space. This amounts to 16 Kbytes of memory assuming a page size of 4 Kbytes. The resulting saving in memory due to demand paging is therefore 20 Kbytes.

It should be noted that some systems disable demand loading for small programs. The reason is that small programs tend to need all their pages anyway and going through all the page fault overhead to load them one at a time actually results in higher overhead and slower execution. For example, Solaris uses the **pgthresh** kernel parameter to decide which programs should be demand-loaded. Its default value is 280 Kbytes, which means that programs such as the Bourne shell, `vi`, and other small utilities would not be demand-loaded assuming that there is some minimum amount of memory free.

3.13.2 Zero-Fill-on-Demand

A similar mechanism to demand paging is used to reduce the amount of memory needed for program data. When you ask the kernel for additional memory using the library routine `malloc`, the kernel only grows the number of page descriptors (and swap space size) of your program. No actual memory is allocated to your process, and the valid bits are set to

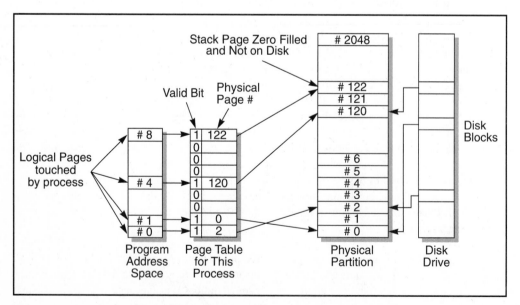

Figure 3.5 Program Image and Physical Memory

zero for all the new page descriptors. The moment any of these new data are touched (by either reading or writing), a page fault is generated. Because there are no file system data associated with these pages, the kernel simply allocates an empty page from the free pool and zeros it out before linking it into the page descriptor table. (BSD calls this zero-fill-on-demand or zfod.) The same thing occurs for stack pages and the initial BSS segment (i.e., global variables in your programs that are not initialized).

What all this means is that when you call the library routine `malloc` to allocate 1 Mbyte of memory, no actual memory is given to your process. Your process memory usage grows only as you access each page.

The dynamic allocation of data pages can result in significant savings in memory usage. This stems from the fact that programs are typically more wasteful of their data segments than text. It is not unusual to see 80–90% of the text size of a large process resident in memory compared to 50–60% of the data segment.

3.13.3 Shared Memory

UNIX supports both explicit and implicit sharing of memory. For example,

> *if you try to run a program when another copy of it is already running, the kernel arranges for both processes to share the same instruction (text) pages.*

This results in significant savings in memory usage and also speeds program start-up time.

Conceptually, sharing text is fairly simple and involves giving a copy of the page descriptors of the already running program to the new process. By doing so, the hardware goes to the same physical memory locations no matter which copy of the process is running. In practice, the job is complicated by the fact that the kernel must keep track of all the users of these shared pages to avoid conflicts. For example, when one process exits, the shared text pages must not disappear with it.

Of course, for shared text to work, the shared pages must be read-only. Otherwise, if one process intentionally or unintentionally modifies its program text, all other copies running in the system would be affected. To solve this problem, by default, all programs in UNIX are created (by the linker) to have read-only text segments that are shareable. This feature can be defeated by using the `-N` option of the linker (`ld`), but we cannot think of any good reason to do so.

3.13.4 Page Caching

The kernel uses all the available memory as a giant cache to reduce the overhead of loading programs into memory. It does this by keeping track of what used to be in memory pages before they were freed. For example, when an invocation of the `ls` program finishes, the kernel frees all the pages belonging to it. However, it holds on to data structures that tell it which memory pages are associated with the disk image of `ls` (really its inode).

If `ls` is run a second time, the kernel simply reuses the free pages in memory to satisfy the text page faults due to demand loading.

Page caching is a very important optimization and improves system performance substantially. You can see its effects by running the `ls` program twice. The first time, you see some disk accesses (as many as 10 or more disk reads are necessary). But the second time, page caching together with the buffer cache eliminate all disk I/O operations. Of course, if you wait too long, the free pages that hold the text pages for `ls` may get reassigned to other processes in the system. So, whenever possible, try to keep multiple invocations of the same program together instead of interspersing it with other programs.

You can instrument the effectiveness of the page caching in BSD UNIX by using the `vmstat` utility, which shows the count of pages reused under the **at** column (see the next chapter).

3.14 Paging and Swapping

Because UNIX allows an unlimited amount of memory to be used by user processes,[14] there must be a mechanism to free space when the physical memory is exhausted. In this section, we describe the algorithm used in BSD, SVR4, and SCO UNIX. Other versions of UNIX use similar schemes, although the exact parameters may differ.

At the heart of the system are two special processes called the pageout daemon and the swapper (you can see them by running `ps`). These processes normally sleep and only wake up when there is a memory shortage. There are four variables that are used to determine the severity of the memory shortage. Table 3.1 shows their names and default settings.

Table 3.1 Default Paging and Swapping Thresholds

Parameter	BSD and SunOS 4.1	SVR4 / Solaris 2.4[a]	Purpose
lotsfree	256 Kbytes	256 / 512 Kbytes	Threshold of paging activity
desfree	100 Kbytes	100 / 200 Kbytes	Potential threshold of swapping
minfree	32 Kbytes	32 / 100 Kbytes	Threshold of severe memory shortage
maxpgio	40 * number of swap devices	40 / 40	Level of excessive pageout I/O activity to swap device(s)

a. Nonserver (workstation) settings. MP machines use higher values.

---

14. Well, it is almost unlimited. The total size is limited by the available swap space and user-defined ceilings on data, stack, and text segments.

Because these parameters can be changed and vendors are constantly tuning their values, you may want to use a debugger to display their current settings (in pages). For example:

```
% echo "lotsfree/D " | adb -k /vmunix /dev/mem | tail -1
_lotsfree:      64
```

The kernel wakes up the pageout daemon when the amount of free memory drops below **lotsfree**. The pageout daemon then scans all the pages in the system looking to see if any of them can be freed. It does this by finding out which ones have not recently been used (NRU algorithm).

The pageout daemon treats text and data pages differently. Text pages are instantly freed because they can be fetched again from the file system if needed again. Data and stack pages, however, need to be saved because there is no copy of them in the file system. These pages are written to the swap partition or file if the latter is supported.

Once a page is freed, the kernel turns off the valid bit for the corresponding page in the user page descriptor table. If the process happens to touch the page before it is given to another process, the page-caching scheme gives the page back to the process by simply turning on the valid bit. BSD calls this optimization a "reclaim" and you can instrument its rate under the **re** column of the vmstat command output.

Scanning for least frequently used pages is a fine scheme except that it works rather slowly. Compounding the problem is the fact that the pageout daemon throttles itself by limiting the number of pages it examines in every pass and the number of I/O requests that it generates (defined by the **maxpgio** parameter). This means that the pageout daemon may be too slow to keep up with the memory demand. A rather drastic solution to this problem is the swapper process, which frees memory using a much more aggressive policy.

The swapper starts to run when the amount of free memory is lower than **desfree**. Instead of looking for individual pages, the swapper looks for entire process images to free. It normally searches for idle processes (those sleeping for longer than 20 seconds). But it gets considerably less choosy about which process to swap under severe memory shortage (called desperation). The definition of a severe memory shortage is somewhat complex (some would call it obscure). It depends on the following conditions to *all be true:*

- There are at least two runnable jobs in the system.
- The pageout daemon is doing more I/O than **maxpgio** *or* the free memory has dropped below **minfree**.
- The average free memory for the last 5 and 10 seconds (30 seconds in Solaris 2.4) has fallen below **desfree**.

Figure 3.6 attempts to simplify the preceding scenarios and show the relationship between available free memory and paging/swapping activities.

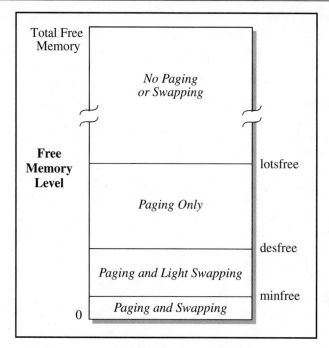

Figure 3.6 Free Memory and Paging/Swapping Activity

If the swapper gets desperate or there are processes to be swapped in, it swaps out the four largest processes regardless of their status.[15] The list may include runnable jobs, which can be a recipe for disaster from a performance point of view. Swapping a process out and then having to swap it back in to run it again causes long delays in its execution (seconds or even minutes). Typical results are text editors that seem to "go away" for seconds at a time and programs that "take forever" to run that normally execute instantly. As a rule,

> *you should avoid swapping at all cost. Even light swapping causes significant performance degradation.*

This is an extremely important observation and perhaps the most important lesson in this text. To better understand it, let's look at why swapping and paging slow down the system.

3.14.1 Performance Implications of Swapping and Paging

When there is no memory shortage, the response time of applications is a function of the CPU speed and I/O wait time. In the simplified case of a CPU-bound job, the only determinant of the response time is the speed of the CPU. As soon as memory drops too low (e.g., slightly below **lotsfree**), the pageout daemon wakes up and starts scanning all the

---

15. The kernel parameter **nbig** determines the number of processes. The default in BSD UNIX is four.

allocated pages in the system. The overhead of this scanning process is negligible, and little impact is felt in the system response time. Assuming that the memory shortage persists, the pageout daemon starts to attack pages that have not been recently touched but that typically belong to sleeping jobs. As such, freeing them is unlikely to cause any slowdown other than the disk traffic generated by the paging out process. This situation is referred to as light paging and is perfectly tolerable.

As the severity of the memory shortage increases, the pageout daemon starts to target pages belonging to programs that are running intermittently such as editors and shells. But as soon as someone generates any input for these processes, they wake up causing page faults and the resulting disk reads before they can continue execution. This contributes to a noticeable but mild increase in response time. This situation should be avoided if possible especially because the amount of memory needed to stop medium to heavy paging is usually not very high.

The worst-case scenario is when the rate of memory usage is higher than the rate at which the pageout daemon is freeing memory. When this occurs, the swapper process invariably wakes up and attacks sleeping jobs. Because these processes in all likelihood have lost most of their pages due to paging, swapping them out does not result in significant savings in memory usage. This makes the swapper more aggressive resulting in swapping of intermittently running jobs. Unlike paging, a swapped-out process cannot run until the system brings back at least some of its pages into memory. This includes the so-called u area (one or more pages holding kernel data structures), the page descriptors, and enough text, data, and stack pages for the process to continue where it left off. Given the busy state of the system at this point, read requests for these pages from the swap device or the file system are bound to be very slow. The result is very large and nondeterministic delays in program response time. This is the reason for our strong recommendation to avoid swapping at all costs.

3.14.2 Swapping and Paging in SCO UNIX

SCO UNIX uses the older (System V.3) style swapping and paging algorithms. Instead of **lotsfree**, pageout starts when the free memory drops below **GPGSLO** (the low water mark). But unlike BSD, there is a hysteresis mechanism meaning that paging will not stop until the free memory increases beyond **GPGSLO** and reaches **GPGSHI** (the high water mark). Another minor difference is that the pageout daemon is called vhand.

The default values for **GPGSLO** and **GPGSHI** are 1/16 and 1/10 of the pageable memory. The latter is defined as the amount of memory available to user processes (i.e., it excludes memory used for the kernel and system data structures).

The swapping operation in SCO UNIX is triggered by a process needing more memory than is available in the system. In this case the process is put to sleep (marked with the **B** status in the ps output), and the swapper looks for low-priority jobs that have been in memory for at least 2 seconds.

3.14.3 Swap Allocation

The kernel preallocates swap space for the entire process image before it runs it regardless of whether it ever needs to swap it out. If the kernel runs out of swap space, it refuses to run new programs (`fork` and `exec` will fail), and memory allocation requests from existing processes will fail. The typical indication is an out-of-core message from the shell, making users think the system is out of physical memory, which is not the case. Due to demand loading, the kernel can run any size program in as little as four or five pages of memory (16 to 20 Kbytes on most systems). So,

> *the size of the largest program that you can run in UNIX is only limited by the amount of free swap space and not the size of the physical memory.*

Because the swap allocation algorithm in UNIX is designed for speed and not space efficiency, you usually need two to four times as much swap space as the total size of all processes in the system. This is specially bothersome in machines with large amounts of physical memory. For example, if your system has 256 Mbytes of memory, you need 1 Gbyte of swap space even though you may never use it! SVR4 and SunOS 4.X are somewhat more frugal in this respect, and you can get away with a factor of 2 rather than 4.

Later implementations of Solaris (from 2.4 on) completely do away with these problems. Swap space in these systems is needed only to cover the difference between the total process sizes and the available memory. So, if you outfit your Solaris system with a sufficient amount of memory to run your workload, you do not need any swap space at all.

3.14.4 The Paged Buffer Cache

As we mentioned in Section 3.5.1, most new implementations of UNIX have integrated the buffer cache with the memory management subsystem. This allocation makes sense because reading and writing files is very similar in nature to demand loading of user program data. By unifying the memory space, the buffer cache no longer needs to have its own dedicated memory region and can grow to the maximum size of physical memory. This, as you will later see, can be as much of a detriment to the system performance as a benefit.

The heart of the integration is the way read and write requests are now handled in the kernel. When a user asks for a disk block to be read, the kernel allocates a region of its *virtual* address space large enough to contain the data to be read from the file system. This is simply done by allocating a chuck of nonvalid page descriptors for the kernel with no memory allocated to them. The kernel then associates this virtual space with the user-requested blocks in the file system. Next, the kernel pretends that the file system data have already been read into the allocated virtual address space and proceeds to copy it out to the user program buffer. This, of course, results in an immediate page fault trap because the kernel page descriptors are not valid. The page fault trap handler looks at the trap type and notices that this is a simple read from the file system. In a manner similar to loading program data, the paging system allocates a page of free memory, links it into the kernel page descriptor, and reads the associated file system data into it. Once the read request is finished, the data are copied from the kernel address space into the user process. The write operation operates similarly except that no physical write request actually occurs to the disk drive. The kernel simply copies the data into the freshly allocated memory after the page fault.

Because the kernel memory management routines already cache program pages, file system data can be reused the same way. Because the page fault handler always checks to see if a copy of the block to be read already exists in the system memory before performing the read operation, the caching function of the buffer cache is preserved.

Note that, without some kind of limit, the paged file data can quickly take over all the available memory. It does not take long for programs to request many megabytes of data to be read or written. No matter how much memory you have in your system, the paged buffer cache quickly fills it with file data.

The system deals with buffer cache overruns just the same as before. That is, the system simply starts paging (and in extreme cases swapping). This turns out to be a poor choice, and early implementations of paged buffer caches suffered from very poor interactive response. The reason was that the pageout daemon would attack program text data in order to deal with the huge appetite of the paged buffer cache. As a result, just about every program in the system would get paged out. Needless to say, the response time would grind to a halt as a result of executing simple, file-intensive commands such as `tar`, `cpio`, and `dump`.

These problems have generated myriads of solutions even when looking at the offerings from the same vendor. Witness the change in the swapping and paging algorithms in every version of Solaris from 2.0 to 2.4. Others such as DEC UNIX and IBM AIX have simply put limits on how large the buffer cache can grow, which creates a "half way" solution. In these implementations, the parameters for the minimum and maximum size of the buffer cache are tunable. Depending on your situation, you may want to reduce the size of the buffer cache to optimize the interactive response at the expense of I/O throughput.

Note that, in addition to the memory thrashing problem, the paged buffer cache scheme is fundamentally less efficient than the older buffer cache code. For example, if you tried to read a block that was already in the old buffer cache, you would only pay the penalty of searching the buffer cache. In the new scheme, you incur a page fault in addition to a similar search performed by the memory management code. Because page faults are rather expensive operations, the new scheme has a substantial cost in terms of CPU usage.

3.15 Multiprocessing (MP) Support

The UNIX kernel traditionally has been designed to execute on a single processor. The reason has to do with the use of many global data structures that could easily be corrupted if more than one CPU attempted to access them. To get around this problem, early multiprocessor implementations allowed only one CPU at a time to enter the kernel. The other

CPUs were allowed to run user code only. If two CPUs attempted to execute a system call, the first one to get there would enter the kernel, and the other would be forced to put its process to sleep and (hopefully) run another process. Needless to say, this approach (which is used in SunOS 4.1) does not work well in system call intensive environments such as general time-sharing and database applications. It does, however, perform satisfactorily in compute-intensive situations where the applications are making few, if any, system calls.

A more modern approach is to rewrite the kernel to protect the various structures and resources so that multiple CPUs can simultaneously execute the kernel code. Some vendors call this Symmetric Multiprocessing (SMP), which means all CPUs are able to execute the kernel code and perform I/O functions.[16]

SMP systems are available from every major UNIX vendor today. But that is not to say that they all work equally well. The effectiveness of an SMP implementation is a function of the hardware concurrency control and careful parallelization of the kernel code. Knowing how well a system is tuned for a multiprocessor environment is critical in gauging how much improvement can be expected from adding more CPUs to a system. This requires full understanding of the hardware architecture and extensive examination of the kernel code, which, of course, is impractical to say the least. Your only solution is to experiment with your work load to see how well the system supports the types of kernel services that you use.

3.16 Threads

The standard process model of UNIX mandates that there be only a single thread of execution in one virtual address space. That is, the program can be doing only one thing at a time. For example, if a process goes to sleep waiting for disk I/O, then it cannot perform any computation during the same time. The standard solution to this restriction is to `fork` additional copies of the program to perform these asynchronous tasks. The problem with this scheme is that sharing data between these programs becomes a problem. A better solution is to enhance the process model in UNIX to include multiple execution paths or threads within a single process image.

Threads, which are sometimes called lightweight processes, allow a single process to have multiple independent threads of execution with seamless data sharing. The entire text and data segment of the process is shared between the threads, allowing direct communication between them (the stack is, however, private to each thread). Threads require less kernel resources than processes due to the sharing of page descriptors and other kernel data structures. Thread creation is typically an order of magnitude faster than forking another pro-

---

16. SMP is usually a hardware terminology that applies to the ability of every CPU in the system to perform the same functions (especially I/O). However, in recent times, it has become synonymous with systems that not only have an SMP hardware but also possess an operating system that allows all CPUs to execute its code.

cess because there is little copying involved. Destruction is likewise quicker because there is no exit overhead.

Threads especially make sense in multiprocessor systems where each thread can be executing on a different CPU. This increases the performance of the application beyond the capabilities of one processor. Vendors such as Convex and SGI go as far as providing compilers that automatically divide portions of a program into multiple threads that execute in parallel without much user intervention.

An important aspect of thread support on MP systems is *gang scheduling*, where a group of related threads are run at the same time. This substantially increases efficiency of the entire process as threads do not waste time waiting for each other. On the other hand, gang scheduling can cause some inefficiencies in interactive situations where multiple CPUs may have to wait for a single CPU that is executing some other job. In addition, gang scheduling reduces the "fairness" of the CPU scheduling because one process may grab multiple CPUs at a time. We expect some major changes in the areas of thread scheduling in the next few years to deal with these issues.

3.17 Kernel Tables

The kernel uses a a number of tables internally to keep track of various events. For example, every time a new process is created (with `fork`), the kernel allocates an entry in the **proc** table. Likewise, if a file is opened, the system needs a **file** table and an **inode** table entry to hold the information about the open file. Another example is the **lock** table, which is used when a process uses the record-locking system calls to control concurrent access to a file.

The space for the kernel tables is typically allocated when the system boots. In most cases, the kernel does not shrink the size of a table. So, if the tables are unnecessarily large, they take away memory that could otherwise be used by user processes. On the other hand, if a table is too small and overflows, the requested service fails. In most cases, some kind of message is printed on the system console. For example, if the **proc** table gets full and a process attempts to execute the `fork` system call, the kernel prints the "proc table full" message on the console and returns a **-1** to the user process (the shells print the "no more procs" message).

Even though the kernel tables are not very large, the default size on some systems is unusually high. To give you a feel for the size of each entry in various kernel tables, we have listed a sample of them in Table 3.2.[17] Keep in mind that the sizes for the individual entries can vary from system to system. In addition, some versions of UNIX (e.g., SVR4) dynamically allocate memory for the **file** and **lock** tables so that there is no need to worry about their sizes.

---

17. There are many more tables in the kernel. We have described only these four because you can monitor their usage and tune their sizes.

Table 3.2 System Table Sizes (in SVR4)

Table	Approximate Size (bytes)
proc	350
inode	250
file	40
lock	44

3.18 Summary

- The kernel is one of the largest consumers of memory ranging in size from 2 to 8 Mbytes.

- User processes consist of text (instructions), data, and stack. The text is by default read-only and shared among all copies of the same program in the system.

- The kernel performs services for user programs through a mechanism known as a system call, which is a slow (indirect) function call into the kernel.

- UNIX heavily relies on the buffer cache to reduce the total number of physical disk (or network) transfers. The newest implementations of the buffer cache are integrated into the paging system, allowing the cache to grow without bounds. This increases the I/O throughput for some applications at the expense of others.

- The heart of the UNIX file system is the inode data structure, which keeps track of all the information about a file including where its data blocks are located on disk. Inodes are kept in an in-memory data structure to speed their access.

- Opening a file requires searching the directory file for its inode. An optimization known as the name look-up cache greatly speeds file name searches by keeping track of frequently referenced file names and their inode numbers.

- The BSD Fast File System provides a substantial boost in performance and reliability over the older System V file system. It is, however, being challenged by newer implementations that provide much faster recovery and dynamic expansion.

- The memory management scheme in UNIX allows gradual, on-demand loading of programs into memory resulting in faster start-up time and reduced memory usage, especially for large programs.

- The paging and swapping processes manage memory shortage problems by swapping either individual pages or complete process images to disk. Even though neither should be tolerated, swapping is especially troublesome when it comes to system performance. Enhancements such as dynamic buffer cache, however, make paging a routine occurrence rather than an indication of actual memory shortage.

- Process scheduling in UNIX is self-adjusting and is optimized more for fairness than real-time response. The schedulers in SVR4 give users a choice of schedulers by providing both time-sharing and real-time facilities.

CHAPTER 4

The BSD
Monitoring Tools

Unlike System V, which has a single monitoring tool (sar), BSD users have to deal with a collection of commands developed over the years. There is a fair amount of overlap between the various tools, which may make the choice of which one to use rather confusing at first (see Table 4.1). Fortunately, in most cases, you can get by with just using vmstat and ps.

Before getting into the details of each command, we should note that the BSD commands have enjoyed little standardization. Each vendor has made its own changes to them mak-

Table 4.1 BSD Instrumentation Tools

Command	Usage
vmstat	General system statistics including CPU, memory, and I/O
iostat	Disk and terminal I/O along with CPU usage
ps	Process status
w	Quick process starts for each user
uptime	CPU load and general system status
pstat	Table sizes and usage

ing it rather difficult to use these tools across multiple versions of UNIX. To simplify things a bit, we point out these differences during the course of this chapter.

4.1 vmstat

vmstat is one of the most complete instrumentation tools in BSD. Its name seems to imply that it can show only Virtual Memory STATistics. In reality, vmstat displays much other useful information such as disk traffic and CPU utilization. The simplified syntax is

  vmstat <-fsi> <interval> <count>

For example,

```
% vmstat 2
procs        memory          page                     disk       faults        CPU
r b w   avm   fre   re at  pi  po  fr  de   sr s0 s1 f0 f1   in  sy  cs us sy id
0 0 0  3092  1048    0  0   0   0   0   0    0  1  0  0  0   18 100  12  1  4 95
0 0 0  3092  1048    0  0   0   0   0   0    0  0  0  0  0   29 638  20  2 11 88
0 0 0  3032  1012    0  0   0   0   0   0    0  0  0  0  0   24 669  19  7 42 51
```

Without any arguments, vmstat shows a single line with most fields being the *average* since the system was brought up. At first, you may think that this is the most desirable mode. However, in general, these data are not very useful because the system load changes drastically during use. Averaging the data for the busy periods, along with the times the machine is idle, normally generates little useful information. Instead, you should be looking at the system statistics during the peak system activity because this provides better clues as to the potential system bottlenecks.

The most common way to run vmstat is to specify an interval over which it averages the results. For example, vmstat 5 displays data averaged over a 5-second period. It will continue to do so until it is killed by the user. Alternatively, you can specify a count of how many lines you want displayed. Either way, the first line of output is again the total system average, which you should typically ignore.

Between intervals, vmstat sleeps (for interval seconds) using no CPU time of its own. You may be tempted to use a small interval to get more frequent updates. But this causes the display to be rather erratic and hard to interpret. In addition, **avm** and **fre** memory statistics (which are averaged by the kernel and not vmstat) are updated only once every 5 seconds. If you use an interval smaller than that, vmstat finds and displays the same value repeatedly (see the **fre** column in the sample output).

The best interval to use depends on which piece of information you are interested in. CPU statistics can be monitored using intervals as small as 2 seconds. On the other hand, disk statistics should be monitored over a 30- to 60-second range.

Instead of going through each item from left to right, let's look at the information vmstat displays in the order that we find most useful.

4.1.1 The CPU Statistics

vmstat shows three percentages for the CPU load. The most important is **id** (idle) which is the percentage of time the CPU was not doing anything in the last interval (i.e., sitting in the idle loop). When the CPU is busy, its usage is divided into two categories: **us** and **sy**. The former stands for user time and indicates the percentage of time the CPU was running user programs. **sy**, on the other hand, stands for system and shows the percentage of time the CPU was running the kernel code.

The sum of all three fields usually adds up to 100%. That is, the system is either idle or running a user process or the kernel. You might wonder why the sum is not always 100%. As a result of the Heisenberg principle, the CPU statistics change as vmstat tries to read them. After all, vmstat is a program itself and the CPU statistics are updated as it runs. In addition, vmstat uses floating-point computations, which can result in round-off errors. However, none of these represents a problem because you should not care about exact value of any of the system statistics. What you are looking for is whether the CPU is busy or not. It makes no difference whether the CPU is 99 or 97% idle. Nonetheless, if you use a large interval as recommended earlier, the discrepancy should vanish.

The **id** value by itself gives you an excellent and quick assessment of the system:

> *if the idle time is above 20%, it can indicate the system is either "I/O bound"[1] or has a memory shortage.*

The reason behind this statement is that if either the memory or I/O becomes a bottleneck, the CPU is forced to wait for them, and this shows up as idle time. As you recall from Chapter 1,

> *the percentage of idle time can be used to gauge how much faster a system can run after all possible optimizations have been performed.*

Because you need CPU cycles to run user programs, system throughput cannot increase beyond the amount of idle time. For example, a system with 20% idle time can run only 20% faster, assuming that you do everything possible to remedy all other system shortages. Put another way, you should not worry about the memory or I/O subsystem performance when the CPU idle time is low (below 10%). You should instead look for ways to increase CPU performance.

Of course, the CPU also idles if it has nothing to do. In this case, the idle time simply indicates excess CPU capacity in the system. To see if this is indeed the case, look at the num-

---

1. The term *I/O bound* is used when the I/O subsystem is the primary bottleneck.

ber of processes waiting for I/O and memory (under the **b** and **w** columns—see Section 4.1.5).

us and **sy** fields break down the CPU utilization. System time (**sy**) is the result of user programs requesting services from the operating system such as reading and writing files and hardware events such as interrupts and traps. Even though there is no good value for this field, well-balanced systems operate with system times below 50%. After all, this is how much of the CPU power is not available to run user applications. In practice, you have little control over the system time because it highly depends on the work load and types of applications being run. Similarly, user time (**us**) is application-specific and not much can be done to change it other than tuning the user applications or eliminating some of them. *Note that if user time is very high (greater than 70%), the kernel is hardly being used and the system performance is completely dependent on the speed of the CPU and the application.* No amount of kernel tuning in this case will result in an appreciably faster system.

4.1.2 Memory Statistics

The **avm** and **fre** fields are the key memory management statistics. **fre** is the amount of free memory in Kbytes. For example, a value of 2048 means that 2 Mbytes of memory are not being used.

You might think that **avm** is an abbreviation for Average Virtual Memory. It is not! Instead, it stands for *Active* Virtual Memory and measures the total sizes of every program that has run in the last 20 seconds. These processes are selected because they are more likely to run again in the future (hence the term *active*).

Note that the total *virtual* size of a process is used in computation of **avm** and *not the amount of memory it is using.* Recall that the demand-loading feature of the kernel makes it possible for programs to use less memory than their total (virtual) size. Therefore, **avm** shows an exaggerated estimate of the memory usage of the active processes in the system.

The system must have at least **avm** Kbytes of memory to avoid severe paging and swapping. This is an important observation because, when the system runs out of memory, performance suffers greatly. Therefore, knowing how much memory is needed to run the current work-load is an extremely important parameter. **avm** gives you this information at a glance.

Despite its usefulness, Sun has deleted the **avm** statistics gathering in SunOS 4.1, and vmstat shows a zero under this field (curiously, the vmstat manual page still claims that this field is valid). The vmstat in Sun Solaris 2.X has completely done away with **avm** and instead shows the amount of free swap space in this column.

Note: If you are using HP-UX, you need to multiply **avm** and **fre** by 4 because the units are in pages and not Kbytes. In addition, HP's version of vmstat has expanded the space for each field so the output extends beyond 80 columns.

4.1.3 Paging and Swapping

vmstat does not directly tell you whether there is a memory shortage or not. To make matters worse, vmstat is incapable of showing the values of **lotsfree**, **desfree**, and **minfree** described in Chapter 3, which set the paging and swapping thresholds. Instead, you have to search for the side effects of paging and swapping in the various fields.

The first indication that paging activity has started is the **sr** column. **sr** stands for scan rate and is the count of pages examined by the pageout daemon to see if they can be freed. The actual value is of little consequence. However,

> *if* **sr** *is nonzero, there is some pageout activity.*

Unfortunately, it is difficult to translate the preceding statement into whether there is a true memory shortage. The reason is that in systems with the paged buffer cache (which includes all the systems that have vmstat), pageout can occur due to simple file activity. So, in practice,

> *it is impossible to distinguish between paging activity due to process memory shortage and simple file access.*

In other words, it is very difficult to tell if there is sufficient memory in the system to run the current work load. The file system paging activity hides any potential memory shortfalls for program text and data. This is an area where the kernel algorithms are running ahead of tools designed to monitor them.

As for swapping, the only indication is the **de** field, which stands for deficit. The swapper process increases deficit before it swaps a process in, and sometimes when swapping a process out.[2] So, **de** can be used as a crude indicator of swapping. Unfortunately, you have to look quickly as the system reduces deficit to zero over a few seconds.

Even though it is possible for the paged buffer cache to cause swapping in addition to paging activity, the situation is rather rare. So, as a general rule,

> *you should always keep* **de** *at zero because it indicates severe memory shortage and swapping activity.*

re is the number of pages reclaimed by the system due to a bad guess on the part of the pageout daemon. A page was freed and then accessed by the process owning it before it was given to another process. Although the reclaim process is an optimization, if its rate is too high, it shows that the pageout daemon is getting too desperate and is attacking pages that are actually in use. In other words, large values of **re** indicate a severe memory shortage.

---

2. The system treats deficit as memory that is in use even though in reality it is not. Swapper (if desperate) increases deficit so that the system does not think the memory shortage has vanished when it swaps out a process. It also increases deficit on a swap-in to make sure at least some amount of memory is reserved for the process.

at is the count of pages that were attached to a process after a page fault. Before reading a page from disk, the kernel first looks to see if any of the free pages in the system contain the required data (i.e., were previously paged in for this or another process). If so, it attaches the page to the process without incurring a disk read. This usually occurs on repeated invocations of the same program (e.g., when you run `ls` twice in a short amount of time). You can safely ignore the attach rate because it has little consequence in system optimization.

pi indicates the total number of pages read in from disk either because of normal program loading or bringing in pages that were paged/swapped out. Because the system does not separate the two activities, not much can be learned from the value of **pi**.

po shows that the pageout daemon is running and is writing memory pages to the swap or, in the case of the paged buffer cache, to the file system. Again, because the paged buffer cache uses the pageout daemon to handle most of its write requests, **po** by itself does not have any useful significance.

4.1.4 Disk I/O

One of the worst enemies of good system performance is the hard disk. Most UNIX systems have disk bottlenecks because of the huge imbalance between the speed of the disk drive and the CPU. This results in longer response time and high CPU idle time.

`vmstat` shows the disk traffic under four columns, typically labeled **d0** through **d3**. But note that system vendors routinely rename these headings. To find them in the `vmstat` output, look for a single letter indicating the type of drive and a number showing the unit number. For example, "s1" might mean SCSI disk 1.

The value displayed under each disk column is the number of transfers per second (tps), on the average, for the particular disk drive. Unfortunately, this field is not as useful as it could be. What you are really interested in is the percentage of time the drive was busy. (System V users can easily get this information from `sar`.) All is not lost, however. Because the maximum number of transfers per second for most modern drives is between 70 and 90 per second, you can easily compute the ratio. For example, if the number of transfers per second is 40, the drive is roughly 50% busy. In general,

> *you should keep the disk drives in your system at less than 25% busy for good performance.*

Once you exceed the 25% threshold, the response time gradually starts to suffer. When the rate approaches 100%, the system becomes completely I/O bound, and the CPU idle time becomes very high. The result is not as bad as a memory shortage but should nevertheless be avoided.

In case you are wondering, `vmstat` is not able to display disk transfer rates for more than four drives.[3] The only way to get around this limitation is to reconfigure your hardware

---

3. This is a kernel limit, which some vendors have raised to eight.

and place the drive that you are interested in at a physically lower unit number.

Another limitation in `vmstat` disk statistics is that it shows the number of transfers *per disk drive and not partitions (logical drives)*. So, if you are using multiple partitions on one drive, you will not be able to narrow the source of the file activity to an individual file system.[4] This, of course, is very annoying because the solution to high disk usage is reallocation of busy file systems to other, less used drives. You are at a significant disadvantage if you cannot identify the busy file systems. The only solution is to study the applications that are running and to try to determine which partitions may be contributing to the high usage.

4.1.5 Process Information

The **r**, **b**, and **w** columns show a summary of the status of processes in the system. The **r** field is the count of processes that are currently runnable. Depending on the implementation, this may or may not include the number of jobs running on the CPU(s). For example, SunOS 4.1 (and most BSD implementations) include both the number of jobs running on the CPU(s) and those waiting in the queue, whereas Solaris excludes the running jobs. That is, if you have a two CPU system and there are five runnable jobs in the system, the SunOS 4.1 `vmstat` would show a count of 5 under the **r** column, whereas Solaris would display only 3.

> The **r** column is a good indicator of whether the CPU performance is a problem or not. High values of **r** (typically greater than four in BSD and four times the number of CPUs in Solaris) cause a noticeable slowdown in system performance as the CPU is forced to jump between runnable jobs.

The **b** field is the count of jobs sleeping at a negative priority. This typically means that a process is waiting for disk, tape, or (rarely) memory.

> High counts in the **b** column together with high CPU idle time indicate that the system is heavily I/O bound.

The ideal count is zero but an occasional nonzero value can be tolerated. The disk statistics should be consulted when the **b** column is nonzero to see which drive is the bottleneck.

The **w** field counts the number of jobs that have run in the last 20 seconds and that are now swapped out. Because the system only swaps out these jobs as a last resort,

> if the **w** column is ever nonzero, the system has a severe memory shortage.

Needless to say, you should never let **w** become nonzero.

Note: We have noticed that the DEC UNIX `vmstat` simply shows the number of sleeping jobs under **w** (even those waiting for user input!). We are not quite sure why anyone would

---

4. The fault really belongs to the kernel for not maintaining the statistics on a per partition basis.

be interested in such data. Likewise, the vmstat in HP-UX 9.01 shows the total number of sleeping jobs under the **b** column, which renders that field useless.

4.1.6 System Call Statistics

User processes request services from the kernel by executing system calls, and vmstat shows their rate (per second) under the **sy** column. Even though high system call rates can significantly slow down the system, there may not be much that can be done to reduce them. After all, this is a measure of how much work the kernel is performing.

The upper bound on the system call rate depends on the speed of the CPU and the type of system calls being executed. Modern CPUs can easily execute in excess of 10,000 system calls per second. So monitor your system frequently to get a feel for what counts are "normal" for *your* environment.

Note that high system call rates invariably force the system time (**sy**) to also increase. **sy** reaches 100% when the system is spending all its time executing system calls.

The -f option of vmstat can be used to see the rates for two system calls, namely fork and vfork:

```
% vmstat -f
3982 forks, 67889 pages, average=17.05
1439 vforks, 210586 pages, average=146.34
```

The output shows the total number of forks and vforks since the system start-up, the total number of process pages involved in all the requests, and the average per call. This option is very useful in detecting whether some application uses the faster vfork or the older fork scheme. Simply run vmstat -f, execute your command, and then follow it with another vmstat -f. Assuming no other activity in the system, the difference between the two samples is the number of fork or vfork requests along with the number of pages involved in the potential copy operation.

Because the BSD kernel does not keep detailed statistics for any other system calls besides fork, you will not be able to display their usage with vmstat or any other similar tool.

4.1.7 Hardware Interrupts

As you recall, most I/O devices cause an interrupt when they finish performing their request. The kernel keeps statistics on these interrupts, which you can display using the -i option of vmstat (run under SunOS 4.1 on a SPARCstation 2):

```
sunset% vmstat -i
interrupt        total        rate
------------------------------------ autovectored interrupts
esp            2307991          0
fd                 274          0
audio              274          0
le             8669780          3
```

```
zs                2453656          0
cgsix                1470          0
clock           275759926        100
-------------------------------- vectored interrupts

--------------------------------
Total           289193371        104
```

The first column is a (cryptic) abbreviation of the device name. In the sample output, **esp** is the SCSI controller, **audio** is for the audio CODEC (the COder/DECoder chip which is a fancy name for an audio digitizer), **fd** is for the floppy disk, **le** is the AMD Lance Ethernet controller, **cgsix** is for the color graphics (GX) adaptor, and **zs** (Zilog SCC) is the serial interface.

Last but not least is the **clock** interrupt generator, which, as you can see in the sample output, is the most frequent (and regular) source of interrupts. The clock source is the main mechanism in UNIX for time-keeping operations. Even though the actual rate varies from system to system (50, 60, and 100 are common choices), its average rate should not change over the life of the system. Any kind of variation causes the system time and date to drift by the same amount.

Note that the list of devices displayed depends on the type of hardware you have in your machine. Refer to the documentation for your system for the list of abbreviations. If that fails, look at the system boot-up messages.[5]

4.1.8 Context Switch Statistics

The kernel keeps track of the number of times it switches from running one process to another, and vmstat shows this information (per second) under the **cs** column. **cs** should be small (less than a few hundred on a single CPU system). Higher rates typically indicated poorly structured application programs (e.g., lack of buffering between client-server programs such as X Window).

Context switches are very expensive operations and waste considerable CPU time. Nevertheless, unless you have the option of modifying the programs running on the system, not much can be done to reduce their rate.

4.1.9 Sun Name Look-Up Cache Information

The SunOS version of vmstat has been enhanced to show the name look-up cache statistics using the -s (summary) option. To see the information, use

```
SunOS4.1% vmstat -s |tail -2
   108425 total name look-ups (cache hits 54%  per-process)
           toolong 12
```

---

5. It is amazing that, given the large amounts of memory in today's systems, the device names remain as abbreviations, when printed both by the kernel and by the utilities.

Even though the total number of look-ups is of little interest, the cache hit rate is of partic- ular importance. The hit rate should be greater than 90% for good performances. The sam- ple output shows a poor rating of 54%.

The display also includes the number of times cache requests were denied because the file name was greater than 14 characters (32 characters in Solaris) under **toolong**. As we men- tioned in Chapter 3, you should keep the number of file names below this limit for good performance.

Note that the name cache statistics are available only in Sun's version of vmstat (in both SunOS 4.1 and Solaris 2.X). The information is absent from other systems that have vmstat (e.g., HP-UX).

4.1.10 Other vmstat Features

When vmstat is first started, it attempts to determine the number of lines on your termi- nal or workstation window. It then nicely reprints its heading when the output gets close to the bottom of the screen. The same thing happens if you suspend (e.g., by typing con- trol-z or whatever your suspend character is set to) and resume vmstat.

4.2 DEC vmstat

The DEC UNIX version of vmstat is a highly modified version of the BSD equivalent. The usage, however, is very similar to BSD:

```
DECbox% vmstat 2
Virtual Memory Statistics: (pagesize = 8192)
  procs    memory        pages                            intr        cpu
  r  w  u  act  free wire fault cow zero react pin pout  in  sy  cs  us sy  id
  2 46 29 3711  118 1164  58K  12K 20K  487  15K 626  12  51  51   1  1  99
  2 46 29 3693  136 1164  100   13  63    1    8   4   7   9  41   0  2  98
  2 46 29 3693  136 1164   53    0  53    0    0   0   3   7  33   0  2  98
```

As we already mentioned, one of the key differences between this version and the BSD vmstat is the fact that the **w** column includes the number of sleeping jobs that are inter- ruptible. These are usually processes that are waiting for routine events such as keyboard input or termination of child processes.

The **u** column counts the number of sleeping jobs that are *not* interruptible. In the BSD kernel, such jobs (shown under the **b** column) are those sleeping for high-priority devices or resources such as disk and memory. Alas, the DEC UNIX seems to put many other pro- cesses to sleep using this scheme, making the information presented somewhat hard to interpret.

The **act** field counts the total number of memory pages in use in the system. It unfortu- nately includes the number of pages used by the paged buffer cache so it cannot be used to

Table 4.2 vmstat Summary

Field	Description
r	Number of runnable jobs waiting for the CPU.
b	Number of jobs sleeping at negative priority (this usually counts the processes waiting for disk, tape, network, or memory).
w	Number of jobs that have run in the last 20 seconds that are now swapped out.
avm	Total "Active" Virtual Memory in kilobytes (size of all processes that have run in the last 20 seconds). The units are in pages in HP-UX.
fre	The amount of free memory in kilobytes. The units are in pages in HP-UX.
re	The number of free pages reused that belonged to same process.
at	The number of free pages reused because another process had already loaded them into memory.
pi	The number of process pages that were brought in from disk.
de	The amount of memory (in pages) that is temporarily reserved just before a process is swapped in and sometimes after a swap out (deficit).
sr	The number of pages that pageout daemon has examined to see if they can be freed (scan rate).
d0-d3	Disk drive activity on drives 0 through 3 (the first letter varies from system to system and indicates the type of disk drive).
in	The number of hardware interrupts per second excluding clock.
sy	The number of system calls (kernel services) per second.
cs	The number of times the system abandoned one process to run another (context switch).
us	The percentage of time CPU spent inside a user process.
sy	The percentage of time CPU spent running the kernel itself.
id	The percentage of time CPU was idle doing nothing.

gauge the memory requirements of the processes themselves. On the other hand, the output nicely shows the page size of the system (8192 in our example) so that you can correctly interpret the memory statistics (which have units of pages).

pin, **pout**, and **free** are comparable to BSD's **pi**, **po**, and **fre**, which show the number of pages being brought in, pushed out, and available, respectively. Because of the existence of the paged buffer cache, not much can be gleaned from the values of these parameters, with the minor exception of **fre**. If this value stays below 128 for long, the system may begin to start swapping, which indicates a heavy memory shortfall. Values above this limit do not have much significance.

wire shows the number of pages that are locked in memory and cannot be swapped. Although the kernel does occasionally lock memory pages (e.g., during an I/O request to make sure that the page doesn't disappear during a transfer due to paging), the unusually high count in this field seems to indicate that pages used by the kernel are also included. In this example, the kernel is using roughly 8 Mbytes of memory, which matches the page count of 1164 shown in the sample output.

fault counts the number of page faults per second. To see what has caused these faults, look at the following fields which show the number of copy-on-write protection faults (requiring physical copying of pages that are being shared) under **cow**, zero-fill-on-demand of new program data pages under **zero**, pages reattached to processes from the free list under **react**, and pages that had to be read in under **pin**. The sum of these fields does not always equal the number of faults because some faults are illegal and are dismissed without any action from the VM system.[6]

The rest of the fields are the same as BSD's vmstat.

4.3 SCO vmstat

Althought it is not a BSD system, the SCO UNIX also includes a variation of the vmstat command. The CPU statistics are identical to BSD with the exception that the system time is shown under the **su** heading rather than **sy**. The **b** column follows the HP-UX lead in that it counts all sleeping jobs so no quick determination can be made as to whether the system is I/O bound or not.

```
# vmstat 2
```

PROCS			PAGING											SYSTEM		CPU		
r	b	w	frs	dmd	sw	cch	fil	pft	frp	pos	pif	pis	rso	rsi	sy	cs	us	su id
0	47	0	98304	0	0	0	0	0	0	0	0	0	0	0	31	6	0	0 100
0	47	0	98304	0	0	0	0	0	0	0	0	0	0	0	45	12	0	5 95
0	47	0	98304	0	0	0	0	0	0	0	0	0	0	0	40	9	0	0 100
0	47	0	98304	0	0	0	0	0	0	0	0	0	0	0	34	7	0	1 99
0	47	0	98304	0	0	0	0	0	0	0	0	0	0	0	44	9	0	2 98

4.4 iostat

As the name implies, iostat shows the system I/O statistics. For good measure, iostat also throws in the CPU utilization. Even though vmstat also displays some of the same information, iostat has a more detailed display.

Typical usage of iostat is similar to vmstat. That is, if no options are specified, it shows the system averages since the system was booted. Otherwise, you can give it a numeric interval and count to get periodic updates. As with vmstat, you need to ignore the first line as it shows the total averages.

---

6. We are just guessing here. The DEC documentation is very vague as to the meaning of these fields.

```
% iostat 2
        tty           sd0              sd1              sd3            cpu
  tin tout bps tps msps   bps tps msps   bps tps msps   us ni sy id
    0   17   3   0  0.0     1   0  0.0     0   0  0.0    0  0  1 99
    0 7448   0   0  0.0   141  30  0.0     0   0  0.0    3  0 37 60
    0 7061  21   3  0.0   111  26  0.0     0   0  0.0    2  0 52 46
    3 7382   5   1  0.0   124  26  0.0     0   0  0.0    1  0 50 48
   10 6145  20   2  0.0   146  27  0.0     0   0  0.0    2  0 40 58
    7 8565   8   1  0.0   119  21  0.0     0   0  0.0    3  0 53 44
    7 8097   0   0  0.0   132  26  0.0     0   0  0.0    4  0 42 54
```

4.4.1 Detailed CPU Usage

iostat shows the CPU statistics on the right-most four columns. The **id** and **sy** fields show idle and system time, respectively, and are identical to vmstat fields with the same headings. Where vmstat shows you a single value for the user time, iostat shows two: **us** and **ni**.

us stands for user time, but, unlike the field with the same heading in vmstat, it does *not* include the percentage of CPU cycles used by jobs that have been niced (either positively or negatively). Instead, the percentage of CPU cycles used by niced processes is displayed under the **ni** column. For example, if you run a single job that uses all the CPU cycles without using the nice command, iostat shows 100(%) under the **us** column. On the other hand, if you use the nice command to run it, then the **ni** column goes to 100(%) and **us** stays at zero. If you run your background jobs niced, you can use this information to see if they are getting any CPU time.

4.4.2 Disk Statistics

tps displays the transfers per second, which is the same as what vmstat presents under the disk columns. But iostat goes on to display two more disk statistics under the **bps** and **msps** columns. These stand for "bytes per second" and "milliseconds per seek," respectively.

bps is a misnomer as it really shows *kilobytes* transferred per second on the average during the last period. The Solaris version of iostat rightfully shows Kps for this reason. You may be surprised to find that **bps** is typically much smaller than the peak transfer rate of your disk drives. The reason is that a busy system does not read blocks sequentially from a disk drive because files for different users are scattered on the surface of the drive requiring extensive seeks. Because no data are transferred when the drive is seeking or waiting for the next block, the *average* **bps** value can be quite low.

msps is an attempt by the kernel to measure the average access time for the drive under actual usage. It turns out that what is really measured is the total I/O time and not just the access time of the drive. Unfortunately, some disk drivers such as Sun's SCSI do not maintain this statistic. As a result, you typically see zeros under the **msps** column making this field useless in practice. The DEC UNIX implementation of iostat goes one step further and omits **msps** altogether.

4.4.3 Terminal Activity

iostat shows the terminal traffic under the **tin** and **tout** columns. **tin** is the count of characters per second transferred into the system. **tout** is the opposite, showing the number of characters per second output from the system. Both **tin** and **tout** include the traffic for serial ports in addition to pseudo terminals, which are used by networking programs (e.g., rlogin) and windowing subsystem (e.g., X Window).

Note that **tin** can be quite high if a port is connected to another computer (e.g., when using a modem). In contrast, human beings cannot type very quickly and **tin** should be small (as an example, a fast 60 words per minute typist can input only five characters per second).

On most systems, each **tin** also causes an interrupt if not buffered by the hardware. These interrupts can significantly slow down the system. A simple modem transfer at 9600 baud can create almost 1000 interrupts per second. System time usually climbs in this situation because each interrupt has to be processed by the kernel. Well-designed systems either have deep buffers (FIFOs) or DMA engines to reduce the interrupt rate by transferring more than one character in each I/O request.

If **tin** is very high (greater than 100 typically) without any modem transfers, then the cause might be "noisy" RS-232 ports. Long, unterminated RS-232 lines (e.g., a turned-off terminal) can cause characters sent on the cable to echo back to the system as either a good character or a parity error. Because both cause an interrupt, the system can slow down substantially even if no one is using it. This viscious circle (positive feedback in engineering terms) will continue forever until someone terminates the line (e.g., by turning on the terminal).

Table 4.3 Iostat Column Headings

Field	Description
bps	Kilobytes per second transferred
tps	Read or write transfers per second
msps	Average time for each transfer (in milliseconds)
us	Percentage of CPU cycles used by processes that are not niced
ni	Percentage of CPU cycles used by processes that are niced
sy	Percentage of CPU cycles used by the kernel
id	Percentage of CPU cycles not used (idle)

4.5 ps

Most people use ps to see what the background jobs are doing and do not think of it as a performance tuning aid. But ps can be used as an effective instrumentation tool given the right options. Specifically, the -u flag provides a very useful listing of processes sorted by their degree of CPU usage[7]:

```
SunOS4.1% ps aux | head -20
USER       PID %CPU %MEM    SZ   RSS TT STAT  START   TIME COMMAND
amirm     2107 67.0  4.0 1048  1208 p5 S     14:41    0:16 large_prog
amirm     2113 30.8  1.6  232   476 p5 R     14:41    0:00 ps aux
root         2  0.0  0.0    0     0 ?  D     Feb  1   0:00 pagedaemon
root         1  0.0  0.0   52     0 ?  IW    Feb  1   0:00 /sbin/init -
root        46  0.0  0.0   68     0 ?  IW    Feb  1   0:00 portmap
root       131  0.0  0.0   56     0 ?  IW    Feb  1   0:01 cron
amirm      169  0.0  0.0 1380     0 co IW    Feb  1   0:04 mwm
amirm      170  0.0  0.0  116     0 p0 IW    Feb  1   0:02 -sh (csh)
root        53  0.0  0.0   40     0 ?  IW    Feb  1   0:00 keyserv
root        79  0.0  0.0   16     0 ?  I     Feb  1   0:03 (biod)
bin         51  0.0  0.0   36     0 ?  IW    Feb  1   0:00 ypbind
root        81  0.0  0.0   16     0 ?  I     Feb  1   0:03 (biod)
root        78  0.0  0.0   16     0 ?  S     Feb  1   0:02 (biod)
root        92  0.0  0.0   60     0 ?  IW    Feb  1   0:00 syslogd
amirm      159  0.0  0.0   40     0 co IW    Feb  1   0:00 /usr/X11R5/bin/xinit
root       108  0.0  0.0  104     0 ?  IW    Feb  1   0:09 /usr/lib/sendmail -bd -q
root       121  0.0  0.8  608   244 ?  S     Feb  1 13:02 automount -v
root       128  0.0  0.0   12     4 ?  S     Feb  1 55:48 update
root       114  0.0  0.0   52     0 ?  IW    Feb  1   0:00 rpc.statd
```

4.5.1 Per Process CPU Utilization

As already mentioned, ps -aux sorts the list of processes by their CPU usage (**%CPU**). Note that it is easy to identify processes that are the highest CPU users because they appear at the top of the listing. Because it is rare to have more than a few CPU-bound jobs in even large systems, you usually want to pipe the output of ps to the head command to see only the top few jobs in our example.

In the sample output, ps shows large_prog and itself as the highest CPU users (with 67 and 31% of the CPU cycles, respectively). For the actual amount of CPU usage rather than a percentage, simply look under the **TIME** column, which shows the accumulated CPU cycles in minutes and seconds.

4.5.2 Per Process Memory Utilization

%MEM shows the percentage of *physical* memory used by each process. These data can be somewhat misleading because ps ignores the amount of memory the kernel steals for itself (which ranges from 2 to 8 Mbytes). In addition, ps does not take into account the text (instruction) size and only sums the stack and data segments for each process. Despite these flaws,

> *the %MEM column can be used to easily identify large processes that are responsible for system paging and swapping.*

---

7. A public domain utility called top shows this ps display continuously.

Note that the sum of **%MEM** values rarely equals 100% because not all the physical memory is allocated to user processes.

SZ is the approximate *virtual* size of a process at the time `ps` was run. Unfortunately, the SunOS version of `ps` excludes the text size in the **SZ** column. While this is a major failing, the text size tends to be smaller and hence less important than the data segment for most programs. You may want to use the text size as displayed by the `size` command and add it to **SZ** manually to get a closer approximation of the memory utilization of the process (this would still miss the sizes of any shared libraries the process uses).

RSS stands for Resident Set Size and is the actual amount of memory in kilobytes that the process is currently using (**%MEM** is computed from **RSS**). **RSS** is a much more useful figure than **SZ** because the latter reflects only the virtual size of the process and not what has actually been paged in. In our sample display, you may see **RSS** figures that are higher than **SZ** for some processes. This is because **RSS** includes the paged portion of the text segment which **SZ** does not (in SunOS 4.1).

Note that it is important to look at the **RSS** when the program is actually doing something useful (i.e., has allocated and touched its data structures). For example, an empty `vi` session uses 460 Kbytes (on SunOS 4.1) but uses 572 Kbytes once you read in `/etc/termcap` with it.

Note that unlike other `ps` displays, you can easily identify who the owner of each process is by looking under the **USER** column. `ps` translates the user id, which the kernel maintains to a user login name by using the `/etc/passwd` file.

STAT shows the current state of a process. Table 4.4 lists the single-letter mnemonics used in this column.

Because a process can be in multiple states simultaneously, you may see more than one letter under the **STAT** column. For example, **IW** indicates a sleeping process that is currently swapped out. Keep an eye on the **RW** combination, which means that the system has swapped out a job that was either running or has recently run. As mentioned before, the system only swaps out runnable jobs as a last resort. Therefore,

*if ps ever shows a process in RW state, the system has a **severe** shortage of memory.*

TT is the abbreviated name of the controlling terminal on which the process is running. For example, if the user terminal device is `/dev/tty00`, `ps` displays "`00`". If the device is the console, `ps` shows the abbreviation "`co`". Devices starting with "`p`" are pseudo terminals used by the networking and windowing programs.

PID is a unique per process identification number that the kernel assigns to each process. You can use it for example to terminate a process (using `kill`) or change its priority (using `renice`).

Table 4.4 Process Status Field

STAT	Description
R	Process is either running or waiting to be run by the CPU
1	Convention used on multiprocessor systems to indicate a process is running on the CPU—can be higher than 1 indicating the CPU number
S	Process sleeping for short amount of time (less than 20 seconds)
I	Processes sleeping longer than 20 seconds (idle)
W	Process swapped out
D	Process sleeping at a negative priority, which typically indicates that the process is waiting for an I/O request from a device such as disk or tape
T	Sleeping process suspended by the user (e.g., ^Z)
N	Process has a positive nice priority
<	Process has a negative nice priority
>	Process has exceeded its soft memory limit
Z	Zombie process waiting for its parent or I/O to finish before exiting
P	Process sleeping because of a pagein request

START simply shows the time (or the date if more than 24 hours have passed) since the process was started.

The **COMMAND** field shows the string that was used to invoke the program. Note that this may not match the actual command typed by the user due to expansion of wild cards (e.g., *.c) by the shell and user aliases (in csh). In addition, user processes can overwrite their command string, which can further distort this information (rcp is one of the standard utilities that modifies its argument string). An alternative is to use the -c option, which extracts the program name from a kernel data structure, which is not subject to corruption by the user process. However, you will not be able to see the arguments used to invoke the program in this case.

4.5.3 Memory Sorted Process Display

In analyzing high-memory usage, you may want to use the -v option to get a sorted output based on the **%MEM** field:

```
sonyBSD# ps v
  PID TT STAT TIME SL RE PAGEIN  SIZE  RSS   LIM TSIZ TRS %CPU %MEM COMMAND
 1016 p0 R    0:24  0 28      0   764  452 14696  128 128 90.4  4.0 ccom
 1019 p1 S    0:00  0 13      0   108   80 14696  120 116  4.2  1.0 csh
 1024 p1 R    0:00  0  0      0   116   96 14696   56  32  0.0  0.9 ps
```

Most of the fields are the same as the ones in the CPU-sorted display just discussed. Of special interest are the **TSIZE** and **TRS** fields, which show the total virtual size of the text segment of the process and how much of it is paged in, respectively. In the sample display (run on SONY's BSD implementation), the C compiler, ccom, has paged in all of its 128 Kbytes of its text segment. Likewise, C shell has paged in 116 Kbytes out of 120 (only one 4-Kbyte page is left untouched). This is fairly typical of most small programs, which have few pages that are fully made up of dead code. This observation applies to ps also, even though its ratio of **RSS** to **SIZE** is smaller. The reason for this discrepancy is that ps samples its own data when it hasn't finished execution. If you could somehow look at ps just before it exits, you would see a very high percentage of its text pages resident in memory.

We should note that the SunOS version of ps is missing both **TRS** and **TSIZ**. Although this is not a big loss in the case of normal UNIX utilities that page in the majority of their text pages, the same cannot be said of some large commercial applications. Although we sympathize with the problem of figuring out how to apportion the text usage of shared libraries, which we suspect is the reason behind the absence of these fields, some approximation of text usage would have been better than nothing.

```
SunOS4.1% ps avx |head
  PID TT STAT   TIME SL RE PAGEIN SIZE  RSS    LIM %CPU %MEM COMMAND
 2155 p5 R     0:04  0  5      2 1048 1196    xx 81.7  4.0 large_prog
 2156 p5 R     0:00  0  0      0  228  468    xx  0.0  1.5 ps
  121 ?  S    13:04  0 28    129  608  248    xx  0.0  0.8 automount
 2157 p5 S     0:00  0  0      0   28  200    xx  0.0  0.7 head
  472 p5 S     0:01  0 16     30   80  176    xx  0.0  0.6 csh
  471 ?  S     0:02  0 24     10   32   48    xx  0.0  0.2 in.telnetd
  169 co IW    0:05 82 58    298 1380    0    xx  0.0  0.0 mwm
   46 ?  IW    0:00 99 99     15   68    0    xx  0.0  0.0 portmap
  170 p0 IW    0:02 99 99      9  116    0    xx  0.0  0.0 csh
```

4.6 DEC UNIX ps

The DEC UNIX version of ps is a single program impersonating both System V and BSD versions. It assumes that you want the BSD behavior if you omit the dash from the list of options:

```
OSF/1% ps aux |head
USER      PID %CPU %MEM   VSZ  RSS TT  S   STARTED        TIME COMMAND
amirm     804 69.0  0.4 1.28M 168K p5  R   17:34:09    0:03.16 runner
amirm     769  0.0  1.0 1.96M 480K p5  S   17:21:13    0:00.30 -csh (csh)
root      768  0.0  0.7 1.34M 344K ??  S   17:21:13    0:00.21 rlogind
root      193  0.0  0.1 1.38M  56K ??  I   13:16:25    0:00.60 /usr/sbin/ypb
root      184  0.0  0.3 1.42M 136K ??  I   13:16:25    0:00.06 /usr/sbin/por
root      205  0.0  0.0 1.28M   0K ??  U   13:16:26    0:00.05 /usr/sbin/nfs
root      123  0.0  0.2 1.34M 104K ??  S   13:16:22    0:00.22 /usr/sbin/rou
root      207  0.0  0.0 1.28M   0K ??  U   13:16:26    0:00.03 /usr/sbin/nfs
root      203  0.0  0.0 1.28M   0K ??  U   13:16:26    0:00.05 /usr/sbin/nfs
```

The **USER, PID, %CPU, %MEM, TT, RSS, TIME**, and **COMMAND** are identical to fields already described for BSD ps. The **STARTED** column is the same as the **START** field in BSD and indicates when the program was invoked. The memory fields (**VSZ** and

RSS) have been nicely enhanced to scale automatically to kilobytes (**K**) and megabytes (**M**) instead of just overflowing as is the case in BSD ps.

The **VSZ** field shows the total virtual size of the process including the sizes for any shared libraries the process may be using. In computation of this field, the entire size of a shared library is used even if the process uses just a single routine out of the whole set. As a result, even small programs tend to have unusually large virtual sizes.

Like its BSD counterpart, the DEC ps command also has a v option:

```
OSF/1% bty[2]% ps avx |head
  PID TT  S            TIME        SL PAGEIN   VSZ  RSS %CPU %MEM COMMAND
    0 ??  R < 130-20:37:59 81616763     0  201M 9.5M  0.0 20.7 [kernel idle]
  370 ??  S <     02:41:51          8  8294 24.0M 3.1M  0.0  6.7 /usr/bin/X11/X
  451 ??  I        0:02.34       2906   844 4.95M 2.1M  0.0  4.5 xterm -C -name
16233 p2  S        0:03.20          3   152 1.09M 1.0M 26.0  2.2 a.out
  434 ??  I        7:04.26       2904  4656 2.53M 760K  0.0  1.6 fvwm
16179 p0  I  +     0:00.42        162   474 1.97M 488K  0.0  1.0 -csh (csh)
16228 p2  S        0:00.27          0   245 1.96M 480K  0.0  1.0 -csh (csh)
16234 p2  R  +     0:00.10          0   177 1.55M 440K  0.0  0.9 ps avx
13137 ??  I        0:06.14       2904    74 2.11M 400K  0.0  0.8 /usr/local/bin/
```

The largest memory user is usually the kernel shown as PID 0. This is a very welcome addition because it immediately tells you how much memory the kernel is using. In our example, it has a resident size (**RSS**) of 9.5 Mbytes.

The **TIME** column shows the amount of CPU time the process has used. In the case of the kernel idle thread, it is the total amount of CPU idle time since the system was booted (in this case, 130 days, 20 hours, 37 minutes, and 59 seconds).

The **S** field is similar to **STAT** in BSD and shows the process state. Most of the states are the same as the BSD version. The exceptions are the plus (**+**) sign, which indicates that the process is the controlling terminal (usually the login shell), and **U**, which means an uninterruptable (i.e., negative priority) sleeping process.

4.7 uptime

uptime is a simple utility that shows a quick summary of the system status.[8] No options are necessary. The following is a typical display:

```
5:39pm  up 20 days, 20:47,  2 users,  load average: 5.00, 3.06, 1.07
```

The number of users in the system is reported along with how long the system has been up. The most useful information, however, is the so-called load averages. The kernel maintains running averages of the count of active jobs in the system (the same processes

---

8. uptime is really a link to the w utility.

counted under the **r** column in `vmstat`) for the last 1, 5, and 15 minutes. `uptime` shows these averages as the last three numbers. The first value is a very useful measure of the current CPU load. As with the **r** field in `vmstat`, the system slows down significantly when the load average exceeds four.

The longer term averages are used to determine whether the system load is increasing or decreasing. In the preceding example the system load is increasing (1 minute average higher than the last two), which means that the situation is worsening (i.e., the CPU load is increasing).

Note that the standard SVR4 version of `uptime` does not show the load averages. But some vendors such as SONY and Sun (in Solaris) have enhanced their version to show this information.

A related utility to `uptime` is `rup`, which gathers the same information from other machines on the network.

4.8 pstat

`pstat` is really a kernel-debugging tool but one of its options, `-T`, is useful for displaying the sizes for selected kernel tables. Using this option, the number of entries in use and the total table size (separated by a slash) can be seen:

```
% pstat -T
168/960 files
600/612 inodes
 66/532 processes
 30/ 68 texts active,   68 used
131/323 00k swap
```

The thing to look for is whether any of the tables are excessively large. The tables that use the most amount of space are **proc** (shown as **processes**) and **inode**. You can safely ignore the rest other than making sure they are large enough as to not cause any system failures.

In addition to table sizes, `pstat  -T` also prints out the amount of free swap space. The units are in hundreds of Kbytes as indicated by the cryptic "00k" notation. In the sample output, the system has used 13.1 Mbytes of swap space and still has 32.3 Mbytes of space left.

4.9 Sun Multiprocessor Statistics

Instrumenting multiprocessor implementations is somewhat difficult due to lack of standard monitoring tools. So, we recommend that you refer to your vendor documentation for up-to-date information on your version of UNIX. We briefly cover the Solaris psrinfo and mpstat utilities in this section.

psrinfo simply shows the type of processor that you are using and its status:

```
Solaris% /usr/sbin/psrinfo -v
Status of processor 0 as of: 08/19/95 15:19:53
   Processor has been on-line since 08/19/95 14:46:38.
   The sparc processor operates at 50 MHz,
           and has a sparc floating point processor.
Solaris% /usr/sbin/psrinfo -v
Status of processor 2 as of: 08/19/95 15:19:53
   Processor has been on-line since 08/19/95 14:46:38.
   The sparc processor operates at 50 MHz,
           and has a sparc floating point processor.
```

mpstat is a utility similar to vmstat except that most of the fields are replaced with various counters that keep track of internal kernel events:

CPU	minf	mjf	xcal	intr	ithr	csw	icsw	migr	smtx	srw	syscl	usr	sys	wt	idl
0	6	0	10	94	42	14	7	2	0	0	300654	38	52	0	9
2	0	0	1	96	41	15	2	2	0	0	29433	3	6	0	91

The right-most columns are the familiar CPU idle, user, and system time. Of special importance is **smtx**, which counts the number of times the kernel attempted to acquire a semaphore for exclusive access to some data structure and its request was denied. This occurs if another CPU is holding on to the same data structure indicating heavy contention for that resource. In an ideal situation, the number of contentions would be zero. In real life, **smtx** values of 100 to 300 can be tolerated. Higher levels indicate lost CPU cycles (which show up as system time) due to the processor having to wait for the other CPU to release the semaphore.

4.10 Summary

As vmstat is the most comprehensive tool in BSD, you should start your analysis with it. The ps command can be used to further pinpoint the cause of high CPU or memory usage. Likewise, the iostat command can show slightly more detailed disk I/O statistics along with terminal traffic. The uptime command can be used as a quick means of getting long-term CPU usage. It is especially useful in gauging whether the state of the CPU usage is improving or getting worse. pstat, while really a kernel utility, can be used to see the usage of a few selected tables.

CHAPTER 5

System V Monitoring Tools

Even though BSD has many instrumentation utilities, System V basically relies on `sar`, which stands for System Activity Report. `sar` can display a comprehensive array of system information and usually with a high level of detail. Most of the credit, however, goes to the System V kernel for maintaining these statistics. After all, `sar` displays only what it reads from the kernel. On the down side, `sar`'s formatting of its output data leaves something to be desired. Although most UNIX tools have a similar reputation, `sar` pushes this to an extreme if you use options such as `-A` (which combines the output from every individual option creating a very confusing listing).

5.1 sar

The `sar` program can be run in two distinct modes. It can be instructed to retrieve system information either already stored in a log file or from the live system. The former actually relies on another program called `sadc`, which is usually run by the `cron` program at regular intervals to collect system data. `sar` can then be used to view the stored information.

The syntax for `sar` is

sar -options <interval> <count>

If an `interval` is used, `sar` sleeps for that many seconds and then prints one line of output. If an interval is specified, then the `count` argument indicates the number of times `sar` outputs its data before stopping. As usual, you should not use intervals that are too small. Otherwise, there is a possibility of getting incorrect and erratic information. Depending on the data being displayed, a value between 2 and 30 seconds is usually sufficient to produce a useful display.

Without the `interval` and `count` arguments, `sar` defaults to reading its data from the log file and not the current statistics (from the kernel). `sadc` conveniently stores a time stamp in the log file, which `sar` prints, making it easy to analyze the data over a long period.

The most useful options in `sar` are summarized in Table 5.1. Although some options such as -p (for pagein) are easy to remember, others such as -g (for pageout) are unfortunately not.[1] Options can be combined to get more information in each sample. But if you do, the output may be difficult to read, especially if more than two options are specified. In addition, the output quickly scrolls off the screen, making it hard to see any trends. Workstation users are better off running multiple copies of `sar` in separate windows, each with a single option. Another problem is that `sar` does not reprint its headings when they scroll off the screen, forcing you to memorize them instead.

Table 5.1 Common `sar` Options

Option	Description
u	CPU usage
b	Buffer cache statistics
c	System call rates
d	Disk I/O activity
g	Pageout information
p	Pagein information
r	Free memory and swap space
q	CPU run queue statistics
v	Kernel table sizes and utilization
w	Swapping statistics
y	Terminal I/O rates (see Chapter 6)
n	Name cache statistics (SCO only)
A	Show all statistics

---

1. Perils of using single-character arguments in UNIX.

5.1.1 CPU Utilization

The -u option is used to get the CPU statistics in combination with other options. Otherwise, -u is the default and need not be specified. Here is a sample output:

```
% sar 2 3
20:08:29    %usr     %sys     %wio     %idle
20:08:31       1       12        0        87
20:08:33       1        5        1        93
20:08:35       1        7        0        93

Average        1        8        0        91
```

User (**%usr**) and system (**%sys**) times are identical to equivalent fields to BSD's vmstat and show the percentage of time spent running user programs and the kernel, respectively. Unlike vmstat though, the total system idle time is broken down into **%wio** and **%idle**. **%wio** shows the percentage of time the CPU was idle waiting for an I/O device. However, only block devices (e.g., disk and tape) are accounted for. Especially lacking is the wait time for network I/O requests (such as NFS). **%idle**, on the other hand, is the percentage of time the CPU had absolutely nothing to do or was waiting on the network. *So, the total CPU idle percentage (as shown in* vmstat) *is the sum of* **%wio** *and* **%idle**.

%wio is quite useful in identifying whether the system is I/O bound (that is, the I/O subsystem is the bottleneck). For example, a **%wio** value of 100 (which forces **%idle** to be zero) indicates that all CPU resources are being wasted and the system is constantly waiting for I/O devices.

> *You should strive to keep* **%wio** *as small as possible. A* **%wio** *value of 50 means the system is running at half speed.*

As mentioned previously, you should not worry about the disk I/O performance when the total CPU idle time (the sum of **%wio** and **%idle**) is less than 10%. Instead, you should try to optimize the CPU performance.

Table 5.2 sar -u: CPU Usage Summary

Field	Description
%user	Percentage of time spent running user programs
%sys	Percentage of time spent running the kernel
%wio	Percentage of time the CPU was idle waiting for an I/O request to finish
%idle	Percentage of time the CPU had no jobs to run (was idle) or was waiting on the network

5.1.2 Buffer Cache Hit Rates

sar -b shows the statistics for the kernel buffer cache:

```
SonySVR4% sar -b 5 3
```

18:12:14	bread/s	lread/s	%rcache	bwrit/s	lwrit/s	%wcache	pread/s	pwrit/s
18:12:19	1	16	95	2	2	0	0	0
18:12:24	8	27	72	5	27	82	0	0
18:12:29	0	0	100	0	0	100	0	0
Average	3	15	80	2	10	77	0	0

In systems with paged buffer caches, the statistics displayed by this option relate only to the small, fixed-size buffer cache that is still left to handle file system ("metadata") traffic. This includes such transfers as reading and writing inodes, indirect blocks, and file system superblocks. Although this information is still useful, the lack of statistics for the paged buffer cache is a major failing. The only exception to this limitation in SGI IRIX 5.X, which shows the combined statistics for both caches. Likewise, in SCO UNIX, the buffer cache is not paged, and hence these statistics related to both file system data access and file contents.

The total number of user read requests is shown in **lread/s** and the number that actually resulted in physical I/O to disk in **bread/s**. sar also displays the ratio of **bread/s** to **lread/s** as a hit rate under **%rcache**. For example, if all read requests were satisfied with data in the buffer cache, **%rcache** would be 100 (best case). Likewise, if **bread/s** and **lread/s** were identical, **%rcache** would be zero (worst case).

> *Note that for good performance, %rcache should be above 80%.*

sar displays the effects of the delayed write policy by showing the rate of user write requests as **lwrit/s** and the number resulting in physical writes under **bwrit/s**. A hit rate is also computed as the ratio of **lwrit/s** to **bwrit/s** and is displayed under the **%wcache** column, even though this is not technically the right terminology for this optimization.

pread/s and **pwrit/s** show the rates for a class of I/O operations (also called raw transfers) that bypass the buffer cache. This method is used by some database applications to get better reliability and performance. If you are not using these special applications, you will only see zeros in these fields.

Table 5.3 `sar -b:` (Meta) Buffer Cache Statistics

Field	Description
lread/s	Number of read operations per second
bread/s	Number of reads that resulted in physical disk I/O
%rcache	Ratio of breads to lreads (hit rate)
lwrit/s	Number of write operations per second
bwrit/s	Number of writes that resulted in physical disk I/O
%wcache	Ratio of bwrits to lwrits
pread/s	Reads from raw devices per second
pwrit/s	Writes to raw devices per second

5.1.3 System Call Rates

Because user programs request services from the kernel in the form of system calls, know-ing which system calls are being executed can be helpful in the analysis of high system time. The kernel keeps track of certain (important) system calls, and `sar -c` can display their rates:

```
% sar -c 2 3
20:10:46 scall/s sread/s swrit/s  fork/s  exec/s rchar/s wchar/s
20:10:48     477      59      25    0.00    0.00   70368    4511
20:10:50     665      98      43    0.00    0.00   62562    8370
20:10:52     913     150      74    0.00    0.00   66347   12415

Average      699     105      49    0.00    0.00   66165    8698
```

The rate of all system calls per second is shown under the **scall/s** column. Typical values for **scall/s** are below the 1000 mark, although fast CPUs can easily exceed this rate. Some system calls such as `fork` (which creates a new process) and `exec` (which runs a new program) can substantially tax the system, and you should keep an eye on their rates. `sar` shows the number of `forks` and `execs` per second under the **fork/s** and **exec/s** col-umns, respectively. As you will see in Chapter 7, it is important for the rate of `execs` to be close to the rate of `forks`. Otherwise, you may need to fine-tune the shell path.

`sar -c` also shows the total number of bytes being transferred between user programs and the kernel under **rchar/s** and **wchar/s**, but there is not much that can be deduced from their values.

5.1.4 Disk Statistics

`sar -d` shows disk I/O information with considerably more detail than BSD's `iostat`. A welcome enhancement is the device field, which has more room and displays a much more meaningful drive name. `sar` shows a separate line of information for each drive config-ured in the system.

Table 5.4 `sar -c`: System Call Summary

Field	Description
scall/s	Total number of system calls per second
sread/s	Read system calls per second
swrit/s	Write system calls per second
fork/s	Fork system calls per second
exec/s	Exec system calls per second
rchar/s	Number of bytes transferred to user programs as a result of read system call
wchar/s	Number of bytes transferred to kernel from user programs as a result of write system call

We recommend that you run this option with a rather large interval of at least 30–60 seconds to get a better view of the overall traffic.

```
Solaris% sar -d 30 1
15:30:35   device       %busy   avque   r+w/s   blks/s  avwait  avserv
15:31:05   fd0              0     0.0       0        0     0.0     0.0
           sd2             87     2.7      82     2377     0.0    33.3
           sd3             87     1.9      80     1766     0.0    23.7
```

Because the CPU is much faster than the disk drive, the system can create many disk requests in the span of time it takes for the disk drive to service just one. To deal with this problem, the system maintains a queue for each drive and links new requests into it while the drive is busy. When one I/O finishes, the kernel picks up the next request from the queue and gives it to the disk controller to process. **avque** shows the average number of requests in the disk queue while the drive was busy.[2]

%busy shows the percentage of time the device was busy servicing a request. This is a very important parameter because it shows how saturated a disk drive is. As a general rule,

you should strive to keep %busy below 25% for optimal system performance.

avwait and **avserv** display the average amount of time a request was waiting on the queue along with the average amount of time it took for the drive to process it. If **avwait** plus **avserv** exceeds 50 milliseconds, the drive is running too slow for good response time (probably due to too many I/O requests).

r+w/s is the number of transfers per second and is identical to a similar field in vmstat and iostat. But here, it is not a key piece of information because you have **%busy**, which gives you the same information but in a more meaningful way.

blks/s shows the amount of data transferred to and from the disk drive. Unlike **bps** in vmstat, the units are in 512-byte blocks and not kilobytes.[3]

5.1.5 Pageout Activity

As you recall, the kernel frees memory by writing out pages of memory to the swap device (or the file system in the case of the paged buffer cache). This operation is called paging out, and sar -g in SVR4 displays the statistics related to this operation.

```
% sar -g 2 3
16:23:18  pgout/s ppgout/s pgfree/s pgscan/s %ufs_ipf
```

2. The system averages the queue size only when it is not empty.

3. The reason for this is historic but one wonders about justification of reporting data in 512-byte units in a modern operating system.

Table 5.5 `sar -d`: Disk Statistics

Field	Description
device	Kernel's notion of the disk drive name
%busy	Percentage of time the drive had anything to do
avque	Average number of requests pending for this device
r+w/s	Read or write operations performed per second
avwait	Average amount of time (in milliseconds) the I/O request was waiting before being processed by the controller/drive
avserv	Average time (in milliseconds) the disk drive (and controller) required to service the request
blks/s	Blocks transferred per second (in 512-byte units)

```
16:23:20     3.00    76.00   141.50   168.50    0.00
16:23:22     0.50     2.50     8.00     8.00    0.00
16:23:24     0.00     0.00     0.00     0.00    0.00

Average      1.17    26.17    49.83    58.83    0.00
```

pgout/s shows the number of times the pageout daemon was activated to free memory. **ppgout/s** is the number of pages that had to be written out to the swap space to free memory. **pgfree/s** shows the total number of pages freed per second (whether they required an I/O or not) by the pageout daemon or the swapper.

pgscan/s is the number of pages examined by the pageout daemon to see if they can be freed and is identical to **sr** in `vmstat`. *If pgscan is nonzero, the pageout daemon is running looking for pages to free.* But note that this does not necessarily mean that there is a memory shortage if your system has a paged buffer cache.

%ufsipf is a key piece of information and indicates how often the kernel had to reuse an inactive inode that had pages associated with it in the buffer cache. This is usually an indication of an inode table that is too small causing useful buffer cache data to be thrown away:

> *%ufsipf should always be zero. Otherwise, the inode table is too small.*

Note that the `-g` option is used to display terminal buffer statistics in SCO's `sar` utility and has nothing to do with paging. Likewise, SGI's version of `sar` uses this option to show the graphics statistics.

5.1.6 Pagein Activity

`sar -p` shows the pagein activity:

```
SonySVR4% sar -p 5 3
```

Table 5.6 `sar -g`: Pageout Summary

Field	Description
pgout/s	Number of pageout requests per second
ppgout/s	Number of pages paged out as a result of each pageout request
pgfree/s	Number of pages freed per second without any I/O to the swap device
pgscan/s	Number of pages examined by pageout daemon to see if they can be freed per second
%ufsipf	Percentage of time an inode was taken off the freelist that had reusable pages associated with it

```
18:33:28  atch/s  pgin/s ppgin/s  pflt/s  vflt/s slock/s
18:33:33    3.85   18.37   29.71    1.36   44.22   22.22
18:33:38    3.21   17.87   34.14    0.20   35.14    6.02
18:33:43    6.13   24.90   38.54    0.00   33.20   20.16

Average     4.43   20.48   34.33    0.48   37.23   15.92
```

Pagein statistics are of little value in system tuning and are only included here for completeness. Table 5.7 describes all the fields if you are curious.

Table 5.7 `sar -p`: Pagein Statistics

Field	Description
atch/s	Pages per second given back to a process after a page fault
pgin/s	Pagein requests per second
ppgin/s	Pages brought in per second as a result of pageins (equal to pgin times fsblocksize/pagesize)
pflt/s	Protection faults per second (copy-on-write page faults typically)
vflts/s	General page fault (valid bit = 0) usually resulting in pagein or zero-fill page
slock/s	Page faults per second as a result of page lock requests (typically initiated by a driver)

5.1.7 Swapping Activity

`sar -w` shows the swapping information. Unlike `vmstat` in BSD UNIX, you can easily see the swapping rates:

```
% sar -w 2 3
20:18:40 swpin/s pswin/s swpot/s pswot/s pswch/s
20:18:42    0.00     0.0    0.58     1.7      27
20:18:46    0.31     0.9    1.25     3.8      39
20:18:48    0.71     2.1    0.71     2.1      74

Average     0.39     1.2    0.91     2.7      49
```

The total number of processes swapped out is shown under **swpot/s**, and the number swapped in under **swpin/s**. To swap out a process, the kernel gathers all its pages (which may number in the hundreds for large programs) and writes them out to the swap device.[4] As a result, **pswot/s**, which is the count of pages swapped out, is usually a large multiple of **swpot/s**. The number of pages brought in as a result of swap-in (**pswin/s**), however, is typically very small. The reason is that when the kernel wants to swap a process in, it brings in only one kernel data structure (the so-called u area, which can be from one to three pages), and lets the user process bring in its own pages one at a time (through demand paging). So, **pswin/s** is usually much smaller than the corresponding **pswot/s** for an equivalent number of swap-ins and swap-outs.

If your version of UNIX is older than SVR4, `sar` displays **bswin/s** and **bswot/s** instead of **pswin/s** and **pswot/s**. The only difference is that the units for **bswin/s** and **bswot/s** are in 512-byte blocks rather than pages. Regardless,

> *you should not see any swapping activity in the output of* `sar -w`. *Otherwise, it indicates a severe memory shortage.*

The last column in this display is **pswch/s**, which shows the number of process context switches per second. We have no idea why it is included under swapping information though. Nevertheless, you should keep an eye on it. It should stay under a few hundred in most environments.

Table 5.8 `sar -w`: Swap Statistics

Field	Description
swpin/s	Processes swapped in per second
pswin/s	Number of pages swapped in per second as a result of swap-ins
swpot/s	Processes swapped out per second
pswot/s	Number of pages swapped out per second
pswch/s	Process context switches per second

5.1.8 Free Memory and Swap Space

`sar -r` prints the amount of free memory and swap space. Note that the units are *not* in Kbytes. The free memory is reported as number of pages and swap space as 512-byte blocks:

```
SonySVR4% sar -r 2 3
18:49:34 freemem freeswp
18:49:36    251   13183
18:49:38    300   13183
18:49:40    293   13183

Average     288   13183
```

---

4. The instruction (text) pages are not usually swapped out.

On systems with paged buffer caches, free memory usually hovers around the `lotsfree` value (in the preceding example it is set to 1024, which roughly matches the display if you multiply the value by 4 Kbytes). The only time lack of free memory indicates a problem is when the value stays below `lotsfree` for an extended amount of time (which triggers swapping). Free swap space, on the other hand, does not have any impact on the performance of the system. But, if you run out of swap space, you will not be able to run any new programs, and the existing processes may fail.

5.1.9 CPU Run Queue Statistics

`sar -q` shows the size of the run queue (where processes wait to be run by the CPU) under **runq-sz** (run queue size) and what percentage of time the queue was nonempty under **%runocc** (run queue occupancy):

```
% sar -q 2 3
20:33:08 runq-sz %runocc swpq-sz %swpocc
20:33:10    1.5     100
20:33:12    1.0      50
20:33:14    1.0      50

Average     1.2      67
```

runq-sz is similar to the **r** column in `vmstat` and indicates how busy the CPU is. Therefore,

> *high values of **runq-sz** (greater than four) mean the system is very CPU-bound.*

The run queue statistics can help you determine quickly if the CPU is saturated. In addition, if you have a multiprocessor system, the run queue size tells you how many additional CPUs you can effectively utilize. For example, if the **runq-sz** size is 3, you can add up to 3 CPUs to the system and have some confidence that they would not sit idle. In this case, you need to run `sar -q` with a large enough interval (at least 60 seconds) to make sure that you are not seeing short-term peaks.

swpq-sz shows the number of swapped-out processes. As such,

> *swpq-sz should always be zero. Otherwise, you have a server memory shortage.*

Table 5.9 `sar -q`: CPU Run Queue Utilization

Field	Description
runq-sz	Average size of the CPU run queue when not empty
%runocc	Percentage of time the CPU run queue was not empty
swpq-sz	Size of the swap queue averaged when the queue was not empty
%swpocc	Percentage of time the swap queue was not empty

5.1.10 Table Sizes

`sar -v` prints the sizes for **process**, **inode**, **file**, and **lock** tables:

```
% sar -v 2 3
20:36:34 proc-sz ov inod-sz ov file-sz ov lock-sz
20:36:36  63/400   0 353/400  0 208/  0  0   1/300
20:36:38  63/400   0 353/400  0 208/  0  0   1/300
20:36:40  63/400   0 353/400  0 208/  0  0   1/300
```

You can ignore the **inode**, **file,** and **lock** tables if you are using SVR4 because the kernel grows these tables as needed. Additionally, SVR4 does not have a limit on the file table size even though `sar` shows it to have a zero size. While the **lock** table is also grown automatically, the kernel imposes a hard limit on how many entries can be used. This is the value that `sar` shows as the **lock** table size. Likewise, the **inode** table is grown dynamically until it hits the kernel parameter, **ufs_ninode**. Note that in Solaris 2.4, the limit has much less of a meaning because the kernel can actually exceed **ufs_ninode**. In either case, the table size shown by `sar` is the value of **ufs_ninode** (400 in our example).

The **ov** columns show the number of times the table preceding that column has overflowed in the past. Needless to say, you need to keep these tables large enough to keep them from overfilling. The correct operation of the system requires that the **ov** columns are always zero.

Table 5.10 `sar -v`: Table Usage Summary

Field	Description
proc-sz	Process table entries used / total size
inod-sz	Inode table entries used / total size (or limit)
file-sz	File table entries used / total size
lock-sz	File locking table entries used / maximum size (or limit)
ov	Overflow counter for the preceding table

5.1.11 Name Cache Statistics

The SCO version of `sar` has a `-n` option, which shows the hit rate of the name look-up cache:

```
# sar -n
14:53:00  c_hits cmisses (hit %)
15:00:02   15274     763 (95%)
15:20:01    9001     601 (93%)

Average    24275    1364 (94%)
```

The key figure is **hit%**, which should always be above 90%. If it drops below this level, the number of name cache entries (S5CACHEENTS) should be increased.

5.1.12 Solaris Kernel Memory Allocator Statistics

If you are running Solaris, you can use the `-k` option of `sar` to view the amount of dynamic data memory that the kernel has allocated for itself:

```
Solaris% sar -k 1

17:47:39 sml_mem    alloc   fail  lg_mem    alloc   fail  ovsz_alloc   fail
17:47:40  357120   354784      0 1769472  1658880      0     2035712      0
```

There are two pools for allocation: small and large. Small buffers are usually 256 bytes or less and large ones are from 512 bytes and up. The total amount of memory to each pool is shown under **sml_mem** and **lg_mem**. In our example, roughly 348 Kbytes (35,7120/1024) are reserved for small buffers and 1.6 Mbytes (1,369,472/1024/1024), for large buffers. You should add these sizes to the kernel size reported at boot time to arrive at the true size of the kernel.

5.2 System V ps

The System V `ps` is rather anemic compared to its BSD counterpart when it comes to performance-monitoring capabilities. The only useful options are `-el`, which provide a complete list of processes (sorted by the rather useless **PID** column) in the system:

```
sunshine% ps -l
 F S    UID   PID  PPID  C PRI NI    ADDR      SZ   WCHAN TTY          TIME COMD
 8 S    900 12552 12550 80   1 20  ff75a800    358 ff75a9c8 pts/2      0:01 csh
 8 O    900 12559 12552 17   1 20  ff73b800    149          pts/2      0:00 ps
```

The first column to look at is **S**, which shows the process status in a similar manner to BSD's `ps` but with different letter mnemonics as shown in Table 5.11.

Absent from the process state is any indication of whether the process is swapped out. For that, you need to look at the Flags field under **F**. Unfortunately, this is a copy of a single-word bit field in one of the kernel structures and its meaning is very system-specific. For example, on SGI IRIX, if bit 4 (hex value 0x10) is set, it indicates the process is resident in memory. In HP-UX, the same information is contained in bit 0. Refer to the `ps` manual page to find the right bit value.[5]

TIME simply shows the accumulated CPU time in minutes:seconds.

C shows the recent CPU usage of a process. On some systems such as HP-UX, SVR4, and SCO UNIX, it indicates the percentage of CPU usage. On Solaris, it is not a percentage

---

5. It is amazing that the user is forced to look up the meaning of each bit manually when `ps` could have easily decoded them.

Table 5.11 System V ps State Flags

Flag	Description
O	Process is currently being run by a processor.
0	Process is currently being run by a processor (SGI only).
R	Process is waiting to be run by the CPU (it is in the run queue).
S	The process is sleeping.
I	The process is being created (Intermediate state).
Z	A Zombie process. It has called exit but is waiting on some event that is keeping it from terminating.
T	The process is suspended (using ^Z for example in C shell). It may also indicate a process that is being traced (by a debugger) in some systems.
X	The process is growing and is waiting for more memory to become available.
B	The process is waiting for more memory (SCO only).

but rather a simple value that counts up to a maximum of 80. The count decrements while the process is waiting on the run queue and is not being run.

PRI is the process priority, but its exact meaning is subject to the scheduler in use. Refer to Chapter 3 on the exact meaning of this value. The same goes for the nice value as indicated by **NI**.

SZ shows the total virtual size of a process in Kbytes. In the standard System V implementation, there is no way to display the actual memory usage of a process (àla RSS in BSD). The SGI IRIX implementation, however, shows this information:

```
iris% ps -l
 F S    UID   PID  PPID  C PRI NI  P    SZ:RSS     WCHAN TTY       TIME COMD
30 S      0 26972   160  0  26 20  *   293:56   88296480 ttyq6     0:01 rlogind
30 S    998 26973 26972  0  39 20  *    90:72   8819a5c0 ttyq6     0:00 csh
30 R    998 28183 26973 23  71 20  0   322:154           ttyq6     0:00 ps
```

Note that the units for both pieces of information (**SZ:RSS**) are in (usually 4-Kbyte) pages and not Kbytes.

If you have an SVR4 system, you want to use the -c option, which shows the scheduler-specific parameters:

```
sunshine% ps -cl
 F S   UID   PID  PPID  CLS PRI     ADDR    SZ    WCHAN TTY       TIME COMD
 8 S   900 12552 12550   TS  59 ff75a800   358 ff75a9c8 pts/2     0:01 csh
 8 O   900 12574 12552   TS  44 ff75d000   149          pts/2     0:00 ps
```

With this option, you can easily see the scheduler class for each process under **CLS** and the scheduler-specific priority under **PRI**. In our example, csh has a Time Sharing (TS) scheduler along with a global priority value of 59 (its scheduler-specific priority was 1 as seen in the previous example without the -c option).

5.2.1 DEC UNIX ps

As we mentioned in Chapter 4, the DEC implementation of ps supports both System V and BSD options. Using its System V syntax (triggered by specifying a dash before the options), we get a display that is a mix of BSD and System V fields:

```
DEC% ps -l
       F S      UID   PID  PPID %CPU PRI  NI   RSS WCHAN        TT        TIME COMM
80808005 I  +   403   762   761  0.0  41   0  456K 89c54448 p0      0:00.33 csh
80808205 S      403   769   768  0.0  41   0  480K pause    p5      0:00.31 csh
80808001 R      403   804   769 98.0  53   0  168K -        p5      3:59.09 runn
```

Here, the **%CPU** field clearly displays the CPU usage of the process. Likewise, the actual memory usage of the process is nicely shown under **RSS**. Also note that the CPU usage shown under **TIME** has a higher resolution of one hundredth of a second as indicated by the format, minutes:seconds.fraction.

5.3 The top Utility

Instead of using the System V ps, you may want to use the much more useful, public domain top utility. It is available from many ftp sites (e.g., eecs.nwu.edu under /pub /top) and runs practically on every UNIX platform. Its display is a combination of uptime and ps:

```
last pid:  3982;  load averages:  0.07,  0.01,  0.00                17:29:45
43 processes:  39 sleeping, 1 running, 3 stopped
Cpu states:  0.2% user,  0.0% nice,  1.4% system, 98.4% idle
Memory: 29M available, 21M in use, 8464K free, 1120K locked

  PID USERNAME PRI NICE  SIZE   RES STATE   TIME   WCPU    CPU COMMAND
 3979 amirm     25    0  472K  768K run    0:00  0.00%  0.00% top-sun4c-4.1.3
 2411 amirm     25    0  364K   0K stop    0:00  0.00%  0.00% vi
 2335 amirm     25    0  364K   0K stop    0:00  0.00%  0.00% vi
  653 amirm      1    0  368K   0K stop    0:00  0.00%  0.00% vi
 3972 amirm     15    0  216K  424K sleep   0:00  0.00%  0.00% csh
```

The display, while similar to BSD's ps, is more readable as seen by the process state, which is clearly spelled out (under **STATE**). The **WCPU** field is the weighted CPU usage, which ps shows under the CPU column (and is used for priority migration). See the top manual page for more information on some useful options (e.g., -I, which omits idle processes making it very useful to spot heavy CPU users).

5.4 Printing System Configuration

Traditionally, it has been very difficult to get the system configuration in UNIX. The kernel usually prints the relevant information when it boots, but there has been no standard mechanism for reading it on-line. Fortunately, in SVR4, you can use the `prtconf` command to get some of the information you may be interested in. The most useful data are the amount of physical memory the system has:

```
sunshine# /etc/prtconf
System Configuration:  Sun Microsystems  sun4c
Memory size: 64 Megabytes
....
```

5.5 Conclusions

Despite its arcane output, `sar` provides just about all the information that is necessary to instrument the system. Time stamps and the ability to log the information to a file for later viewing make the information even more useful.

Beyond `sar`, your options are very limited in System V. The `ps` command, while somewhat useful, is clearly deficient compared to its BSD counterpart for not sorting its output. So, you may want to use the public domain `top` utility instead.

CHAPTER 6

UNIX Terminal Support

Even though ordinary ASCII terminals are not very glamorous these days, they still serve a large number of UNIX users. And despite heavy inroads from graphical interfaces, there is still a larger number of UNIX users who interact with their system using the traditional line-oriented commands. In addition, anytime you use any modems connected to your system, you are dealing with the character-oriented interface of UNIX. The part of the kernel responsible for these services is called the terminal or tty section.

6.1 The Kernel tty Support

User data arrives in the system usually in the form of a hardware interrupt from an RS-232 serial port. The serial port interrupt handler captures the input character and passes it the upper-level tty routines. The processing of the character from here on depends on what mode the port is in.

UNIX allows tty ports to be in either line- or character-oriented (also known as cbreak or raw) mode. The former requires that the system buffer each character input by the user. When a new line or carriage return is typed, the entire buffer is then passed to the user process (which retrieves the data as a result of a read system call issued on the tty port). The kernel takes care of echoing the characters (by writing them back to the tty port) and handling special characters such as backspace and tabs. The burden on the system is very minimal because the user process remains inactive (sleep) while the kernel handles the entire processing.

Because hardware interrupts generated by the input characters are serviced regardless of what the system is doing, character echoing always appears instantaneous in line mode. Additionally, because the kernel code is not paged or swapped out, memory shortages have no impact on this process. The mechanism works so well that users are not able to detect that the system is busy by simply looking at the character echo time.

6.1.1 cbreak and raw Character Processing

Character mode (turned on by using the cbreak or raw flags on the tty port—see the stty manual page) is used by programs that need access to each keystroke as it is typed and cannot wait for the entire line. These include full-screen editors such as vi and Emacs in addition to communication programs (cu, tip, and uucp). In this mode, the kernel has to pass each character to the user process as soon as it arrives. This means that the process is awakened after each input character incurring the overhead of a full-context switch.

Even though the kernel can be instructed to echo characters in raw or cbreak modes, most applications usually do not choose to let it do so. As a result, if any echoing is required, the application program takes care of it. The job is not especially complicated and simply requires that the echo character be written back to the tty port (using a write system call, of course). From a performance point of view, however,

> echoing characters in the application program is far more expensive than the kernel echo processing in the normal, line-oriented mode.

The overhead has to do with the expensive context switches in addition to the extra write system call – none of which is required when the kernel handles the echo. To put things in perspective,

> typing characters at a vi session can easily consume ten times more CPU cycles than doing the same at the shell prompt (where the kernel echoes the characters).

Echoing characters in the application process also suffers from jittery and non-real-time response. The reason is that user processes, unlike a kernel interrupt thread, are subject to paging and swapping in addition to priority migration. If a process cannot run due to a CPU bottleneck or being swapped out, the character echoes will stop. For a good example of this, try to input a line in vi when there is a severe memory shortage. Character echoes usually stop for long periods of time. A less severe situation occurs during high CPU load. In this case, character echo is simply sluggish.

Even though it is unlikely that you will be able to convince users to stop using their favorite editor and use a line-oriented one (does anyone still remember ed?), you should be able to use the information in this section in your capacity planning. If you are planning to run strictly character-oriented applications, then you should count on much higher overhead per user. In addition, you need to invest in extra memory capacity to make sure that you do not get into severe swapping or paging. The same goes for the CPU horsepower. You may need a faster CPU to provide the same crisp response that users are accustomed to in the line-oriented mode.

6.2 Serial Port Input Mechanism

Serial port traffic can create a significant amount of work for the CPU. A port operating at a baud rate of 19,200 can receive almost 2000 interrupts/sec. Considering that the normal interrupt rate in most systems is less than 200/sec, this is indeed a quantum leap in system load. Because interrupt processing is very expensive in general (measured in thousands of instructions), this translates to rather high CPU overhead. Aside from performance considerations, getting an interrupt per character can also lead to data loss. If the CPU is too slow to respond to an interrupt, the input data may simply get lost.

The solution to these problems is a well-designed serial port interface. As a minimum, the serial interface chip should buffer the input characters while the CPU is busy. Then, when the CPU finally acknowledges the interrupt, it can pass all the stored characters to the CPU at once. This is exactly how typical serial port chips work in a typical PC. The standard 16540 PC serial port chip (the UART) has a very small FIFO buffer and is unable to handle data transfers above 9600 baud. The much improved, 16550 UART has a much deeper FIFO that enables it to keep up with higher baud rates. Many well-designed workstations have additional DMA logic that enables them to use the main memory as a giant FIFO. As a result, they create the least amount of CPU overhead and do not lose data even in the most extreme situations.

6.2.1 Serial Port Output Mechanism

To output anything on a serial port, user programs have to issue a write system call, passing a string of bytes to be output and a byte count. The kernel copies the user string into an internal buffer (called a clist in case of BSD and a stream buffer for System V—see the next section) and allows the user program to continue execution without delay. The kernel then feeds the hardware one byte at a time or a complete string depending on the intelligence of the output device. As with input, getting an interrupt per output character can be fairly CPU-intensive. Fortunately, most serial controllers can accept multiple characters per write request, which reduces the overhead to negligible levels. As a result, modern CPUs can easily saturate a serial port even at the highest baud rate settings.

6.3 Character Buffering

Like all modern operating systems, UNIX allows users to type ahead, meaning that characters can be input while the system is busy doing something else. This means that the data need to be stored somewhere until a process wants to read them. Additionally, when a user requests a string of characters be written to a port, the system tries to buffer it first and lets the process continue execution while the serial port slowly drains. This is necessary because outputting 80 bytes on a fast 19,200-baud port still takes 0.04 second, which is an infinity in CPU cycle terms.

The traditional method for buffering characters in UNIX is the clist (Character LISTs) data structure, which is still used in BSD and System V.3-based systems. The clists simply contain a small array of bytes holding from 28 bytes in SunOS 4.1 to 72 bytes in SONY's BSD port (NEWS OS 5.X). To find the actual size on your system, simply search through the kernel include file, `param.h`:

```
SunOS4.1% grep CBSIZE /usr/include/sys/param.h
#define CBSIZE  28                /* number of chars in a clist block */
```

You need to add 4 bytes for a pointer at the beginning of each clist to arrive at the actual amount of memory occupied by each clist. The pointer is used to link a sequence of clists in order to construct larger buffers than the `CBSIZE` parameter. For example, if you attempt to output 40 bytes in SunOS 4.1, you will tie up two clists for a total storage requirement of 64 bytes.

The clists are statically allocated by the kernel with the count limited by the tunable parameter, **nclist**. In configuring the number of clists, keep in mind that

> *if the kernel runs out of clists, it throws away all incoming characters. On output, the process is put to sleep until a clist is freed.*

Running out of clists is rare on most systems because clists are used only for a short amount of time. In rare cases, however, when a process is too slow to read its data from the kernel, a large number of clists may stay in use, causing a shortage in the system. One situation where this might occur is when multiple serial ports are used for high-speed modems on CPU-bound systems. In this situation, you may want to reconfigure your kernel to increase the number of clists.

6.3.1 Monitoring Terminal Traffic

To see how much terminal I/O is occurring in System V, use `sar -y`:

```
% sar -y 2 3
20:11:54 rawch/s canch/s outch/s rcvin/s xmtin/s mdmin/s
20:11:56      0       0      88       2       1       1
20:11:58      1       0      42       2       2       2
20:12:00      5       0      94       5      10      10

Average       2       0      73       3       5       5
```

rawch/s is the total number of input characters per second received into the system. The input could have come from serial ports or pseudo ttys (used by the networking subsystem and X Window).

canch/s counts the number of characters per second that were processed and passed on to user processes. This is usually a subset of the raw input characters.

outch/s shows the total number of characters per second transmitted by the system.

rcvin/s and **xmtin/s** show the number of hardware input and output interrupts per second, respectively. You can find out if your system has intelligent serial ports by looking at the ratio of characters received per transmitted character versus the interrupt rate. In the preceding sample output, you can see that the system transmitted a large number of characters for every interrupt indicating that the hardware either has a DMA channel or a large output buffer.

The last column is **mdmin/s**, which is supposed to show the number of interrupts from modem devices. Because modems are usually attached to serial ports, most vendors simply make **mdmin/s** a copy of **xmtin/s**.

Table 6.1 `sar -y`: Terminal Statistics

Field	Description
rawch/s	Number of characters per second input on terminal or workstation window
canch/s	Number of characters per second available for user input after processing
outch/s	Number of characters per second output by the system
rcvin/s	Number of interrupts per second generated by input devices
xmtin/s	Number of interrupts per second generated by output devices
mdmin/s	Same as **xmtin/s**

6.4 The Streams Facility

If you are using System V, chances are your system does not use the older clist scheme. Instead, it employs a completely new mechanism known as streams. Streams were initially designed for the networking subsystem where the stackability of streams modules was an elegant solution to the layered architecture of the networking services.

There is little difference between the clist-based tty code and the new streams modules replacing them due to the need for backward compatibility. The only exception is in the area of memory allocation where streams use a dynamic buffer management algorithm.

In BSD, when a user types a single character, an entire clist is used to store it. This can waste a lot of memory. In contrast, the streams buffering scheme used in System V.3 has buffer sizes of 4, 16, 64, 128, 256, 512, 1024, 2048, and 4096 bytes. So, a single byte could be stored in a 4-byte buffer saving a considerable amount of memory over the BSD scheme.

The solution in System V.3 is not perfect, however. The system divides its streams buffers into a high-priority and a low-priority pool. But the majority of the kernel code requests low-priority buffers meaning that about 20% of the buffer pool typically gets wasted. In addition, the buffer allocation scheme is not capable of merging smaller buffers to create larger ones. Nor does it look more than one size beyond the requested one to see if a buffer is available. This means that memory requests can be denied even if there are many buffers of larger sizes available. In addition to all these limitations, the total count of each stream buffer is fixed by kernel configuration. Tuning the buffer sizes means knowing which sizes are in use, which is not always easy to determine in a dynamic environment.

SVR4 solves these problems by using a new streams allocator. To begin with, it dynamically grows the streams buffer pool and, if needed, shrinks its size. The system also does away with the fixed-size "buckets" and attempts to allocate just what the caller needs. The result is a much more efficient allocation of memory.

The System V.3 implementation is used in SCO UNIX and (sometimes in) SunOS 4.1. To see how the streams buffers are allocated in SCO UNIX, use the `crash` utility (you can also use `netstat -m` if the networking subsystem is installed):

```
# crash
dumpfile = /dev/mem, namelist = /unix, outfile = stdout
> strstat
ITEM                    CONFIG   ALLOC    FREE      TOTAL     MAX    FAIL
streams                    128      83      45        168      83       0
queues                     512     386     126        387     386       0
message blocks            2275     213    2062      28554     274       0
data block totals         1820     262    1560      27779     274       8
data block size    4        64      51      13        672      60       8
data block size   16       384       2     382        975      11       0
data block size   64       512      37     478      20035      47       0
data block size  128       448     111     337        397     120       0
data block size  256       208      26     182         82      27       0
data block size  512        88      12      76       1012      31       0
data block size 1024        52       0      52          5       1       0
data block size 2048        52      23      28       4565      26       0
data block size 4096        12       0      12         36       1       0

Count of scheduled queues:    0
```

In this display, the total number of buffers configured for each size is shown under **CONFIG** followed by the number currently in use under the **ALLOC** column. Of special interest is the number of 2048 byte buffers, which are used to contain full Ethernet packets that have a maximum size of 1500 bytes. Also pay particular attention to the **FAIL** column, which indicates the frequency of allocation errors due to lack of space. Because the System V.3 kernel always looks ahead to the next available size, if you see failures in consecutive sizes (e.g., 2048 and 4096), try increasing the size for the smaller bucket first.

To see some of the same information in SunOS 4.1, use `netstat -m`:

```
SunOS4.1% netstat -m
...
streams allocation:
                                          cumulative   allocation
                      current   maximum        total     failures
streams                    13        13           80            0
queues                     46        46          304            0
mblks                      23       145      1471623            0
dblks                      23       145      1471623            0
streams buffers:
external                    0         0            0            0
within-dblk                 0        98       612785            0
size <=     16              5       126       204203            0
size <=     32              0         4        43054            0
size <=    128             18       135       610319            0
size <=    512              0         1          589            0
size <=   1024              0         1          661            0
size <=   2048              0         1            2            0
size <=   8192              0         1           10            0
size >    8192              0         0            0            0
```

Note that in SunOS 4.1 the streams facility is used only by the System V Streams interface for user program. It does not replace the older, BSD-style, tty subsystem.

6.5 Summary

- Serial ports use a considerable amount of CPU cycles if not properly designed. But even a simple enhancement such as a deep FIFO can result in a sharp reduction in the interrupt rate and CPU usage.

- `raw` or `cbreak` modes used by some applications (such as `vi`) require character processing by the application program, which translates to much higher CPU usage than the kernel doing the same.

- Clists are fixed-sized buffers that are used to buffer characters in BSD and older versions of System V UNIX. You should make sure that you have sufficient memory allocated to clists; otherwise, you could lose input data and experience delays on output.

- Streams replace the older tty code in UNIX. The streams memory allocated in SVR4 is far superior to the BSD's clist scheme and System V.3's fixed-size allocator.

CHAPTER 7

Optimizing the System

By now, you should be able to identify resource shortages that lead to poor system performance. In this chapter, we focus only on optimizing the base system and leave the networking and windowing subsystems to later chapters. As you will see, it is very important to start with a tuned system before attacking performance problems in these other areas.

In tuning your system, there are three major areas to worry about: memory, CPU, and disk. Memory shortages often make the system disk bound because of the paging activity. So, be sure to attack them first as we do here.

7.1 Identifying the Memory Shortfall

Before getting started, we need to emphasize the difference between a true memory shortage and one caused by the paged buffer cache. Systems employing these caches will always be short of memory and can page on a continuous basis. Although difficult to ascertain, knowing whether paging or swapping activity has been caused by the paged buffer cache or lack of memory for user programs can be very important. The reason is that adding memory to a system that lacks memory for user processes results in a substantial improvement on its response time. But the improvement will be much less pronounced if paging is a result of simple file activity caused by the paged buffer cache. As an example, if the processes in the system need 40 Mbytes of memory to run and you have only 32 Mbytes available to them, your system will perform very poorly. But, if you run the same work load in a 64-Mbyte system and then enlarge the memory to 80 Mbytes, you will see only small improvement because the extra memory is only increasing the buffer cache hit ratio.

In addition to enough space for user processes, you must have extra memory for the kernel especially because none of it ever gets paged or swapped out. Determining the kernel size was discussed in Chapter 3 and involves looking at the console messages. But note that the value extracted using this method is the starting size of the kernel. We recommend that you add at least 30% to it to account for dynamic memory allocation for uses such as streams buffering. As a conservative estimate, you may want to allocate 8 Mbytes for the kernel.

Next, you should determine the memory requirements of user processes. This is very easy if your system has a `vmstat` that includes the **avm** field. If this is the case, simply use that figure (keep in mind that the units for **avm** in `vmstat` output of HP-UX are in pages that are 4 Kbytes each). Otherwise, you must add up the process sizes manually. To do this, use the `ps` command and look at the **SIZE** field. We recommend to use the **SIZE** data instead of **RSS** because the latter is accurate only if the process has touched (i.e., paged in) all its data space. This is something that cannot be easily determined unless you are quite familiar with the behavior of each application in your system. The down side to using the **SIZE** field is that it could give you slightly exaggerated numbers. However, because some systems such as SunOS 4.1 exclude the text size in their `ps` display, the number can actually be quite close to what you want.

Instead of computing the total process sizes manually, let the system do the work. If you have a system V machine, use[1]

```
ps -elf | awk '
{ s += $10}
END {printf "Total Memory Usage = %d, 80%% = %d\n", s , s*0.8}'
```

And for BSD use

```
ps -axl | awk '
        { s += $8 }
END {printf "Total Memory Usage = %d, 80%% = %d\n", s , s*0.8}'
```

Before using either one of these scripts, run the `ps` command with the specified options and make sure that the **SIZE** data appears in the appropriate column (10th in System V and 8th in BSD).

The script prints both the total size and 80% of it. The latter can be used as a more aggressive target for memory usage, which may result in light paging activity.

To see if you have a severe memory shortage, add the process sizes to the kernel size and compare it to your physical memory. To determine the latter, you could look at the hard-

---

1. You may have to modify the script slightly to work on SGI IRIX.

ware, but it is more accurate to ask the kernel for the information. Unfortunately, even though the memory size is available inside the kernel, there is no standard mechanism to extract it. The most reliable way is to look at the system messages as the kernel boots. If your system has dmesg, you can use it on-line to do the same. For example

```
SunOS4.1% /etc/dmesg |grep mem
mem = 32768K (0x2000000)
```

The number displayed is in kilobytes. To convert it to megabytes quickly, just ignore the right-most three digits (in this example, the system has 32 Mbytes of memory).[2]

Depending on your UNIX implementation, you may have other tools available to you to print the same information. For example, on SGI IRIX systems, you can use the hinv program to get a complete description of your system hardware:

```
iris% hinv
...
Main memory size: 16 Mbytes
```

If the amount of physical memory is less than the minimum system requirements, you will suffer from paging and swapping. In general, the amount of physical memory in your system should be 20–50% higher than the minimum in order to guarantee enough headroom for peak usage and allowance for the paged buffer cache (assuming it exists).

7.2 Solving Memory Shortages

The solutions for a memory shortage are rather obvious. Either increase the amount of physical memory in your system or decrease the system memory requirements. The first solution is the most effective and usually easier to apply. As of this writing, memory costs are under $30/Mbyte for PCs and most workstations. This means that

> it may be more cost-effective (for small systems at least) to purchase additional memory than to spend many hours trying to squeeze the last byte out of the system.

Then again, if you have to buy memory for 50 workstations, you may want to look at the other alternatives. Additionally, if the maximum memory capacity of the system has been reached, you have no choice but to reduce the memory usage. This is especially true for older PCs where the maximum memory is often limited to 16 Mbytes.

Reducing the system memory requirements involves either shrinking the kernel size or user work load. Most people focus on the former, but, despite its large size, there is little opportunity for reducing the kernel size by more than a few hundred kilobytes. This

---

2. Of course, this technique ignores the fact that each kilobyte is 1024 bytes and not 1000. But for this purpose, it is close enough.

amount is rarely enough to stop swapping or heavy paging activity. On the other hand, changing the user work load can result in significant memory savings. The down side is the potential for lower productivity and impact on the user community.

7.3 Streamlining the Kernel

The UNIX kernel is always resident in memory and is never paged or swapped.[3] The only components of the kernel that get swapped out are the user page descriptors and the per-process data structure called the u-area (which is typically 4–8 Kbytes). The rest of the kernel remains resident in memory at all times occupying a fair amount of memory.

Reducing the kernel size requires reconfiguration of the system. The procedure for this varies from system to system. Some, like Solaris, let you reconfigure the kernel by simply editing a text file and rebooting the system. Others require that a new kernel be built and the system booted from it. Regardless of the approach, you should be able to change the system configuration to remove unneeded kernel modules or to reduce the size of kernel data structures to save space.

The largest memory consumer in the kernel is the older static buffer cache if it exists. Because changing the buffer cache size can impact the I/O performance of the system, we have dedicated a separate section later in this chapter on how to best tune its size.

Once you go beyond the buffer cache, the opportunity for saving much memory drops sharply. The savings are measured in kilobytes and not megabytes. Nevertheless, let's take a look at your possible options.

7.3.1 Tuning the Kernel Tables

Because the kernel allocates space for many of its internal tables (i.e., data structures) "statically" at boot time, any memory allocated to them cannot be used by user programs. This is the case even if the tables are completely empty. As a result, eliminating waste in kernel tables has been a popular method for reducing the kernel size. However, we feel that this technique is outdated and at times downright dangerous. To begin with, these tables do not occupy significant amounts of memory by today's standards. Sure, on a 4-Mbyte system of the early 1980s, reducing the kernel size by 100 Kbytes was significant. (You could add a few more users to the system.) However, most systems running UNIX today have 16 Mbytes or more, and this kind of saving would be insignificant.

 If you are still determined to proceed to reduce the kernel table sizes, heed this warning.

> *Making kernel tables too small may have catastrophic results ranging from system crashes and hangs to program failures.*

---

3. The exception is IBM AIX, which can swap out some pieces of the kernel. But these segments are often small.

In general, the kernel has little (if any) recovery code if a table becomes full. Depending on the table, the failure can be either soft (a system call fails) or hard (system crashes). Although neither one of these failures is very desirable, system crashes are especially unwelcome. So, you should be careful when shrinking tables that lead to hard failures. To help you in this regard, we have listed a handful of common kernel tables along with size and failure modes in Table 7.1. The list is short because the rest of the kernel data structures are not documented and their usage is heavily subject to change.

Just in case we have completely scared you away from touching the kernel, we should remark that, in some cases, reducing kernel tables can be a reasonable approach to saving memory. For example, it is doubtful that you could get in trouble if you cut the proc table size in half when only 200 out of 1000 are in use. Just do not try to fine-tune its size to 201!

The first step in adjusting the size of a table is knowing its highest usage count. Unfortunately, this is easier said than done. Even though you can instrument the size of some of the kernel tables, it is hard to know when they are at peak usage without intimate knowledge of the user applications and the kernel. The best solution is to monitor each table under various load conditions and use the highest figure that you see. Because this method is not foolproof, we recommend that you add at least 30% to the maximum size just to be safe. You need to be especially cautious with tables whose usage cannot be instrumented. In these cases you may be better off living with the default values shipped with your system.

Table 7.1 Common Kernel Tables

Kernel Parameter	Size[a] (bytes)	Min Size	Typical Size	Comments
nproc	350	50	500-1000	process table size: Cannot execute new programs (fork fails) if full.
ninode, ufs_ninode	75	100	500-1000	mode table size: Cannot open new files if full.
nfile	12-40	100	400-600	file table size: Cannot open new files if full.
flckrec	44	10-50	N/A	Used mostly by third-party applications. Use their recommendation for size.
ncallout/ ncall	20-28	30-50	100-200	System panics (i.e., crashes) if too small. Should be increased with more device drivers. No longer used in Solaris 2.2+.
nbuf	1096	100	1000+	number of buffers: System hangs if set too low.
nbuf	120-200	100	1000+	number of buffer headers: If set to 0, kernel automatically determines the size.
s5cacheents	72	ninode	2*ninode	Speeds file name lookups.
nregion	68	100	3.3*nproc	Used on System V.3 systems (SCO and HP-UX).
NBLKnnnn	4–4096			number of streams, buffers: Dynamic in SVR4.
nhbuf	16			Should be one quarter to half of **nbuf**.

a.Size is approximate and depends on kernel implementation.

As for monitoring table usage, System V users are better equipped in this regard. The kernel keeps track of both usage and overflow status of the tables, which can be displayed using `sar -v`. If the **ov** field is nonzero, it indicates that the table has overflowed and you actually need to increase its size and not decrease it.

In BSD systems, the `pstat` command can be used to get table usage similar to `sar -v` but without overflow status. Instead, the kernel typically prints a message on the console (a copy of which is usually located `/usr/adm/messages`). Because overflow detection is more difficult in BSD, we recommend that you leave yourself more of a safety margin (perhaps 50%).

Once you have determined the proper table size, you must reconfigure the kernel to change the size of the specific table. Because these are private kernel data structures, vendors feel free to modify, rename, or eliminate them from release to release. So refer to the reconfiguration guide in your system documentation before changing any parameters. Also note that some newer systems such as SVR4 and Solaris dynamically allocate space for some tables (e.g., file) so that you do not need to worry about their size. We suspect that this trend will continue and that, by some time in the future, all kernel tables will be dynamically allocated. BSD 4.4 is an example of such a system, but it will be a while before other systems follow its lead.

7.3.2 Tuning the MAXUSERS Parameter

Many vendors use a configuration parameter called **MAXUSERS** to set the sizes of their individual kernel tables. Despite its name, **MAXUSERS** has nothing to do with the number of users allowed in the system. Instead, this parameter is used as a variable in determining the proper size for each table. Unfortunately, each UNIX implementation uses its own ad-hoc formula for this purpose. For example, one version may allocate 10 proc structures per **MAXUSERS** and another may use 20. It is not clear which formula is correct because each system, application, or user is different. Vendors know this and try to err on the side of being conservative. As such, setting **MAXUSERS** to the correct number of users often results in tables that are too large. One would also wonder about the right value of **MAXUSERS** on a single-user workstation. Setting its value to 1 would surely result in tables that are too small.

Our advice is to start with a reasonable value for **MAXUSERS** (the number of users on a multiuser system and the number of windows in a workstation) and then override the size of any table that is too large. If all the tables seem too large, reduce **MAXUSERS** and start over.

If you are using Solaris 2.2 or later, the **MAXUSERS** parameter is set automatically by the kernel to the amount of memory in the system (in megabytes) minus 2. So, if you have 32 Mbytes of memory, **MAXUSERS** will be set to 30. We are not quite sure if this is an improvement over the old scheme. Nevertheless, you can override it by setting **MAXUSERS** to whatever you like in the kernel configuration file, `/etc/system`.

7.3.3 Removing Kernel Modules

Another option for saving memory is reconfiguring the kernel to remove any unnecessary modules or services. For example, if you are not connected to a network, you can remove the networking code (TCP/IP) and NFS. In addition, you can eliminate unneeded device drivers (these are kernel routines used to access hardware devices). In our example, you can take out the Ethernet driver because it is used only by the networking software.

Keep in mind that most device drivers are less than 50 Kbytes in size so the savings in memory will be small. And, if you ever decide to use the device, you have to take the time to reconfigure the kernel and reboot the system.

7.3.4 Limiting the Paged Buffer Cache Size

Because the buffer cache has a huge appetite for memory, limiting its size can free a substantial amount of memory for user processes. Even though the smaller buffer cache may slow down file system access to some extent, reduction of paging and swapping will more than make up for that loss in most cases.

To start, subtract the minimum memory requirements computed in Section 7.1 from the total physical memory. Then, set the buffer cache size to 90% of this value. For example, if you have a 64-Mbyte system and the kernel and applications need 32 Mbytes, set the buffer cache to 0.9 * 32 Mbytes or 29 Mbytes.

The procedure for limiting the size of the dynamic buffer cache is not well-documented and varies from system to system. On HP-UX (9.01), you can change the kernel parameter **bufpages** to limit the buffer cache size. The units are in 4-Kbyte blocks, so if you like to have a 4-Mbyte buffer cache, set **bufpages** to 1024.

In DEC UNIX, the dynamic buffer cache is referred to as the UBC (Unified Buffer Cache) and its size is determined by the **ubcminpercent** and **ubcmaxpercent** kernel tunable parameters. As the names imply, you can set the upper and lower limits of the buffer cache size. The upper limit sets the maximum percentage of memory that the buffer cache can grow to. The minimum size guarantees that there is always some amount of space allocated to the buffer cache. The defaults for **ubcminpercent** and **ubcmaxpercent** are 10 and 100%, respectively. We recommend that you leave the minimum alone and shrink the maximum to the number recommended previously but express it as a percentage of total memory (in our example, 45%).

We are not aware of any scheme to limit the size of the buffer cache in either standard SVR4 or Sun Solaris. The Solaris 2.3 performance guide states that modifying **bufhwm** changes the size of the buffer cache – it does not. This parameter changes the size of the older, fixed-sized (meta) buffer cache, which is kept around for special occasions such as reading file system superblocks. The paged buffer cache bypasses this mechanism, so this limit does not apply. Fortunately, Solaris and SunOS use an aggressive policy of freeing buffer cache pages, which seems to work well, obviating the need to limit the buffer cache size.

Aside from the paged buffer cache, the older, meta buffer cache can also be tuned to use less memory. See Section 7.7.6 on how to do this.

7.4 Reducing the User Memory Usage

Once you have optimized the kernel for memory efficiency, the next place to look is the user applications. There are two areas worth looking at:

- eliminating redundant processes and
- changing the work load

Redundant and idle processes can hog (hold on to) large amounts of memory without getting any useful work done. Even though the memory pages used by these processes are the first to be stolen by the pageout process, there is no guarantee that their usage will drop to zero. Specifically, the pageout daemon does not touch the u-area of a process, which holds the kernel data structures, nor does it do anything about the space taken by the process page tables. The u-area alone is a minimum of one page, meaning a loss of at least 4096 bytes. Although this may not seem like much, the total wasted space can climb to almost 1 Mbyte if you have 256 idle processes. Although the swapper does free these resources, it gets invoked only if there is a very severe memory shortage.

Having a high number of idle processes may seem like an unusual situation, but we have seen many examples of it. The most typical situation is an environment where a shell script is used to start a program that interacts with the user and rarely, if ever, finishes execution. The result is a shell that sits idle for the entire login period. The solution to this problem is very simple. Just have the shell exec the new program on top of itself. To do this, just precede the command line for the specific program with the keyword exec. This technique instructs the shell to skip calling fork and just execs the program on top of itself. Aside from saving memory, you also reduce the start-up time because you avoid the fork overhead.

Another related situation is nesting of shell scripts. Instead of running a shell script separately, use the dot (.) in Bourne shell or the source command in C shell to have the current shell execute the script. Otherwise, another shell is forked off to execute the script. Again, this approach not only reduces memory usage but also gets rid of the fork and exec sequence resulting in lower CPU usage and faster execution time.

7.4.1 Changing the Work Load

Changing the system work load can be a very effective method of reducing the overall memory usage. The most common technique is to postpone the execution of memory-hungry programs by scheduling them to run off hours when no one is using the system. This, in essence, averages out the peak memory usage over a longer period, reducing its harmful effect. The ps command can be used to determine the large processes, which are good candidates for this purpose.

Keep in mind that only large reductions in memory usage can stop swapping and heavy paging—eliminating small programs does not help. In general, look for processes that are at least 0.5 Mbyte in size. Keep in mind that due to sharing of text, additional copies of a program take up less space than the first copy. So, getting rid of them may not result in significant savings.

If it is not possible to run a program at a later time (or not at all), you can reduce the peak memory usage and actually increase system throughput by running your work load sequentially rather than in parallel. This may not seem intuitive because running programs sequentially usually results in longer execution time (due to less efficient use of the CPU). To clarify this point, let's look at an example.

Assume that you want to run two copies of a 7-Mbyte, CPU-bound program. If the system has more than 14 Mbytes of free memory, the total runtime will be roughly twice as long as running just one copy (because each gets 50% of the CPU time). Now, if you run the same two copies when the system has only 8 Mbytes of memory free, there will be a memory deficit of 6 Mbytes causing a significant amount of paging/swapping activity. Because the system slows down in an exponential manner when it is very short of memory, the total runtime will be three or more times longer than running just one copy. In this case if you run the programs sequentially, the system will not run out of memory, and the runtime will be just twice as long. Ironically, this is what older and less fashionable batch-mode mainframe operating systems used to do.

Most implementations of UNIX include a rudimentary utility aptly called `batch` that can simulate a batch environment. To use it, simply give it the name of a command to run or type in a sequence of commands at its prompt followed by control-d. For example,

```
# batch
at> find /home -name foo >/tmp/find.out
at> <EOT>
warning: commands will be executed using /bin/csh
job 765584707.b at Tue Apr  5 15:25:07 1994
```

As you might suspect from the `at>` prompt, `batch` is just a simple interface to the `at` command. (For more information and some important restrictions, see the `batch` manual page.) There are commercial queueing systems (such as HP's NQS) that are considerably more sophisticated than `batch` and allow you to specify priorities and other characteristics for the submitted jobs.

Finally, no matter how intuitive it might seem,

> *do not lower the priority of memory-hungry applications. Doing so only lengthens their execution time and, hence, the amount of time they hold on to their pages.*

You should let these processes run as fast as they can so that they finish execution and free their memory.

7.4.2 Tuning the Paging/Swapping Subsystem

We cover this section last because it is usually not wise to attempt to tune the memory management code. The algorithms used for paging and swapping are not guaranteed to stay the same and, as a matter of fact, are subject to very frequent changes. Nevertheless, if you have tried everything else and can take some chances with your experimentations, you may want to look at tuning this part of the system. In this section, we focus on tuning the paging/swapping system for SunOS 4.1 and SVR4/Solaris, which are fairly well documented. For other systems, refer to your system documentation on how to perform these steps.

Tuning the paging system means balancing peak response against the average response time. By having the pageout daemon start early (i.e., when there is more free memory available), you leave a larger pool to draw from when the need arises. This lowers the amount of time a process must wait for memory to become free. On the other hand, by having the pager anticipate these shortages, you potentially create more traffic on the system, which increases the average system response time.

In general, the paging threshold should be set to a value slightly above the size of the largest program that you are likely to run. For example, if your most common application is an X Window program that uses 2 Mbytes of memory as soon as it starts, you should set **lotsfree** to 2.25–2.5 Mbytes. This technique guarantees that when this program starts execution, it doesn't have to wait for the pageout daemon to free memory before it runs.

 *Before setting **lotsfree**, always make sure that it is higher than **desfree**. Otherwise, you risk causing unpredictable results from system hangs to other anomalies. Likewise, the swapping threshold **minfree** (which we do not recommend changing) should always be lower than **desfree**.*

If you are using SVR4 and Solaris, we recommend that you fix an oversight that limits the paging rate to a very low value. The parameter, **maxpgio**, in the original BSD implementation was scaled by the number of swapping disk drives in the system. This scaling was lost in the translation to SVR4. In addition, the original formula assumed rather slow drives that could only handle 60 transfers per second. Modern, high-performance disk drives can easily reach 90 or more transfers per second.

To compute the correct value for **maxpgio**, you need to determine the number of swap drives in your system and whether they are dedicated to swapping or are shared with file system access. If they are dedicated, then simply multiply their number by 80–100, depending on how fast your drives are. If they are being shared, use the BSD figure of two thirds as the multiplier. For example, if you have two dedicated high-performance (7200 RPM) disk drives exclusively for swapping, **maxpgio** should be set to 200. If one of the drives is shared with an active file system, then lower the value to 66+100 or 166.

Another parameter that reduces thrashing due to swapping in BSD-derived systems such as SunOS 4.1 is **maxslp**. The swapper picks its candidates to swap out from the pool of processes that have been sleeping longer than **maxslp**. With its default of 20 seconds, programs that run on a regular basis but sleep longer than this value tend to get swapped in and out constantly. You may want to increase **maxslp** to a number greater than 30 seconds to avoid having programs such as update experiencing this problem. Setting **maxslp** to 128 completely disables this facility, which may be useful for dealing with processes that sleep for longer than 127 seconds.

7.5 Lowering CPU Usage

The most clear indication of a CPU shortage is the lack of idle time followed by the CPU load average climbing (displayed by uptime in BSD systems and sar -q in the form of run queue length). The first step in solving this problem is to use the ps command to identify which processes are heavy consumers of CPU. The -u option in the BSD ps nicely shows the top CPU users (affectionately called the CPU hogs) in a sorted display. System V users are not as fortunate because ps does not show the CPU utilization as a percentage of total available. One solution is to run the ps command multiple times in a row and look at the **TIME** column to see which processes are accumulating CPU time. Alternatively, you can use the following script to highlight processes that are either running on the CPU or waiting for it:

```
IRIX% ps -el | awk '{if ($2 == "R" || $2 == "O" || $2 == "0") print;}'
38 R    0   301    1  0 20 20   *   470:264          ?       36:01 mediad
30 R  998   695  608 42 81 20   *   281:66           pts/3    0:01 heavy_co
30 R  998   696  608 12 66 20  0   322:153          pts/3    0:00 ps
30 R  998   690  608 40 80 20   *   281:66           pts/3    0:26 cpu_hog
```

You may want to run this script a few times in a row to make sure that you catch the processes that run intermittently but often enough to be heavy CPU users.

A better approach to finding CPU hogs in System V (or even BSD) is to use the public domain top utility. This program continuously shows the top CPU users, making it easy to spot them.

Once you find the offending programs, you can use these techniques to reduce their impact on the system:

- postpone their execution,
- temporarily stop them,
- change their priority,
- optimize the programs, or
- get additional or faster CPUs.

Let's look at each one of these in detail.

7.5.1 Postponing or Suspending Program Execution

The easiest way to deal with high CPU usage is to use the `at` command to postpone the execution of CPU-bound jobs. (The previously mentioned `batch` facility can also be used for this purpose.) Alternatively, you can suspend the execution of a program momentarily using the `kill` command. No, we are not suggesting that you really destroy these programs (although that would also solve the problem!). The `kill` command is a misnomer as its main job is to send a signal to a process—not just kill it. The name comes from the fact that the default argument is signal number 15 (`SIGTERM`), which tells the process to terminate itself. Here, we are interested in two other signals, `SIGSTOP` and `SIGCONT`, which suspend and resume the execution of a process respectively. The syntax is very straightforward. To stop a process, use[4]

```
% kill -STOP <pid>
```

The `pid` is the process identification number and can be extracted from the `ps` display (under the **PID** column). By suspending long-running background jobs until the system work load reduces, you can effectively eliminate poor response time during peak use. Once the system load reduces to a reasonable level, resume the execution of the process by

```
% kill -CONT <pid>
```

One potential pitfall with this scheme is that the process may be using the `STOP` and `CONTINUE` signals for its own use. If this is the case, sending these signals may change its operation. Even though this situation is rare, you should first test this procedure with your desired applications in a nonproduction environment to make sure that there are no ill effects.

7.5.2 Changing Process Priorities

If you cannot kill or stop high-CPU consumers, you may want to lower their priority to reduce their impact on the system. As you recall, the priority of a process in UNIX depends partially on its nice value. So, by specifying a different nice value other than the default (0 in BSD and 20 in System V), the process gets less CPU cycles than others in the system. This is an especially good technique to use on background, CPU-intensive jobs, which by their nature do not have users waiting for their response.

If you are using the C shell, you can use the internal `nice` and `renice` commands to change the nice value of a process. The difference between the two commands is that the `renice` command can be used to change the nice value of a running process. (It requires the process id that you can get from the `ps` command.) The `nice` command, on the other hand, starts a program at the specified nice value. The simplified syntax for the commands are

```
% nice <priority> command
% renice <priority> pid
```

---

4. We are using the preferred symbolic names of these signals rather than their numeric values. The `kill` command accepts both styles.

If no priority is specified, the default value is +4 (slightly lower than normal priority). For example, if you want to compile a large program in the background at a low priority, use

```
SunOS4.1% nice cc -O big.c &
```

In BSD, the range of allowable nice values is from -20 to +20 (-20 to +19 in SunOS 4.1 and SGI IRIX). Negative numbers are used to increase the priority of a job (making it more likely to get the attention of the CPU) but require superuser privileges.

If you are using System V, the kernel internal range of nice values is from 0 to +39 with the default of 20. The value specified in the `nice` command is a change to the current setting. For example, if you specify a nice value of -5, the nice value drops from 20 to 15. As with its BSD counterpart, specifying negative increments requires superuser privileges.

Note that the `renice` command is a recent addition (first appearing in SVR4) and may not be present in some System V implementations.

If you are not using the C shell, you have to use the stand-alone `nice` utility, which has a rather confusing syntax (note the additional dash):

```
% nice -<priority> command
```

In this case, `nice -5` actually means a nice value of +5! If you want to specify a negative nice value, you must use double dashes (e.g., `nice --5`). Note that the default parameter value is also different and is set to +10. Luckily, the `renice` program (if it exists) has the same syntax as the one built into the C shell.

7.5.3 Tuning the Scheduler

As with the paging algorithms, modifying the scheduler, as tempting as it may seem, should be used as a last resort. While the algorithms are not as fluid as the ones in the paging subsystem, measuring the effects of any changes can be next to impossible. The reason is that it is very hard to measure the process response times (i.e., on every context switch) in UNIX. Without any kind of feedback loop, it is silly to attempt to adjust the scheduler parameters.

The only time we recommend any changes to be made to the scheduler is when your work load is very static and you can easily measure the improvement in the form of faster completion of a set of commands. Needless to say, no scheduler tuning should be attempted unless you are completely out of CPU cycles (i.e., 0% idle time). Nor should you worry about a system that has only a single runnable job.

Note that some UNIX schedulers are not tunable. The best example is the BSD scheduler used in SunOS 4.1, which cannot be modified without access to the UNIX sources. Fortunately, some newer implementations such as SVR4 and IBM AIX are highly configurable.

One parameter worth experimenting with is the time slice. The standard value used in most schedulers is optimized for interactive response at the expense of long-running, CPU-bound jobs. For these other processes, a longer time slice would be more optimal because it would increase the cache reuse resulting in (slightly) faster performance.

Changing the time slice in SVR4 may not be due necessarily to its "inverted" time slice structure. But because long time slices are not reached until the process reaches fairly low priorities, you may want to increase the time slice for higher-priority levels. To do this, use the `dispadmin` command to extract the current parameters and save them in a file. Then using your favorite editor, modify the required values and save the file. The last step is to use `dispadmin` yet again to change the current system parameters using the file as input.

Note that any changes made are temporary and will be lost on the next reboot. To make the change effective all the time, simply include the last step in one of the `/etc/rc.x` files.

In SCO UNIX, the **MAXSLICE** kernel tunable parameter determines the maximum time slice for all processes in the system regardless of priority. Its units are the kernel clock interrupt rate that is typically 100/sec. So, setting **MAXSLICE** to 100 results in the maximum time slice being increased to 1 second.

The IBM AIX has a dedicated utility for modifying scheduler parameters called, appropriately, `schedtune`. To change the systemwide maximum time slice, you simply use the `-t` option and specify a value in terms of the 10-millisecond clock ticks. As with SCO UNIX, using a value of 100 would result in a time slice of 1 second. To restore the system to the original default, simply use a value of zero.

7.5.4 Optimizing Programs

If you have access to the program sources for the CPU hogs, you may want to follow the procedures outlined in Chapter 13, to optimize them to run faster. This would not only reduce the load on the system but also improve the responsiveness of the programs themselves.

7.5.5 Reducing The exec and fork Rates

If the system time is high, you may want to look at the number of `fork` and `exec` calls. As you recall, these are some of the most expensive system calls and, if used unwisely, can waste a substantial amount of CPU cycles. Because the main user of `exec` and `fork` is the shell, you need to make sure its `PATH` variable is set correctly.

All modern shell implementations cache the file names in each `PATH` directory internally. This is a huge improvement over the older versions, which did an `exec` in each path directory until they found the executable. One problem remains, however, and that is the treatment of the current directory or dot (.) in the `PATH`. Suppose that you have the following path variable (the C shell syntax shown):

```
IRIX% set path=(. /usr/ucb /bin)
```

Now, let's run the `ls` command repeatedly (e.g., `repeat 22 ls >/dev/null`), which lives in `/bin` directory and look at the system call rates at the same time:

```
IRIX% sar -c 5 1
16:37:44 scall/s sread/s swrit/s  fork/s  exec/s rchar/s wchar/s
16:37:49    1701     333     337    4.39    8.78   26163    7209
```

As you see, the rate of `execs` is twice as high as `forks`. Now, let's rearrange the path so that the dot appears at the end:

```
iris3% set path=(/usr/ucb /bin .)
```

Now if we run the same sequence again, we see that the `fork` and `exec` counts match:

```
iris3% sar -c 5 1
16:38:59 scall/s sread/s swrit/s  fork/s  exec/s rchar/s wchar/s
16:39:04    1724     327     331    4.39    4.39   26127    7173
```

The reason for the higher rate of `execs` in the first case is that the shell does not cache the contents of the current directory (because its contents can change all the time). So, it has no choice but to try to `exec` any executable in it first, before moving to other directories in the PATH. So, our recommendation is to

always place the current directory (.) at the end of your PATH.

Note that this advice also makes sense from a security point of view because placing the dot at the beginning of your path makes you vulnerable to Trojan horses (programs that impersonate standard UNIX utilities in order to gain access to the system).

Yet another manifestation of this problem is when you specify directories that do not start with slash (e.g., `foobar/test`). The shell treats these the same as the dot and does not cache their contents resulting in excessive exec calls. So, make sure any relative paths are also placed at the end of the PATH.

Another good practice is to place directories with a large number of executable files at the end of the path. This reduces the search time required for the shell to find the path for a cached command name. The impact, however, is rather small because the algorithm uses hashed lists that shorten the search list. To find the full path name for the programs that you usually run, use the `which` command:

```
% which vi
/usr/ucb/vi
```

In shell scripts, you may want to override and minimize the PATH variable inside the script to only those directories that are needed for the executable in the script. This is especially useful if the standard login path is very long.

Aside from the `exec` rate, you may also want to monitor the number of `fork` system calls by themselves. Interactive users rarely generate high `fork` rates. So, if you see consistent high counts (e.g., greater than 4/sec), the traffic is in all likelihood generated by shell scripts. Try to modify the shell scripts to not call others (which invokes additional copies of the shell). If you use shell scripts interactively, see if you can use the aliasing feature of your shell to perform the same functions. Aliases are interpreted by your current shell and run considerably faster than equivalent shell scripts. They also result in significant memory saving because no additional shells need to be run to execute them.

7.5.6 The Console Output Overhead

A rare but perplexing problem with system performance has to do with console output generated by the kernel. To write anything to the console, the kernel uses a stripped down version of the user level `printf` library routine. But unlike its user counterpart, this `printf` can consume huge amounts of CPU time.

For reliability reasons, the kernel `printf` uses polled I/O meaning the CPU disables interrupts and waits for the console device to accept the output string byte-by-byte. During this time, no process is running, and the system ignores all I/O interrupts. This means that all system activity essentially grinds to a halt for the duration of this operation. If the output is to a slow serial port, the delay can be very long especially if the console messages are repeated multiple times.

Note that the I/O mechanism is completely different if you just try to use the console as a login terminal. In that case, the normal interrupt-driven I/O structure is used, which means that the impact is not as severe. However, some workstations have very poor console drivers and use high amounts of CPU cycles to do simple jobs such as scrolling. An example is the console on Sun systems where a FORTH (language) interpreter handles the actual I/O. Although not as slow as the kernel `printf`, this mechanism still leaves something to be desired from a performance point of view. Fortunately, if you use the console under a window system such as X, the overhead drops considerably.

7.5.7 The Inode and Name Lookup Caches

The name lookup cache speeds path name to inode translations. Because this is a very frequent operation (every file opened in UNIX goes through this translation potentially multiple times), enlarging the lookup cache size eliminates expensive directory searches. This usually results in lower CPU usage and, occasionally, reduced disk I/O.

Before modifying the size of the cache, instrument its effectiveness using the appropriate tool. For example,

```
SunOS4.1% vmstat -s |grep lookup
   370715 total name lookups (cache hits 85%  per-process)
```

The hit ratio should be 90% or better. If it is not, you should reconfigure the kernel to increase the lookup cache size. The configuration parameter is usually called **ncsize** (**S5CACHEENTS** in SCO UNIX) with its default value usually equal to the number of inodes, which itself is derived from **MAXUSERS**. Because the name cache data structure is rather small (e.g., 44 bytes in SunOS 4.1 and 40 bytes in SCO UNIX), you should not be too shy about increasing its size. In addition, you should configure the size of the lookup hash table to one fourth (on single-CPU systems) to one half (on MP systems) of the total cache size in order to keep the search time low and avoid lock contention in multiprocessor systems.

Keep in mind that the kernel does not cache file names longer than 14 characters (32 in Solaris). So, you should try to keep your file names (and especially symbolic links) shorter than this limit for good performance.

Because the name cache maps file names to in-memory inodes, you should also keep the sizes for the lookup cache and inode table in proportion. In general, the inode table should be double the size of the name cache size (the exception is Solaris 2.4 where you can get away with equal sizes).

The kernel configuration parameter for the inode table size is usually called **ninode** or **ufs_ninode** as in the case of SVR4 and Solaris. Because the inode cache is indirectly tied to the paged buffer cache (the kernel throws away cached contents of a file if its inode is needed for another purpose), you must make sure that the inode table is proportional to the buffer cache size and usage. If you are running SVR4 or Solaris, you can monitor the number of times a good inode is reused by using `sar -g` and looking at the **%ufs_ipf** field. Increase the inode table size until this field drops to zero under all load conditions.

Even though the inode table entries are much larger than the lookup cache, you should nevertheless be rather aggressive with its size. Each entry uses anywhere from 250 to 512 bytes, so if you have lots of memory, increase the inode table to a few thousand entries.

7.5.8 Reducing the Interrupt Rate

Another area that you should pay attention to is the interrupt rate. Look at the number of interrupts per second. If it exceeds a few hundred, you may have too much activity on your serial ports. PCs are notorious for having poor serial port interfaces that generate high interrupt rates. A good clue is if the system time is high without any process accumulating CPU time. If this is the case, you may want to postpone any high-speed modem activities (e.g., UUCP or `tip/cu`) or get "smart" serial cards with on-board buffering.

7.6 Increasing CPU Cycles

Alas, the best option in dealing with high CPU utilization is to get a faster CPU. The added CPU power can speed up your system whether you are running one job or many or are system-bound or user-bound.

The question often comes up as to whether you are better off getting a faster CPU or, if your system supports it, adding more CPUs. Before answering this question, we need to look at how and when additional CPUs help your system.

7.6.1 When to Add More CPUs to a System

Before considering adding more CPUs to a system, you must first make sure that they will actually have something to do:

> *because each CPU must have an independent process to run, the optimal number of CPUs for a system is equal to the number of runnable jobs.*

This is a very important rule and is derived from the fact that few applications can be partitioned to run on multiple CPUs (ask your application vendor to see if the application is multi-threaded and, hence, can use more than one CPU). None of the standard UNIX utilities, for example, run on more than one CPU at a time.

Given the preceding rule, if your system has three runnable jobs, you will not be able to use more than three CPUs. If you exceed this threshold, some of the CPUs will sit idle with nothing to do.

To determine the number of runnable jobs, look at the load average of the system using `uptime`. If your system lacks this utility, run `vmstat` or `sar` with a long interval (at least 30 seconds) and look at the number of runnable jobs or the length of the run queue, respectively. Note that these data can be a bit misleading because the processes currently running by a CPU are not counted in some systems. In such cases, these numbers indicate the number of additional CPUs you can add to the system. For example, if the run queue length is 4 on a three-CPU system, the optimal number of CPUs would be seven.

7.6.2 Degree of Speed-Up in Multiprocessor Systems

In an ideal world, the performance of a multiprocessor system would scale linearly as the number of CPUs is increased. That is, going from two CPUs to four should result in a two-fold speed-up in throughput. In real life, resource conflicts between the CPUs cause inefficiencies that reduce the incremental improvements. The most common culprit is the need for concurrent access to the same piece of data by more than one CPU. It is usually not desirable to have one CPU modify a piece of data while another is attempting to either look at or modify the same data. The solution is to serialize this process by allowing only one CPU to access the data at a time. This means that a CPU may potentially have to wait for another one before continuing its work from time to time (using a mutex, lock, or semaphore). If this situation (commonly referred to as lock contention) occurs frequently, then the efficiency of the system goes down as the CPUs waste their cycles waiting on each other.

In the simplest case of a single-CPU system, there are no conflicts, and the efficiency is obviously 100%. As the number of CPUs is increased, the probability of conflicts increases.

How far you can go before the efficiency drops too low (i.e., additional CPUs actually slow down the system rather than speed it up) is highly implementation-dependent.

One determining factor is the UNIX kernel, which is very prone to lock contention because it has many data structures that must be protected against simultaneous access. As a result, the efficiency of a multiprocessor machine is substantially lower in a system-bound environment where conflicts are very likely. On the other extreme, if you have a number of user-bound processes that make few system calls, the conflict rate is extremely low due to a lack of dependencies between them. So in general,

> *machines with high user time can achieve much higher throughput in a multi-processor environment than system-bound environments.*

What this means is that heavily user-bound applications make perfect candidates for MP systems (see Figure 7.1). For example, a four-CPU system can produce almost four times as much work as a single-CPU system if there are four 100% user-bound jobs for it to run. We say *almost* because the ultimate efficiency of such a system depends on shared hardware resources (namely memory and caches) between the various CPUs. Fortunately, modern MP implementations have large secondary caches that reduce the memory bus traffic to a point that you get fairly reasonable speed-up as new CPUs are added (at least until you approach 8 to 16 CPUs).

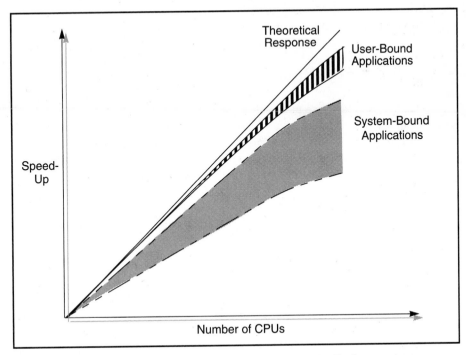

Figure 7.1 Degree of Speed-Up in Multiprocessor Environments

Determining if a system-bound machine can benefit from additional CPUs is a fairly difficult and uncertain job. The speed-up is a function of the system calls that the application makes along with how efficiently the kernel has been tuned by your UNIX vendor.

A safe bet is that you are not going to see a linear speed-up even under the best circumstances. As a general rule, systems that allow a large number of processors in the system (e.g., 16 or more) tend to be more tuned and provide much better efficiency, especially in smaller configurations (e.g., up to four CPUs). Even so, we recommend that you stay away from the last 25% of the CPU capacity of your system where the payoff will likely be small.

If you are running older, less optimized kernels, the efficiency drop will occur much sooner. For example, the single-semaphore implementation of SunOS 4.1 where only one CPU can execute the kernel code at a time means that you are unlikely to see any improvement once you go beyond two or three CPUs in a system-bound environment. Such systems are useful only if the percentage of user time is very high.

Now going back to the original question, if you have a choice of adding CPUs to an old system versus getting a faster CPU, always opt for the latter because a faster CPU improves a CPU-bound system regardless of whether it is user- or system-bound. The performance improvements of a multiprocessor system are much less certain and are highly application-dependent as we just discussed. Multiprocessor systems make sense only when the fastest CPU offered by your vendor is inadequate for your job and you need to use more of them to get the required throughput.

7.7 Improving File System Performance

After memory shortage, the most typical cause of slow response time is a saturated disk subsystem. Being much faster than the disk drive, the CPU can quite easily idle waiting for slow disk requests to finish. The result is a slow response time that can become erratic if the number of I/O requests climbs very high. Our general rule is that the fastest disk subsystem is one that is not being used!

To start, make sure that your system is I/O bound by examining the CPU idle time (it should be above 20%) and the disk subsystem (the number of I/Os greater than 25–30 transfers/sec on at least one of the drives). For example,

```
SunOS4.1% vmstat 30
 procs     memory        page            disk          faults      cpu
 r b w   avm   fre   re at  pi po fr  de  sr d0 d1 s2 d3  in  sy  cs  us sy id
 0 1 0     0 13344   0  0   0  0  0   32    0104  0  0  0 423 315 210   0 28 71
 1 1 0     0 13356    0652   0  0  0   16    0101  0  0  0 430 466 229   1 30 68
 0 1 0     0   612   0 11   0  0  0   16    0103  0  0  0 416 306 204   2 31 68
```

In this example, the idle time is almost 70% with drive zero (**d0**) completely saturated at over 100 transfers/sec (this is a high-performance SCSI drive) and we see that there is one I/O bound job (under the **b** column).

To verify an I/O-bound situation in System V, run `sar` with a 30-second interval and examine the CPU idle time and the number of transactions/sec (**r+w/s**) using the `-d` option. For example,

```
IRIX% sar -d 30 2
18:18:28  device   %busy  avque  r+w/s  blks/s   w/s  wblks/s  avwait  avserv
18:18:58  dks0d1     99    1.3     60    2141     60    2141     5.4    16.6
18:19:28  dks0d1     99    1.3     60    2147     60    2147     5.2    16.5

18:19:28  device   %busy  avque  r+w/s  blks/s   w/s  wblks/s  avwait  avserv
Average   dks0d1     99    1.3     60    2144     60    2144     5.3    16.6
          dks0d2      0    0.0      0       0      0       0     0.0     0.0
          dks0d4      0    0.0      0       0      0       0     0.0     0.0
```

In this example drive one (**dks0d1**) is 99% busy with 60 transfers/sec (this is *not* the same disk drive used in the previous example and, as you can see, is much slower).

There are many ways to deal with disk bottlenecks. Let's look at some common techniques.

7.7.1 Balancing Multiple Drives

If you have more than one disk drive in your system, it is very important that the disk traffic be spread equally among them. In most multidrive systems, one or two drives get accessed constantly while the rest go idle. The cause is usually poor disk space planning. To avoid it, keep in mind that

> *each disk drive should have only one active partition on it.*

An active partition is one that gets used very frequently. Examples include /tmp, /usr, and the project directory where work gets done. These partitions should be placed on drives that have otherwise rarely used information (e.g., old projects or reference material). If you cannot find material that is less frequently used, you may want to leave the space empty. This is a good reason for selecting the right size disk drive for the application rather than a huge one that would make you feel guilty about leaving empty space.

Applying the preceding rule after you have configured the partitions on your disk drives can be painful because it requires saving and restoring entire file systems. So, do your planning ahead of time and do not randomly place file systems on any drive that happens to have a spare partition on it.

To check that you have balanced the disk I/O effectively, run `iostat` or `sar` and look at the number of transfers/sec over a 1-minute interval. You should see roughly equal numbers for each drive. Do not be disappointed if you cannot achieve this goal all the time because this technique does nothing to reduce the traffic from a single-file system. The RAID systems can be used to deal with these balancing problems.

7.7.2 Using Disk Striping or RAID to Balance Disk Traffic

One problem with balancing disk drives manually is that as the disk usage changes, the configuration may become suboptimal, requiring the load to be rebalanced. An example would be an inactive file system that suddenly becomes a heavily accessed partition causing the drive to seek from one active partition to another constantly. A RAID controller or software disk striping can solve this problem by constantly distributing the transfers across multiple drives even though the user thinks it is accessing a single (logical) drive.

Another advantage of RAID or disk striping is that it can spread disk traffic caused by accessing even a single file. Manual tuning, on the other hand, gets impossible in such situations.

Another motivation for using a software striping scheme or a RAID controller is in those cases in which the user disk I/O load cannot be predicted in advance. A good example is an NFS server serving many users running different applications. In this environment, it may be very difficult to guess which file systems will get heavily used.

The main drawback to disk striping is lower reliability. RAID systems do not have this problem but cost more due to higher media cost (additional drives for parity) and higher controller cost. So, you need to weigh these factors before deciding on these solutions.

7.7.3 Optimizing Single-Drive Systems

Most UNIX users are not fortunate enough to have more than one drive in their system.[5] Given the high volume of disk traffic in most UNIX systems, a single-drive machine is bound to perform poorly, especially in the standard configuration used in most systems. You get poor file system performance on a single-drive system because, by definition, you have more than one active partition on the drive. Fortunately, some steps can be taken to minimize the constant seeking between the partitions resulting in better (but not ideal) performance.

Figure 7.2 on page 165 shows a typical partition layout recommended by most system vendors. The root (/) and user (/usr) file systems are provided by the vendor and contain the operating system and utilities. The second partition is for swapping, and the user files are placed in the remainder of the drive under /home partition. Although this disk layout is optimal from a space allocation point of view (the first three partitions are of fixed size

---

5. Some users are unfortunate enough to have systems that are running diskless, which is the worst environment to run UNIX from a performance point of view.

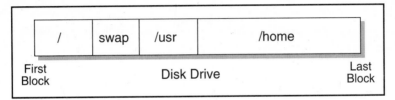

Figure 7.2 Poorly Configured Single-Drive File System Partitioning

so it makes sense to put them at the beginning), it provides for very poor disk I/O response.

The problem is that there is a good chance that the accessed files are in different partitions. For example, when a user invokes a UNIX utility that operates on a file in /home, the drive must seek to /usr or / to demand load the program. Then, any output that needs to be is stored in /home, which causes a long seek back to the end of the drive. The situation gets much worse in the case of a program such as the C compiler, which generates intermediate files that may have to be written to the /tmp directory.

A much better solution is to combine /usr and /home file systems into one (larger) partition (starting where /usr is located now). By combining these file systems, the kernel accesses files that are much closer to each other, especially if you are using FFS or some derivative of it. The drawback to this solution is that the system is harder to maintain. By mixing /home with /usr, it may be more difficult to upgrade the operating system because you have to extract user files before recreating the /usr partition. In addition, full backups require saving standard system files that rarely change. So, you need to weigh the speed improvements versus such inconveniences.

Another option is to locate the swap partition at the end of the drive on systems that have lots of memory (and hence are less likely to swap). Better yet, if you are sure you will never swap or page program memory (i.e., you have more memory than the minimum requirement specified in Section 7.1), use a simple file for swap. This has the added advantage of freeing the swap space for other use. *By moving the user files closer to the beginning of the drive, you also get the higher throughput available from the outer tracks of a modern ZBR disk drive.*

A somewhat more expensive but optimal solution may be to buy a small drive dedicated to /tmp (and possibly to the swap partition). This would double the disk bandwidth resulting in even shorter compile times. This brings us to another important disk optimization rule:

> *you get better performance out of two smaller disks than one larger one, assuming the performances of the drives are similar.*

So, instead of buying one 4-Gbyte drive, you may want to opt for two 2-Gbyte ones. This would give you much more freedom in choosing the location of your active partitions. The drawback is a slight increase in total cost.

7.7.4 Sun's tmpfs File System

RAM disks, a popular concept in the PC world, use the main system memory to emulate a disk drive. Because there are no mechanical seeks required to access data in a RAM disk, their random access time is far superior to real disk drives. Unfortunately, UNIX demands are much higher than PCs, making it difficult to set aside enough memory for a reasonable size RAM disk.

Instead of providing a pure solution, some vendors have focused on hybrid implementations that provide most of the performance of a RAM disk but without the size restrictions. One such solution is Sun's tmpfs. This type of file system uses the swap space as the storage medium with the buffer cache providing the high-speed access mechanism. The speed comes from the fact that write requests are delayed and not written to the swap device unless the buffer cache fills up. If this does occur, some of the requests will make it to the swap partition. This is a departure from a true RAM disk, where none of the disk requests are ever written to a physical medium. As such, the performance of tmpfs to some extent depends on the speed of the swap device.

File systems that have many small and short-lived files make the best use of tmpfs. Examples include /tmp whose size is rarely more than the available physical memory, and the lifetime of many files in it (e.g., those generated by the compilers) is relatively short. On the other hand, if your file system is very large and files remain in it for an extended amount of time, the performance of tmpfs will be almost as poor as a disk-based file system because the swap device will be heavily accessed in the process. This is especially bad in diskless environments where the swap partition is a remote disk connected to the local system via Ethernet. But note that, even in this environment, converting /tmp to tmpfs is beneficial.

Despite its speed advantages, tmpfs has one major drawback.

> *Despite using the swap partition as a "back up," tmpfs is volatile. Its contents do not survive a reboot, a system crash, or even a simple unmount.*

So, be careful about which files you put in tmpfs. Even innocent-looking file systems such as /var/tmp hold potentially precious data such as the vi recover files that allow you to get copies of files that you were editing before a system crash. You may also want to warn your user community that the specific file system is temporary because users are known to create directories in file systems such as /tmp and expect them to be there forever.

By using the swap partition as the storage medium, tmpfs file systems can potentially grow to the maximum size of the available swap space. We say *potentially* because tmpfs can use only swap space that is not already allocated to user programs. So, if you plan on using tmpfs, make sure to increase the size of the swap space first. Use the pstat -s command (in SunOS 4.1) or sar -r (in SVR4 or Solaris) to make sure that there is adequate space available:

```
SunOS4.1% pstat -s
9196k allocated + 2720k reserved = 11916k used, 34160k available
```

In this example, the machine has 34 Mbytes of free swap space. Assuming that you have run `pstat` during peak system load, you could safely create a `tmpfs` that can grow to 25 Mbytes (about 25% set aside just in case).

In Solaris, there are no less than three mechanisms for displaying swap space. The one we recommend is `sar -r`:

```
Solaris% sar -r 1 1
17:23:44 freemem freeswap
17:23:45     349   203680
```

Because the units are in 512-byte blocks, the free swap space is 101 Mbytes, which is easily big enough for a `tmpfs` file system.

To use `tmpfs`, simply specify `-t tmp swap` to the `mount` command followed by the directory where you want the file system placed. For example

```
SunOS4.1# mount -t tmp swap /foo
```

In this case, a `tmpfs` file system is created, which can be accessed by using `/foo`. If you are running SunOS 4.1, there are instructions in the `/etc/rc` file on how to mount `/tmp` as a `tmpfs` file system. Essentially, you put an entry in `/etc/fstab`, which looks like

```
swap /tmp rw 0 0
```

Then, in `/etc/rc` simply uncomment the line that does

```
mount /tmp
```

In Solaris, `/tmp` is mounted by default as `tmpfs`. So be careful not to place large files in `/tmp`, use `/var/tmp` instead.

7.7.5 Tuning the Paged Buffer Cache Size

As you recall, the buffer cache in UNIX is highly effective in reducing disk traffic. Obviously, the larger the buffer cache, the higher its hit rate. Because the paged buffer cache can use all of the available memory, increasing its size simply involves adding more memory to the system. But note that once the buffer cache reaches a critical size, enlarging it beyond that point results in only little, if any, reduction in disk I/O rates. Finding this point requires trial and error and, of course, an ample amount of free memory to use in the experimentation.

The job is complicated by the fact that most implementations of the paged buffer cache do not maintain any hit rate statistics. The standard `sar -b` command shows only the statistics for file system metadata cache and not the paged buffer cache. The only major exception to this is the SGI IRIX where `sar -b` shows the combined statistics for both types of operations. So, if you are using IRIX, simply watch **%rcache** when running `sar -b` with a long interval (at least 30 seconds) and strive for a hit rate of at least 80%. On other systems, you are stuck with monitoring disk I/O rates and trying to reduce the transfers per second by enlarging the buffer cache.

7.7.6 Tuning the Metadata Buffer Cache Size

As mentioned earlier, the older style buffer cache (which we call the metadata cache) still exists in systems with paged buffer caches. Its role is to cache file system access requests such as reading and writing inodes, directory (and symbolic link) contents, indirect blocks for files, superblocks, and cylinder group information.

Unlike the paged buffer cache, you can instrument the effectiveness of the metadata cache in most implementations, but the procedure varies from system to system. For example, in DEC UNIX, you must use the `dbx` debugger to fetch the statistics as shown in the following script (must be superuser to run this):

```
echo "p bio_stats" | dbx -k /vmunix /dev/mem 2> /dev/null | awk '
/hits/ { h = $3}
/getblk_misses/ { m = $3}
END { printf("Metadata cache Hit ratio = %d\n", h / (h + m) * 100 )}'
```

In this case, the statistics are printed for the total runtime of the system, which is appropriate for this kind of data.

In System V implementations, use `sar -b` but make sure to run it over a long period to get good averaging:

```
Solaris% sar -b 30 2
16:34:39 bread/s lread/s %rcache bwrit/s lwrit/s %wcache pread/s pwrit/s
16:35:09     11      96      89      7      18      59      0       0
16:35:39     11     109      90      7      20      64      0       0

Average      11     102      89      7      19      62      0       0
```

In Solaris, you can use the (undocumented) -k option of `netstat` to retrieve accumulated statistics similar to OSF/1:

```
Solaris% netstat -k |more +/biostat
...skipping
biostats:
buffer_cache_lookups 20505 buffer_cache_hits 18606 new_buffer_requests 0
waits_for_buffer_allocs 0 buffers_locked_by_someone 24 duplicate_buffers_found 0
```

A quick `awk` script can turn these data into a hit rate:

```
netstat -k |awk '
/buffer_cache/ {l = $2; h = $4}
END {printf("Metadata cache Hit ratio = %d\n", h / l * 100 )}'
```

Running this on the same system results in

```
Metadata cache Hit ratio = 90
```

Regardless of which method you use, make sure the hit rate is above 90%.

In DEC UNIX, the **bufcache** parameter sets the size of the metadata cache. The value indicates the percentage of physical memory available for the metadata cache. This makes it rather hard to tune because on large memory systems, even 1% may be too high a value, especially if your application is not very file-intensive. Likewise, the default value of 3% seems too high for systems with large memories and few file systems. Setting aside almost 4 Mbytes on a 128-Mbyte system can be wasteful.

In SunOS 4.1, the kernel **nbuf** variable sets the size of the metadata cache. If the value is set to 0, the kernel determines the size for you. Before reducing its size, display its configured and current (kernel determined) value using adb:

```
SunOS4.1% echo "nbuf/D; nbuf?D" | .s adb -k /vmunix /dev/mem
physmem 1fe5
_nbuf:
_nbuf:              61
_nbuf:
_nbuf:               0
```

The first value displayed (61 in this case) is the number of 8-Kbyte buffers allocated to the metadata cache. The second value is the configured value. Because it is zero in this case, the kernel has used its own formula for computing it (which is usually a percentage of the total available memory in the system).

Because there is no way of displaying the metadata statistics in SunOS 4.1, we recommend that you stay on the conservative side and use the default values except when you have a lot of memory. In this case, the size used by SunOS is too large. So, you may want to adjust it if you have over 128 Mbytes of memory. To do this, use the adb debugger yet again (which must be run as root).

 Note that using the adb debugger to patch the kernel is inherently dangerous. Make sure that you type the following command exactly, and with all the same capitalizations. In addition, you should make a backup copy of your kernel and completely test the patched version to make sure that it is working correctly before using it in a production environment.

Now let's change the default value of **nbuf** to 100 (which sets aside 800 Kbytes). The value is specified as 0t100, which indicates to adb that it is a decimal number. adb confirms the change by displaying the old and new values (in hex format unfortunately):

```
SunOS4.1# echo "nbuf?W 0t100" |adb -wk /vmunix /dev/mem
physmem 1fe7
_nbuf:              0x3c              =              0x64
```

Note that you must reboot your system for this change to take effect.

In SVR4 (and hence Solaris), the kernel allocates memory as needed for the metadata cache up to the size specified by the kernel parameter, **bufhwm** (which stands for Buffer High Water Mark). The units for **bufhwm** are in kilobytes in Solaris and in percentage of physical memory in standard SVR4. The allocation is done in units of **p_nbuf**, which defaults to 100 buffers. The current number of buffers allocated can be seen by looking at the **nbuf** variable (which has units of pages).

7.7.7 Adjusting the Buffer Cache Size in SCO UNIX

As of this writing, SCO UNIX uses a fixed-size buffer cache, which means that you can easily tune its size. Before reconfiguring it, however, you should look at the current size of the buffer cache by examining the console output when the system boots. Use the following command if you do not want to reboot your system:

```
# /etc/dmesg |grep bufs
kernel: i/o bufs = 200k
```

Alternatively, you can search the saved version of the console messages using

```
# grep bufs /usr/adm/messages
kernel: i/o bufs = 200k
```

The value reported is the total amount of memory (in kilobytes) permanently allocated to the buffer cache. The size defaults to 10% of the available memory with an upper bound set by the **MAXBUF** kernel variable (default is 600 Kbytes). If you use the tunesh utility as recommended by SCO, the buffer cache size will be set to 200 Kbytes if you have 8 Mbytes of memory or less and 300K if you have more. We find this formula suboptimal for performance reasons. Specifically,

> the default buffer cache size is too small for a system with greater than 16 Mbytes of memory. We recommend a buffer cache of at least 1 Mbyte in these systems with larger sizes highly desirable if there is sufficient memory left for user processes.

Given the low disk I/O performance in some PCs, a large buffer cache is a must for good performance. Use sar -b with a 1-minute interval and examine the hit rate. It should be above 80% for good performance.

In enlarging the buffer cache, take care not to take memory away from user processes. Decrease the buffer cache size as soon as you see any sign of paging or swapping. In addition, do not let the total kernel size go beyond 16 Mbytes because some PC disk controllers cannot make DMA transfers beyond this point. SCO UNIX solves this problem by copying the specific buffer to a temporary place in the lower 16 Mbytes before initiating the I/O. Needless to say, this is going to hurt the CPU performance greatly. Given this restriction, the buffer cache size is limited to about 13 Mbytes in these systems, which, fortunately, should be sufficient for most environments.

Changing the kernel parameters for the buffer cache size is very easy in the SCO UNIX, thanks to the availability of the menu-driven `sysadmsh` utility. Simply select `System->Configure-> Kernel` and then choose the option for tuning kernel parameters. This option prompts you for each kernel parameter and then rebuilds a kernel that must be booted before the changes take effect.

The parameter to change for the buffer cache is the **nbuf** variable, which sets the number of 1-Kbyte buffers in the buffer cache. So if you would like to configure the buffer cache size to be 1 Mbyte, set **nbuf** to 1024. Because the ultimate size of the cache is limited by **MAXBUF**, make sure that you also set it to a reasonable value (e.g., the same as **nbuf**).

If you make large increases in the buffer cache size, you may also want to increase the size of the kernel variable, **NHBUF**. This sets the number of "hack buckets," which are used to speed buffer cache searches. The value should be a power of two and we would go along with the recommendation of SCO to set it to one quarter of **nbuf**.

7.7.8 Optimizing the Cache Flush Parameters

The kernel flushes delayed write requests to disk on a frequent basis. The mechanism in BSD is fixed, and not much can be done about it. In contrast, the scheme used in System V (which includes SVR4/Solaris and SCO UNIX) has tunable parameters for the flushing mechanism.

The first parameter, **NAUTOUP** (SCO) or **autoup** (SVR4/Solaris), determines the age of a buffer before it is written to disk. The default for this parameter is typically 30 seconds, making the behavior similar to the traditional aging scheme used in UNIX.

Increasing the age time for buffers increases the efficiency of the buffer cache because it potentially eliminates write requests for files that get deleted before the time expires. On the other hand, the longer aging means that your system is more vulnerable because more data can be lost in case of a system crash. So, you must balance the two needs. We recommend that you keep **NAUTOUP** below 60 seconds because the improvements beyond this point will be minimal, but the risk of data loss increases sharply.

To limit the amount of work that needs to be done to scan the memory pages in use, another parameter, **BDFLUSHR** (SCO) or **tune_t_flushr** (SVR4/Solaris), sets how often the kernel invokes the `bdflush` (SCO) or `fsflush` (SVR4/Solaris) processes, which are responsible for scanning dirty buffers. The default for this parameter in SVR4 is 1 second but has been increased to 5 seconds in Solaris.

The flush rate should be set relative to the aging time (**NAUTOUP** or **autoup**). If, for example, the aging rate is set to 50 seconds, with the default value of 5 seconds for **tune_t_flushr**, dirty buffers get written every 50 to 55 seconds but in a very gradual manner (i.e., every 5 seconds). Now, if you increase the flush rate to 50 seconds, buffers will be aged from 50 to 100 seconds with very large write traffic generated every 50 seconds—a rather undesirable effect.

In general, it is a good idea to keep the flush rate much smaller than the aging time, especially if you have a large buffer cache. This would allow dirty buffers to get written on a gradual basis instead of creating a large peak. Remember that writing just 4-Mbytes worth of data generates over a thousand (4 Kbyte) disk requests! If during this period you try to access the disk, you may potentially have to wait 10 seconds (assuming a 10-millisecond average access time) to read something from your disk drive.

7.7.9 Choosing Between a RAM Disk and the Buffer Cache

Given the option of a RAM disk (or Sun's `tmpfs`) and a larger buffer cache, which one would you choose? The answer lies in the specific way each one improves the system performance. The major benefit of the buffer cache is that it reduces disk traffic *on all the disk drives in the system*, including networked requests in case of NFS.

Another advantage of the buffer cache is that it makes efficient use of main memory in that it is never empty. Its main disadvantage is that no matter how large, the buffer cache can not totally eliminate disk I/O. The so-called dirty buffers (write traffic) eventually will have to be written to disk as a result of a `sync` or a file system flush.

The strongest reason to use a RAM disk is that it completely eliminates disk I/O requests for files contained in it. Data written to a RAM disk reside in memory and never cause any disk traffic. In addition to higher throughput, a RAM disk is very predictable, making it a good option for real-time systems. Aside from volatility, the major drawback of a RAM disk is its inefficient use of main memory. As with most file systems, RAM disks will only be partially full wasting the unused memory space.

So, even though there is no question about the superiority of a RAM disk from a performance point of view, you must find a way to deal with its drawbacks. If you can find a set of frequently used files that you do not mind losing and have lots of unused main memory, by all means use a RAM disk. Otherwise, stay with the buffer cache. In most environments, it makes sense to actually use a mixture of the two: put heavily used, small files in a RAM disk and let the buffer cache take care of the rest.

7.8 Tuning the System V File System

The traditional System V file system is notorious for fragmentation, which is the result of almost random allocation of disk blocks after some period of use. This causes many unnecessary seeks, significantly lowering disk throughput.

The most effective but time-consuming approach to optimizing System V file system is to back it up, recreate it, and reload its contents. For obvious reasons, we strongly recommend that you verify the integrity of your backup before destroying the old file system.

Perhaps the best approach is to avoid the System V file system altogether and use the BSD Fast File System or any other high-performance file system available to you. Although FFS provides an immediate boost, there are some additional steps you can take to optimize its performance further.

7.9 Tuning the Fast File System

Before attempting to modify any of the FFS parameters, you should look up the current settings for your file systems. This can be done by running the /usr/etc/dumpfs program. Unfortunately, dumpfs is not universally available on all systems that have FFS (e.g., SVR4), and we know of no easy way of getting the same information without it.

The output of dumpfs is very long because it displays the entire structure of the file system and not just its key parameters. Fortunately, the most important values are shown first, and you can either use grep or head to find what you need. For example,

```
den# /usr/etc/dumpfs /dev/rsd2c | head -16
magic    11954   format  dynamic  time     Wed Nov  9 19:39:48 1994
nbfree   60577   ndir    3        nifree   247283  nffree  13
ncg      138     ncyl    2208     size     533232  blocks  500093
bsize    8192    shift   13       mask     0xffffe000
fsize    1024    shift   10       mask     0xfffffc00
frag     8       shift   3        fsbtodb 1
minfree 0%       optim   time     maxcontig 7       maxbpg  2048
rotdelay 0ms     rps     60
ntrak    7       nsect   69       npsect   69        spc     483
trackskew 0      interleave 1
cpg      16      bpg     483      fpg      3864      ipg     1792
nindir   2048    inopb   64       nspf     2
sblkno   16      cblkno  24       iblkno   32        dblkno  256
sbsize   2048    cgsize  2048     cgoffset 40        cgmask  0xfffffff8
csaddr   256     cssize  3072     shift    9         mask    0xfffffe00
cgrotor  6       fmod    0        ronly    0
```

As you can see from our example, dumpfs requires the partition name as its argument because it reads the file system information directly from the disk drive. You can get the name of the disk partition by running the mount command. Note that you will most likely need to have root privileges to run dumpfs due to the permission modes on the disk partition.

Despite the volume of information displayed by dumpfs, you need to focus on only a few fields. We have listed the most useful ones along with their description in Table 7.2. They

Table 7.2 `dumpfs` Fields

Field	Description
nbfree	Number of large blocks (usually 4K or 8K) free—also shown by `df`
ndir	Total number of directories
nifree	Number of free inodes—also shown by `df -i`
ncg	Number of cylinder groups
bsize	Size of the large blocks (in kilobytes)
fsize	Size of the fragment (in kilobytes)
fpg	fragments per cylinder group (equal to the cylinder group size if fragment size = 1024 bytes)
rotdelay	Spacing between sequential blocks on disk in milliseconds
rps	Disk drive speed in revolutions per second (i.e., disk RPM/60)
minfree	The amount set aside, which is usable only by superuser

should be self-explanatory with the exception of **rotdelay**, which we will describe in Section 7.9.3.

7.9.1 Optimizing the Block and Fragment Sizes

The FFS allows the file system block size to be increased to improve performance. The default block size is typically 4096 bytes but can be changed to 8192 bytes or even larger on some systems. Larger blocks reduce fragmentation at file level because more of the file data are clustered together (in one block). In addition, because the first 12 blocks of each file can be accessed directly using the information in the inode, larger blocks also minimize the need to fetch indirect blocks in order to access most files. For example, with an 8-Kbyte block, you can access files up to 96 Kbytes without indirection, whereas with 4-Kbyte blocks you are limited to only 48 Kbytes.

Note that enlarging the block size also increases the size of the fragments, which have a minimum size of one eighth of a block. Because the majority of UNIX files are very small, larger fragments are bound to increase waste.

Speaking of fragments, you may also want to increase their size. The advantage here comes from the fact that the FFS maintains the free space in the file system in terms of fragments and not blocks. So even if the application requests a full block to be written, the FFS must scan the file system free list (which is kept as a bit map) to find eight adjacent fragments (with the default fragment size). By increasing the fragment size, you minimize this search time. The highest performance is achieved when the fragment size is set to the same value as the block size.

Of course, the drawback to enlarging the fragment size is a fairly substantial increase in file system waste. On the average, the waste would be equal to 50% of the fragment size times the number of files in the file system. So, if your file system has few files and ample space, you may want to build it with large fragments. On the other hand, if you have a file system with many small files (e.g., the news directory) that are accessed infrequently, the smallest fragment size will be appropriate.

Changing the block or fragment size requires that you rebuild your file system from scratch. So, it is best to plan for this before you create your file systems by examining your usage based on the preceding criteria. To change the block size, you need to specify the -b option of newfs. Likewise, the -f option specifies the fragment size. If you are using some other command to make your file system, refer to its documentation on how to set these parameters. Note that the automatic OS installation scripts of most vendors do not allow you to specify any of the file system parameters. This means that you have to live with the default sizes for these partitions.

7.9.2 Using tunefs to Set FFS Parameters

When told about a file system tuning program, most people think of a program that defragments files. Unfortunately, such is not the case with tunefs. Despite its lofty sounding name, its capabilities are limited to changing a few of the FFS parameters. Specifically, you can modify **minfree** (the amount of free space not available to normal users), **maxbpg**, and **maxcontig** (see below).

Note that tunefs needs to be run on an *unmounted file system* because it modifies the disk image directly (i.e., it uses the raw disk interface). Although you do not get any errors and tunefs appears to work on mounted file systems, the changes will not take effect. The reason is that the kernel caches in memory the superblock that contains the parameters that tunefs modifies. Hence, changing their values on disk will not have any effect. What is worse, the kernel writes out the (modified) superblocks on the next sync request, which erases any changes made by tunefs on the disk drive. So, be sure to unmount the file system first before running tunefs. As a consequence, you cannot run tunefs on the root file system because it is permanently mounted. This means that you are at the mercy of your vendor to have chosen the right values for you. Because the root partition is usually small and not used frequently, this may not be much of a problem in practice.

Running tunefs is very easy and requires only the name of the raw partition and the option for the parameter that you want to change. For example, to set the percentage of space set aside for superuser access only, use the -m option:

```
# tunefs -m 5 /dev/rsd1f
minimum percentage of free space changes from 10% to 5%
should optimize for space with minfree < 10%
```

As you see, tunefs prints the old value before changing it, which is a nice way of confirming that the change has taken effect. If you really want to be sure, simply run the command twice and the second time you should see the same value for old and new.

By the way, ignore the advice given by `tunefs` to change the optimization policy to space when you decrease **minfree** below 10%. The FFS used to have an optimization policy, which helped it decide whether it should grow a fragment by allocating a full block (optimization = time) or using a larger fragment (optimization = space). This mechanism is no longer effective because the FFS in the majority of cases grows a fragment into a full block right away. So, you can safely ignore the message along with a similar one coming out on the console from time to time (indicating that optimization has changed from time to space and vice versa).

As you recall, the FFS works better when it has plenty of space in its cylinder groups so that it can pick the optimal one for new files and directories. As such, it limits the size of large files so that they cannot fill an entire cylinder group by themselves. Once this limit is reached (determined by the parameter, **maxbpg**), FFS switches to another cylinder group, and the process continues.

The default for **maxbpg** per `newfs` documentation is one quarter of the cylinder group size. But as you notice from our sample `dumpfs` output, this is not the case. Indeed, the default value (at least in SunOS 4.1, BSD 4.4, and DEC UNIX) is *fixed* at the number of blocks that can fit in one indirect block. On a file system with an 8-Kbyte block, **maxbpg** always is 2048 regardless of the cylinder group size. Using this value, files are broken into 16-Mbyte chunks. This is much larger than the typical cylinder group size (roughly 3.8 Mbytes in our example), which means that **maxbpg** does not have the intended effect. Despite this bug, we recommend that you leave **maxbpg** alone because it does not come into play except for very large files and, in that case, it is not clear that you would want to add many unneeded gaps to these files. If you do want to experiment with changing **maxbpg**, use the `-e` option of `tunefs`:

```
SunOS4.1# tunefs -e 4096 /dev/rsd2c
maximum blocks per file in a cylinder group changes from 2048 to 4096
```

The **maxcontig** parameter indicates the number of contiguous blocks allocated to a file (see the next section) before a rotational delay is inserted. But once you set the **rotdelay** parameter to zero (see the next section), this parameter does nothing. So, some systems such as SunOS 4.1 and Solaris use **maxcontig** to specify how many blocks are read ahead on each sequential access. The default is 7, which, using 8-Kbyte blocks, means that 56 Kbytes are read ahead each time. This is probably optimal in most environments and should not need to be changed. If, however, you are using software disk striping, then the value may need to be scaled by the number of drives in the cluster. For example, if you are using one logical drive that consists of four physical drives, enlarging **maxcontig** to 28 maximizes the throughput on each drive.

7.9.3 Rotational Latency Optimization

The rotational latency parameter in FFS is a crude way of indicating block interleaving in your file system. This mechanism is no longer necessary because most new implementations can "chain" or cluster disk requests together allowing disk blocks to be accessed consecutively. Because the units of **rotdelay** are in blocks (but expressed in milliseconds), any value other than zero means that the FFS will be at least skipping every other block when allocating space to a file. Nonzero **rotdelay** values therefore mean that your disk throughput is at most 50% of the available disk bandwidth.

You can take a chance and set **rotdelay** to zero using tunefs to see if you get higher performance:

```
# tunefs -d 0 /export
rotational delay between contiguous blocks changes from 0ms to 0ms
```

After running tunefs (and remounting the file system), test your file access speed by timing how long it takes to create and read some large files. If the file system slows down as a result of the change, set the delay back to the original value—your drive and controller are just too slow to keep up. Invest in a new disk controller and drive.

7.10 Upgrading the Disk Subsystem

Remember that, as with the CPU, upgrading your disk drives may provide a faster path to better file system performance in some cases. We recommend that you invest in the faster 7200-RPM drives available from many vendors (SEGATE, MICROPOLIS, IBM, QUANTUM, etc.) for your active partitions. These drives would make a big difference, especially if you are still using 3600- or even 4500-RPM 5.25-inch drives. Because these newer drives use ZBR, you should place your most important files in at the beginning of the drive.

CHAPTER 8

TCP/IP Architecture and Optimization Techniques

In this chapter we cover both the architecture and helpful hints for optimization of the TCP/IP networks. NFS, which is a close sibling of TCP/IP, is covered in Chapter 9.

Before starting, we should note that, by its very nature, network management and tuning is a complex task requiring a good understanding of the various protocols and networks involved. Even though we cover the information necessary to optimally design, configure, and optimize networks of UNIX systems, the coverage will be brief when it comes to issues unrelated to performance. In these cases, you are much better off referring to other texts specially written to cover these topics (see the bibliography at the end of this text).

8.1 TCP/IP Basics

The protocol suite typically referred to as TCP/IP is actually comprised of many distinct modules. These include two basic classes of service: TCP (Transmission Control Protocol) and UDP (Unreliable Datagram Protocol). The latter is much less known but is quite important because it provides the foundation for NFS.

Both TCP and UDP allow user applications to send and receive data to and from other systems across arbitrary network configurations and topologies. The difference between them lies in the type of service provided. TCP guarantees delivery of user data (which is called a packet or datagram) to its destination regardless of system or network errors.[1] UDP, on the other hand, makes only a best attempt at delivery of the data. Specifically, it is possible for UDP packets to get lost, duplicated, or corrupted (if checksums are turned off—see Section 8.3). It is the responsibility of the application or higher-level services using UDP to make sure that the integrity of the data is kept. As an example, NFS uses its own protocol to deal with losses at the UDP layer. Both TCP and UDP use the IP (Internet Protocol) layer as their low-level packet handler (see Figure 8.1).

Along with the basic protocols, the networking suite in UNIX also includes the so-called r commands (`rcp`, `rlogin`, `rsh`, etc.) and a number of other services (such as `ftp` and NIS). All these services are implemented as user-level programs on top of TCP. The only exception is `tftp` ("trivial" File Transfer Program), which uses UDP and is necessary for diskless booting. See Section 8.7 for a description of how some of these tools operate.

Before getting into the specifics of each protocol, let's first look at how user programs access these services.

8.2 Sockets

Sockets provide a programming interface (an API) to the underlying networking code. They are not part of the protocol suite but have become a UNIX standard, especially in BSD-derived systems. Sockets operate in two domains: UNIX domain and Internet domain.

UNIX domain sockets are used as a means of communication between processes in the same system. Often referred to as InterProcess Communication or IPC, UNIX domain sockets do not use either TCP or UDP. The kernel simply handles the data transfer internally. As an example, BSD-derived systems use UNIX domain sockets to implement

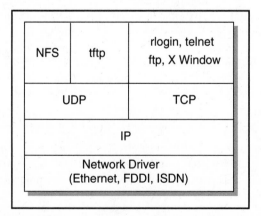

Figure 8.1 The UNIX Networking Suite

---

1. Of course, nothing can guarantee delivery of data to a dead host or network, TCP included.

pipes, which is not to say it is a good idea from a performance point of view. Using sockets to implement pipes, while elegant, is not the most efficient approach. Socket-based pipes are usually three to four times slower than older, but more efficient pipe code still resident in many System V variants.

Internet domain sockets are used to interface with the networking protocols. There are various types of Internet domain sockets, but the most common are Stream and Datagram. Stream-based sockets are connection oriented links (i.e., operate between two specific hosts) and are usually used on top of TCP. Datagram sockets, on the other hand, are connectionless and allow each packet to be sent to a different host. UDP connections use Datagram sockets.

Sockets are used in a manner similar to normal file operations. But instead of calling `open`, user programs issue a `socket` system call to get a socket handle (similar to a file descriptor) to use in the follow-on operations. The `write` and `read` systems calls can easily be used to operate on sockets allowing any application to send and receive data over the network. The actual usage is somewhat more complex than file handling because the system needs to be told what protocol needs to be used in addition to the endpoints of the connection.

8.2.1 Reading and Writing Sockets

When you write to a socket, the kernel copies the user data into an mbuf or streams buffer (depending on the implementation) and then passes it to the related protocol. The user data must be copied because they may have to be retransmitted long after the user process is finished with them. This means that sockets are a fairly CPU-intensive form of IPC. Although modern CPUs have made this overhead less painful, the impact is still significant.

Received data are likewise stored in a kernel buffer until the user process empties it by reading from the socket. This is necessary because low-level protocols have no concept of user program address spaces and, hence, must store the data in intermediate buffers until the upper-level protocols decide where the data should go.

To keep the memory requirements from becoming too large, the kernel puts a ceiling (or high water mark) on how much data can be outstanding in each socket connection. If the process attempts to write more to the socket than this limit, it is put to sleep until the socket drains to a low water mark. On the input side, socket overflows can lead to data being thrown away depending on the protocol (see the specific section for the socket limits in each protocol).

8.3 The UDP Protocol

As we mentioned, UDP provides a connectionless scheme for data transmission. This means that unlike TCP, there is no need to establish a connection between the nodes. The price for this flexibility is that UDP makes only a best attempt at delivering the data. While UDP adds special checksums to the end of the packet so that the receiver can check the integrity of the data, it does not verify that the packets actually arrive at their destination. Furthermore, UDP checksuming is optional, meaning that the receiver can simply ignore it. This was initially done for backward compatibility with some early UDP implementations that incorrectly computed the checksum. (This is no longer a valid reason because these implementations are extinct.) However, some vendors disable UDP checksuming to get better performance because computing it on each incoming packet is fairly CPU-intensive.

There is no well-defined way to determine if UDP checksuming is turned on in a system. One (undocumented) way is to use a debugger to display the value of the kernel variable, **udpcksum** (**udp_cksum** in SunOS 4.1). If the variable is set to 1, checksuming is enabled. Otherwise, it is not. Some examples follow:

```
SunOS4.1# echo "udp_cksum?D" |adb /vmunix
_udp_cksum:
_udp_cksum:      0                              # checksum OFF

iris5.2# echo "p udpcksum" |dbx -k /unix /dev/kmem
dbx version 3.18 Feb 14 1994 00:52:47
Type 'help' for help.
1                                               # checksum ON

DEC UNIX# echo "p udpcksum" |dbx -k /vmunix /dev/mem 2>/dev/null
dbx version 3.11.4
Type 'help' for help.

stopped at  [thread_block:1461 ,0xffffffff0009ac18]     Source not
available
1                                               # checksum ON

Hp-ux9.01# echo "udpcksum?D" |adb /hp-ux /dev/kmem
udpcksum:
udpcksum:        1                              # checksum ON
```

A better way might be to use a LAN analyzer and decode the individual UDP packets. If the checksum field is zero, the UDP checksuming is disabled.

Turning off UDP checksums is relatively safe because there are various constancy checks at the low-level network interfaces. Even so, we do not recommend that you turn off checksuming unless you have a very simple, single-segment network. It is definitely advisable to turn on checksuming if you use high-error-rate wide-area networks (WANs).

Once again, toggling UDP checksuming requires that you use the undocumented scheme of patching the kernel with a debugger. To make a temporary patch, use the following script (**caution:** the /W command must be typed in uppercase):

```
SunOS4.1# echo "udp_cksum/W 1" |adb -wk /vmunix /dev/mem
physmem 1fe7
_udp_cksum:      0x0              =           0x1
```

Or on HP-UX:

```
Hp-ux9.01# echo "udpcksum/W 1" |adb -w /hp-ux /dev/kmem
udpcksum:        1              =        1
```

Note that you need superuser privileges for the preceding commands to work. In addition, the change is temporary and will be lost when you reboot your system. This can be an advantage in that it allows you to turn checksuming on and off dynamically to see if there is a noticeable performance difference. To turn the checksuming off, just replace the 1 with a 0.

To make a permanent change, change /W to ?W *but make sure that you make a backup copy of your kernel first and fully test your changes before trusting the patched version.*

UDP performs demultiplexing on the received packets so that the data are delivered to the right socket (and process) that is waiting for it. The process is awakened after queuing the data on its socket structure. As with all sockets, the input packets hang around until the process frees each one by reading it from the socket. The maximum amount that can be pending on a receive socket is set by the kernel variable **udp_recvspace**. Likewise, the maximum queued on a transmit socket is limited by the **udp_sendspace** variable.

The default values for the UDP socket send and receive buffers vary from system to system. Again, the only way to see their values is by using a debugger:

```
SunOS4.1# echo "udp_recvspace?D" |adb /vmunix
_udp_recvspace:
_udp_recvspace: 18032
```

As you can see, the default value in SunOS 4.1 is very small (essentially two 8-Kbyte packets plus the protocol overhead). While this is fine for the r commands, it is extremely small for NFS servers which, by nature, use 8-Kbyte requests. The default has been sharply increased in most other implementations such as AIX, DEC UNIX, and BSD 4.4. All set the UDP receive buffer size to 41600. Even this higher value is too small to accommodate faster networks such as FDDI and Fast Ethernet. In these cases, the receive buffer size should be at least 64 Kbytes, preferably, 128 Kbytes.

AIX has a nice utility for changing networking parameters called no. To modify the receive buffer space, use

```
% no -o udp_recvspace=XXX
```

Note that **udp_recvspace** must be smaller than the maximum bytes allowed pending on the socket. The later is defined by the **sb_max** parameter, which can likewise be changed with the no command.

Keep in mind that UDP drops packets because they are not being consumed fast enough by the upper-level protocols. The culprit is usually a system that is starved for CPU cycles and is too busy to run the code that empties the socket.

8.4 The Internet Protocol

The Internet Protocol is the foundation upon which both TCP and UDP operate. Its main job is to pass and receive data packets to and from the network driver, which in turn communicates with the hardware.

When a packet is received from the network, the device driver fields the interrupt, copies the packet into a network buffer, and (if required) passes the packet to IP. The driver does not call the IP routines directly. Instead, it queues the packet for IP and simply returns after setting off a special software interrupt, which occurs when the (network) hardware interrupt is finished processing. This allows the IP code to run at a much lower priority level, reducing the chances of losing hardware interrupts due to the length of time it takes to process packets.

IP looks at the protocol field in the packet to detect which protocol the packet belongs to. The packet is then linked into the appropriate protocol queue, and the protocol layer is notified of the arrival of the packet.

Note that IP has a self-imposed limit on the number of packets that can be outstanding in its queues. The network drivers check the maximum queue length before appending any packets to it. Once this limit is reached, any incoming packets are dropped. The limit for the queue is usually based on the kernel parameter, **ipqmaxlen**. The default in BSD UNIX, which is the same value used in SunOS 4.1 and SGI IRIX 5.2, is 50 packets. The default in DEC UNIX is a much larger value of 512, which we prefer.

On transmit, IP simply hands the packets to the network driver if they are smaller than the maximum packet length on the specific network. If the size exceeds the maximum size (which is usually referred to as the Maximum Transmission Unit or MTU), IP fragments (breaks up) the data into multiple packets to be transmitted. When the packets are received by the target host's IP layer, they are reassembled into a single packet. Therefore, the packet fragmentation/reassembly is completely transparent to upper levels. The most common user of this mechanism is NFS, which uses packet sizes of roughly 8 Kbytes, which is larger than the MTU of Ethernet (1500 bytes) for example.

Another function of IP is packet routing. If you have two separate physical networks, IP running on a system connected to both networks can handle packet transfers between them. See Section 8.12 on how to use this feature to increase your network bandwidth.

Because IP must look inside each packet to see if it belongs to the current host as part of its routing function, it needs to make sure that the received packet is indeed a valid IP packet. To do this, IP adds its own checksums to each packet as it transmits them and checks their validity on received packets. Note that this checksum is limited to the IP portion of the packet (20 bytes). The remaining portion of the packet (which presumably contains data from TCP or UDP layers) is not protected by the IP checksum. In addition to checksums, IP also performs other sanity checks such as making sure the length field in the packet header matches the actual size of the received packet.

8.5 The Transmission Control Protocol

TCP provides a reliable and error-free communication mechanism between two nodes. The packets are guaranteed to reach their destination even in the face of catastrophic (but temporary) failures of the network. To achieve this feat, TCP uses a so-called positive acknowledgment scheme. When TCP sends a packet of data to a remote host, it does not throw away the data immediately. Instead, it sets off a timer and waits for the remote host to acknowledge the receipt of the packet using a special response packet called an acknowledgment packet or ACK for short. If the ACK does not arrive within the allotted time, TCP retransmits the data. Eventually, if no response is received, the connection is dropped, and the sender gets an error.

Because networks can corrupt contents of packets in addition to outright losing them, TCP computes a checksum (a 16-bit sum of all the data in the packet) and transmits it along with the packet. The receiving host recomputes the checksum of the packet and compares it to the value already stored in the packet to detect whether the packet needs to be kept or thrown away (dropped).

Due to the fact that it takes a finite amount of time for a packet to transmit from one host to another, it is possible for a (late) ACK to arrive at the sender right after a time-out, and hence retransmission. The result is that the receiving host gets a duplicate packet. To deal with this problem, the TCP specification requires that the receiver keep track of the data that have been received and throw away any duplicate packets. The same code is also able to handle packets that arrive out of order.

8.5.1 TCP Flow Control and Acknowledgment Scheme

From a performance point of view, waiting for an ACK before transmitting a packet is very inefficient. The network sits idle for the amount of time it takes for the receiving host to acknowledge the packet. To get around this, the TCP protocol allows the sender to transmit multiple packets before having to wait for an ACK. For this to work, the sender needs to hold on to all the outstanding packets that have not yet been ACKed just in case it needs to retransmit any of them. Because it is possible for packets to arrive out of order, the receiver has to also buffer all the packets until it gets a complete sequence of them.

To limit the total amount of memory needed to store these packets, the receiver advertises the total number of bytes that the sender may transmit before an ACK is received. This is called a window size and is the basic mechanism for flow control in TCP.

To avoid causing additional network traffic, the window size information is not transmitted by itself. Instead, it is included in the acknowledgment packet sent for the previous packets. The receiver can also advertise a window size of zero, which forces the sender to wait for another acknowledgment packet before transmitting. This is useful when all the system buffers are exhausted, and no capacity is left for new packets. The default window size is implementation-dependent (e.g., in SVR4 it is six times the MTU of the network being used).

To reduce the protocol overhead even further, the receiving host is not obligated to ACK each packet. Instead, it can wait and send one acknowledgment packet for a sequence of bytes received in multiple packets. This sharply decreases the number of ACKs, helping to reduce network clutter.

TCP sports an adaptive retransmission scheme that uses variable time-outs to cope automatically with various network types and conditions. The algorithm in TCP bases the time-out value on the running average of the round-trip delays of the previously transmitted packets. The average is used as the basis of time-out value for each new transmission. If a packet is successfully acknowledged within the allotted time, TCP updates the average and continues with the next packet. Otherwise, it retransmits the packet and waits for an ACK again after doubling the time-out value. This process continues until the maximum retry count is reached, at which point the connection is dropped.

Adaptive retransmission helps to reduce network congestions while increasing throughput. The algorithm automatically adjusts to various load conditions and network speeds and always uses an optimal time-out value. This is important when you consider that TCP must operate on everything from slow serial ports running at 960 bytes/sec all the way up to FDD at over 10 Mbytes/sec. Without adaptive retransmission, you would have to set the time-outs manually for each network type. This would be adequate if the network was always idle and there were no intermediate routers with nondeterministic response times. Given that even local area networks are subject to large variations in response times, the adaptive scheme in TCP is almost a necessity in every environment.

Note that using the correct time-out value can have a significant impact on network performance. If the time-out is set too low, the sender retransmits a packet if the network or the receiving host is too busy to respond in time. Sending a duplicate packet to be processed is the last thing that a busy network or host wants to see. It simply aggravates an already bad situation. On the other hand, if the time-out is set too high, recovery time from packet losses will be too high. This in turn translates to slow response time if packet loss is high (a situation very common in WANs).

A related optimization to the adaptive time-out mechanism is slow start. Once an ACK is received for a retransmitted packet, TCP starts transmission at a slow pace and gradually works its way back to full rate. The assumption is that the retransmission is due to network congestion, and slowing down the transmit rate can help to alleviate it.

8.6 Physical Interfaces

So far we have discussed the operation of the protocol layers without regard to the specific networks involved. Indeed, most of the networking code is written in a way that is independent of the physical network. But from a performance point of view, the various networks in use vary considerably. So, let's look at the a sampling of networks in use in UNIX systems starting with the most poplar, the 10-Mbit Ethernet.

8.6.1 Ethernet

The Ethernet interface began in the early 1980s and quickly gained momentum. Today, the popularity of Ethernet has spread to most tiers of computing thanks to the availability of very-low-cost controller chips (about $15 each as of this writing).

The Ethernet network is based on a concept known as Carrier Sense-Multiple Access/Collision Detection (CSMA/CD). This means that before a station (also called a node) can transmit data, it must first listen to see if any other node is already transmitting. This is necessary because all nodes share the same wires, and if two or more try to transmit at the same time, both of their packets get corrupted. The formal name for this failure is a *collision*.

Once a node detects a collision, it goes into a back-off mode. This requires that the node wait a random amount of time before retransmitting. Standard practice is to pick a pseudo random time (usually based on some interval counter inside the Ethernet chip) and then double the time with each consecutive collision. This is commonly referred to as a binary back-off algorithm.

Note that the collision handling is done entirely at the Ethernet hardware level and the networking software in UNIX does not get involved until the Ethernet chip exhausts its maximum retry count (which can be up to 16 times). If the hardware is unable to transmit the packet, it will notify the kernel in the form of a hardware interrupt. The Ethernet driver fields this interrupt and simply increments an error counter (which can be viewed by running `netstat -s`) and otherwise ignores the error. It is the responsibility of the upper-level networking protocols to retransmit the packet if required. In the case of UDP, the packet will be lost forever. However, protocols such as TCP and NFS retransmit the data resulting in no perceived error at the user level.

8.6.2 Performance Considerations of Ethernet

The Ethernet network has a maximum theoretical speed of 10 Mbits/sec. Due to inherent overhead in each packet (e.g., for destination address and checksums plus a required inter-packet gap), the best achievable throughput is usually around 9 Mbits/sec or 1.1 Mbytes/sec. Note that this assumes zero collisions and only one sender. Although most well-designed UNIX systems have no problem achieving these rates, some low-end PC Ethernet cards run as slow as 0.5 Mbits/sec.

Being a CSMA/CD-type network, Ethernet gets blamed for instability and poor performance under heavy loads. It turns out that in practice this is not the case. A somewhat recent study has shown that even in a worse-case situation (25 concurrent hosts transmitting minimum-sized packets of 64 bytes), the collision rate climbs to only about 10%. This dispels the common myth that the collision rate of Ethernet rises to 50% or more under such loads.

The reason for the low rate is the effective collision detection mechanism in Ethernet. Because each host listens before transmitting, stations simply take turns accessing the wire. The collisions occur only in a small timing window when two hosts try to grab the network at identical times.

Care must be taken in interpreting these data. It is by no means desirable to have 25 hosts transmitting simultaneously. Although the throughput of the Ethernet drops only by the 10% collision rate, the bandwidth available to each host is only 36 Kbytes/sec. No user will tolerate such slow data transfer rates. So, even though the basic Ethernet design is not flawed, its bandwidth is very limiting especially in modern systems where a single host can saturate the entire network.

In general, we recommend that you place only one active Ethernet node (e.g., an NFS server) per Ethernet segment. Any more than this and you are dividing your total bandwidth by the number of active hosts.

8.6.3 FDDI

The FDDI (Fiber Distributed Data Interface) network runs at a peak speed of 100 Mbits/ sec or roughly 12 Mbytes/sec. The original specification called for fiber optic cabling due to its much higher bandwidth and noise immunity. Because fiber optic cabling is considerably more expensive than standard copper cabling, another variation of FDDI known as CDDI (Copper-Distributed Data Interface) allows transmission on high grade (Category five) copper wire. Even so, the cost of FDDI networks remains much higher than Ethernet (due to the increased cost of the controller), which is responsible for its scarcity so long after its introduction.

FDDI uses a token-passing scheme instead of CSMA/CD to arbitrate access to the physical media. Stations can transmit only if they are holding a token, which gets passed around between all the nodes. Token-passing networks degrade more gracefully under heavy loads than CSMA/CD but have higher latencies under light loads because nodes must wait for their turn (token).

Note that unlike Ethernet, we are not aware of any systems that can pump out data continuously at the theoretical FDDI speed of 12 Mbytes/sec. As of this writing, most systems peak out at around 8 Mbytes/sec. In general, FDDI has roughly six to eight times higher throughput than Ethernet. This makes it suitable for environments where large amounts of data are being transferred. Examples include NFS file servers used in data-intensive scientific/visualization areas in addition to Computer Aided Design where file sizes can easily grow to hundreds of megabytes. Although you can use FDDI for less demanding applications, the price/performance will likely be poor due to relatively high investment required for the FDDI connection. As an example, you may be better off buying a local hard disk for an NFS client than giving it a faster, FDDI connection to a remote NFS server.

8.6.4 100-Mbit Ethernet

A recent entry to the high-speed networking world, 100-Mbit Ethernet should gain acceptance much faster than FDDI mostly because of the low cost per station. There are two variations being proposed for adoption: Fast Ethernet and VG-AnyLAN. Support for Fast Ethernet seems much stronger than VG-AnyLAN as of this writing.

Fast Ethernet has many profiles allowing connection, including use of two pairs of Category four wiring or one pair of Category five. There are also provisions for fiber connection, although we expect the demand to be lower in this profile due to the higher cost.

As of this writing, Fast Ethernet adaptors are becoming available for many platforms at unusually low costs. A PCI card, for example, can be purchased for about $200 for PCs, which is also backward-compatible with 10-Mbit Ethernet. Due to the compatibility with existing network, we strongly recommend that you start investing in these dual-standard adaptors instead of saving a few dollars and buying a 10-Mbit card. Another reason for recommending these adaptors is that early benchmarks show that 100-Mbit bus-mastering PCI cards achieve almost 6 Mbytes/sec, almost six times faster than 10-Mbit Ethernet—a major step up.

8.6.5 ISDN

Integrated Service, Digital Network or ISDN networks are slowly becoming popular as a replacement for the standard dial-up phone lines. They provide much higher speeds albeit at a higher cost. The standard ISDN line known as 2B+D provides two ("B") channels of 56 (or sometimes 64) Kbaud plus a low-speed ("D") channel.

Using TCP over ISDN is uneventful because, as we discussed, TCP self-adjusts its time-out mechanism to match the longer round-trip delays. But keep in mind that the link is 100 times slower than Ethernet. So, you may want to compress your files when you move them across ISDN.

If you decide to use NFS over ISDN, take care to set the time-outs correctly. Otherwise, the slower speed will cause heavy retransmissions (see Chapter 9). In addition, ISDN, like all other slow links, can become congested quickly, leading to long and painful delays. So, keep your file transfers to a minimum.

8.7 Networking Applications

As we previously mentioned, the TCP/IP suite also includes a set of user services such as `rlogin`, `rcp`, `rsh`, `telnet`, and `ftp`. These programs usually work in tandem with another daemon (server) process on the remote system.[2] To get a feel for how these programs work, let's take a look at what happens when you run the `rlogin` program.

The main task for `rlogin` is to run programs on a remote system but have the keyboard input and screen output happen on the local system. When you invoke `rlogin`, it opens a TCP connection to a remote server on a specific TCP port for the `rlogin` service. A pro-

---

2. The fancy name for this type of architecture is client-server.

cess known as `inetd` is typically listening for connection requests at this port. Once the connection request is made, `inetd` runs a copy of `/etc/rlogind` process on the remote host and goes back to listening for more connection requests.

On start-up, the remote `rlogind` process creates a pseudo tty and becomes its master. A pseudo tty is a simple terminal loopback inside the kernel. It has two endpoints: a master and a slave. Any data written to the master port appear as input on the slave side. Likewise, any data written to the slave side appear as input on the master side. The `rlogind` process then forks off a shell on the slave pseudo tty port. The pseudo tty fools the shell into thinking that it is dealing with a real serial port. But in reality, the port only exists in the kernel. Any output generated by the shell simply appears on the master port being controlled by `rlogind`.

On the local system, there are two copies of `rlogin` running, one to handle input and another to handle output. When the user types something on the local system, the `rlogin` process associated with input takes the character and transmits it to `rlogind` using the TCP connection. `rlogind` in return writes the character to the master port of the pseudo tty. By doing so, the character instantly appears as input on the slave side of the tty. Once a carriage return is typed, the remote shell (or any other program that is running) sees the entire line as input as if someone had typed it on the remote system. The shell then executes the command and writes its output to the slave port. `rlogind` sees the same data as input on its master port, which it reads and transmits using TCP to the output `rlogin` process. This `rlogin` then displays the data on the local system.

Note that the local `rlogin` process sends each character to the remote system *as it is typed*. This happens regardless of whether the remote process wants them one at a time (i.e., is in `cbreak` or `raw` mode) or not. As a result, every time you type a character on the local system, a TCP packet is generated and transmitted to the remote system. Any echoing required is done by the remote system. In case of the shell, the pseudo tty port is in line-oriented mode causing the remote kernel to echo the character. The returning echo character is read by the `rlogind` process, which transmits it to the local system. Including the required ACKs, *a total of three TCP packets are generated for each character typed on the local system*. Needless to say, this results in tremendous overhead when compared to data coming from a simple serial port connected to the remote system.

The reason for transferring characters one at a time is that the local process has no idea what type of program is running on the remote system. Because some of the programs may require characters one at a time (e.g., `vi`), `rlogin` simply uses the most common denominator of always sending characters as they are typed.

Because the packets involved in transferring user-typed characters back and forth are small (60 bytes each on an Ethernet network), they do not necessarily load up the network. The real problem is that the entire chain of events must happen quickly (less than 50 milliseconds ideally) and predictably. Otherwise, the character echoes will seem sluggish. These conditions are not hard to meet in lightly loaded client and server systems. Things fall apart, however, if, for example, the remote system runs out of memory and swaps out the `rlogind` process. In this case, all terminal input and output seem to cease on the local `rlogin` process. Severe slowdowns could also occur if the round-trip delays of packets become very large, as is usually the case in Wide Area Networks such as the Internet. And just in case you are wondering, the `telnet` program works substantially the same as `rlogin`. So, you will not save anything by using it.

While not much can be done to reduce the overhead of these services, it is useful to be aware of their toll on the system performance in capacity planning. If the majority of your users are remotely logging into a system (e.g., using a terminal server in a database environment), then plan on using a faster CPU with a larger amount of memory. As a general rule, each user logged in through `rlogin` or `telnet` creates about ten times more overhead than a standard serial port.

In general, we do not recommend that you place more than a few hundred `telnet`/`rlogin` users on an otherwise idle 10-Mbit Ethernet network. Take care to also account for an extra memory usage of about 100 Kbytes per user taken for the `rlogind/telnetd` programs (in contrast, there is no memory required for support of serial ports).

8.8 Monitoring the Network with netstat

`netstat` is a one-stop network diagnostic and monitoring tool. To monitor network traffic, use the `-i` option:

```
SunOS4.1% netstat -i
Name  Mtu   Net/Dest    Address       Ipkts    Ierrs Opkts   Oerrs Collis  Queue
le0   1500  sun-ether   mt            48629676 3     25223689 24    1304610 0
le1   1500  mt3-ether   mt3           60063575 53    62443204 3     1188459 0
le2   1500  mt4-ether   mt4           87832075 48    56973686 25    739473  0
le3   1500  hp-ether    mt0           54941349 3     106958938 12   836709  0
lo0   1536  loopback    localhost     3236400  0     3236400  0     0       0
```

The output shows the list of available networks (**Name**), their Maximum Transmission Unit (**Mtu**), and the total network statistics since system start-up. The latter is broken up into the total number of packets received (**Ipkts**), input errors (**Ierrs**), output packets (**Opkts**), output transmission errors (**Oerrs**), transmission collision rate (**Collis**), and number of dropped packets due to the IP queue being full (**Queue**).

The network **Name** is predefined by the kernel (really the network driver). It typically indicates the driver name (`le` in our case) along with the unit number. The designator, `lo0`, is the loopback driver. It is used to simulate a network connection within the same system. This lets you, for example, `rlogin` to your own system. Other services such as NFS and X Window also use this connection. Refer to the chapters covering these topics for the performance implications of the loopback connection.

The input and output packet counts are the number of packets transmitted or received. This information is useful in determining which one of the networks (if there are more than one) is the busiest and potentially needs attention. Unfortunately, there are no statistics kept on the packet length, type, or peak rate, making these data much less useful than they could be.

Input errors is a catch-all, implementation-dependent field that is used to count anything that leads to a packet being thrown away. This includes lack of network buffer memory, packet length errors (e.g., a packet whose size is smaller than the minimum Ethernet packet size), and failure of other network-specific consistency errors. Input packet errors should be very small, preferably zero. Otherwise, it could be a sign of packet corruption by routers or gateways or a shortage of network buffers.

Output error count is also very implementation-dependent. It is generally the number of times the interface controller refused to transmit a packet due to an error of some kind. For example, in the case of the popular Lance Ethernet controller (`le` in Sun Systems), this could include loss of carrier, maximum retry count (16) exceeded on collision, or time-out on a memory (DMA) transfer. In practice, output errors occur due to faulty network transceivers, wiring, or other severe problems. As with input errors, this field should be zero or close to it.

The **Collis** column shows an estimate of the number of collisions experienced by an Ethernet network. If the collision rate is above 1%, it indicates that there are multiple active nodes on the network, which is something you should avoid. In our sample output, the `le0` Ethernet segment experiences a high collision rate of 5%.

The queue full field indicates the number of times a packet was dropped due to the IP queue being full. Despite being very useful, the count is maintained only by the Serial Line IP (SLIP) layer. Especially absent are statistics for Ethernet and higher-speed networks. This means that, in practice, this field will always be zero unless you are using SLIP. Perhaps for this reason, most vendors have removed this field from their `netstat` display. The exception is SGI IRIX, which not only maintains the count but also shows what the maximum IP queue size is set to if you use the `-iq` option:

```
iris6 1% /usr/etc/netstat -iq
Name Mtu   Network     Address          Ipkts Ierrs    Opkts Oerrs q max drop
ec0  1500  mt3-ether   iris6           660060     6   726460     0  0 50   0
lo0  8304  loopback    localhost       236063     0   236063     0  0  0   0
```

Here, the maximum IP queue length is shown as 50 under **max** and the current number of entries waiting, and the number dropped due to the queue being full under the **q** and **drop** columns, respectively.

8.8.1 Real-Time Network Monitoring

If you specify a time interval along with `-i`, `netstat` starts with the summary information followed continuously by per-interval statistics:

```
SunOS4.1% netstat -i 3
```

```
    input   (1e3)      output           input  (Total)    output
packets errs   packets errs   colls  packets errs  packets errs  colls
55058106 3       107156829 12      836776 256361557 108   256521680 65     4111659
16       0    23       0     0      310     0     304     0     0
10       0    22       0     0      244     0     244     0     0
```

By default, the display includes only the packet traffic for the first network configured in the system (1e3 in our example) and the sum total for all (under **Total**). To see the statistics for other networks, use the -I option:

```
SunOS4.1% netstat -I le0 -i 2
    input   (1e0)      output           input  (Total)    output
packets errs   packets errs   colls  packets errs  packets errs  colls
49217610 3       25659224 24      1324178 256374053 108   256534722 65     4111877
32       0    25       0     0      86      0     85      0     0
18       0    11       0     0      53      0     53      0     0
```

The two **errs** fields under the input and output columns are identical to **Ierrs** and **Oerrs** discussed earlier. Similarly, the **colls** column is the same as the **Collis** field.

8.8.2 Network Summary Information

The kernel networking code maintains many other statistics, which can be viewed by netstat using the -s option. The output is fairly long but is broken nicely into specific protocols. Let's start by looking at the IP statistics:

```
SunOS 4.1% netstat -s | more +/ip
ip:
        32178708 total packets received
        0 bad header checksums
        0 with size smaller than minimum
        0 with data size < data length
        0 with header length < data size
        0 with data length < header length
        1297451 fragments received
        0 fragments dropped (dup or out of space)
        25 fragments dropped after timeout
        1339201 packets forwarded
        0 packets not forwardable
        0 redirects sent
        0 ip input queue drops
```

The **fragments dropped after time-out** field indicates that IP could not reassemble a fragmented packet on receipt. Some of the packets were never received causing IP to drop the rest. This has a large impact on NFS performance, which heavily relies on fragmentation (its transfer size is roughly 9000 bytes—higher than the MTU of most networks).

Another useful piece of data is **ip input queue drops.** This counts the number of times a packet was dropped by the network driver because the IP maximum queue size (**ipqmax-len**) had been reached.

Most of the other IP fields are consistency checks and should be zero. Other values could be a sign of data corruption by intermediate routers or gateways.

The next piece of data to look at is the UDP statistics. Here the most important field is the number of socket overflows:

```
SunOS4.1% netstat -s
udp:
        0 incomplete headers
        0 bad data length fields
        0 bad checksums
        264 socket overflows
```

As you can see from the sample output, the socket overflow count is nonzero. Because NFS is the main user of UDP, refer to Chapter 9 to see what can be done to remedy this situation. The other fields indicate consistency errors in the received packets and should be zero. Otherwise, data corruption is occurring in the network with the possible cause being faulty routers and gateways. Resolve these problems before addressing performance issues.

The TCP statistics are very verbose, keeping track of many events:

```
SunOS4.1% netstat -s |more +/tcp

...skipping
tcp:
        1782440 packets sent
                911432 data packets (132971195 bytes)
                16185 data packets (655547 bytes) retransmitted
                486378 ack-only packets (462831 delayed)
                90 URG only packets
                382 window probe packets
                358154 window update packets
                9819 control packets
        2141257 packets received
                767663 acks (for 132969417 bytes)
                6498 duplicate acks
                0 acks for unsent data
                1722716 packets (606838567 bytes) received in-sequence
                12070 completely duplicate packets (3179069 bytes)
                461 packets with some dup. data (36576 bytes duped)
                7963 out-of-order packets (2014807 bytes)
                30 packets (23 bytes) of data after window
                23 window probes
                3197 window update packets
                116 packets received after close
                1 discarded for bad checksum
                0 discarded for bad header offset fields
                0 discarded because packet too short
        3026 connection requests
        3500 connection accepts
        6406 connections established (including accepts)
```

```
     6935 connections closed (including 151 drops)
     166 embryonic connections dropped
     732411 segments updated rtt (of 750451 attempts)
     16445 retransmit timeouts
             26 connections dropped by rexmit timeout
     28 persist timeouts
     488 keepalive timeouts
             333 keepalive probes sent
             36 connections dropped by keepalive
```

Before getting into the details of the important fields, we should point out that the performance of TCP is not nearly as important as UDP and IP. TCP is used only by the r commands and X windows, none of which rely on sustained, long-term traffic. Nevertheless, problems experienced by the TCP protocol are an indication of the overall health of the network so they merit some consideration.

The **retransmit time-outs** indicates the number of times a packet failed after the second or more retries. Because the count excludes the first retry attempt, even small counts indicate some amount of network congestion.

You may also want to look at the number of data packets retransmitted. The ratio of these packets to **packets sent** should be less than 1%, although you may not have much control over this parameter if you are using busy WANs such as the Internet (the sample output was extracted from an Internet gateway).

As with the other protocols, TCP performs a number of consistency checks on its received packets, the results of which are reflected in the discarded packet statistics. Once again, all these fields should be zero or you have a faulty or conjested network.

8.9 The ping Command

While the `ping` utility is usually used to see if some remote host is alive, it also has uses in performance monitoring. `ping` operates by sending an ICMP echo packet to a remote host and waiting for a response. Once the response arrives, `ping` prints out the round-trip delay. By looking at how long it takes for a response to come back, you get a quick view of the network (and remote host's) response time.

The syntax for `ping` is very simple. Just specify the host name of the machine that you want to ping along with the -s option (some systems such as DEC UNIX default to -s; check with the `ping` manual page):

```
SunOS4.1% ping -s wy
PING wy: 56 data bytes
64 bytes from wy (192.9.224.121): icmp_seq=0. time=2. ms
64 bytes from wy (192.9.224.121): icmp_seq=1. time=2. ms
64 bytes from wy (192.9.224.121): icmp_seq=2. time=2. ms
```

```
^C
----wy PING Statistics----
3 packets transmitted, 3 packets received, 0% packet loss
round-trip (ms)  min/avg/max = 2/2/2
```

As you see in the sample output, `ping` runs indefinitely until you interrupt it (with control-c in our example), at which point it prints a summary of its statistics (you could also specify a count instead of interrupting `ping` manually). The response time, shown after **time=**, is typically 1–2 milliseconds on Ethernet networks. Higher values are usually seen on slower networks (e.g., 1.44-Mbit T1 links). Note that anything higher than about 30 milliseconds means that your `rlogin/telnet` sessions will be noticeably slow (we use the 30-millisecond number instead of 50 because there is one more packet involved in an `rlogin/telnet` session than the simple echo in `ping`).

Another piece of data to look for is the variations in response time. Specifically, there should be little difference between **min**, **avg**, and **max** (i.e., low standard deviation). In addition, the packet loss percentage should be zero. Higher values indicate routers or gateways that are dropping packets.

8.10 Monitoring Burst Response Using spray

As the name somewhat implies, `spray` is designed to generate network traffic on demand. You have full flexibility in choosing the packet length, the delay between packets, and the total number of packets to be transmitted. This makes `spray` very useful in detecting whether a network, together with a remote host, can handle large volumes of data. `spray` can also be used to see how a networked application behaves under very high network load by simulating background traffic.

Before using `spray`, *we should caution you that forcing packets onto a network can in some situations cause applications to fail (e.g., due to NFS time-outs from an overwhelmed NFS server). So, only use spray in a nonproduction environment where loss of data is not critical.*

The simplest way to run spray is by just specifying a host name. `spray` will then continuously send the default packet of 86 bytes to the remote machine:

```
sunshine# spray venus
sending 1162 packets of lnth 86 to venus ...
        in 0.8 seconds elapsed time,
        287 packets (24.70%) dropped
Sent:    1449 packets/sec, 121.7K bytes/sec
Rcvd:    1091 packets/sec, 91.7K bytes/sec
```

The key field is the number of packets **dropped** (24.7% in our example). Ideally, you should see zero packets dropped. But in practice, the loss can be high if the sender (running `spray`) is much faster than the remote host.

While the default packet size is fine for checking interactive (e.g., `rlogin` and X window) response, you should use larger packet sizes to test NFS servers. This is done by using the `-l` option:

```
SunOS4.1% spray -l 1024 id2
sending 97 packets of lnth 1026 to id2 ...
        in 0.1 seconds elapsed time,
        no packets dropped
        1067 packets/sec, 1069.5K bytes/sec
```

In this example, the sender is a Sun SPARCstation 2 and the remote host is a much faster Sun SPARCstation 10. As a result, not only is the packet loss zero, but the throughput of 1069.5K is superb for our (unloaded) Ethernet network. Note that it usually does not make sense to send packets larger than the MTU of the network because doing so results in a mixture of packets being sent due to IP fragmentation (unless, of course, the length is a multiple of MTU).

8.11 Network Optimization Basics

Let's start by stating the most important rule about network performance:

The fastest network is one that is not being used!

The reason for such a bold statement is that even the fastest network is going to be orders of magnitude slower than the system memory and, in some cases, the disk drive. As you recall, fetching data from a remote host across FDDI runs at a slow pace of only 6–8 Mbytes/sec. Compare this to the 80–100 Mbyte/sec rate memory speed of even low-end PCs, and you quickly realize that the network can be a real bottleneck if not used carefully. The situation is, of course, much more grim in the case of very high-performance systems and the slow, 1-Mbyte/sec Ethernet, which is four to eight times slower than the data rate of a modern disk drive. So the key in network optimization is to reduce the usage of the network itself because anytime the CPU waits on it, the application performance drops by a large factor.

Needless to say, before trying to optimize your network, make sure that it is indeed the bottleneck. We find that people are quick to blame the network for performance problems instead of actually analyzing the situation. So be sure to monitor the other system resources before worrying about the networking subsystem. As a case in point, memory shortages could easily dwarf any network bottlenecks.

Yet another false network performance problem is faulty wiring and interfacing. While most of these low-level, physical problems lead to total network failures, some manifest themselves as poor performance. For example, a poorly terminated Thinnet Ethernet network can cause heavy packet losses. But if you are using NFS or TCP, these protocols automatically retransmit the packets until they eventually succeed. Because this happens after many, long time-outs, the result is a network that appears slow even when it is being lightly used. To detect these problems, look at the low-level checksum failures with `netstat` or a LAN analyzer.

The key to good network performance is minimization of packet traffic and latency. This is best done as part of the planning effort before a network is initially set up. Try to think of the possible uses of the network in advance because reconfiguring the network later can be painful and disruptive (and, as a result, gets postponed indefinitely). Keep in mind that it does not take much to destroy the balance of a network completely. A simple act of moving a few files from a client to an NFS server can substantially increase network traffic, causing a major slowdown for all the existing users. So, plan changes to the network as carefully as the initial design.

8.12 Breaking Up a Network to Improve Performance

Dividing a network into multiple independent segments can improve network throughput by increasing the maximum potential bandwidth. For example, by breaking up a single 10-Mbit Ethernet network into four segments, you quadruple the maximum bandwidth available to you to 40 Mbits/sec. This is perhaps the most powerful technique in dealing with a saturated network.

The main drawback to breaking up a network is that you must find a way of connecting the segments so that you still have full connectivity. The most common techniques follow.

- **Repeaters**. These devices connect two segments, but because every packet is transmitted from one segment to the other, *no performance gain is achieved*. As such, repeaters should be used only to physically extend a network (e.g., between buildings using optical repeaters).

- **Bridges**. The classical bridge simply gets around the physical (length or node) limitations of a network by taking every packet from one network and transmitting it on another. The device interprets the physical layer data and, hence, is independent of the protocol involved. This type of bridge provides no performance enhancements because the traffic is not isolated to a specific network. These bridges should be used only with protocols that do not support routing. Because IP already includes routing capability, standard bridges are not a good choice in UNIX networks.

- **Hub**. This device simply converts a bus-based network such as Ethernet into a star configuration. This process removes the reliability problems that you run into with bus-mode configurations where one faulty node can bring down the entire network. The most common hub solution is 10BaseT, which allows twisted-pair cabling to be used to interconnect the various Ethernet nodes. Like bridges, hubs do nothing to lower the overall traffic so its use is primarily for reliability (and, in some cases, solving physical length restrictions).

- **Learning or Smart Bridges**. These devices keep track of the nodes on each network and, over time, learn where each packet needs to go. As such, packets destined for the local network segment are not retransmitted on the alternate segment. Because the network traffic on each segment is localized, the total available bandwidth is increased. The drawback to these devices is that, if not configured correctly, the network is subject to packet storms and loops. In addition, the configuration protocol is often proprietary, forcing you to stay with one vendor in some cases.

- **Ethernet Switch or Switching Hub.** This is a variation on the standard hub where the device can actually filter some of the packets between nodes. This is usually done by taking a multiport hub and dividing it into separate virtual networks/circuits. A packet transmitted by a node in one virtual net can only be received by nodes in the same group. The result is an increase in total bandwidth proportional to the number of virtual networks. As with learning bridges, the protocol for configuring these devices is usually proprietary.

- **Dedicated Routers.** These devices handle packet movement between the networks at the protocol layer. Unlike bridges and switching hubs that for example look at the Ethernet destination address to figure out where to send a packet, routers look at the protocol-specific data to find the destination. In the case of TCP/IP, the router decodes the IP header in order to find out whether the packet should be transmitted on the alternate segment (called a subnet in this scheme). This means that packets destined for other nodes on the same segment as the receiver stay in the same segment. As such, routers do increase the overall bandwidth by localizing traffic on the individual segments.

   The drawback to routers is that, because of the additional processing required for each packet, they tend to either run slower than learning bridges or switch hubs or be more expensive for equivalent performance. This is offset by the fact that routers can be configured using standard protocols (such as SNMP). In addition, routers do not suffer from packet storms or other similar problems and, as such, are excellent building blocks for enterprise-wide networking solutions.

- **UNIX Routers.** Because of the inherent routing capabilities of IP, standard UNIX systems can and are used heavily as routers. The virtues of this solution are also the source of its problems. Even though any old machine with two network interfaces can be used as a router, the performance of these systems leaves something to be desired. You need a fairly fast CPU along with optimized Ethernet hardware to provide low latency packet routing under UNIX. For example, on an Ethernet network, the routing rate must match the worst case situation of 15,000 packets per second. A 486 PC with an ISA bus controller will not even be able to achieve half this rate. On the other extreme, a SPARCstation 10 or a Pentium PC with Localbus Ethernet cards can easily run at these speeds. The other problems with using a UNIX router, namely reliability and start-up time, are harder to solve. UNIX systems tend to have more things that can go wrong with them (e.g., hard disks that crash) and recovery time from a system crash can be lengthy. On the plus side, a UNIX router can also be used to run applications such as NFS but, then again, that may slow down its routing performance.

No matter which solution you pick, make sure that cross traffic between the segments is minimal, especially if you use a router. Specifically, the hosts in a subnet need to be selected carefully so that they primarily communicate with each other and not with hosts on other segments. An example would be an R&D organization where the hardware and software development teams are in two subnets.[3]

If the isolation principle of subnets is not obeyed, network performance can suffer greatly. Indeed, a cluster of subnets may actually run slower than a single, larger network. To see why, consider that, even assuming an infinitely fast router, the transmission of a packet from a host on one subnet to another on a different subnet will always be twice as long as a single segment (because the packet must be transmitted twice: once on the local subnet and, the second time, on the remote subnet). Given the fact that real-life routers do not have zero latencies, you need to be even more careful in how you use your subnets. As a general rule,

> *if more than 30% of the packets in one subnet is destined for another, you are better off combining the two.*

So subdivide your network only if most of the traffic can be localized in the specific segments/subnets. You should do this analysis at the planning stage because finding this problem (at least with UNIX tools) can be rather difficult. Avoid common mistakes such as placing NFS clients and servers on different segments. If you do need to allow clients to access a common NFS server from multiple subnets, make sure that your server sits on all the subnets (by adding more network interfaces to it). That way, the packets would not need to be routed between the subnets to get to the server.

8.13 Performance Summary

- There are two major types of networking services available in UNIX: UDP and TCP. UDP provides a connectionless and unreliable transport mechanism, whereas TCP guarantees data delivery.

- Sockets are a standard mechanism to interact with the networking subsystem but consume a high amount of CPU time due to copying of user data in and out of the kernel.

- UDP checksuming, although desired, is turned off in some systems for the sake of CPU efficiency.

---

3. Assuming the typical organization where hardware and software people do not talk to each other!

- The IP protocol, which the network drivers interact with, is the layer below TCP and UDP. Its main function is packet buffer and routing. To reduce memory usage, IP drops packets once its queue becomes full.

- The TCP protocol sports sophisticated, adaptive error recovery and flow control, allowing it to deal with varying network speeds and loads.

- The Ethernet network, although more robust than first thought, is too slow at 10 Mbits/sec to satisfy the needs of modern computer systems.

- FDDI, although faster than Ethernet, has received lukewarm reception because of the much higher cost of fiber optic cable and adaptors.

- 100-Mbit Fast Ethernet promises what FDDI could not deliver. A fast replacement for 10-Mbit Ethernet on the desktop. It does this with excellent performance and very low cost.

- ISDN, although relatively slow at 128 Kbits/sec, is still much faster than typical modem dial-up speeds. Its acceptance has increased sharply recently because of widespread use of the Web.

- Networking applications such as `rlogin` provide their magic by using a client-server architecture. A daemon on the remote system fools application programs into thinking that they are interacting with serial ports. Although the magic works effectively, it does so at very high CPU cost resulting from per-character handling of input data.

- `netstat` is the main monitoring tool in UNIX and can be used to detect the collision rate of Ethernet networks. Any rate higher than 1% should be investigated. The `-s` option can be used to find UDP socket overflows that harm NFS performance.

- The `ping` and `spray` can be used to check the response time of networks and remote servers.

- Your main option for increasing network performance is to subdivide your networks. Routers and switching hubs provide the best solution in this area.

CHAPTER 9

NFS Architecture and Optimization Techniques

The Network File System (NFS) protocol was designed by Sun Microsystems to allow almost transparent file access across a network. The motivation came from the proliferation of workstations and their accompanying administrative overhead and cost. The NFS designers chose what could be called a 99% solution in providing transparent access to remote files compared to local hard disks. Full compatibility was compromised to a small extent in order to get higher performance (more on this later).

Even though NFS was designed to be portable and able to run on a range of operating systems, it has enjoyed a majority of its success on UNIX platforms. NFS uses the UDP protocol and is most commonly used on top of Ethernet, although it has no dependency on it. To understand the performance implications of NFS, we first need to look at how the protocol works.

9.1 The Basics

The first thing to note about NFS is that it is not a single protocol but a suite of protocols working in tandem. The suite consists of RPC and XDR layers operating on top of UDP/IP. The RPC or Remote Procedure Call layer is both an error-free communication mechanism and a programming interface. The interface provided is in the form of simple function calls, and hence the name Remote *Procedure Call*. The eXternal Data Representation (XDR) layer translates the arguments passed to the remote system and the data returned to a common format so that binary data can be interchanged between machines with different byte ordering and number representation. In addition to emulating the function call interface, the RPC layer is responsible for error recovery so that requests and their responses are guaranteed (within reason) to reach their destinations.

The NFS protocol is simply a set of (14) RPC calls that a compliant NFS server must support. The calls resemble typical file system operations such as `open`, `close`, `creat`, `remove`, and `mount`.

The NFS protocol is said to be stateless, which means that the server does not keep track of requests made by the clients. The implication is that every request must be self-contained. This is in sharp contrast to local file operations, which are very stateful. For example, when you read a file on a local hard disk, the kernel maintains an internal seek pointer, which tells it where the next read operation should occur. In the case of NFS, the server does not maintain the seek pointer, and it is the responsibility of the client to send the seek pointer along with each read request to the NFS server.

The stateless nature of the NFS server makes crash recovery trivial because the server does not lose any data when it reboots. On the other hand, the lack of state breaks certain UNIX semantics. The best example is file locking, which restricts access to certain portions of a file. This operation has to be performed by the server because clients do not talk to each other and, therefore, cannot find out if anyone else has a portion of a file locked. Because of the lack of state on the server, standard file locking does not operate across NFS. Sun's solution to this problem is an external process called the lock manager, which clients have to communicate with to perform this function. Although this solves the functionality requirements of locking, the performance characteristics leave something to be desired because all lock requests are processed by a slow remote process.

9.2 RPC Performance Considerations

Even though the NFS RPC code is able to deal with network errors, its retry mechanism is not nearly as sophisticated as those in TCP. Basically, RPC sends out a request and then waits for an ACK. The initial time-out value is based on the `timeo` parameter specified when the NFS partition is mounted. If an ACK is received before the time-out expires, RPC retransmits the request and repeats the process after doubling the time-out value (using exponential back-off). The maximum number of retries is determined by another mount parameter, `retrans`.

Although TCP adjusts its time-out value depending on the average round-trip delay on the specific connection, the initial time-out value in RPC is fixed. In addition, RPC lacks the slow-start mechanism after time-out.

The rigid time-out and lack of slow-start means that NFS is not the best protocol to use on slow or congested networks. Specifically, WANs, which are subject to long and variable delays, make poor transports for NFS. Studies have shown that running NFS on top of TCP (which is rarely available) does indeed produce better throughput under adverse conditions. So, unless you are desperate, we do not recommend that you run NFS over a WAN.

As with all error recovery procedures, it is possible for a slow server to get duplicate packets if it does not respond within the time-out period. Unlike TCP, early NFS implementations did not detect this and actually performed the operation twice. The assumption was that there was no harm in repeating these operations because all file operations are idempotent (i.e., can be repeated without harm). This turns out not to be true. Even though you can, for example, write the same file block twice, it is certainly not correct to remove the same file twice. The second invocation would result in an error because the file does not exist.

Note that, in addition to causing incorrect operations, duplicating requests causes additional load on the server and the network. Because a late ACK is a sign of a busy server or network, sending duplicate requests in such an environment is only going to make matters worse.

Fortunately, the majority of NFS implementations today have a request cache that keeps track of recently completed RPC operations. This allows the server to check for duplicate requests. If a match is found, the request is thrown away. Note that the cache holds only the requests for a short period of time (a few seconds). This would allow it to detect similar operations that are done intentionally. Going back to our previous example, if you remove a file and then repeat the operation a few minutes later, you would indeed expect to get a "file not found" error. If the cache were kept valid forever, the second request would incorrectly succeed.

Note that, strictly speaking, the request cache violates the stateless nature of the NFS protocol because the server is now keeping track of history. But unlike other kinds of state information, losing the request cache (due to a reboot for example) is not catastrophic. The worst that can happen is that the server performs a few duplicate requests before its cache gets updated.

9.3 Impact of the NFS Block Size

To maximize network efficiency, NFS by default uses an 8-Kbyte block size (you can use the `rsize` and `wsize` options of the `mount` command to change the block size for reads and writes, respectively). Note that the block size is somewhat independent of the actual read and write system calls issued by user processes on the client machine. For example, if the user process requests 1 Kbyte to be read, the NFS client actually issues an 8-Kbyte request to the server. Once the data arrive (into a buffer cache data block), the kernel copies the first kilobyte to the user process and holds the rest in a buffer. Follow-on read requests are satisfied out of the buffer (cache) until there is a need for another block, at which point another 8 Kbytes of data are read from the server.

The large block size substantially increases throughput *on networks with very low error rates* such as an unloaded Ethernet network. On other networks, however, the larger block size can significantly work against you. The problem stems from the fact that few network interfaces are able to deal with 8-Kbyte packets. As you recall, the IP layer breaks up any request passed to it that exceeds the MTU of the network in question. In the case of Ethernet, IP breaks the NFS RPC request into six fragmented packets because the MTU of Ethernet is 1500 bytes. Imagine what happens if any of the fragments get lost. Because IP is not able to reassemble the original packet, it drops all the remaining fragments. This causes a time-out at the RPC layer *and retransmission of the entire 8-Kbyte packet,* even though only a small segment of it was actually lost.

This problem has rather severe implications in practice, stemming from the fact that packets typically get lost because of network congestion. Because losing one packet leads to six more being retransmitted, NFS manages to increase network congestion substantially at the worst possible time. The retransmission potentially leads to more congestion, which causes more packets to be lost and so on. Even though the exponential back-off and eventual termination of the request (in error) does allow the network to recover, it may happen too late. In sharp contrast, services using TCP (e.g., `ftp`) do not suffer from this problem because TCP itself breaks up the request into segments, and the retransmission is based on segments and not entire blocks.

Even though the typical lightly loaded Ethernet network loses fairly few packets, the same cannot be said of the slow WANs that run much slower than Ethernet. Their low speed causes them to become congested sooner and suffer more because of the avalanche effect mentioned previously. The only cure is to decrease the read and write block sizes (see Section 9.9.2 on how to tune the NFS block size for your network).

9.4 NFS Caching

One of the early goals of NFS was to provide comparable performance to local hard disks. This was a noble goal and rather feasible in the early 1980s when the typical file system throughput was only 200 to 400 Kbytes/sec on a local disk (and well within the ability of the Ethernet network to handle). Even so, achieving this goal was difficult given high network latencies and protocol overhead. If every block had to be fetched from the server, the throughput would be far lower than a local disk. The solution was to allow clients to cache most data they read from the server. The caching aspects of NFS have been a key to NFS's success despite the ever-increasing performance of UNIX systems and essentially constant speed of the typical Ethernet network.

There are two basic levels of caching in NFS: file and directory attributes plus file contents. As with most caches, consistency is the critical component. So, let's take a look at how each one of these caches works and how they solve this problem.

9.4.1 Attribute Caching

One of the most frequent operations in UNIX is inode access and manipulation. For example, when you run `ls -l`, there is a `stat` system call executed on every file name in the current directory. The `stat` system call simply returns the inode structure to `ls` allowing it to display all the file or directory attributes. Other `stat`-intensive applications include `make` and `find`.

Nondirectory operations can also require frequent inode manipulations. For example, on a local file system, every read to a file causes the access time in the inode to be updated. This is a fast operation because it involves updating the specific field in the in-core inode data structure, which requires no disk I/O. In NFS, however, the inode for the file resides on the remote server. Without some kind of caching, every read operation requires an RPC request to update the inode access time. Needless to say, this would be rather slow.

The solution to these performance problems is the attribute cache. The NFS clients are allowed to retain inode information for any remote files or directory that they access. This means that after the first (slow) access to an inode, follow-on operations run much faster. Given the commonality of many UNIX file names, the cache has a fairly high hit ratio.

The problem with caching inodes is that the data could become stale if another client modifies the same inode on the server. Without any kind of invalidation, the local client continues to see the old data. The solution in NFS is to limit the amount of time that a client can keep an attribute in its cache. The default is to cache file attributes for a minimum of 3 seconds, but it can be changed by using the `mount` parameter, **acregmin**. Directory attributes are cached for a longer period of 30 seconds by default and, likewise, can be changed by using the `mount` parameter, **acdirmin**.

The caching time is extended if a file or directory attribute is modified by the same client. The time extension is limited by the **acregmax** parameter for regular files (with a default of 60 seconds) and by the **acdirmax** parameter for directories (which also defaults to 60 seconds). The idea here is that if a client is accessing a file inode now, it will likely do so again in the near future.

Because there is no mechanism to invalidate a cache entry if it has been modified on the server, it is possible to get into compatibility problems. This shows up when, for example, you edit a file on one client and then try to compile it using `make` on another. Quite often, `make` does nothing because it thinks that file has not been modified. The reason for this inconsistency is that the first client (running the editor) has cached the file attribute and has not flushed (written) it to the server.

To get around the attribute caching problems, you can use the `noac` flag when mounting an NFS file system. This totally disables attribute caching on the client, which addresses the compatibility problem. *But keep in mind that this option significantly increases the load on the server while at the same time lowering the throughput on the local client.* The option should be used only if concurrent updates are made to the same set of files on a frequent basis. A better work-around may be to set the attribute cache times to a small value. This way, the changes make their way to the server quickly but without substantially compromising performance.

9.4.2 File Data Caching

Even though attribute caching is very helpful, the bulk of data being exchanged between a server and client is file contents. To speed up these requests, NFS allows clients to use their buffer cache to store data read from the server. This results in a substantial performance boost because the high hit ratio of the buffer cache hides the long latencies of accessing a remote server.

Again, because the data are being cached on the local client, there is a possibility that the client data could get out of sync with the server. To solve this, NFS checks the attribute cache for a file before trusting the contents of the buffer cache. If the modification time in the attribute cache is later than the time the data block was cached, an RPC read request is sent to the server, and the cache block is invalidated. Because the attribute cache can get out of sync for 3 seconds by default, so can the contents of the files. So, if you modify a file on one client, it takes 3 seconds by default for the change to appear on the server.

Note that the server always returns the file attributes along with any read data to the client. These are used to update the client attribute cache and are helpful in keeping the attribute cache more up to date. In addition, the update helps to limit the amount of time the buffer cache of the client stays out of sync with the server.

Unlike read, the write treatment in NFS is quite harsh when compared to local file systems. Instead of delaying them, client write data must be sent to the server synchronously and be written to the remote server's disk before a process can continue execution. This is done to make sure that other clients can see the write data quickly and that the data are on a stable storage (i.e., disk rather than memory) before the process goes away. This is more time-consuming than it would seem at first glance. Not only does the client have to send an RPC request for each write operation, but the server is obligated to flush the file inode and any indirect blocks in addition to the write data itself. *This means that each client write request translates to two or three disk requests on the server.* This is in sharp contrast to local writes, which get delayed and do not need to be written to disk for a while (if ever).

To lessen the impact of slow writes, a special process known as `biod` (`nfsiod` in DEC UNIX) is created at system start-up, which acts as an agent for the process doing the write request. So, instead of forcing the process to wait, the request is handed to `biod`, which handles the transfer and the wait for response. Meanwhile, the process can continue execution.

By running more than one copy of biod, you allow more asynchronous writes to occur simultaneously. For example, if you are using four biod processes, the client can have at most five outstanding write requests (four handled by biods and the last one by the process itself).

Another optimization is to allow partial writes (less than a full block or typically 8192 bytes) to stay in the client entirely (i.e., delayed writes are used just like the local file systems). To lower the chances of getting too far out of sync with the server, any partial write buffers are written to the server when the file is closed.

Note that the biods also help speed up read requests. This has to do with the way normal sequential file access is done in the kernel. To increase drive throughput, the kernel reads ahead sequential blocks. For example, if you try to read block two after reading block one, the kernel anticipates that you will be reading block three next and starts that disk read before the request arrives from the user. This overlaps the read of the next block with the processing of the previous one, which increases throughput. When reading NFS files, the biod process handles the read-ahead block, which provides a similar kind of concurrency that you would get when accessing local drives.

Note that even though the biods increase the utilization of the client CPU, they do little to speed the write requests themselves. On a very write-intensive application (e.g., a simple cp command writing to an NFS file system), the biods quickly back up, waiting for the server to finish. The throughput in that case is simply a function of turn-around time for each request. This results in rather dismal throughput figures. *On a typical Ethernet network, the write throughput is around 200 Kbytes/sec or almost one fifth of the maximum network bandwidth.* If you, on the other hand, use rcp to copy the same data around, the throughput easily would be four to five times higher! This brings us to the most important rule in this chapter:

> *NFS should not be used for write-intensive applications.*

At its current rate, NFS write speed over Ethernet is more than ten times lower than local hard disks. Therefore, from a performance point of view, you are much better off adding a hard disk to a client than using space on a remote server. This especially makes sense for directories such as /tmp, which are constantly being modified with temporary files.

Some vendors have capitalized on this major deficiency in NFS performance. Legato Systems, for example, sells an NFS accelerator called PRESTOSERVE, which captures write requests into a battery-backed RAM buffer and immediately sends an ACK to the client. The requests are then written gradually (in the background) on the server. This turns NFS writes into delayed writes (on the server), which are substantially faster as far as the client is concerned. In addition, the bursty nature of NFS traffic means that the small (2 Mbytes typically) RAM is sufficient for good performance in most environments. The battery back-up more or less guarantees that the data are safe even if there is a power failure, thus preserving the spirit of the NFS design.

9.5 Server Processing

When NFS RPC requests arrive at the server, a special process known as `nfsd` is listening for them. `nfsd` is a system process that, like `biod`, spends all its time in the kernel. UDP wakes up `nfsd` when there is any data for it to process. The `nfsd` process then calls the routine in the kernel to handle the specific RPC request.

Just as with `biod`, you can have more than one copy of `nfsd` running in the system. This provides more concurrency in processing NFS requests, which is important because a single server may have to handle requests from many clients simultaneously. By allowing separate threads of execution in the kernel, the CPU processing of the requests can happen concurrently with the I/O requests. In addition, if any requests can be satisfied out of the server cache, it can be processed without having to wait for a previous request that involved disk I/O.

9.6 Monitoring NFS Performance Using nfsstat

`nfsstat`, which is the main tool for monitoring NFS performance, shows the generic RPC statistics in addition to detailed information about the specific RPC requests used by NFS. Both pieces of data are further broken down into client (requests this host has made to a remote server) and server (NFS requests serviced by this host).

Note that it only makes sense to look at the server information if the command is run on an NFS server. Likewise, there is no need to look at the server statistics on a client-only system. Because `nfsstat` cannot gather information from remote systems, you must run it manually on each host to collect overall statistics for the network.

Without any options, `nfsstat` prints the RPC and NFS statistics for both the client and the server. Because few systems act as both a client and a server, it is usually more appropriate to use either `-c` or `-s` option to narrow the display to client or server, respectively. Another useful option is `-z`, which zeroes out all the (kernel) RPC and NFS statistics. This lets you set a reference point before running a benchmark or work load. Yet another useful option is `-m`, which displays some of the `mount` parameters along with the round-trip response time for some specific RPC commands.

9.6.1 Client-Side Statistics

As we mentioned, the `-c` option shows the client-side information:

```
SunOS4.1% nfsstat -c

Client rpc:
calls     badcalls retrans  badxid   timeout  wait     newcred  timers
1122059   81       249      13       324      0        0        2534

Client nfs:
```

calls	badcalls	nclget	nclsleep			
1121974	4	1121594	0			
null	getattr	setattr	root	lookup	readlink	read
0 0%	443379 39%	6797 0%	0 0%	300167 26%	28614 2%	11036 0%
wrcache	write	create	remove	rename	link	symlink
0 0%	306822 27%	3410 0%	984 0%	361 0%	19 0%	0 0%
mkdir	rmdir	readdir	fsstat			
5051 0%	5046 0%	5183 0%	5105 0%			

The first set of information is general RPC counts. Because other applications besides NFS may use RPC, these counts are usually a bit higher than total NFS RPC calls. The key fields here are the total number of calls (**calls**), retransmissions (**retrans**), responses to RPCs that are *not* pending (**badxid**), and time-outs (**timeout**).

The total number of calls is just a simple count of every RPC request ever received. A similar field (under **Client nfs**) shows the number of RPC calls specifically generated by NFS. If this number is small (e.g., below a few thousands) and the client has been up for a while, it indicates the client does not actively use NFS.

The **timeout** field indicates the total number of times an RPC request has failed due to a time-out. The RPC code retransmits a request until the maximum count (as set by the mount parameter, **retrans**) is exhausted. Each retransmission causes the **retrans** count to be incremented except for the last retry. The final retry is counted as a **badcall**. For example, if the NFS file system is mounted with a **retrans** count of 16 and the server goes down, the client time-out count will go up by 16; the **retrans** count, by 15; and **badcalls**, by 1.

The **badxid** field counts the number of RPC responses that have arrived but have no corresponding RPC requests waiting for them. This event usually occurs when a duplicate response arrives for an RPC request. Surprisingly, the NFS code treats these responses as bad RPC calls causing **badcalls** to also be incremented in addition to **badxid**.

In addition to all the previously stated situations, the **badcalls** field gets incremented if an RPC response packet fails any of a number of consistency checks such as the request being smaller than the minimum RPC request length and header data being wrong (e.g., not XDR-decodable).

The interdependency between all these statistics makes it hard to understand the relationship between all these parameters. To keep things straight, just remember the following formula:

$$\textbf{badcalls} + \textbf{retrans} = \textbf{badxid} + \textbf{timeout} \qquad (9.1)$$

Note that you always get some residual error and retransmission rates in the RPC (and NFS) statistics. These occur due to occasional server reboots and other known failures such as network cables being disconnected and reconnected. So, do not be alarmed if these values are nonzero.

Beyond RPC counts, `nfsstat` also shows the usage pattern for various NFS operations. Table 9.1 shows each call and the corresponding UNIX file system operation that invokes it.

In general, the call counts for `write`, `lookup`, `readlink`, and `null` are the ones to watch for because they give you clues as to the inefficient usage of NFS.

Table 9.1 NFS Operations, Their Corresponding System Calls, and Example Utilities

NFS RPC Operation	Unix File System Operation	Unix System Call	Example Utilities
null	Used by the automounter to find remote NFS servers		automound
getattr	Read file/directory inode	access, open, stat	ls -l, make
setattr	Set file/directory inode data	chown, chmod, truncate	chmod, chown
root	Obsolete—no longer used	N/A	N/A
lookup	Find and return the handle for a file	open	Any program that uses file
readlink	Look up a symbolic link	readlink	ls -l
read	Read a block of a file (usually 8 Kbytes)	read, exec	Any program that uses file
wrcache	Not currently used	N/A	N/A
write	Write one block to a file (usually 8 Kbytes)	write	Any program that uses files
create	Create a file	creat, mknod, open	Programs that create files
remove	Remove a file	unlink	rm
rename	Change the name of a file/directory	rename	mv
link	Create a new (hard) link to a file	link	ln
symlink	Create a symbolic link	symlink	ln -s
mkdir	Create a directory	mkdir	mkdir
rmdir	Remove a directory entry	rmdir	rmdir
readdir	Read the contents of a directory	getdentrs, getdirentires	ls, sh
fsstat	Read file system attributes	ustat (Sys V), stafs (BSD)	df

9.6.2 Server-Side Statistics

The server statistics can be displayed using the -s option. As with client-side, you can use the -n option to just see the NFS statistics:

```
SunOS% nfsstat -s

Server rpc:
calls       badcalls    nullrecv    badlen      xdrcall
17870106    0           0           0           0

Server nfs:
calls       badcalls
17870106    92
null        getattr     setattr     root        lookup      readlink    read
34426   0%  6062967 33% 168341  0% 0   0%       6567714 36% 623485  3% 2314951 12%
wrcache     write       create      remove      rename      link        symlink
0   0%      1061426  5% 115614  0% 56202   0%   5601    0%  8636    0%  13   0%
mkdir       rmdir       readdir     fsstat
10109   0%  5873    0%  801749  4% 32999   0%
```

The **calls** field shows the total number of requests for all RPCs and those for NFS only. If the call counts are low and the server has been up for a while, it indicates that this server is not heavily used.

badlen and **xdrcall** in the RPC information count the number of times an RPC request was received but did not have the proper length or its header could not be decoded by the XDR layer, respectively. Possible causes are data corruption on the network. This field should be zero especially in a LAN.

The NFS version of **badcalls** counts those calls that did not match valid NFS requests.

As with the client-side information, the rates for each NFS request are printed under the NFS heading. Note that this information is the summary of activity on behalf of all clients. In order to figure out why certain percentages are too high, you must run nfsstat -c on each client serviced by this server—a very tedious process.

9.6.3 Round-Trip Statistics

SunOS and Solaris sport a dynamic retransmission scheme to avoid the performance problems that occur due to fixed time-out values. In addition, the read and write RPC requests are broken into smaller packets if the request must travel through a gateway or router. The kernel maintains the round-trip delay for RPC operations and the current read and write buffer sizes. The SunOS implementation of nfsstat includes a -m option that shows this information:

```
den[5]% nfsstat -m
/ from wa3:/export/root/den (Addr 192.9.213.70)
Flags: hard nocto  read size=8192, write size=8192,  count = 5
Lookups: srtt=7 (17ms), dev=4 (20ms), cur=2 (40ms)
```

```
Reads: srtt=7 (17ms), dev=4 (20ms), cur=2 (40ms)
Writes: srtt=33 (82ms), dev=6 (30ms), cur=7 (140ms)
All: srtt=7 (17ms), dev=4 (20ms), cur=2 (40ms)
```

The output shows the statistics for all file systems mounted in the system. The first line shows the mount point, the server name, and the exported directory along with the server's IP address. The next line shows some of the mount options. The **count** field, by the way, is the same as the retransmission count.

The most useful information is the smoothed, round-trip time (**srtt**) for `lookup`, `read`, and `write` RPC calls. The relevant times are reported in parentheses and have units of milliseconds. The sample output verifies the fact that write operations are indeed slow, showing a round-trip delay that is four times slower than reads (33 versus 7 milliseconds). In general, write response over 100 milliseconds is considered too slow. Look-ups and reads should be faster than 50 milliseconds.

Besides the **srtt**, the output also includes the estimated deviation from average (**dev**) along with the time-out value for the next transmission (**cur**).

You may want to ignore entries with addresses that start with an IP address of 127. These NFS servers are, in reality, the automounter impersonating a remote server. There is very little significance to their information other than noticing how long it takes to do an operation if you first have to wait for the file system to be mounted. See Section 9.10 for a more complete explanation of how the automounter works.

9.7 Optimizing NFS Servers

Assuming that you have configured your NFS network correctly (see Client Optimization in the next section), you should follow these recommendations to get the best performance from your network.

- **Invest in client buffer caches instead of the server.** The server buffer is not very effective for multiple reasons. The write requests are not delayed and simply use up buffer space. On reads, the server cache is secondary, backing up the first-level cache in the client. The skimming effect together with multiclient (i.e., random) access means very low hit rates for the server buffer cache. What all this means is that you may be better off spending your money on client caches instead of investing in large memory servers.

- **Invest in an NFS write accelerator product such as the Legato Prestoserve.** These devices convert synchronous writes into reliable delayed writes, which eliminates one of the worst bottlenecks in NFS. A similar but cheaper approach (especially on PCs) is to invest in a caching disk controller with write-behind caching.

- **Substantially increase the size of the inode and name look-up caches.** The standard configuration for these tables is usually too small for good performance given the high frequency of file look-ups on NFS servers. Given the small sizes for these tables, you should not be shy about increasing their size to very large numbers (e.g., to 5000 or higher).

- **Run write-intensive applications directly on the server.** Examples would be news and mail gathering programs. If you run these applications on an NFS client, the performance will be very low due to slow NFS writes. If you run the same applications on the server, their writes will be delayed in addition to bypassing the NFS and network overhead. The result is much faster throughput. Another similar misuse is extraction of large directories using `tar` and `cpio` programs. Again, these programs should be run on the server instead of the client.

- **Optimize your disk subsystem.** Use a cluster of smaller drives instead of a single larger one. This is especially useful in an NFS environment where the disk I/O is fairly random. The larger number of drives allows more requests to be processed in parallel. You may also want to use disk striping or hardware RAID solutions to spread disk I/O from one file system to multiple drives.

- **Keep in mind that the premium paid for a high-performance disk drive pales in comparison to the total cost of your NFS server.** So, spend the extra amount of money and invest in the fastest disk drives (and controllers) you can buy. Fortunately, the price of high-performance drives (with 7200 RPM and 8-millisecond seek time) is falling rapidly, so the premium should not be too high.

- **Optimize the number of `nfsd` daemons on your server.** The key thing to remember here is that if you do not have enough `nfsds` running in your system, the NFS UDP socket may overflow causing the requests to be thrown away. To check for this, use the `netstat` command discussed in Chapter 8:

```
SunOS4.1% netstat -s |grep overflow
   8 socket overflows
```

- **If the count is nonzero, then your server is not keeping up with the requests.** This can be remedied by increasing the number of `nfsds`. The only drawback to doing this is the increased CPU overhead because all the `nfsds` fight over the same requests. In implementations such as SunOS and Solaris, the `nfsds` use kernel threads and have much less context switch overhead than standard user processes used in some other implementations. So, on Sun platforms, do not be shy about having tens or even hundreds of `nfsds` (on large servers, of course).

- **Do keep in mind however that each `nfsd` uses between 8 and 24 Kbytes of memory.** So a hundred of them might use up to 2.4 Mbytes of memory.

- **Note that the preceding guideline applies to systems that are dedicated NFS servers.** If you would like to run other applications on your server at the expense of NFS performance, then you should back off on the number of `nfsds`. This would throttle the CPU usage of NFS, leaving more cycles for other uses.

9.8 Optimizing the Network for NFS Usage

We have already covered general techniques for optimizing your networks in Chapter 8. But we would like to emphasize a few important points here.

Make sure that you test your server with `ping` or `spray` before investigating NFS-related problems. Take care to use a large transfer size rather than the default. For example,

```
SunOS% spray -l 8192 wa
sending 12 packets of lnth 8192 to wa ...

        in 10.0 seconds elapsed time,
        2 packets (16.67%) dropped
Sent:   1 packets/sec, 9.6K bytes/sec
Rcvd:   0 packets/sec, 8.0K bytes/sec
```

As you can tell, this server does very poorly with such large transfers. Ideally you should see zero packet loss.

Given the heavy network load of NFS, avoid using gateways and routers between clients and servers. Remember the proximity principle: the closer the data (which is on the NFS server) to where it is needed (the client), the faster the response time. Note that even if you have a high-performance dedicated router, you still pay the latency penalties of two-network access for each packet (one on each segment).

Note that we are not saying that subnets are not good. On the contrary, by isolating the traffic from individual NFS servers, you boost overall network bandwidth significantly. Just be sure to put the clients for an NFS server in the same subnet.

Another point to keep in mind is that slow links, which by their very nature become congested quickly, make for very poor NFS response. The large transfer sizes and fixed time-outs in NFS almost guarantee long and unpredictable latencies. In addition, if the network gets used by other programs (e.g., a large `rcp`), NFS transfers grind to a halt.

9.9 Optimizing NFS Clients

The goal in configuring an NFS client is to reduce its reliance on the server. Recall that if you are using Ethernet, your write throughput is only 10–20% of a local disk. This means that a very write-intensive application runs up to ten times slower across NFS even when the network is otherwise idle! Even though the read speed is better, it is less than a half to a quarter of what you could get on local drives. Directory look-up operations are even worse than read and writes. The fastest `getattr` operation still takes a few milliseconds to execute when sent over the network, whereas a local call takes a few *micro*seconds. This is the reason that inode-intensive applications such as `make` and `find` run so much slower across NFS.

Once you have identified the frequency of various NFS requests made by a client, use the following techniques to reduce their rates.

- **Use local disks when no data need to be shared.** Given the very low cost of disk drives today, do not use NFS servers simply for client data that do not need to be shared. The original motivation behind NFS was to save money on disk drives, but this is no longer true. If you amortize the cost of the disk driver storage over the entire NFS server, you will see that the cost per megabyte of data on a server is much higher than a local disk. Therefore,

  store data only on an NFS server that needs to be shared with other clients.

  So, before placing any data on a file server, stop and think about whether the data need to be viewed by other clients. If that is not the case, place it on the local machine. This would also satisfy the proximity principle of placing data closest to where it is needed, the client. This placement not only boosts the performance of the specific client but also lessens the load on the server, which speeds access by other clients as well.

- **Do not use NFS for temporary storage.** As we mentioned before, /tmp should be on a local (or RAM) disk if possible. Of course, if you follow this logic, diskless systems also do not make sense in performance-sensitive environments. It is bad enough to throttle your fast CPUs with local disks, let alone NFS on a 10-Mbit Ethernet.

  Especially sinister is the usage of NFS for diskless paging/swapping. To allow swapping, diskless clients swap to a file located on a remote NFS server. Considering that swapping to a file is slower than a raw partition even on a local drive, you can imagine what happens when you add the network overhead. The situation is even worse than it seems because swap files are very large and hence always have indirect blocks that need to be updated on every write. Add to that the synchronous inode update, and you wind up with a swapping rate that is many times slower than it would be on a local machine. To make matters worse, diskless clients will (at least occasionally) page/swap if you have a paged buffer cache no matter how much memory you have in the system. So, it is really best to use a local hard disk for swapping regardless of the memory usage.

  Note that we are not saying that diskless machines should not ever be used. They are fine as long as they are not running file-intensive applications.

- **Use short path names.** Because each component of a path name must be sent to the server before a file can be opened, avoid the use of path names with many components (i.e., highly nested subdirectories). To see if this is a problem in your clients, use nfsstat and look at the **lookup** rate. If it is higher than 20% of the total number of calls, your path names have too many subdirectories in them.

- **Do not try to solve the previous problem by using symbolic links on NFS partitions.**

  Symbolic links are never cached on the client and are sent to the server for lookup regardless of how often you access them.

The reason has to do with a design decision that lets the NFS server interpret the meaning of a symbolic link. To see how frequently you are accessing symbolic links, look at the **readlink** rates in the client using `nfsstat -rc`. If it accounts for more than 5% of the total calls, symbolic links are being used too often.

- **Optimize the PATH variable on the client system.** Otherwise, a large number of look-up commands are sent to the server every time a user tries to run something.

- **Use cachefs on Solaris 2.3 and later to speed access to mostly read-only NFS files.** The `cachefs` file system stores blocks read from one file system (in this case, NFS) on another faster file system (typically the Fast File System, which is called UFS in Solaris/SVR4). Subsequent reads are satisfied out of the local copy of the files, eliminating costly network transfers. The nice thing about `cachefs` is that a single local file system can cache data from multiple NFS file systems. `cachefs` is a generic facility and can also be used to speed access to other slow file systems such as CD-ROM.

Take care not to use `cachefs` on file systems that are frequently modified (e.g., `\tmp`). Writes to cached file systems are sent both to the local device and the remote server, meaning that the NFS write penalty actually increases rather than decreases. This more than negates any advantage from read caching. See the `cfsadmin` manual page for more information on how to use `cachefs` under Solaris.

9.9.1 Optimizing Client NFS Performance

Once you have minimized NFS usage as much as possible, it is time to optimize NFS itself. The key areas are the number of `biods`, setting the right attribute cache validation times and optimizing the NFS block sizes.

Recall that the `biod` processes provide read-ahead and asynchronous write operation for the client. The key to determining the right number of them is to balance the need of the client against the server load. Increasing the number of `biods` boosts the client throughput (up to a point) by overlapping NFS I/O requests. But doing so also increases the number of concurrent requests that the server must handle. This is a critical point because

there is no client scheduling in the server.

This means that the server simply processes requests on a first-come, first-server basis. If you have a fast client creating many NFS requests, it could easily monopolize even a fast server, reducing the bandwidth available to other clients. Even with the default number of four `biods`, a single client can saturate not only the server but also an entire Ethernet network. Reducing the number of `biods` gives a better chance to other clients to access the network, especially if it is low speed. So, you may want to actually reduce the `biod` count on a client to indirectly reduce its access rate to the server.[1]

---

1. This, of course, assumes that you can find a user who thinks his work is less important than another!

Even though you can totally eliminate the `biods`, we recommend that you leave at least one running. This would provide some amount of double-buffering, which substantially improves throughput at the server and the client without putting undue strain on either the network or the server.

If you have an environment where only one or two clients are active at any one time, you may want to increase the number of `biods` so that the clients get the best throughput. The right number of `biods` is system-specific and depends on how aggressive the client file system code is when it comes to read-ahead. For example, Sun systems read 56-Kbyte chunks of a file at a time (determined by the **maxcontig** parameter). Because each `biod` handles one 8-Kbyte transfer, for best read performance you need at least six `biods` (the last one, for a total of seven, will be handled by the application itself).

Note that unless you have a faster network than 10-Mbit Ethernet, you are not going to see much difference past four to six `biods`. The network transfer rate quickly becomes a bottleneck in these cases.

9.9.2 Optimizing the NFS Block Size

The default block size of 8 Kbytes in NFS makes operations efficient because it reduces the number of RPC requests for large transfers. However, as you recall, the large block size can be too much of a good thing if any of the partial segments are dropped. So, on congested or very slow networks, you may want to reduce the block size. If the block size is reduced to the maximum packet size (MTU) of the network, the problem with dropped partial segments is completely eliminated. But the solution is not perfect. Smaller packets mean more overhead in the form of increased network load (due to increased ACK count and additional per-packet overhead). The result may actually be higher network usage. So, you may need to experiment with the packet size to see if it has a positive effect.

To get the MTU size for the network, use the `netstat` command:

```
% netstat -i
Name  Mtu   Net/Dest     Address      Ipkts    Ierrs Opkts    Oerrs Collis Queue
le0   1500  wa3-ether    den          1798348  0     1210910  14    6539   0
lo0   1536  loopback     localhost    28538    0     28538    0     0      0
```

Once you determine the MTU size, you can then change the read and write block sizes in the `/etc/fstab` or `/etc/vfstab` files, depending on which one exists on your system (see the corresponding manual page). Because the block size cannot be changed dynamically, you need to unmount and remount the file system each time.

9.9.3 Reducing the Number of getattr Calls

If `nfsstat -cn` shows a high percentage of `getattrib` calls (greater than 20%), you may want to increase the validity times of the attribute cache for both files and directories. But keep in mind that extending the time also increases the time that the clients will stay out of synch. If you are using diskless workstations, you may want to sharply increase the cache times for any nonshared directories such as /tmp and /var/tmp (you may want to mount them separately from the root file system if that is where they are located). This would not only reduce the **getattr** frequency but also increase the efficiency of the client buffer cache because its data are also kept valid for longer periods of time. Because it is unlikely that any other clients would be interested in the contents of /tmp of another machine, this optimization has little risk.

If you are using SGI IRIX, another alternative is to use the mount flag, **private**, which delays all write requests and does not flush anything on close. Needless to say, this significantly speeds access to the specific file system but almost completely compromises data sharing. It is a fine choice for /tmp and other directories whose contents do not need to be shared. But keep in mind that unwritten data to an NFS server will get lost if the system crashes.

9.9.4 Choosing the Best Time-Out Value

Due to the fixed algorithm used in RPC for determining time-outs on lost packets, it is very important to select an optimal value for your network and server response time. Setting the time-out value too low can cause frequent retransmissions that exacerbate network congestions. You can tell if this is a problem when the **badxid** count is nonzero.

In selecting the time-out value, keep in mind that it may be best to err on the high side. This would guarantee that retransmissions will not occur because of an impatient client. The drawback will be that the recovery time in cases of true packet losses will be longer.

The only way to fine-tune the time-out value is by experimentation. Prepare some kind of test load and run it each time after adjusting the time-out value and use nfsstat -z to zero out the statistics between trials (you must be root to use this option). Then monitor the **badxid** count and keep increasing the time-out until the count stays at zero.

You may want to use a binary search to reduce the number of time-out values that you have to try. This is a technique for quickly zooming in on the right value. Instead of going up or down 1 millisecond at a time, go up by a factor of two, or down to the halfway point. For example, if the current time-out value is 40 milliseconds, use a value of 80 initially. If the **badxid** drops to zero, reduce the time-out value to 60 (the midpoint between 80 and 40) and monitor **badxid** again. If the new value causes **badxid** to become nonzero, then use 80. Otherwise, use 60. You can continue this process to fine-tune the value further, although it is not necessary to arrive at an exact value.

9.10 Automounted File Systems

Mounting large numbers of NFS file systems at system start-up can be painfully slow especially if some of the mounts fail. For this reason, Sun invented an automounting mechanism that mounts NFS file systems on first reference and unmounts them after a certain period of inactivity (the default is 5 minutes in SunOS 4.1).

The automounter (shown as `automountd` in `ps` displays) works by impersonating a remote NFS server for every file system specified in its configuration file. This means that anytime you touch a file system to be mounted, the kernel sends the RPC message to the `automountd` process (on the same system) thinking it is the remote server. The automounter, in turn, creates a symbolic link and does a real NFS mount of the file system to where the link points (this is the reason automounted file systems always start with `/tmp_mnt`). Once the mount succeeds, the automounter returns a message to the kernel indicating that the target file to be accessed is a symbolic link and this fools the kernel into accessing the newly mounted file system.

Although the automounter is very useful from a system management point of view, it does exert a certain performance penalty if you are not careful. Because the automounter code is not in the kernel, the system incurs an extra context switch and an RPC request to talk to it. This is not a big problem if it occurs only when the file system is first mounted. Even though this is indeed the case with most referenced file names in an automounted file system, there are situations where the automounted gets called on every look-up operation. Take the following program, for example:

```
#include <sys/types.h>
#include <sys/stat.h>

main()
{
    struct stat buf;
    register i;

    for(i = 0; i < 5000; ++i)
        if (stat("/users/amirm/book/testprogs/foo", &buf) < 0)
            perror("automount");
}
```

The program simply stats (gets the inode contents) of the file `foo` in the specified directory. The initial path, `/users/amirm`, is an automounted file system, which in reality is mounted as `/tmp_mnt/users/amirm`. The program takes 13 seconds of elapsed time and 6.5 seconds of CPU time to run on our sample system. Now if we add `/tmp_mnt` to the beginning of the path in `stat`, the program takes only 2.0 seconds to run and consumes only 1.9 seconds of CPU time!

The reason for the large difference in execution time is that, in the first case, the automounter must constantly translate the symbolic link (`/users/amirm`) to the real mount point (`/tmp_mnt/users/amirm`). This requires a full-process context switch (to run `automountd`) plus the RPC overhead of the `readlink` request (sent over the loopback driver). In the second case, no translation is needed, and the program runs much faster (especially because the file attribute for file `foo` is cached after the first request on the local client).

To avoid this kind of overhead, try to use relative path names where possible. For example, instead of constantly accessing the file `/apps/foo`, try changing the directory to `/apps` first and then access the file as simply foo. You could also add the prefix, /tmp_mnt, to the file name to arrive at the actual mount point (/tmp_mnt/...), but we are not sure if this convention is guaranteed to stay valid forever.

Another issue with the automounter is the time-out value for unmounting a file system. The automounter attempts to unmount file systems under its control after a preconfigured time (usually 5 minutes). If any file is open on the specific file system being unmounted, the kernel refuses the unmount request and the automounter retries later. If the unmount does succeed, the file system will, of course, need to be remounted if it is accessed again. Even though the default inactivity value is fine for most environments, you may want to increase its values in situations where an application accesses its files less frequently than this period. To see if this is occurring in your environment, run nfsstat -s on your servers and look at the count for the **null** request. The automounter uses the **null** NFS protocol request to see if its target file server is alive. As such, the count of these requests indicates how often the automounter has attempted to mount a file system. In general, the ratio of the **null** procedure call to the total number of calls should be less than 0.1% (you need to divide the two numbers yourself because the percent display in nfsstat does not show fractions of a percent).

9.11 Other Network File Systems

The shortcomings of the current NFS protocol has prompted development of new file-sharing services that do not suffer from some of the same problems. Because these newer protocols have not achieved widespread use, we only briefly cover them here.

9.11.1 AFS and DCE

The Andrew File System (AFS) is currently marketed by Transarc Corporation and is available for many UNIX platforms. AFS is a stateful implementation and allows each client to use its buffer cache to the fullest extent. Specifically, the clients are not required to flush their write requests to the server as they do in NFS. Instead, they get permission from the server for exclusive access to certain portions of a file. Once the (lock) request is granted, the clients are not only free to cache data corresponding to these blocks, but they can also delay the write requests (i.e., hold the blocks in their local buffer cache). In addition, AFS allows clients to extend their buffer cache storage capacity by using local hard disks. The advantage here is that a single disk can be used to buffer the most frequently used blocks from many file systems. All this adds up to a performance advantage (especially in write-intensive environments) over the current NFS implementation.

The Distributed Computing Environment from OSF includes a somewhat modified implementation of AFS, which shares all the preceding qualities. Before you switch to AFS or DCE remote file services though, we should note that they are not in widespread use yet.

9.11.2 NFS 3.0

NFS 3.0 is Sun's answer to AFS and DCE. It is an upgrade of the NFS protocol, which allows write-request and local hard disk caching. It can also run on top of other protocols such as TCP, so it should be able to perform much better over slow lines and congested WANs. As of this writing, NFS 3.0 is not commonly available, and its merits remain to be seen. Fortunately, some features of NFS 3.0 (e.g., local disk caching) have found their way into Sun's Solaris implementation.

Given the high reliance of UNIX systems on NFS services, we hope that a new improved protocol does become available regardless of whether it is NFS 3.0 or AFS.

9.12 Summary

Optimizing networks requires starting with a highly tuned base system. The next step is optimal configuration of the network topology to limit traffic to localized subnets. With an efficiently running network, you can shift your focus to NFS. Reducing dependence on NFS, especially when it comes to write traffic, goes a long way toward optimizing system response time.

CHAPTER 10

X Window and MOTIF

Over recent years, there has been a major shift from ASCII terminals to bit-mapped graphical displays. The trend started with the advent of UNIX workstations in the early 1980s and has caught on across the entire range of UNIX computer systems. Even the traditional multiuser systems have adopted this technology with the availability of so-called X terminals.

Early graphical systems were proprietary extensions to UNIX, but the industry now has uniformly adopted X Window (X) developed by Massachusetts Institute of Technology (MIT). It can be argued that X owes its popularity to the fact that it was freely available to the industry at large and not purely to its technological superiority. Even though we do not discuss the general merits of X, we are concerned about its architecture as it relates to system and graphical performance. We should note that our comments relate to implementation of X on top of UNIX and may not necessarily relate to versions of X running on top of other operating systems.

Graphical systems, and X window implementations specifically, have traditionally been equated with poor performance when compared to the older ASCII terminals. Although there are a lot of reasons for the performance loss, much of the blame lies in the fact that it takes considerably more system resources to move individual dots than fully formed characters on screen. This overhead once prompted an ASCII terminal vendor to make a clever observation that cating a file to screen, which used to be a 100% I/O-bound process, is a completely CPU-bound activity on a bit-mapped workstation! In addition to the CPU resources, X window systems have an insatiable appetite for memory compared to traditional systems. The additional memory usage can lead to heavy paging and swapping activity with the resulting poor response time blamed on X.

10.1 X Window Implementation Under UNIX

The X window implementation in UNIX is not part of the kernel and simply consists of a set of cooperating processes. Figure 10.1 shows the set of processes involved in X.

The X server process is the heart of the system and controls all access to screen(s) and input devices such as keyboard and mouse. An X application (commonly called a client) needs to communicate with the X server in order to both display data and get user input.

The type of display services provided by the X server are fairly low level. For example, the X server does not know anything about pull-down menus and input buttons. Providing these higher-level features is the responsibility of the client applications. In practice, there are toolkits (a set of library functions) that allow programmers to implement these functions easily.

Separating the display and input services from user clients in the form of another process (the server) causes even simple requests to turn into complex events. As an example, let's look at what happens when a user inputs a character to be echoed by an X client on an otherwise idle system.

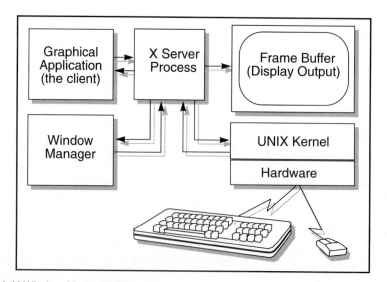

Figure 10.1 X Window Under UNIX

The kernel receives an interrupt when the key is pressed on the keyboard. This causes the X server to wake up and receive the scan code for the key pressed by the user from the kernel. The server then passes the scan code to the client and goes back to sleep. The pending data for the client cause it to wake up requiring yet another context switch. The client examines the scan code and, assuming that it does not have to perform any special functions (e.g., scroll the window), asks the server to display the corresponding character (usually a certain font). The client then goes to sleep waiting for further user input, and the server runs again after another context switch. Displaying a character on a bit-mapped frame buffer requires that each pixel (PIcture ELement or single dot on screen) comprising the specific font to be drawn one at a time. Even for a small 9x11 font, this requires 99 bits or almost 13 bytes to be written to a monochrome screen. On a common 256-color screen, the number of bytes climbs by a factor of 8 to 104, assuming that there is no hardware assist. As you can see, this process is very CPU-intensive in addition to having high latencies. To put things in perspective, Table 10.1 shows the comparison of CPU overhead for a process echoing a character received from an ASCII terminal (in cbreak/raw mode) versus an X client doing the same.

For an easy benchmark, execute cat /etc/termcap in one window and, in another window, run vmstat or sar and monitor the CPU usage. You probably see that the entire CPU cycles are consumed by this simple process (i.e., 0% idle time). In contrast, if you run the same command on a serial port on most workstations, the amount of CPU time used will be negligible. In fairness, we should note that many of the CPU cycles are spent in the server while it waits in a tight loop for the frame buffer to display the pixels.

Table 10.1 Overhead of Echoing a Character

User Interface	Number of Processes	Context Switches	System Calls	Bytes Transferred
ASCII Terminal	1	1	2	2
X Window	3	3	6+	104+

10.2 The Window Manager and Toolkits

The developers of X avoided the user interface wars early on by not selecting any "look and feel." Instead, each client can define whatever user interface it chooses. For example, a selection button can be round or square or have a 3D or a 2D look among many other choices. To avoid duplication and ease the programming effort, a number of libraries or toolkits that provide such functions as pull-down menus, buttons, and text input windows are available. The most popular toolkits today are OpenLook and MOTIF. OpenLook has been promoted by Sun Microsystems and, as such, is mostly available on Sun platforms (but it is being phased out in favor of MOTIF). MOTIF is a product of the Open Software Foundation and has become a de-facto standard in the industry. Both of these toolkits are in turn built on top of the Xt and Xlib toolkits (see Figure 10.2 on page 228).

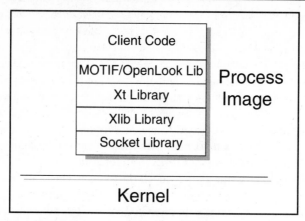

Figure 10.2 Typical X Client Layers

In addition to the clients, a special process called the Window Manager handles the overall look of the system. The Window Manager provides such services as starting new clients, minimizing windows (also called iconifying), moving and resizing client windows, and destroying clients. Again, the X window system does not care which Window Manager you chose to use. The common choices are OpenLook, MOTIF, and Twm (an older window manager bundled with X window system).

10.3 Performance Considerations

The inefficiencies in the X design hover around its interprocess communication scheme, client scheduling, and memory usage. To understand what causes these problems, we need to look at some key aspects of the X design.

10.3.1 Client-Server Communication in X

X is a distributed graphical system, meaning that it does not require that the client and server be on the same system. This allows clients to run on systems that do not have any display capabilities (e.g., large compute servers) and communicate with the server in a workstation or a dedicated X terminal. Most implementations of X windows use the BSD socket mechanism as a means of communication between the clients and the server. Sockets are a programmatic interface to the underlying networking code in UNIX and were already described in Chapter 8.[1]

New clients establish connections with the server as part of their initialization code. The DISPLAY environment variable (or the command line option `-display`) tells the client

---

1. System V machines use the streams connection, which has a different interface but works similarly to sockets for the purposes of this discussion.

where the X server is located. The client uses a UNIX domain socket if the X server is on the local system or a TCP streams connection if the X server is on a remote system.

After a client establishes the connection, it typically sleeps waiting for input data from the X server socket connection. Because the server must service requests from many sources, it can go to sleep only if it has no data pending on any of its client socket connections or input devices. To detect activity on these ports, the server uses the BSD `select` or System V `poll` system calls. These system calls put the server to sleep if there is no pending data for it. But as soon as there is any input (e.g., the user types something) or a client sends a request to it, the server wakes up and handles the event.

Even though the distributed nature of X is quite beneficial, the choice of socket interface puts additional, and possibly unneeded, burden on the system. When the client and server are located on different systems, the socket mechanism is a natural choice. However, the majority of X users have a workstation or PC that hosts both the server and clients. In these systems, sockets are a very high overhead mechanism for interprocess communication because they require the data from one process to be copied into and out of the kernel before being passed to another process. A more optimal solution might have been a shared memory interface between the client and the server. This would have avoided all the copying operations and the socket code overhead. Indeed, this is an enhancement that is included in the X implementation from a few vendors.[2]

To avoid having to store large amounts of data, the kernel limits the amount of data that a process can send to another process using sockets to typically 2048 bytes. If a process attempts to send more than this limit, the kernel breaks up the request into multiples of the maximum size and forces the sender to sleep while the receiving process drains the socket. This leads to additional context switches and higher CPU usage. For example, assume that the client wants to send 9000 bytes of data to the server (e.g., on a screen redraw). The kernel copies 2048 bytes of the data into one of its buffers and wakes up the server after putting the client to sleep. Once the server empties the socket, the client runs again and is able to copy the next 2048 bytes. The result is five context switches to process a single request.

Ironically, the limited kernel buffering is a requirement for smooth operation of X. Because clients usually have equal or higher CPU priority than the server (a very likely scenario because the kernel penalizes the server for running very frequently), they can generate a considerable amount of display output before they lose the CPU. Because the user does not see anything until the server processes the client requests and writes them to the frame buffer, deep kernel buffering causes the display to be bursty and not smooth. This tends to bother most users who have come to expect the output from their programs to come out in a similar manner to old terminals (i.e., one line at a time rather than a complete screenful). By forcing clients to go to sleep after they have filled their socket buffers

---

2. The speed-up is limited to large transfers (typically bit maps) because sockets are still used to wake up the server/client when data arrive.

(regardless of their scheduling priority), the system inadvertently assures that the server runs frequently enough for a reasonable update rate.

10.3.2 The X Server and Kernel Scheduler Conflicts

Recall that, in the case of ASCII terminals, there was no single thread of execution. That is, as lines were typed at the terminal, they were passed to their individual processes, which all ran according to their scheduling parameters. *In contrast, the X server process receives input and output activities for all clients.* Unlike the kernel, the X server has no knowledge of the client CPU scheduling parameters (e.g., user nice and priority values) and uses a simple round-robin scheduler in handling keystrokes for multiple processes. This dual scheduling system can cause anomalies in user response time.

When the server wakes up as a result of the `select` or `poll` system call, *it scans all the socket connections (that have data) linearly* and sequentially processes any requests that it finds. The problem with this scheme is that it ignores the kernel process priorities. The result is that it is possible for the output of a low-priority job to come out before that of a higher priority one. The effect can be annoying if the output of a simple `ls` gets delayed due to a background job that is running in another window and is sending lots of output to the screen. In practice, this anomaly is not very severe because the amount of output generated by a client is more or less proportional to its priority. Nonetheless, we would like to see a tighter connection between the kernel and the X server schedulers.

Another problem is caused by the kernel priority migration scheme. Because the X server has to service requests for all the clients in the system, it uses a considerable amount of CPU time. This in turn results in a substantial lowering of the server's priority, which has the harmful effect of allowing clients to queue up large amounts of output before the server gets to run. The visual effect would be a bursty display with occasional pauses. Fortunately, this effect is not very pronounced because clients are forced to sleep once they fill up their rather small socket buffers. But relying on such an obscure side effect of the networking code is rather dangerous. Indeed, we have seen socket implementations that cause havoc in X response time due to very deep buffering before a client suspension. The right solution would have been special scheduling of the server when it comes to priority migration.

10.3.3 Memory-Related Problems

Even more serious than CPU scheduling is the fact that the kernel treats the X server just like any other process when it comes to paging and swapping. When the kernel searches for large jobs to swap out, it usually picks the X server due to its large size (4 Mbytes and up) and its often sleeping status. This has serious repercussions because swapping the server causes screen activity for *all* clients to halt. To make matters worse, due to its size, the server can take a long time to swap or page back in.

Yet another problem is the fact that the kernel is unaware of the relationship between the server and clients. As a result, it may swap the X server but keep all the clients resident in memory. This, of course, is inefficient because the clients cannot display anything nor receive input when the server is swapped out. It would be much better to keep the server in memory and swap out some unimportant clients like `xclock`.[3] A related problem surfaces when the `xterm` terminal emulator gets swapped/paged out but the shell or the editor that is running within it stays resident in memory.

The clients themselves cause performance problems due to their unusually high memory usage compared to their ASCII counterparts. The little icon showing a graphical clock on your screen uses up to 1.4 Mbytes of memory.[4] By contrast, the `date` utility, which shows the same information (albeit in a much less elegant way), uses less than 10 Kbytes of memory. The same holds true of text editors, Email programs, and other common applications that have character-based counterparts.

The much larger size of X clients makes them excellent targets for the kernel swapper and paging algorithms. X clients, like most applications, spend the majority of their time waiting for user input. If there is any sort of memory shortage, the kernel frees the majority of their memory pages because they are not being touched while they sleep. Once the user tries to interact with the client (which can be as simple as clicking in a window), many pages have to be brought back in before the user sees any output. The problem is much more severe on systems that have dynamic buffer caches. In these systems, the simple act of reading and writing files causes the buffer cache to grow and create a memory shortage. Workstation users may be better off disabling a dynamic buffer cache or at least putting a cap on its maximum size for good response time.

The Window Manager does not escape this problem either and is especially susceptible to memory shortages. It is an ideal process for the kernel to swap out because it is large and sleeps all the time waiting for user input. But nothing is more annoying than clicking on an icon and waiting many seconds for the Window Manager to swap back in simply to pop up a menu.

10.4 Optimizing Your System for X

One of the most common performance problems in X window systems is the lack of system memory. The symptoms are long, multisecond delays when you try to move windows or pull down a menu. Usually associated with this delay is a large amount of disk I/O because the client or the X server get paged back in. Use the techniques described in Chapter 7 to determine the memory requirements of your system. As a general rule, X window systems require a minimum of 16–24 Mbytes of memory to run. This amount would be adequate for the UNIX kernel, a handful of xterm clients, and a few small pro-

---

3. Ironically, `xclock` rarely gets paged/swapped out because it runs regularly to update the time.

4. Measured on a Sun SPARCstation 2 running SunOS 4.1.

grams. Running any commercial applications would quickly push this number higher as even small MOTIF applications require 4 Mbytes or more to run.

Beyond memory, two other factors have an impact on the X performance: CPU speed and graphics controller efficiency. High CPU performance is required to handle the overhead of the client-server communication along with the server and client code. In our experience, to get good response out of X and MOTIF, you need a minimum of 30 Specint of performance (see Chapter 11). This is the level of performance provided by faster PCs (66–100-Mhz 486 and Pentium) and mid to high-end workstations (e.g., Sun SPARCstation 10/31).

The graphics controller (if it exists) can contribute to slow display response. If you see windows being painted slowly on a consistent basis, your graphics controller is too slow. In this case, a faster graphics controller speeds up X more than a faster CPU. The most visible performance aspects of a graphics controller are its copy or blt (read blit) rate along with its text output speed. See Chapter 11 for suitable X window benchmarks to gauge this.

If you cannot get a faster graphics card, try to reduce the display depth (i.e., the number of colors) so that the amount of data that needs to be stored and copied is reduced. For example, going from 24 bits (16 million simultaneous colors) to 8 bits (256 simultaneous colors) can result in a substantial speed-up because only one third as many bits need to be changed in every display update. This technique is especially useful in PC graphics cards that can be run at a higher depth but do so only at a high-performance penalty. If you are unsure as to the current display depth configured in your system, use the following command:

```
% xdpyinfo | grep "depth of root window"
   depth of root window:    8 planes
```

In this example, the display device is configured for 8 planes or 256 colors. Refer to your system documentation on instructions for reducing the display depth.

10.5 Optimizing X and MOTIF

Although X is highly monolithic and nonconfigurable, there are a few things that you can apply to your system to make sure it is running as efficiently as possible. Let's look at them one by one.

10.5.1 The Display Variable

As mentioned before, X allows the output device (i.e., the X server) to be on a remote host. The DISPLAY environment variable is used to tell the X client where the X server is located. The format follows:

```
<hostname>:display.screen
```

For example, to display on a workstation named speedy in Bourne shell, you would use

```
DISPLAY=speedy:0; export DISPLAY
```

or, if you are using the C shell

```
setenv DISPLAY speedy:0
```

The special host name, `unix`, is reserved and indicates that the server is on the same machine as the client. So, to display everything on the local system, you would set the DISPLAY variable to `unix:0`.

A frequent mistake is to set the DISPLAY variable to the name of the current host (e.g., `speedy:0` if `speedy` is the name of the current machine). From a *functional* point of view, this is the same as using `unix:0` but entirely another matter when you look at the impact on system performance. When you specify `unix:0`, the clients use the UNIX domain sockets to communicate with the server. These sockets are more efficient than the TCP streams sockets used to communicate with X servers on other systems. Specifying the name of the current host in the display parameter makes both the client and X server think that they are on separate machines across a network when in reality they are not.

Even though you would think that this operation (i.e., trying to open a TCP connection to the local system) would fail with an error, it does not. When a process writes to a socket that is associated with a TCP connection on the current host, the kernel networking code is smart enough to know that the data are destined for the current host and does not try to send the data out on the wire. Instead, it queues the data back up on the current system as if an outside host had sent the data. This feature is typically referred to as loopback mode.

So, even though the data get routed correctly between the server and clients in the loop-back mode, the path through the kernel is considerably longer than using simple UNIX domain sockets (see Figure 10.3 on page 234). The main reason is that the kernel does not figure out that the packet is destined for the current system until it has executed just about all the TCP/IP networking code and is ready to send the packet out on the network. This additional code increases the CPU cycles executed compared to the much simpler UNIX domain sockets. So,

> *if you are using a workstation and your machine is the display server, make sure that you set your display variable to* `unix:0`.

The performance difference ranges from 10% (on a Sun SPARCstation 2) to virtually none on some systems (e.g., HP735 workstation running HP-UX). Another bonus that you get for using `unix:0` is that you can start many more clients because the kernel limit for TCP streams sockets is much lower than UNIX domain sockets.

10.5.2 Reducing xterm Memory Usage

Lack of memory is the most common source of poor performance under X. Unfortunately, other than eliminating some of the clients, there are not too many ways to reduce the total memory usage. The only exception is the `xterm` terminal emulator.

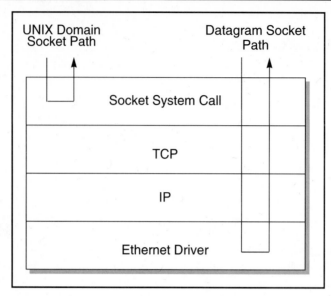

Figure 10.3 Kernel Execution Path for UNIX Domain and Datagram Sockets in Loopback Mode

Many users turn on the scroll bars on xterm windows so that previously scrolled-off data can be viewed again. The number of lines saved is programmable, and most users set it to 1000 lines or more. This feature requires that xterm save its entire memory buffer for each line including all the blank pixels. What the xterm manual page does not highlight is that these line buffers can be rather large. Typical sizes range from 220 bytes per line on SunOS 4.1 to 440 bytes on HP-UX 9.0. Quick computation shows that *saving 1000 lines would increase the size of* xterm *on HP-UX by almost half a megabyte per* xterm. If you have ten xterm windows, you tie up 5 Mbytes of memory just for this purpose. If the number of saved lines is raised to 10,000, it would result in 50 Mbytes of memory being wasted just for scrolled-off text!

The number of saved lines in xterm is usually set with the resource value **savedLines** in the .Xdefault file in your home directory or some other alternate location, in case of systems with desktop managers such as HP-VUE. Find the right resource file and reduce the number of saved lines to something reasonable. For example,

```
Xterm*savedlines: 100
```

After changing this value, you need to restart to your X server. If you know the name of the resource file, the following command may also work:

```
xrdb -load .Xdefaults
```

Alternatively, you can override the resource value by using -sl option of xterm. This may be useful for starting special xterm sessions where you do need to keep longer history. For example,

```
xterm -sl 5000 -e make
```

Of course, the final selection of the number of saved lines is a personal choice and needs to be traded off against the available memory.

10.5.3 Avoid Using MOTIF xterms

Perhaps the most heavily used X application is the `xterm` terminal emulator. Even casual users have half a dozen or more windows open at any one time, making `xterm` one of the heaviest memory users. Of particular concern is the new MOTIF-based `xterms`, which are starting to appear on many UNIX systems. Although these programs seem to work and look the same as the original `xterm`, they use considerably more memory to run. A case in point is `hpterm` in HP VUE, *which is 10 to 15 times larger than* `xterm` *on the same system!* To be fair, `hpterm` does include additional functionality including HP terminal emulation in addition to standard VT100. But if you do not need the additional features, make sure to use `xterm` instead. Similarly, `scoterm` in SCO UNIX commands double the memory usage of `xterm`. To their credit, the SCO documentation does recommend to use `xterm` for the same reasons stated here.

10.6 X Terminals

The network architecture of X lends itself nicely to the idea of having dedicated X window servers. An X window terminal hosts the X server and the networking protocols (usually TCP and DECnet), which makes it capable of displaying data from remote clients. X terminals are gradually replacing traditional ASCII terminals as their costs approach their older cousins. This has given new life to the old idea of time-sharing systems where a central system serves a number of users. All this occurs at a time when most users have been convinced that the ASCII terminals should be replaced with a PC or low-cost workstation.

The industry is divided over whether to use a network of diskless workstations being served by a file server or a high-performance compute server connected to a cluster of X terminals. The decision need not be a religious one, however, because each approach has its advantages and disadvantages. To understand them, we need to look at how each solution addresses the client-server problem.

10.6.1 Advantages of X Terminals

X window terminals are probably the cheapest way to run an X server. Although you can easily run an X server on any PC or workstation, chances are that the final cost will be higher than for an X terminal, assuming comparable performance. The lower cost is the result of needing fewer hardware components and lower horsepower in a dedicated X terminal. Additionally these devices need not concern themselves with expansion buses, large power supplies, huge memory capacity, or floating-point hardware. As a result, X terminals can reach fairly low cost points (in some cases approaching the cost of some high-end ASCII terminals of the early 1980s).

Being a dedicated device, X terminals can run any operating system and, as such, they can side-step the problems of running X on top of UNIX, which we described earlier. Even though some vendors do indeed use UNIX as their operating system, they make extensive modifications to it to optimize it for running the X and networking protocols.

X terminals also have a number of advantages over diskless workstations, some of which are not so obvious. In a network of diskless workstations, anytime you run a new (i.e., not recently executed) program, it needs to be read over the network before it can be executed by the local system. Take for example the `ls` command. Assuming that it has not been run recently (otherwise it would be cached on the local machine), the system needs to transfer its entire text and data segments over the network before it can execute. Because the typical `ls` program is roughly 40 Kbytes, you wind up transferring a lot of data across the network just to see a few hundred bytes of output. If the same command is executed on a remote system and its output displayed on an X terminal, the only data transferred over the network are the display characters. Although the output does include the X protocol overhead, it is still far less than 40 Kbytes. The smaller data transfer results in lower traffic on the network and, hence, faster response time.

X terminals can also save you a considerable amount of money by eliminating redundant resources in the network. Two key areas where this occurs are the main memory and CPU cycles. The savings in memory stems from the fact that users of the same program can share its text segment on the compute server. After all, they are all running the same program on the same machine—only their output is being sent to different machines. The same situation in a network of individual workstations requires that each machine have enough memory to keep a distinct copy of the application. The cost savings can be significant if the application is large. Take even the most minimal situation where each workstation is running a copy of the Window Manager and a few copies of `xterm`. Assuming that you have 50 workstations, this could add up to roughly 30 Mbytes of memory being wasted on the many text copies of the Window Manager and `xterm`.

The X terminal vendors like to point out that if you look at a network of workstations, you would find that, on the average, the CPUs on most systems are over 90% idle. So theoretically, you could get away with having just one or two compute servers instead of many individual machines. As you can tell from the tone of this paragraph, we are not sure if the CPU savings come for "free" or at the expense of user productivity. To understand this issue and other deficiencies of X terminals, we need to look at what makes them unsuitable in some environments.

10.6.2 Disadvantages of X Terminals

Many virtues of X terminals stem from the fact that they localize the computing resources instead of replicating them as is the case with a network of diskless workstations.

Although it is true that a distributed environment is very wasteful, its excess capacity can handle peak loads much better. The response time of a central machine serving many X terminals will, by definition, be unpredictable because you never know when someone else starts one or more resource-hungry jobs. As a result, users tend to like their diskless workstations better, even though they use only 10% of its resources on the average. They know when their machine slows down and why (i.e., because *they* ran one or more programs).

A less important but nonetheless visible problem with X terminals is that they present an inefficient paradigm for certain client-server applications. A case in point is the Window Manager. On a diskless workstation, the Window Manager is able to display all its output on the local frame buffer without going across the network. The X terminal, however, would have to get its data from the remote window manager running on the compute server, making it incur large network latencies. Because the window manager runs frequently and users equate its response time with the speed of the system, an X terminal can make a system seem slower than it really is. This is the reason that some X terminal vendors now allow the Window Manager and some other clients to run inside the terminal. Even though this works for standard X clients like the Window Manager, the solution does not address some display-intensive, third-party applications.

10.6.3 Which Environments Are Best of X Terminals

By now you must be wondering when it makes sense to use an X terminal or a diskless workstation. Our opinion is to follow this simple rule.

> *If price/performance is more important than absolute speed, X terminals provide the best possible solution. On the other hand, if you care only about creating the fastest possible computing environment without much regard to cost, a carefully configured network of (hopefully) diskful workstations is best.*

10.7 Performance Tips Summary

- X Window systems are very resource-hungry. For good performance, make sure that you have plenty of memory (at least 24 Mbytes) and a fast CPU (at least 30 SPECint).
- Reduce the display depth to speed pixel operations. Get a faster graphics card if this does not solve the problem.
- Set your DISPLAY variable to unix:0 if you are running on a workstation.
- Avoid using MOTIF xterms.
- Use only X terminals if absolute performance is not an issue but cost is.

CHAPTER 11

Industry Standard Benchmarks

As you are probably well aware, the computer industry is a highly competitive market. Thanks to operating systems such as UNIX, the market lacks any sort of brand loyalty. Customers are free to choose systems that provide the best price or performance often with little regard to who makes them. This freedom, however, complicates the buying decision. Because no computer is perfect in every regard, it is very important to choose a system that can run *your* application well at the prices you can afford. This, unfortunately, is easier said than done. It is unlikely that you can get performance results for your application workload on your target systems. This is where computer benchmarks and metrics come in. They allow you to compare a range of systems, executing the same set of programs that hopefully resemble yours. This latter caveat is the key to using benchmark results correctly.

In this chapter we describe the most common benchmarks and measures used in the industry along with some pitfalls associated with their use. As you go through this chapter, it may appear that we are overly harsh in pointing out the weakness of each benchmark. As an excuse, we would like to point out that the people who know the most about benchmarks are the ones who criticize them the most. On the other hand, those who know the least trust them the most! Understanding what a benchmark really shows is perhaps the most important concept in this chapter because it will help you determine whether its results are applicable to your environment. To be fair, designing good benchmarks is a difficult task that is hampered by the need for portability and wide availability. Even though this excuses the benchmark developers, it does not relieve you of the responsibility of interpreting their results correctly.

11.1 Benchmarks Versus Real Applications

Determining the performance of a complex computer system is not always an easy task. Contributing to this difficulty is the way the performance of each system is rated by hardware vendors, which is almost always based on some kind of benchmark result. So, before we get into the specifics of each benchmark, here is a word of advice first.

> *Computer performance metrics are usually based on benchmarks that attempt to, but rarely resemble, your own work load. You should always try to evaluate a system using your own application(s). No benchmark ever accurately predicts the performance that you get from a system unless the benchmark includes your application (which is rarely the case).*

Of course, the preceding suggestion is not always feasible because your workload may be too complex to duplicate easily on the target system. Also, if you are not spending large amounts of money, the vendor may be reluctant to let you stage your application on its system. One alternative may be to contact the developer of any commercial application that you are using and ask for performance data. Often, developers have benchmark data for the different platforms that their software runs on. But be forewarned that the software vendors may not always be forthcoming with this information because they do not want to appear to be taking sides with any one vendor. So, be persistent.

11.2 The Megahertz Rating

Before the advent of universally accepted benchmarks, systems were rated using their system clock frequency. It was thought (incorrectly) that a system running at 4 MHz would be faster than one operating at 1 Mhz, regardless of any architectural differences. As you recall from Chapter 2, the clock frequency is only one variable that determines the speed of a CPU. Because CPUs vary drastically in the amount of work they do in a single cycle, using the clock frequency to gauge the performance of a system is clearly wrong. As an example, it would be wrong to compare the clock speed of a superscalar RISC CPU that can execute up to six instructions in parallel with that of a CISC CPU that takes more than one cycle to execute just one instruction. The former may be faster even if it runs at one quarter of the clock speed. Despite these problems, this measure still serves a useful purpose:

> *the clock frequency can be used to reliably compare systems of identical components where the only variable is the CPU clock speed.*

This is fortunate because it seems that the clock speed in the only performance metric specified in the PC world. You simply cannot go wrong assuming that a 120-MHz Pentium system is faster than a 60-MHz Pentium machine. The only thing to keep in mind is that the speed-up is not necessarily 100% due to differences in bus clock, memory, and cache controller speeds. Furthermore, the improvement in performance will most likely be application-dependent.

There is, however, one trap in using the clock frequency as a figure of merit in the PC world. This occus when vendors compare clock speeds of CPUs that appear to be identical in architecture (i.e., have the same name), but in reality they are not. This happened to some extent with Intel 486-compatible CPUs that sported the same instruction set but lacked some major components (e.g., the lack of floating-point processor in IBM's Blue Lightning processor). This situation is getting much worse as the PC CPU vendors diverge even further as they compete with the Intel Pentium. The AMD K1, Cyrix M1, and Nex-Gen 586 have radically different architectures but will be marketed as direct replacements for the Pentium. So, even in the PC business, it is no longer wise to trust the CPU clock speed as a performance measure.

11.3 Simple MIPS

During the late 1970s and early 1980s, vendors were faced with the daunting task of differentiating systems that used wildly varying architectures. Out of this confusion, the concept of Millions of Instructions executed Per Second or MIPS was born. Interestingly enough, although the term indicates how many millions of instructions the CPU supposedly executes per second, it fails to specify *which instructions* are being timed. Imaginative vendors took advantage of this situation and picked the fastest instruction in their CPU, which usually turned out to be the NoOp.

As the name implies, NoOp stands for No Operation and simply tells the CPU to ignore the instruction and continue execution. As you can imagine, knowing how fast a CPU can do nothing is of little value when running actual applications, which are filled with instructions that take many more cycles than NoOp. This trend made this original MIPS rating pretty useless. As you will see later, the MIPS rating was later reincarnated in the form of the Dhrystone benchmark.

11.4 The Whetstone Benchmark

The first alternative to the simple MIPS rating was the Whetstone benchmark. This is a FORTRAN program, which was written by H. J. Curnow and B. A. Wichman in 1976, to measure the speed of a system running scientific applications. There are two flavors of Whetstones: a single-precision version that uses 32-bit floating-point variables and another, which is called double-precision and uses 64-bit variables. The benchmark's aim was to exercise the most commonly used operations in scientific applications such as addition and multiplication.

Unfortunately, Whetstones also includes a heavy dose of transcendental functions (i.e., sine and cosine). These functions are usually very slow because, unlike add and multiply, there is no direct hardware support for them in the CPU. As a result, the time for these functions dominates the overall results. To make matters worse, transcendental functions are rarely used in typical applications—including highly scientific ones. As this major flaw was known only to a handful of experts, Whetstone results were highly relied upon in early 1980s. Even today, the Whetstone results are published in most vendor performance reports. But, in our opinion,

Whetstones is now completely obsoleted by SPEC and should not be used.

11.5 The Linpak Floating-Point Benchmark

The Linpak benchmark was written by Jack Dongarra of Argon National Laboratory in 1976 to measure the speed of an algorithm that solves a set of linear equations. It turns out that this is a very common operation used in many computationally intensive scientific applications. Thanks to its roots in real scientific applications, Linpak results can be very useful and give a very good first-order estimate of the floating-point performance of the system.

The Linpak benchmark lends itself nicely to vectorization, which is a technique used to speed up similar arithmetic operations on many elements of an array (e.g., adding all the elements together). Superscalar processors and multiprocessor architectures tend to also do well for the same reason. It is not unusual to achieve near-linear speed-up as the number of CPUs is increased (at least until the memory subsystem runs out of bandwidth).

Linpak comes in two versions: the 100×100 and the "anything goes" 1000×1000. In the first version, the data set is a 100×100 matrix, and the vendors are allowed to substitute whatever code they like for four of the core routines. These so-called BLAS (Basic Linear Algebra Subroutines) functions are almost always replaced by highly tuned assembly language routines instead of trusting the (FORTRAN) compiler with it. In the larger case, the matrix size is increased to 1000×1000, and vendors are free to make whatever modifications they choose. In addition to using faster BLAS routines, the benchmark is often modified so that the access pattern of the matrix fits better in the cache or the stride (i.e., interleave) of the memory subsystem. As a result, the 1000×1000 numbers are often much higher than the 100×100 case and usually show the absolute best results that can be achieved.

The Linpak rating is stated in megaflops (abbreviated to MFLOPs) due to the fact that each operation involves one FLoating-point OPeration (a FLOP). Because the total number of floating-point operations to solve the linear equations is known, Linpak arrives at its megaflop rating by dividing the total number of floating-point operations by the amount of time the benchmark takes to run.

It would have been nice if Linpak had used a different name for the results because MFLOP is also a metric used to rate the peak floating-point rating of the hardware in a similar manner to MIPS. That is, the CPU clock is divided by the number of cycles taken by a simple operation such as add, and the result is presented as MFLOPs. For example, if a CPU runs at 80 MHz and can perform an addition of two floating-point registers in 4 cycles, the CPU is said to have a 20-MFLOP rating. But this peak MFLOP rating is of little value because it does not represent realistic applications. The Linpak 1000×1000 results better represent the actual peak rating possible while executing "real" code. So, do not trust the MFLOP rating unless the vendor specifies that it was generated by Linpak.

Note that Linpak can be run as either single precision (32-bit variables) or double precision (64-bit variables). However,

> *because single precision rarely has enough accuracy for scientific computations, only double-precision Linpak numbers should be looked at unless you are sure your application uses single-precision numbers.*

The Linpak benchmark was the first "reasonable" industry benchmark and was widely used until the introduction of the SPEC CPU suite, which includes Linpak as one of its components.

11.6 Dhrystone and the New MIPS

As realistic as Linpak is, many vendors dislike it because it predicts the performance of only a certain class of scientific applications. It was definitely a poor fit for early PCs, which did not even have a floating-point processor and hence could not even reach 1 MFLOP at the time (early 1980s). Nor was it any use to anyone running integer code (e.g., the entire UNIX kernel and majority of UNIX utilities). So, the Dhrystone benchmark was born.

Dhrystone was originally a little-known ADA benchmark written by Reinhold Weicker in 1984. It did not gain notoriety until Rick Richardson translated it to C and posted it to the Internet in 1986. Users were encouraged to run the benchmark on their favorite system and mail back their results. Due to ease of compilation and execution, Dhrystone quickly caught on, and, in a relatively short time, results were generated for every computer from the smallest PC to the largest supercomputer. Unfortunately, some early bugs were found in the first version, which caused incorrect results to be reported. So, version 1.1 was posted to deal with these problems.

The popularity of Dhrystone quickly prompted many vendors to try to optimize their systems to generate the fastest results. Some compiler optimizers, for example, could detect that Dhrystone was not using the results of certain loops and completely eliminated the functions resulting in much exaggerated Dhrystone ratings. As a result, Dhrystone was upgraded to version 2.1 to deal with these "smart" compilers. However, in the process, the benchmark ran slower, and you could not compare the result of Dhrystone 1.1 to 2.0.

With the advent of the Dhrystone benchmark, a new MIPS metric was also born:

> *by dividing the number of Dhrystones reported by the result from the DEC VAX 780 minicomputer, a MIPS rating can be computed for the system.*

The rationale behind this was the (incorrect) belief that the VAX 780 was a 1-MIPS computer and, therefore, could be used as reference in this case. The VAX generated approximately 1540 Dhrystones (version 2.1). So, if a system could generate 15,400 Dhrystones, it was thought to be a 10-MIPS computer. Recent analysis shows that the VAX 780 was actually a 0.5-MIPS system and not 1-MIPS. But no one has bothered to change the standard so the preceding formula still holds.

As with Whetstone, Dhrystone measures characteristics of the system that only few people truly understood in the early days. Quick profiling of the benchmark shows that Dhrystone spends the majority of its time copying 100+ byte strings around. Although we do not claim to know how this may have been a common operation in ADA, it is certainly not something that is often used in everyday UNIX applications.

Studies have shown that, even though UNIX does indeed spend a considerable amount of time copying bytes around, the average string size is a much smaller 14 bytes. Above all, *Dhrystones is an integer benchmark meaning that it uses no floating-point computations.* Therefore, it is totally unsuitable for predicting system performance in a scientific and engineering environment. To make matters worse, some vendors have put special hooks in their compilers to generate special code for the large copy operation with the single purpose of getting better Dhrystone numbers.

Because Dhrystone did not use floating-point computations, many supercomputers that are optimized only for floating-point generate Dhrystone ratings slower than some workstations costing a fraction of the price. But the workstation vendors had their own reasons for not liking Dhrystone because their RISC processors had blazing floating-point performance, which was being totally ignored by Dhrystone. These deficiencies prompted a group of vendors to design the SPEC suite to replace Dhrystone. Unfortunately, in the early 1990s, interest in Dhrystone was suddenly revived, and the industry regressed back to using Dhrystone version 1.1. That's right, version 1.1 and not 2.0.[1]

> *You would do well to ignore Dhrystone ratings completely. At best, Dhrystone gives an exaggerated rating of the integer performance of a system.*

The best and only useful CPU benchmark today is the SPEC CPU suite as described next.

---

1. The name of the vendor who set this precedent in 1990 will remain unmentioned here, but, hopefully, they know who they are!

11.7 The SPEC CPU Benchmark

As we eluded to earlier, dissatisfaction with the benchmarks in the early 1980s led to the formation of the System Performance Evaluation Cooperative (SPEC). The core members of the group consisted of MIPS (now part of Silicon Graphics), Sun, DEC, and HP. The group's noble goal was to design a suite of benchmarks that were based on real-life applications, albeit, in a simplified form to aid in portability across different platforms.

The industry was asked to donate their applications for inclusion in the benchmark. But because many software vendors consider their code proprietary, the submissions were generally from communities where there was a generous amount of public domain code. With the scientific community falling in this category, the resulting suite became highly floating-point-specific. Out of the original suite of ten benchmarks, six were floating point and only four used integer code.

Based on pressure from many directions, SPEC initially gave in to the idea of deriving a single figure of merit for the entire suite. The SPECmark, as it was called, was derived by computing the geometric mean of all ten numbers. Geometric mean is a statistical method that generates a conservative average that is less affected by one high number than a simple average would be. *The vendors were still required to report all ten numbers to the SPEC committee, which printed them in its newsletters.* So, in theory, the users could look at the specific benchmark that best represents their application. We say *in theory* because in practice users completely ignore the individual results and focus on the single SPECmark. Due to the higher percentage of the floating-point benchmarks and also the fact that new CPUs have increased their floating-point speed faster than integer performance, the overall SPECmark was more representative of the floating-point speed of the system than integer.

The SPEC CPU suite was updated in 1992 and renamed SPEC92. To reduce confusion, the name of the original SPEC CPU suite has been changed to SPEC89. The number of benchmarks has also increased to 20, and there is no longer a single figure of merit. Instead, there is a Specfp92 and a Specint92, which are geometric means of all floating-point (CFP92) and integer-intensive (CINT92) benchmarks, respectively. Vendors are discouraged from combining the two numbers, although some privately quote Spec92 numbers anyway.

Note that the SPEC suite generates only timing results for each benchmark and not the SPECmark value usually reported. To arrive at a specific SPECmark, a similar scheme to Dhrystone is used where the time for the DEC VAX 780 is again used as one SPECmark machine.

Table 11.1 shows sample performance data for a number of computer systems. Note that no attempt has been made to pick systems of equal value so the chart should be used only on an informational basis. See Chapter 12 for a more complete listing of SPEC results sorted by each computer vendor.

Table 11.1 SPEC92 Results for Some Sample Systems

System	Processor	Clock Freq.	Specint92	Specfp92
Compaq SystemPRO/XL	Intel Pentium	66.7	65.1	63.6
SGI Indigo2	MIPS R4400	150	85.9	93.6
Compaq DeskPro	Intel 486DX2	66	32.2	16.0
IBM RS/6000 580	Power	62.5	73.3	134.6
DECstation 3000/500	Alpha	150	84.4	127.7
HP 735	PA7100	99	80.6	149.8
Sun SS10/52	SuperSPARC	45	58.1	78.4

As you can see from the sample results, some systems have Specint and Specfp results that are close to each other, whereas others have been more optimized for floating point (at the expense of integer) performance. In deciding which set of numbers to believe, you need to look at the application set that you run as described in the following section.

11.7.1 What the SPEC Suite Measures

Table 11.2 shows the list of benchmarks in SPEC92 along with a brief description of each one. Do not be discouraged if you are having difficulty figuring out just what most of these benchmarks are measuring. You are not alone! Even though the SPEC integer and FP benchmarks (which SPEC calls CINT and CFP) are immensely more useful than all the other CPU benchmarks in the industry combined, it is hard to corollate their results with real-life applications. For example, because there is no desktop publishing application in SPEC suites, it is sometimes difficult to see how such an application would perform in a system. Even where there is a match as in the case of the gcc C compiler, the results should not be generalized. Specifically, it is unlikely that the performance of a system running gcc can be extrapolated to other compilers in the system. The gcc results are only a gross estimation of the actual performance you might get. Having said this, the data are much more valid than, say, Dhrystone or, worse yet, Linkpak in this case.

Another problem is the freedom that vendors take with respect to compile/link options when building binaries from the SPEC sources. Some use as many as 10–15 flags to compile each benchmark. Worse yet, the flags vary from benchmark to benchmark. SPEC's solution to this problem is to require that vendors specify all compiler and linker options when they report their results. Although this is a step in the right direction, we are not sure that it solves the problem. Specifically, it is doubtful that an average user or even an experienced software developer would know what such options as `xlygetvalue`, `-aggressive=a`, or `mP2OPT_conditional_lim=TRUE` really mean.[2]

---

2. Flags taken at random from the *SPEC newsletter,* Volume 5, Issue 3.

Table 11.2 Spec92 Benchmarks and Their Functions

Benchmark	Type	Language	Size[a]	Description
Espresso	Integer	C	0.3	A PLA electronic circuit generation and optimization program
Li	Integer	C	0.2	A small lisp interpreter (Xlisp) solving the "nine queens" problem on a chess board
Eqntot	Integer	C	0.4	A CAD tool that translates Boolean equations into truth table; spends most of its time in quicksort
Compress	Integer	C	0.5	Clone of the UNIX compress utility working on a 1-Mbyte file (20 times)
Sc	Integer	C	0.3	A spreadsheet program calculating various formulas such as amortization and SPECmarks (heavily relies on the curses library)
Gcc	Integer	C	0.9	The GNU C Compiler compiling its own sources down to Sun-3 assembly language
Spice2g6	Float-64	FORTRAN	8.4	The Berkeley analog circuit simulation program mostly doing an LU decomposition
Doduc	Float-64	FORTRAN	0.4	Monte Carlo simulation kernel (Physics)
Mdljdp2	Float-64	FORTRAN	0.5	Simulation solving equations of motion for the interaction of 500 atoms (Quantum Chemistry)
Wave5	Float-32	FORTRAN	14.6	Solves Maxwell's and particle equations to simulate a plasma (Physics)
Tomcatv	Float-64	FORTRAN	3.8	Two-dimensional "mesh generator" and solver (CAD)
Ora	Float-64	FORTRAN	0.2	A ray-tracing algorithm used in calculating reflections (3D Graphics)
Alvinn	Float-32	C	0.6	A neural network trainer (Robotics)
Ear	Float-32	C	0.2	A human ear simulation (Signal Processing)
Mdljsp2	Float-32	FORTRAN	0.4	Simulation solving equations of motion for the interaction of 500 atoms (Quantum Chemistry)
Swm256	Float-32		3.8	Shallow Water Modeling using Finite Difference method (Weather Prediction)
Su2cor	Float-64	FORTRAN	4.4	Solver for masses of elementary particles (Quantum Physics)
Hydro2d	Float-64	FORTRAN	0.6	Solves fluid dynamic equations using Navier-Stokes method (Physics)
Nasa7	Float-64	FORTRAN	3.1	The NASA benchmark suite consisting of 7 programs, which include Linpak & Complex FFT
Fpppp	Float-64	FORTRAN	0.6	A solver taken from the public domain program Gaussion88 (Quantum Chemistry)

a.Static size measured in megabytes on SUN SPARC.

Another problem is the technique of invoking a preprocessor to rewrite the benchmark effectively so that it better fits in the CPU caches (using the so-called blocking schemes). This has a dramatic effect on some benchmarks resulting in two- to fourfold speed-up. A prime example of such an effect was the matrix300 benchmark, which allowed vendors to achieve SPEC ratings of four to five times the average for the system. The problem was so pronounced that the SPEC committee eliminated matrix300 from Spec92.

Even though vendors are not allowed to modify any part of the benchmark, such auto-mated (i.e., compiler-directed) modification of the program is allowed. The justification is that these preprocessors can indeed be useful in real-life applications. Although this is true, the preprocessors are often expensive options that are not shipped with the system or the standard compilers. Additionally, only a subset of real-life floating-point applications can benefit from these preprocessors. Yet, they manage to largely inflate the value of Specfp to an extent that can be misleading.

To its credit, SPEC has developed a new baseline result system where vendors are restricted to only a minimal set of required compiler and linker flags. These results should be much closer to what you can achieve with standard tools provided with the system. Unfortunately, the baseline results are not frequently reported (at least not in the popular press), and vendors usually tout only their highly optimized, traditional results.

Due to the difficulty of interpreting individual results, users have all but given up on look-ing at the individual numbers and always use the single figures of merit. Because reporting the results of the entire suite is one of the strengths of SPEC, in Table 11.3 we try to give you some pointers as how to corollate the results of individual benchmarks to the perfor-mance you are likely to get with your own application. Again, keep in mind that no bench-mark predicts the performance of your application with 100% accuracy. There is simply no replacement for running your own application on the target system. But, if this is not possible (as is often the case), the following analysis should help you avoid making any catastrophic mistakes.

11.7.2 SPECrate for Multiprocessor Systems

An early complaint against the SPEC CPU suite was the fact that it was single threaded. That is, it executed sequentially and, hence, did not take advantage of more than one CPU. So, a new measure (not benchmark) was invented to deal with this problem. SPECrate_int92 and SPECrate_fp92 measure how many SPECmarks the system can exe-cute in a given amount of time (1 week in the current version). This is done by starting multiple copies of the program until the execution time exceeds the allotted time.

Given the large caches of today's multiprocessor systems, the SPECrate results usually track the number of CPUs in the system. For example, the DEC 7000/610 AXP system generates 3251, 6436, 12709, and 19180 SPECrate_int92 for 1, 2, 4, and 6 CPUs. In gen-eral, we feel that SPECrate exaggerates the effectiveness of MP implementations.

Table 11.3 Typical Applications and Their Relationship to SPEC CPU Benchmarks

Category	Type	Spec Benchmarks	Correlation	Comments
UNIX Kernel	Integer	Specint	Good	System calls and kernel execution profile not represented
UNIX Utilities	Integer	diff, gcc, specint	Good	Little I/O or system call in the suite
File Server/ NFS	Integer	Specint	Fair	No I/O or networking code (Use SPEC SFS instead)
C Compiler, Assembler & Linker	Integer	gcc, Specint	Good	gcc not the main compiler used in most systems. No benchmark for make
Desktop Publishing	Mostly Integer	Specint	Fair	Graphics output not represented
Digital Simulation & Synthesis	Integer	Specint	Very Good	Good correlation in practice despite lack of direct representation in the benchmark
Electronic PCB Design (Routing)	Integer	Specint	Good	Good correlation in practice despite lack of direct representation in the benchmark
Analog Simulation	Float	spice2g6, Specfp	Very Good	
Database Access	Integer	Specint	Fair	No I/O or context switch benchmarks
3D Graphics	Float	ray, Specfp	Fair	Performance often limited by the 3D hardware and not the CPU
Mechanical CAD (2D)	Float	Specfp	Fair	Drawing operations not represented
Mechanical CAD (3D Solid)	Float	ora, Specfp	Fair	See 3D graphics
Materials Analysis (e.g., FEA)	Float	Nasa7, Specfp	Very Good	
Flight Simulation	Float	Specfp	Fair	I/O and context switch time not represented
Statistical & Financial Modeling	Float & Integer	Specfp & Specint	Good	

Although user-bound applications will probably track the results of SPECrate to some extent, system-bound environments for which many multiprocessor systems are designed are likely to fare much worse.

11.7.3 How to Obtain SPEC Benchmarks

You can contact SPEC to become a member and receive the newsletters that include the latest reports from various vendors. You can reach SPEC at

> SPEC [Standard Performance Evaluation Corporation]
> c/o NCGA [National Computer Graphics Association]
> 2722 Merrilee Drive
> Suite 200
> Fairfax, VA 22031
> USA
> Phone: +1-703-698-9600 Ext. 325
> FAX: +1-703-560-2752
> Email: spec-ncga@cup.portal.com

The costs for various SPEC suites as of this writing are listed in Table 11.4 (accredited universities receive a 50% discount).

The *SPEC Newsletter,* which contains articles about the SPEC benchmarks and latest official results for various systems, comes out quarterly and costs $550 per year. It is a worthwhile publication if you have any interest in this field. Alternatively, you can join SPEC as a full member, which gives you voting rights and early access to all the benchmarks and, of course, subscription to the newsletter. There is an initiation fee of $1000 for membership and annual dues of $5000.

Of course, you should contact SPEC directly to get the most up-to-date pricing on all their products and services. We should note that, to their credit, the SPEC suites have been priced just to cover the administrative costs of running the organization. This is shown again in the pricing of the latest version, SPEC95, which covers only media costs.

In addition to the SPEC organization itself, SPEC results are available from all major system and CPU vendors. If you have access to the Internet and the World Wide Web, you

Table 11.4 Typical SPEC Benchmark Suite Pricing

Benchmark Suite	Benchmark Description	Source License
CINT92	CPU-intensive integer suite	$425
CFP92	CPU-intensive floating-point suite	$575
CINT92 & CFP92	Combined CINT92 and CFP92	$900
SDM	UNIX software development suite	$1450
SFS	NFS benchmark suite	$1200

may want to look at the performance data on `http://performance.netlib.org` where a copy of the SPEC results is available.

11.8 SPEC SDM Multiuser Suite

One of the first criticisms voiced by the industry against the SPEC CPU benchmark was the fact that it was a strictly CPU benchmark and did not address other parts of the system (most significantly, the I/O subsystem). SPEC's solution was to produce the SDM multiuser benchmark.

SDM contains two kernels, both of which are based on rather old UNIX benchmarks. The first kernel is called SDET and is based on what used to be a proprietary benchmark from AT&T by the name of Gaede. This benchmark uses a mix of UNIX commands (such as ed, make, cc, rm cd, echo, ls, cpio, and pr) to simulate per-user load. The results of SDET are reported as the number of scripts executed per hour. There are no actual terminals involved, and each user is really a shell script. As a result, there is no think time between commands nor are there any realistic keyboard input streams.

As is probably apparent by now, we are not great fans of simple-minded benchmarks such as Gaede. The profile of the UNIX tools used to simulate user load does not match usage of any modern UNIX environments that we are aware of (e.g., how many users still use *ed* as their main editor?[3]). The same can be said of the frequency of each command (e.g., four pr commands versus two greps). Some commands such as echo are now built into the shell, so timing the speed of the stand-alone utility is uninteresting. Although these faults are understandable given the age of Gaede (circa 1982), we are surprised that the command set as a minimum was not updated after adoption by SPEC. Given these problems, we are sorry to say that it is hard to put considerable value on the results of this benchmark.

The other benchmark in SDM is an updated version of the MUSBUS benchmark developed by the Monash University in Australia which is renamed to Kenbus1. Although still based on a UNIX command set (rm, cp, export, mkdir, cc, ed, grep, chmod, cat, and ls), this benchmark is much more sophisticated than SDET. Specifically, it tries to simulate an input stream by feeding characters one at a time to the scripts using a pipe connection. (The typing rate is a reasonable 3 characters/sec). Like SDET, the results of Kenbus1 are reported as the number of scripts executed per hour. But note that the results of the two benchmarks are independent and should not be compared to each other.

Despite its sophistication, Kenbus1 unintentionally puts a heavy emphasis on the performance of the pipe system call because all user input and output are done using pipes. As the number of users goes up, most of the CPU cycles are consumed copying bytes from one user space to another. Because some pipe implementations are very slow (e.g., in

---

3. Or have ever heard of this program!

BSD), these systems face a handicap even though the performance of pipes is of little consequence in most environments. Just as with SDET, the command set in Kenbus1 is dated, and the frequency used (e.g., five `rms` to one `grep`) is not very defensible.

The bottom line is that neither of the benchmarks in SDM is an accurate model of what happens in a typical multiuser system today. The classical UNIX multiuser system has either transformed into a server system connected by Ethernet to many X terminals (or workstations running X) or one that is used as a database server. The former is likely to be executing many larger X applications across the network presenting a load that is substantially different than what is modeled. The latter is much better benchmarked using the TPC suites than SDM.

Perhaps for these reasons, SPEC SDM has not garnered the kind of wide appeal that the CPU suites have achieved. More work is needed in this area to develop a benchmark that more closely simulates modern UNIX multiuser environments.

11.9 SPEC SFS NFS Benchmark

Since the introduction of NFS, users have been searching for file servers that could host their files in one central location but with minimal impact on system performance as perceived by individual clients. However, evaluating NFS servers is quite difficult because we are not just looking at an individual system but also a cluster of machines connected with networks that have their own complex characteristics.

Lack of a suitable benchmark led some vendors to invent their own. One such effort was the Nhfsstone benchmark, which was developed by Legato Systems—a vendor specializing in NFS accelerators. This benchmark has been adopted by SPEC and renamed to SFS. The are some small, but significant, differences between the two suites, which make it impossible to compare their results. But, because SFS has completely replaced Nhfsstone, this is not much a problem.

SPEC SFS (also known as Laddis) uses client workstations and a target file server to simulate a typical program development environment. The model for this environment has been derived from traces of actual systems where the frequency of various operations (e.g., `read`, `write`, `unlink`) and their sizes were recorded (e.g., block size for each read and write). One or more client workstations are used to generate these requests.

In an interesting twist, SFS does not use the client NFS code to generate the NFS requests. Instead, the benchmark contains its own NFS client protocol stack. This is necessary because generating file server traffic using a standard NFS client can be quite difficult. Normal file operation may or may not result in actual requests to the server due to the client's buffer cache. By bypassing the client file system and NFS code, SFS can generate the exact number of NFS operations in its profile with guaranteed repeatability (at least from the client's point of view).

Going around the client NFS code means that the `biod` daemon running on the client also gets bypassed. To compensate for this, SFS models the asynchronous nature of the `biod` daemon internally. The number of `biod`s is specified in a configuration file, and SFS uses it to figure out how many transactions can be outstanding at any one time.

Note that SPEC does not mandate that vendors use any specific hardware or network for this benchmark—only that they must specify it in the report. Therein lies our main criticism against SFS. In a quest to get the highest possible ratings, vendors have picked very large configurations to run SFS (see Table 11.5). We doubt that these configurations match even the largest file servers in the field. In addition, there is no consistency among vendors, making it impossible to do an "apples and apples" comparison. For example, some vendors use FDDI networks when running the benchmark, whereas others use Ethernet. The same goes for vendors who use unusually high numbers of network adaptors. Because of these issues, the SFS results have not proven as useful as they could be. Hopefully, over time, the industry will converge on a standard hardware and network configuration.

As you can see from Table 11.5, the results of SFS are reported in units of "SPECnfs_A93 Ops/Sec". To generate this rating, the number of clients (and, hence, the number of requests sent to the server) is increased until the average response time for each request exceeds 50 milliseconds. The maximum number of requests per second is then reported along with how many "SPECnfs_A93 users" the system can handle. The number of users is computed based on the assumption that each user makes on the average 10 requests/sec. So, the number of users is a simple division of SPECnfs_A93 Ops/Sec by 10.

11.10 X Window Benchmarks

The state of the art in graphics benchmarks falls considerably shorter than suites such as the SPEC CPU benchmark. The industry (especially the X terminal market) has strongly endorsed two micro benchmarks, `xstone` and `xmark`. They are called micro benchmarks because they time only individual X operations rather than a profile of calls used in a typical application. Although micro benchmarks can be useful, they are not nearly as valuable as a full-blown application benchmark in judging the performance of a system.

Table 11.5 Sample SPEC SFS Ratings

System	CPUs	Disks	Networks	"SPECnfs_A93 Users"
Auspex NS 6000	4 (FPs)	60	8 (Ethernet)	131 @ 48 ms
Sun SPARCserver 1000	8	34	2 (FDDI)	140 @ 31.2 ms
Sun SPARCserver 2000	8	66	2 (FDDI)	242 @ 35.4 ms
HP 9000 Model H60	1	32	1 (FDDI)	131 @ 48 ms

xstone (which is an X client) is run on one system, and the output is usually sent to the X server (over the network in the case of X terminals). Despite its popularity, we are unsure as to how useful the profile of operations used in xstone is.

xmark is not really a benchmark by itself. Instead, it summarizes the data reported by the standard x11perf benchmark, which is part of the X distribution by MIT. x11perf exercises the speed of many of the X operations and reports how many were executed per second. xmark takes this output and assigns weights to each one of the operations. Highest weights are assigned to scrolling, line drawing, and text output.

The problem we have with xmark is that it includes many X operations that are either not used in typical applications or their usage is so infrequent as to make their speed irrelevant to application performance. For example, we are not sure if anyone cares about how fast a server can fill a 100-pixel ellipse. Yet, the weight for this operation is *one third of text display* and *line drawing,* both of which are very common operations.

Instead of relying on xmark or xstone, we recommend that you get a copy of the x11perf itself and analyze its detailed results yourself. If you are running a drawing-intensive application (e.g., Electrical CAD), pay particular attention to the rate of 10- and 100-pixel solid lines. The speed of these operations determines how fast the server can display complex drawings, which usually consist of many 2D vectors (lines). Look for a 10-pixel line speed of at least 300,000/sec.

For normal, everyday use, look at the text display rate. "Char in 80-char line (TR-10)" measures how fast you can display text. This is a very common operation and comes into play when you scroll text in a window (e.g., by moving the scroll bars in xterm). The rates for this operation need to be surprisingly high for fast display response. To see why, assume that you want to scroll the text in a window that has 80 lines by 120 characters by holding down the scroll key (e.g., the j key in vi). If the keyboard repeat rate is 10 characters/sec, you need to output text at a speed of 96000 characters/sec. If the text drawing rate is slower than this, scrolling will fall behind the input rate—a rather annoying experience.

The NoOp benchmark is also important to look at (in a workstation environment) despite the fact that its name implies otherwise. The benchmark times how long it takes to send a message to the server, which does nothing. Even though this may not seem valuable, the speed of the NoOp test indicates how fast the communication mechanism (including context switches) operates. This test also gives the upper bound of how fast the X operations could go. For example, if you see 1 million NoOps/sec rate and a single pixel drawing operation of 800,000/sec, you can assume that the small pixel drawing operations are bound by the speed of the protocol and not the hardware drawing speed. Note that the NoOp speed is a function of the speed of the CPU and the efficiency of the kernel code in dealing with UNIX domain socket connections.

11.11 Database Benchmarks

The database community has traditionally been obsessed with the term Transactions Per Second (tps) with the same fervor that the rest of the computer community treats MIPS. Just the same, tps started as a vague measure often specified by hardware vendor without hardly any details as to how it was measured. Needless to say, this led to much confusion and made system comparisons very difficult.

The first step in arriving at a useful tps rating was a proposal by Jim Gray of Tandem in the form of a DebitCredit benchmark. This was based on his earlier work at IBM on a similar benchmark called TP1. Although his work was a step in the right direction, the benchmark led to many misleading published results due to lack of audit and "simplification" performed by some vendors.

The DebitCredit benchmark and subsequent auditing requirements led to the formation of the Transaction Processing Performance Council and its now famous TPC benchmarks. As of this writing, there are three variations (TPC-A, TPC-B, and TPC-C) and work continues on TPC-D.

Like Gray's proposal, the TPC benchmarks include provisions for calculating the cost of the benchmarked system so that a "$/tps" ratio can be computed. The cost computation is based on the nondiscounted purchase price of the complete hardware, software (operating system and database), connecting terminals (if applicable), and 5-year maintenance cost. Although it is doubtful that this is the actual cost that you will pay (e.g., the full list price of the base system price is used without any discount), it does standardize the calculation technique. Even though this is not a perfect metric, it does avoid the problem of vendors inventing their own measures (as is the case with "$/Specint").

Another side benefit of the $/tps measure is that it motivates the vendors to keep their benchmarked system configurations as small as possible. So, we consider this a positive attribute of the TPC benchmarks as long as you keep in mind that it should be used only for comparative purposes and not as a way to actually compute the price of a target system.

The TPC requires "full disclosure" of all factors involved in the benchmarking effort from configuration of the system to any actual tuning performed on it. This should make it easy for users to validate and, if desired, duplicate the results. The TPC started by only recommending that the benchmark results be audited by an outside firm to remove any doubts concerning validity of the results. As of 1994, the guidelines have been changed, and the audit process is now mandatory. These measures go a long way toward gaining user confidence in the results generated by the suites despite the monetary overhead it creates for the vendor. Indeed, support for TPC benchmarks has been strong, especially in the case of TPC-A where results are available for over 150 systems as of this writing.

Note that TPC benchmarks are not tied to any one database software. Any database program that is capable of running the benchmark can be utilized. So, care should be taken to look only at the results generated using your desired database program. Because some databases are more tuned for one hardware platform than for another, the results of a TPC run on, say, Oracle should not be extrapolated to others like Sybase, Informix, and Ingress.

11.11.1 TPC-A

The TPC-A benchmark simulates a banking system where a single-transaction type (making a deposit) is performed repeatedly. The deposit affects three (indexed) files: the depositor (to update his account balance), the teller, and branch data. In addition, a fourth file is updated (sequentially) to keep a history of all the transactions.

To simulate user input, another system (also called the RTE or the Remote Terminal Emulator) must be used to handle the generation of transactions. The TPC allows the RTE to be connected to the system under test (SUT) using either a local area network (usually Ethernet) or a wide area network. The results of the benchmark have to include the designation "TPC-A-lan" or "TPC-A-wan" depending on the type of network used. In practice, the industry has heavily favored the LAN version, and the results are simply specified as TPC-A.

To make the benchmark more realistic, each transaction in TPC-A must be followed by a 10-second "think time." This means that to generate one transaction per second, you need ten terminals driving the database server. In order to get higher transaction ratings, the number of terminals needs to be increased. But before doing so, the specification requires that the database files also grow to be more representative of larger systems.

To measure the infamous TPS rating, the load on the database server is increased until the response time of 10% of the transactions exceeds 2 seconds. Put another way, the benchmark considers an under-2-second response time for 90% of its user community as the highest level of tolerance for delay.

The TPC-A benchmark turns out to be very disk-intensive and does fairly little processing of data. The various index files are constantly updated because every transaction requires modification of many database files. It could be argued that in a real-world situation, at least some of the transactions would be queries and not require immediate writes. For this reason, high tps reports also accompany very large disk configurations to cope with the high volume of disk writes required to sustain high transaction rates.

The system cost formula has also suffered from a huge reduction in the cost of the core system and is often dominated by the price of user terminals and disk drives. Hardware vendors try to use the cheapest terminal prices they can find in TPC-A cost computations even if this means that they have to use another vendor's product. These limitations in TPC-A have led to the development of the TPC-C benchmark described in Section 11.11.13.

11.11.2 TPC-B

The TPC-B benchmark is essentially the same as TPC-A with the exception that the transactions are generated on the same system that is running the database software. This in essence models a batch-oriented environment. For this reason, the system cost does not include the price of the user terminals making the cost of the disk drives stand out. Because TPC-B uses the same type of transactions as TPC-A, its performance is also largely limited by the disk subsystem.

As of this writing, TPC-B is gaining momentum rapidly, but the volume of results still lags behind TPC-A.

11.11.3 TPC-C

The TPC-C benchmark is radically different from TPC-A and TPC-B and models an order-entry system. The transactions are against a "company" that warehouses a stock of 100,000 items and fills orders against them. Like the other TPC benchmarks, the database is scaled for higher transaction ratings.

TPC-C addresses one of our main criticisms against TPC-A and TPC-B in that it uses five transaction types (new order, payment, order status query, delivery, and stock-level query). The transaction types are picked either randomly based on a weighted distribution or sequentially from a random set.

Like TPC-A, this benchmark requires an RTE simulating user terminals. The response time is measured at the terminal, but in an interesting twist, the 90% response time threshold is not used for all the transactions. Based on a real-life situation, the stock-level query can stand delays of up to 20 seconds, whereas the other transaction types must complete in under 5 seconds. There are also other parameters such as query-specific think time, minimum mean of think time distribution, and the transaction mix. In short, TPC-C attempts to provide a much more realistic Online Transaction Processing (OLTP) benchmark than TPC-A or TPC-B. Unfortunately, as of this writing, TPC-C results are spotty. Over time, we hope to see more TPC-C results than the more simple-minded results of TPC-A and TPC-B.

11.11.4 Applicability of TPC Results

As we already mentioned, TPC-A and TPC-B suites are perhaps much more disk (write)-intensive than even real-life banking environments, let alone other transaction processing situations. But, more importantly, we worry about the extent to which vendors resort to hand tuning their systems and databases to achieve the highest number of transactions per second.

It is not uncommon for a system vendor to spend months setting up one of their most complex configurations in order to beat another vendor's highest numbers. Some configurations include tens of disk drives, many megabytes of memory, and eight or more processors pegging the system price close to $1M in some cases. In addition, the database server is highly tuned by experts who know "what knobs to turn" to get the best TPC performance. We doubt that many users have such budgets or access to this level of expertise both at the UNIX system level or the database server. Although these exercises can be useful in detecting the headroom (future capacity for expansion) for a system, we would like to see smaller configurations also tested.

As for applicability, we are not aware of any studies correlating the performance of real systems to TPC results (specially TPC-A and TPC-B). So, you may be better off using the result as just a gross estimation of your target system. As another guide, you may want to look at the SPECint/SPECrate of the CPU. The reason is that transaction processing systems (i.e., databases) can be very CPU-intensive. To reduce latency and improve performance, database vendors usually split the server process into multiple copies, each serving a specific number of users. This causes a fair number of context switches, especially if the ratio of number of users is high compared to the available number of CPUs. Context switches are very CPU-intensive and, although not directly measured by any benchmark in the SPECint suite, usually track the overall performance of the CPU in well-designed systems.

It goes without saying that you should trust only the TPC results from vendors if they are run using your desired database program. Even though database vendors are always tuning their software, performance still varies among them. In addition, some are more tuned (hand optimized) for one system than another. In other words, do not try to extrapolate the results to other database systems.

11.11.5 Getting More Information on TPC

Additional information about the TPC benchmarks can be attained by contacting

> Shanley Public Relations
> 777 North First Street, Suite 600
> San Jose, CA 95112-6311
> Phone (408) 295-8894
> Fax (408) 295-2613

11.12 Proprietary Benchmarks

In this chapter, we focused on benchmarks that are widely available. There are also a number of proprietary benchmarks that also exist in the market. The best-known is the AIM benchmark. The AIM suite VII is a multiuser benchmark available from AIM Technologies. It attempts to measure the performance of the system using synthetic work loads. We call them synthetic because the benchmarks are not really based on actual applications but on simplified models of each. Over the years, AIM suite VI has enjoyed wide popularity, and the results are available for many systems.

To get more information about AIM suite VI or their other benchmarks, contact AIM technologies at

AIM Technology
4699 Old Ironsides Dr., Suite 150
Santa Clara, CA 95054
Phone: (408) 748-8649, (800) 848-8649 (outside CA)
Fax: (408) 748-0161
Email: benchinfo@aim.com

If you are interested in AIM suite VI results only, you can get a low-cost subscription ($29.95 plus shipping for five quarterly issues) which includes certified results from various vendors.

11.13 Conclusions

Although the current crop of computer benchmarks are not perfect, they allow you to choose your systems more wisely. In evaluating the results, it is very important to understand what the benchmark actually measures as opposed to what it claims to do. This is useful in determining whether the results are applicable to your situation.

CHAPTER 12

Choosing the
Right Hardware

By now, you should be familiar with the techniques involved in analyzing performance problems. If our experience is any indication, there is a good chance that the source of your performance problems is the hardware and not UNIX. To that end, in this chapter we discuss the current, high-volume architectures that run UNIX as of this writing.

12.1 Understanding Design Cycles

One of the most common questions users are concerned with is which system is the fastest. Unfortunately, there is no easy answer to this question. Although you can look at the performance results of competing systems and pick the highest performing one in the list, your selection will be wrong in a few months. This has to do with the skewed design cycles of computer and CPU manufactures.

Assuming that the competing companies all have competent designers, each will be aiming to produce a system that outperforms all others when it comes to market. Because the hardware manufactures do not synchronize their efforts for obvious competitive reasons, their products are bound to come out at different times. Given the fact that the basic semiconductor technology is also constantly improving, a later design will be able to use more advanced technology than one started a year earlier. The process is typically shown as a sinusoidal phenomenon with each vendor holding the title for the fastest systems for a few months at a time (see Figure 12.1).

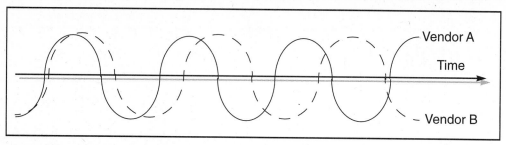

Figure 12.1 Sinusoidal Design Cycles

Note that we are not saying that this rule is always true. Indeed, it is possible for a manufacturer to fall behind the technology curve and not be able to catch up with the others. You can tell if this is occurring if a vendor is not able to outperform its competitors over a period of 1–2 years. A prime example is the Motorola 68K series, which has fallen behind the technology curve (the latest 68060 processor, while quite useful in embedded systems, struggles to achieve one third of the best performing processor today). Of course, you do not need the fastest system to get the best price/performance ratio. So if the latter is more important to you, then a slower performing system may still be a good buy.

12.2 Survival of the Fittest

In the 1970s and early 1980s, there were many CPU architectures. Today, the total number can almost be counted on one hand. The reason has to do with software availability. Third-party application developers only target systems that have high volumes. New architectures face the proverbial "chicken and egg" problem in that they are not able to get software "ported" to their systems because they have not sold many systems yet. But, if they do not get the software, they cannot gain the volume they need. Although heavy monetary investments can jump start this process, it is not always entirely successful.

In the following sections, we will point out the fastest and best systems out there. But you should keep in mind the software availability issue. It does not make any difference how fast a system is if your favorite software does not run on it.

In choosing your application software, you may want to check to see how many hardware platforms it runs on. By selecting a software package that is available on many platforms, you broaden the number of systems that you can potentially purchase. This may become very important if you "run out of horsepower" on your first platform.

12.3 Selecting the Best Architecture

As we mentioned, your foremost criterion in selecting your system should be software availability. The next step is to decide whether you care about lowest price, price/performance, or absolute performance regardless of cost.

PCs clearly hold the record for the lowest-priced systems and have maintained this lead mainly due to huge volumes and heavy discounting. However, the majority of PC UNIX applications are targeted toward commercial (i.e., multiuser) environments, and there is a total absence of engineering and scientific applications. For this reason, PCs do not make a direct replacement for the traditional workstation, although the situation may change in the future.

Entry-level workstations often provide the best price/performance, although in some situations PCs can give them heavy competition. Absolute highest performance has been the realm of high-end RISC workstations and multiprocessor servers, and the trend seems to indicate that the situation will remain the same for the foreseeable future.

12.4 X86 PCs

Even though PCs are best known as DOS and Windows machines, large numbers are also being used to run UNIX. As a general rule, PCs provide the best performance for the lowest-price category (systems under $5000). They do not have the highest performance (RISC processors hold that record) and, surprisingly, do not always provide the best price/performance. Nevertheless, their extremely low cost makes them a very attractive choice if you are on a budget.

In choosing a PC over other systems, keep in mind that the benchmark results for PCs may not be representative of the system that you purchase. A case in point is the SPEC CPU benchmark results. The only data available are for a handful of systems (see Table 12.6),

Table 12.1 Performance of X86 Offerings (as of mid-1995)

System	Clock Speed	SPECint92	SPECfp92
Xpress Desktop Pentium with 1 Mbyte L2 cache	120	140.0	103.9
Xpress Desktop Pentium with 1 Mbyte L2 cache	100	121.9	93.2
Xpress Desktop Pentium with 1 Mbyte L2 cache	90	110.1	84.4
Xpress Desktop Pentium with 512 Kbytes L2 cache	120	133.7	99.5
Xpress Desktop Pentium with 512 Kbytes L2 cache	100	118.1	89.9
Xpress Desktop Pentium with 512 Kbytes L2 cache	90	106.5	81.4
Xpress Desktop Pentium with 512 Kbytes L2 cache	75	89.1	68.5
Xpress Desktop Pentium with 256 Kbytes L2 cache	66	78.0	63.6
Xpress Desktop Pentium with 256 Kbytes L2 cache	60	70.4	55.1
SNI PCE-5S Pentium	100	96.2	81.2
SNI PCE-5S Pentium	90	86.3	81.2
Compaq System PRO/XL	66	65.1	63.6
486 DX4	99	~48	~24
Compaq DeskPro 486 DX2	33/66	32.2	16.0

which, although similar, are unlikely to be identical to the "no name clone" system that you may be buying. Indeed as you see in the performance data (which were gathered from the Intel Web database), Intel has not even published data for the 90-, 100-, and 120-MHz systems with 256 Kbytes of cache, even though this is by far the most common PC configuration. Even if Intel had included such data, you would be hard pressed to extrapolate the results to any system other than the one Intel has benchmarked (which, in all likelihood, is based on the Intel chip-set). In contrast, workstation vendors release benchmark results for the identical system that you are purchasing so you are more likely to get what you expect.

Given the large volume of PC sales, there are usually three classes of performance available. As of this writing, the low-end consists of 66- and 100-Mhz 486 and compatible processors. The mid-end is occupied by 60- and 75-MHz Pentiums. The top-end currently belongs to 90–133-MHz Pentiums. We do not see any benefit in buying low-end systems because the price advantage is fairly small and is typically dwarfed by the cost of a fully configured system. The small savings are also wiped out by the loss of productivity especially if you use floating-point applications for which the 486 is a poor fit.

12.4.1 The Intel P6

The successor to the Pentium is the P6, and its performance takes off from where Pentium ends. The P6 is initially clocked at 133 MHz using a 0.6-micron design. We expect Intel to shrink P6 quickly and volumes to really start on one of the first high-volume, 0.35-micron lines (where the 120-MHz processors are produced today). The P6 has almost twice as many transistors as the Pentium (5.5 million versus 3.3 million). In an unusual twist, the P6 consists of two pieces of silicon: the processor and 256 Kbytes of secondary cache. By putting the L2 cache on the same substrate, Intel is able to run the bus clock at much higher speeds than would be possible on an external PC board. As a result, the P6 enjoys a much higher bandwidth to the CPU than the Pentium. The higher bandwidth is necessary because the P6, despite its higher performance, has only a 16-Kbyte L1 cache on board.

The estimated performance of P6 at 133 MHz is 200 SPECint92 and 170 SPECfp92. The higher performance is a function of more aggressive superscalar design than the Pentium (three instructions executed in parallel versus two on the Pentium). While the integer performance is very competent, the floating-point performance does not break new ground compared to RISC offerings. As the clock speed quickly ramps up to 150 and then 200 MHz, Intel will continue its pressure on the RISC vendors to keep improving their performance or risk getting run over.

12.4.2 Picking the Right PC System

Selecting the best performing PC system can be quite challenging. It is nearly impossible to find UNIX performance data, so you are stuck evaluating systems based on DOS or Windows benchmarks. Extrapolating the data from these benchmarks to the performance that you can get under UNIX can be impossible at times. This is especially the case with graphics cards that have optimized Windows drivers but often have only functional drivers for UNIX. Another problem with some benchmarks such as the CPU performance meters is that they are the glorified versions of the old NoOp test. They are too simplistic to show the difference between various memory subsystems, for example. Although this hadn't been an issue in slow, 486-based systems, it is definitely a problem in Pentium and P6-based machines.

All is not lost, however. As far as the base motherboard is concerned, select a PCI system that either comes with or allows expansion of the L2 cache to 512 Kbytes or more. The normal cache size of 256 Kbytes is too small to keep the processor satisfied. If possible, make sure that the cache is write-back and that it uses synchronous SRAMs. Even though your PC vendor is unlikely to know this information, some detailed product reviews in the *PC Magazine* do include such information in their comparison tables or side-bar articles.

For memory subsystem, see if you can find a system that supports the EDO type DRAM. These devices not only run faster but their support indicates that the memory controller is of a newer design (such as Intel's Triton chip-set) and, hence, has a better chance of offering good PCI performance and reduced memory latency. While we are on this subject, note that the low price offered on your PC is almost always with 8 Mbytes of memory, which is inadequate for running UNIX. Make sure that you have at least 16 Mbytes and, preferably, 32 Mbytes of memory, especially if you are planning to run X.

Be especially careful of some cacheless Pentium systems that have started to appear of late. These machines (which are usually based on the 75-MHz Pentium) rely on the internal cache of the Pentium and do not sport any kind of secondary cache. Despite the use of faster EDO DRAMs, these machines are bound to perform poorly in many applications. So, be sure to ask if your system includes a secondary cache and, if so, how much it includes.

On the issue of disk storage, we recommend that you stick with PCI SCSI controllers, even though the enhanced IDE drives also provide good performance. At the low-end of the price spectrum Enhanced IDE drives are bound to be faster, but there are simply no high-end solutions comparable to the top of the line, 7200-RPM SCSI drives as of this writing. Along these lines, do not buy the packaged disk drive offered with most preconfigured systems. These are usually low-speed IDE or SCSI drives. Instead, invest in a high-performance (preferably, 7200-RPM) drive.

12.5 Selecting RISC Systems

RISC systems currently hold the speed records for both integer and floating-point performance. Most of these systems have efficient I/O subsystems that outperform all but the best PC solutions. This is fortunate because availability of third-party hardware is very limited on these systems compared to PCs.

The pioneer in this market is Sun SPARC, which was followed by MIPS. HP PA is also an early RISC adaptation, although its current PA-RISC systems bear little resemblance to the first-generation systems. IBM and DEC architectures are the latest to join the fury.

12.6 Sun SPARC

Being one of the earliest commercial implementations of RISC technology, the SPARC architecture sports a large installed base. The key to its continued success is software availability. The performance of the latest SuperSPARC (used in SPARCstation 20s) lags somewhat behind other architectures as of this writing. Even though SuperSPARC is a superscalar design, its clock speed remains very low (only 75 MHz as of this writing) compared to other competing systems. Although the floating-point performance is respectable, the SuperSPARC integer speed is only fair by today's standards.

The price/performance of SPARC systems remains respectable, especially if you consider the availability of a large amount of low-cost, third-party hardware. In addition, Sun sells fairly cost-effective multiprocessor systems. The additional processors come in handy when there is more than one runnable job in the system and, hence, are perfect for database servers and multiuser applications.

The Sun offerings fall into two classes: the entry-level systems, which use a highly integrated CPU complete with memory controller and I/O bus (called the MicroSPARC or uSPARC), and the high-end versions, which use a multichip solution (the standard chipset used in SPARCstation 10 and 20s). Although the entry-level systems do achieve fairly aggressive price targets, their performance is unexceptional (see Table 12.6). The high-end systems, on the other hand, use fairly large secondary caches, which result in good floating-point performance.

In choosing a SPARC system, pay particular attention to the size of the secondary cache. Models such as the 10/40 and 10/41 are differentiated only by the sizes of the their secondary caches. As you can see from Table 12.6, the larger cache results in a 10% speed-up in floating-point speed.

12.6.1 Sun UltraSPARC

Sun's answer to the performance challenges of other vendors is the all-new UltraSPARC. Based completely on a CMOS technology (SuperSPARC uses BiCMOS), the chip is expected to produce 240 SPECint92 and 350 SPECfp92. This is quite a jump from the SuperSPARC offerings, increasing performance level by a factor of three. The initial clock speeds are expected to be around 140–167 MHz and scaling up to 200 MHz over time.

An interesting aspect of the UltraSPARC is new instructions optimized for video decompression and compression for teleconferencing applications. If and when such applications become popular on the desktop, this feature should differentiate Sun from some of its

Table 12.2 Performance of Sun SPARC Offerings (as of mid-1995)

System	Clock Speed	SPECint92	SPECfp92
Sun 20/71	75	126	121
Sun 20/61	60	88.9	102.8
Sun 10/51	50	73.0	84.4
Sun 20/50	50	69.2	78.3
Sun 10/41	40	53	67
Sun 10/40	40	50.2	60.2
Sun 10/30	36	45.2	54.0
Sun 5 (uSPARC)	85	64.0	54.6
Sun 4 & 5 (uSPARC)	70	57.0	47.0

competitors (although others such as SGI are also working on similar features). The main enabling technology here is fast arithmetic operations on smaller data types (e.g., 16-bit operands), which is common in audio and video applications.

The foundry for the UltraSPARC is once again Texas Instruments, which is the current supplier for the SuperSPARC. The design is based on a 0.6-micron process that TI has been using for its high-end DSP (Digital Signal Processor) so volume availability should not be a problem this time around (lack of volume at high clock speeds was a major problem with the SuperSPARC).

12.7 HP PA-RISC

The PA-RISC architecture dates back to early years of RISC, but the latest generations (up to ninth at last count) are radically different from older CPUs bearing the same designation. The new designs are superscalar and run at fairly high clock speeds (up to 125 MHz as of this writing).

The most radical difference between PA-RISC and other architectures is the lack of primary cache in the CPU. HP takes advantage of the fact that the primary cache on the CPU is never large enough for floating-point-intensive codes or even some large, "ill-behaved" integer applications. By eliminating the primary cache, HP avoids the miss penalty of the on-board CPU cache before accessing the external cache. Elimination of the primary cache allows chip real estate to be used for very fast floating-point units. The resulting systems have excellent floating-point performance with very good integer speed (see Table 12.6). HP continues this trend of focusing on data access speed and latency as is evident in the newer 7200 architecture.

The down side to HP's architecture is the cost of the external cache RAMs. The speed of static memories required for some high-end systems (e.g., the 120-MHz 7200) is a super-

Table 12.3 Performance of HP PA-RISC Offerings (as of mid-1995)

System	Clock Speed	SPECint92	SPECfp92
HP K100/200/400	100	136.0	217.0
HP 735/125	125	136.0	201.0
HP 735/99	99	109.1	167.1
HP 755/99	99	109.1	167.1
HP 9000 GHI60	96	82.0	171.8
HP 9000 HI50	96	78.2	141.6
HP 712/80	80	84.3	122.3
HP 715/	80	83.5	120.9
HP 725/75	75	80.3	126.8
HP 715/100	100	100.1	137.0
HP 712/60	60	58.1	79.0
HP 715/64	64	66.6	96.5
HP 715/33	33	24.2	44.0
HP 725/50	50	36.9	70.0
HP 750	66	48.1	75

fast 6 nanoseconds. These devices cost considerably more than the "garden variety" 12- to 15-nanosecond chips used as secondary caches on other systems. The cost of the external cache has primarily relegated HP systems to the mid- to high-end range.

Another potential threat to HP is the ever-increasing chip densities, which allow competing architectures to constantly increase their primary CPU caches. We are not sure whether HP can keep its advantage once primary caches cross the 128-Kbyte barriers. Of course, HP can also follow the same scheme and use on-board caches as evidenced by the small on-board "assist" cache of 2 Kbytes in its 7200 CPUs. This latter cache, by the way, solves a potential problem with the external direct-mapped caches, which are very prone to thrashing.

In addition to good CPU performance, HP systems also have hardware-assisted 2D and 3D graphics built in. The 2D performance is extremely competent (over one million 2D lines per second) and provides for "snappy" X window performance. With the addition of a software package, the system can provide adequate 3D performance for such jobs as mechanical CAD without the added cost of 3D graphics hardware.

Being compatible with older designs, PA-RISC has a good software library. But note that while the older applications do run on the new systems, the performance that you get will not be as high as recompiled code. Fortunately, the majority of PA-RISC applications are optimized for the new architecture, so this should not be an issue.

As of this writing, PA-RISC systems are available only from HP and Convex. The latter specializes in large multiprocessor systems (up to 128 processors) targeted toward scientific applications.

12.7.1 HP PA-8000

True to its form, HP's next-generation offering is a cacheless CPU that relies on a very high-speed, external, one-level cache. Unlike the PA-7200, however, the PA-8000 uses an extremely aggressive superscalar design. The result is very high floating-point speed with respectable integer performance. The down side is that HP's target introduction of PA-8000 is almost a year later than some of its competitors (such as DEC 21164 and Sun's UltraSPARC). So, HP's advantage may not be as large as it may seem. Nevertheless, PA-8000 gives HP a solid enough footing to continue its high-performance (and rather high-cost) offerings.

12.8 IBM Power

IBM's reentry into the RISC market (after the failed RT attempt) has been quite successful. The Power series consists of a range of designs, all sporting superscalar architectures that excel at floating point. The integer performance, however, is only average. But given the wide range of systems available, it is possible to get systems with good integer performance, albeit at high prices.

The so-called RS/6000 series uses an enhanced MicroChannel bus for I/O expansion, which has reasonable speed but, in its current form, has lower performance than other PC class buses such as PCI and VL. Software availability is good and especially strong in the commercial sector as expected from IBM's lineage.

Of special interest is the new PowerPC venture together with Apple and Motorola. A single-chip processor called the 601 is available at this time, which produces lower floating-point and integer performance as compared to the multichip solutions. However, the CPU real estate is quite small and, even with the advanced five-layer process, has excellent price/performance characteristics. The 601 processor is at the heart of the Power Macintosh systems, which should increase its appeal, although most of those systems will be running Mac OS and not UNIX.

A variation of the 601 named the 603 sports lower power consumption with some loss in performance. It is suitable for portable workstations and other battery-operated systems. An upgrade to the 601 is the 604 processor, which significantly boosts the speed of this series. It produces 160 SPECint at 100 MHz. Beyond the 604 is the 620, which sports performance slightly higher than the Intel P6 systems that it will be competing with.

A high-end chip-set from IBM called the POWER-2 is at the heart of the best performing IBM systems (e.g., Model 990 and 590). The performance comes at a high cost though because of the number of chips involved in the design.

Table 12.4 Performance of IBM Power (RS/6000) Offerings (as of 1995)

System	Clock Speed	SPECint92	SPECfp92
RS/6000 990 (POWER-2)	72	126.0	260.0
RS/6000 590 (POWER-2)	66	117.0	242.6
RS/6000 570	50	57.5	99.2
RS/6000 25X (Power PC601)	66	62.6	72.2
RS/6000 220	33	20.4	29.1

12.9 DEC Alpha

DEC Alpha is the newest RISC architecture and is characterized by unusually high clock speeds and an instruction set that lacks any kind of byte addressing. The high clock speed is the result of an advanced semiconductor process currently available only from DEC. The slowest clock speed is 150 MHz with high-end systems as of this writing clocking in excess of 275 MHz. The high clock speed results in high heat dissipation, which can be overcome with proper cooling techniques.

The Alpha systems excel in floating-point while providing excellent integer performance. SPECmark results are available for all DEC systems, making it easy to pick the right machine (see Table 12.6). Being a new architecture, software availability is not as good as other systems, so make sure your application runs on Alpha before committing to it.

12.9.1 DEC Alpha 21164

DEC's next-generation offering is in the form of another high-clock-speed, superscalar design named the 21164. The 21164, like its competitors, substantially increases the transistor count to 9.3 million compared to 2.8 million on the older 21064. In a new twist, the

Table 12.5 Performance of DEC Alpha Offerings (as of 1995)

System	Clock Speed	SPECint92	SPECfp92
DEC 3000/900	275	189.3	264.1
DEC 3000/700	225	162.6	230.6
Alphastation 400 4/233	233?	155.2	181.2
Alphastation 200 4/233	233?	157.7	183.9
Alphastation 200 4/166	166?	116.2	134.8
7000/610	160	132.6	200.1
3000/800S		138.4	187.6
DEC 3000/600		87.6	165.2
2000/300 & 500		81.0	110.2

21164 includes *two* levels of cache on chip. This was thought necessary because a very large primary cache would have had too high a latency (the 21164 has 96 Kbytes of secondary cache *on chip*!). The primary cache is kept at a small size of 16 Kbytes, and the CPU has direct support for a third-level cache. The chip is laid out on a 0.5-micron, four-layer process and, true to DEC's previous processors, runs at high clock speeds of 266 and 300 MHz initially.

Being a four-instruction issue, superscalar CPU, the 300-MHz 21164 produces 330 SPECint92 and 500 SPECfp92. The 266-MHz part reaches 290 SPECint92 and 440 SPECfp92. Without sounding too much like a DEC advertisement, the 21164 has created a wide gap between it and all the competing architectures. It is the first processor to break the 1 *billion* instructions/sec peak rate (300 MHz times 4 instructions/cycle). Considering that it has already started shipping (as of June 1995), it deserves attention if you cannot wait for the offerings from other vendors.

Perhaps the only drawback to the 21164 is the fact that, as of this writing, it is available only in DEC's high-end systems.

12.9.2 SGI MIPS

This architecture was also an early commercial implementation of RISC and used to sport the title of being the fastest RISC until the arrival of IBM, HP, DEC, and Alpha architectures. The current R4400 processor is superpipelined and excels at integer performance. The R4400 also has respectable floating-point performance but cannot keep up with the fastest offerings from other vendors. SGI, who bought the MIPS computer company that developed this technology, is hard at work to fix the floating-point deficiencies. At the high-end the R8000 (formerly called the TFP) produces very high floating-point performance but with average integer performance. See the next section on the follow-on to the R4400 called the R10000, which addresses the integer performance.

The R4400 comes in two versions: the R4400PC and R4400SC. The former lacks an external cache controller and, as such, turns in lower floating-point performance. The higher-end R4400SC can have as much as 4 Mbytes of secondary cache, which can practically contain most applications (and benchmarks!).

The R4400 CPU has been shrunk twice already, bringing its (internal) clock speed from an initial speed of 100 MHz (on a 0.8-micron process) to 200 MHz (using an advanced 0.40- to 0.45-micron technology). The cache size has also received a much needed boost from the initial size of 16 Kbytes (8 Kbytes for instructions and 8 Kbytes for data) to 32 Kbytes (split equally yet again). This was necessary because the direct mapped L1 cache on this CPU does not enjoy as high a hit rate as the competing primary caches on other CPUs (which are often two- or four-way set associative).

Yet another offering in the MIPS camp is the R4600. Despite the similarity in the name, however, the R4600 is a new design based on a simple, pipelined design. It does not use superscalar or superpipeline schemes, and, as such, its performance is *below* that of the

R4400 (at the same clock speed). Its major advantage over the R4400 is in die size and cost. The per-chip pricing is $250, which is one quarter of the R4400. As a result, you see the R4600 in lower-end systems from SGI and other vendors.

Volume shipments of UNIX MIPS systems are available from a number of vendors besides SGI, including Pyramid Technology, Tandem, Siemens Nixdorf (in Europe), SONY, and NEC (in Japan) among other vendors. Each one of these systems has its own characteristics. SGI systems are quite strong in 3D graphics and parallel processing. Tandem specializes in fault-tolerant systems, and Pyramid and Siemens Nixdorf systems are multiprocessor servers used in commercial markets typically running database applications. SONY and NEC are primarily 2D workstations used in a wide range of applications (in Japan).

12.9.3 SGI/MIPS R10000

The R10000 attempts to fix the performance deficiencies (especially in floating point) of the R4400 by using a very aggressive superscalar design (much like the HP8000). Although details are sketchy as of this writing, the chip is estimated to produce around 300 SPECint92 and 600 SPECfp92 at 200 MHz. This should bring the performance of the MIPS architecture up to par with other competing designs.

Table 12.6 Performance of MIPS-Based Systems (as of mid-1995)

System	Clock Speed	SPECint92	SPECfp92
SGI Power Challenge (R8000)	75	108.7	310.6
Indigo2 Extreme (R4400) with 1 Mbyte L2 cache	200	141	143
SGI Indigo2 (R4400)	150	90	87
SGI Challenge L/XL	150	93.7	97.1
SGI Challenge	100	62.4	66.5
SGI IndyPC (R4600)	100	62.8	49.9
Indy R4400 with 1 Mbyte of L2 cache	175	122.6	115.5
Indy R4400 with 1 Mbyte of L2 cache	150	91.7	97.5
Indy R4600 with 0.5 Mbyte of L2 cache	133	113.5	73.7
Indy R4600	133	84.9	61.0
Indy R4600	100	62.8	49.9

12.10 References

Dick Pountain, "Different Kind of RISC," *Byte*, August 1994.

The Web pages of the represented system and chip vendors.

SPEC results from `ftp.cdf.toronto.edu` in pub/spectable.

CHAPTER 13

Optimizing User Programs

One subject often overlooked in performance tuning is the optimization of individual programs. No amount of kernel tuning can make a user-bound process run faster because it does not spend any time in the kernel. In this chapter, we focus on tools and techniques available for instrumenting and optimizing user programs. Unlike system tuning, program optimization requires modifications to the source code of the application. Therefore, the techniques described here do not apply to commercial "shrink-wrapped" binary applications for which you do not have the sources.

The best way to understand how to use the various tools involved in optimizing user programs is to apply them to a sample program. The following program is a classical sort application. It initializes a rather large array of short integers in descending order (lines 9 and 10). It then uses the bubble sort algorithm to convert the data in the array to ascending order.

The main work is performed in the sort routine, which scans the array and swaps any two consecutive elements that are in the wrong order. After performing this operation n–1 times, the array is fully sorted.

```
1   #define COUNT 5000
2   short array[COUNT];
3
4   main()
5   {
```

```
 6        register i;
 7        int intcmp();
 8
 9        for(i = 0; i < COUNT; ++i) /* initialize the array in rev. order */
10            array[i] = (short)COUNT-i;
11
12        sort(array, COUNT);
13
14        if(array [0] != 1 || array [COUNT-1] != COUNT)
15            printf("Sort failed!\n");
16    }
17
18    sort(array, nel)
19    short array[];
20    int nel;
21    {
22        register i, j;
23        --nel;
24        for (i = 0; i < nel ; ++i)
25            for( j = 0; j < nel; ++j)
26            {
27                if(array[j] > array[j+1])
28                {
29                    swap(&array[j], &array[ j+1]);
30                }
31            }
32    }
33
34    swap(first, second)
35    short *first, *second;
36    {
37        short temp;
38        temp = *first;
39        *first = *second;
40        *second = temp;
41    }
```

13.1 Basic Time Measurements

Before attempting to modify the program, we need to identify whether it can benefit from any optimization. After all, if the program runs in 0.1 second, there is little reason to worry about it. You do this by using the time command.

13.1.1 The Time Commands

The time command, which is available in all variants of UNIX, can be used to measure the CPU usage and total elapsed time of a program. The situation is rather confusing, however, because there are three versions of the time command *all with the same name:*

- /bin/time or /usr/bin/time utility
- the csh built-in time command

- the `ksh` built-in `time` command

The difference between these versions is the resolution of the reported data. The `time` command in the C shell reports elapsed time only in seconds, whereas `/bin/time` (or `/usr/bin/time`) reports all statistics with one decimal place. The Korn shell `time` command goes one step further and reports all times with two decimal places. We find the lack of resolution in the C shell `time` command to be a problem when timing programs that execute in less than 1 minute. So, we recommend that you use the other two versions. Because built-in commands take precedence over executables in the PATH environment variable, you need to specify the full path name of the stand-alone time utility (e.g., `/bin/time`) if you like to use it in either shell. The typical syntax for all versions is the same:

```
time <command> <command arguments>
```

Now let's run the `time` command on our sample program:

```
SunOS4.1% /bin/time cpu_hog
        12.1 real        12.0 user        0.0 sys
```

The output shows the total elapsed time (also called the wall clock time) as **real** and the CPU usage under **user** and **sys** (see Table 13.1). As you might have already guessed, **user** is the amount of CPU time spent running the program itself (i.e., in its own address space) and **sys** is the amount of CPU time spent in the kernel on behalf of this process. Our sample program is using 12 seconds of actual CPU cycles executing the program. The system time in this case is minimal and can be ignored. As a general rule,

> *programs with high user time (double the system time) are good candidates for source-level optimization.*

Based on this rule, our sample program makes an excellent candidate for optimization. Programs with a high percentage of system time can also be optimized by reducing the number of system calls they make, although this may be difficult in practice. The majority of system calls in programs are for I/O, which makes them hard to eliminate. Exceptions are when the system calls can be grouped (e.g., reading 4096 bytes once instead of issuing 4096 one-byte reads).

Programs that have a high percentage of idle time are poor candidates for source-level optimization. The idle time is the difference between the total elapsed time and the sum of user plus system times, assuming that you are running on a stand-alone system with no

Table 13.1 Fields Reported by the Time Command

Field	Description
User	Total amount of time spent in user code (in seconds)
System	Total amount time spent in the kernel (in seconds)
Real	Total elapsed time (in seconds)

other programs using CPU time (see Section 13.9.1). Because idle processes do not consume any CPU cycles, optimizing them makes no sense.

13.1.2 System V Timex

One drawback to the standard `time` utility is that it accounts only for the CPU usage of the command it is running. It is impossible to time a process that forks off another process to do the actual work. A good example is an X window client that makes requests to the X server to perform the output processing. If you use the `time` command on an X client, you get only the timing data for the client and not the CPU resources used to run the X server. The solution is to use `timex`, which looks at the impact of a process on the system as a whole and is able to account for all its CPU usage (and other resources).

The `timex` utility (which is a link to the `sar` command) takes a snapshot of the entire system, runs the program (or programs), takes another snapshot, and reports the difference between the two samples. As a result, the entire CPU utilization is computed regardless of how many processes are involved. Because `timex` is built on top of `sar`, it can also report on other activities such as disk I/O.

It makes no sense to run `timex` on our sample program, but if you do have a client-server situation, you may want to use `timex` to see the total CPU usage. We should also note that `timex` is available only in System V implementations.

13.2 Profiling Programs

Once you have identified that a program is a good candidate for source-level optimization, it is then necessary to figure out *where* the program is spending most of its time. The task is simplified by the fact that programs typically spend the majority of their time in a handful of functions. Studies show that even very large programs have fewer than ten hot spots where most of the CPU cycles are spent (you often hear the 90/10 rule, which indicates that 90% of the CPU time is spent in 10% of the program). More often than not, only one or two routines need to be optimized to achieve significant speed-up.

Identifying the amount of time spent in each routine is called profiling. This is done by using the `prof` utility, which gives basic timing and call counts for each function. BSD systems (and some System V vendors such as SONY, SGI, and HP) include a much more sophisticated profiling tool called `gprof`, which not only gives the timing for each function but also the relationship between the routines in a program. The significance of the latter becomes clear later in this chapter.

13.3 Simple Profiling Using prof

The `prof` utility provides the call count for each routine and the amount of time spent in each. In order to use `prof`, a program needs first to be compiled using the `-p` option of the

C compiler. For languages other than C, refer to the reference manual of the specific compiler to see how profiling can be turned on (also see Section 13.10). Often, cc can be used to compile programs other than C. If that is the case, -p should also work for them.

Care must be taken to not only compile but also link the program with -p. Otherwise, the library routines that handle the statistics gathering and storage will not be linked into your program (see Section 13.9.2). So, if you use cc -c to compile each source file individually, your final cc to link the application also needs a -p. In the case of our sample C program, we need to simply add -p to our compile line:

```
% cc -O -p cpu_hog.c -o cpu_hog
```

This generates the cpu_hog executable as before, but the new version includes both a function call counting mechanism and library support to save profiling data.[1] To gather the statistics, we need to run the program first. Upon execution, a profiling file is created in the current directory of the process. The default name of this file is prof.out. You may want to run ls -l on it to make sure that prof.out is indeed created. If prof.out does not exist, check to see that you have specified the profiling option correctly and have write permission in the current directory (the touch prof.out command should succeed without any errors).

Once prof.out is created, you need to run prof to analyze its contents. To do this, you need to specify the name of the program that generated prof.out and, optionally, the name of the profiling file if you have renamed it (a useful practice for different runs of the same program). Typical usage is

```
prof [a.out] [prof.out]
```

Note that prof does very little sanity checking on the profiled data. Specifically,

> *if you give prof the name of a program different from the one that generated prof.out, you simply get garbage data. The same thing happens if the profiling subsystem is not operational (e.g., in the case of languages other than C).*

So, you may want to experiment with a well-known program (such as the example in this chapter) before trusting the data.

prof generates a sorted output of each routine in the order of CPU time consumed (from highest to lowest):

```
SunOS4.1% prof cpu_hog
 %time  cumsecs  #call   ms/call  name
  40.7    9.13                     mcount
  34.5   16.87        1   7740.00  _sort
  24.8   22.4212497500     0.00    _swap
   0.0   22.42        1      0.00  _exit
```

---

1. Some compilers do not allow optimization (-o) to be turned on with the profiling option. This is unfortunate because nonoptimized code may have a different profile.

```
        0.0     22.42    1       0.00    _main
        0.0     22.42    1       0.00    _malloc
        0.0     22.42    1       0.00    _on_exit
        0.0     22.42    1       0.00    _profil
```

The first column shows the percentage of total time used by the function listed on the right (under the **name** column). The second column, **cumsecs**, shows a running total of the amount of time used by each function. To get the actual time spent in a function, simply subtract its time from the one before it. For example, to calculate the amount of time used in sort, subtract 9.13 from 16.87.

As the list is sorted by **%time**, the highest consumers of the CPU time are easily found at the top of the list. Notice how the amount of time spent in each routine drops rapidly as you go down the list. In our example, mcount and sort are shown as the highest consumers. The mcount routine is the profiling function added to your program and, as you can tell, uses a lot of CPU cycles in our examples. In general, you should fold the contributions from mcount into the rest of the program to nullify its effect. In our example, the program actually uses 41% less CPU time (the contribution from mcount) than shown. So, the real **%time** for sort is closer to 58% (16.87 - 9.13) / (22.50 - 9.13) * 100.

prof also displays the number of calls for each function under the **#call** column. If the call count is absent, it indicates that the routine was not compiled with -p (or that the routine is written in a language that does not support profiling). The timing information, however, should still be accurate.

In addition to the call count, prof computes the amount of time used in each call (under **ms/call** or milliseconds per call) by dividing the total time by the number of calls to it. So, this should be taken as average time and not minimum or maximum.

Before diving into the source code, let's look at the gprof utility, which gives you much more insight as to *why* each function is being called.

13.4 Call Graph Profiling with gprof

One problem with prof is that it indicates only the number of times a function is called but not who called it. Because reducing function call counts is one of the most useful techniques for reducing execution time, lack of this information can be a major hindrance.

The solution is to use a "call graph" profiler, which not only provides timing data but also completes call tree of who calls who and how many times. To enable call graph profiling, the program needs to be compiled using the -pg option:

```
% cc -O -pg cpu_hog.c -o cpu_hog.p
```

Do not make the mistake of reversing the letters g and p by specifying -gp no matter how logical this may seem. The compiler happily accepts -gp, but no profiling data are generated. The reason is that the -g option tells cc to add debugging information to the executable, and any letters specified after it (as in the case of -gp) are quietly ignored.

As with -p, you also need to link the program using -pg and let your program exit normally. The profiling data are then saved in the file, gprof.out in the current working directory of the process.

To see the profiling information, you need to run the gprof utility. Its usage is similar to prof but has a few additional options that you may want to use. Especially welcome is the -b option that tells gprof not to print a rather lengthy description of each field. The other useful option is -z, which instructs gprof to show only routines that are never called. This is useful in identifying "dead code" in programs, which you may want to remove to save some memory.

Now let's examine the output generated by gprof[2]:

```
SunOS4.1% gprof -b cpu_hog
granularity: each sample hit covers 2 byte(s) for 0.07% of 14.89 seconds
                                   called/total       parents
index  %time   self descendents  called+self   name          index
                                   called/total       children
                                                     <spontaneous>
[1]     98.2   0.00    14.62                    start [1]
                0.00    14.62      1/1             _main [2]
                0.00     0.00      1/1             _on_exit [130]
                0.00     0.00      1/1             _exit [124]
-----------------------------------------------
                0.00    14.62      1/1             start [1]
[2]     98.2   0.00    14.62      1          _main [2]
                8.12     6.51      1/1             _sort [3]
-----------------------------------------------
                8.12     6.51      1/1             _main [2]
[3]     98.2   8.12     6.51      1          _sort [3]
                6.51     0.00 12497500/12497500    _swap [4]
-----------------------------------------------
                6.51     0.00 12497500/12497500    _sort [3]
[4]     43.7   6.51     0.00 12497500          _swap [4]
-----------------------------------------------
                                                     <spontaneous>
[5]      1.8   0.27     0.00                    _moncontrol [5]
                0.00     0.00      1/1             _profil [131]
-----------------------------------------------
                0.00     0.00      1/1             start [1]
[124]    0.0   0.00     0.00      1          _exit [124]

granularity: each sample hit covers 2 byte(s) for 0.03% of 31.25 seconds
   %   cumulative   self              self     total
  time   seconds   seconds    calls  ms/call  ms/call  name
```

2. We have removed blank lines and miscellaneous functions generated by the runtime linker to save space.

52.4	16.37	16.37				mcount (44)
26.0	24.48	8.12	1	8115.67	14621.21	_sort [3]
20.8	30.99	6.51	12497500	0.00	0.00	_swap [4]
0.8	31.25	0.27				_moncontrol [5]
0.0	31.25	0.00	2	0.00	0.00	_getfreehdr [121]
0.0	31.25	0.00	2	0.00	0.00	_sbrk [122]
0.0	31.25	0.00	1	0.00	0.00	.udiv [6]
0.0	31.25	0.00	1	0.00	0.00	.umul [7]
0.0	31.25	0.00	1	0.00	0.00	_demote [123]
0.0	31.25	0.00	1	0.00	0.00	_exit [124]
0.0	31.25	0.00	1	0.00	0.00	_free [125]
0.0	31.25	0.00	1	0.00	0.00	_getpagesize [126]
0.0	31.25	0.00	1	0.00	0.00	_insert [127]
0.0	31.25	0.00	1	0.00	14621.21	_main [2]
0.0	31.25	0.00	1	0.00	0.00	_malloc [128]
0.0	31.25	0.00	1	0.00	0.00	_morecore [129]
0.0	31.25	0.00	1	0.00	0.00	_on_exit [130]
0.0	31.25	0.00	1	0.00	0.00	_profil [131]
0.0	31.25	0.00	1	0.00	0.00	_putfreehdr [132]

```
Index by function name
   [6] .udiv              [127] _insert          [132] _putfreehdr
   [7] .umul                [2] _main            [122] _sbrk
 [123] _demote            [128] _malloc            [3] _sort
 [124] _exit                [5] _moncontrol        [4] _swap
 [125] _free              [129] _morecore         (44) mcount
 [121] _getfreehdr        [130] _on_exit
 [126] _getpagesize       [131] _profil
```

The key to deciphering the rather complex output is learning the formatting conventions that gprof uses. Each function (separated by a set of dashed lines), which we call the main entry, is listed along with a set of functions above and below it (all indented). For the main entry, the output shows the amount of time spent in this routine (under self) and the accumulated time spent in all the routines it calls.

By looking at the function entries above the main entry, you can see who is calling this function, the number of calls to it from each one, and the amount of time spent in the main entry on behalf of each caller. This makes it very easy to identify the most frequent callers of a function.

Listed below the main entry are the routines called by this function. Again, the call count is broken down for each function along with the amount of time spent in each.

To understand gprof output better, let's take a look at an example:

```
                 8.12       6.51       1/1            _main [2]
   [3]    98.2   8.12       6.51       1             _sort [3]
                 6.51       0.00 12497500/12497500    _swap [4]
```

In this case, sort is the main entry. It is called by main only once, and no other routine calls it (indicated by the total call count of one). It calls swap 12,497,500 times and is the sole caller of it because the total calls to swap equal the ones made from sort. sort uses a total of 8.12 seconds, of which 6.51 seconds are spent in swap. swap itself does not use a significant amount of time (shown as 0.00 seconds).

gprof shows the tag, <spontaneous>, if it cannot determine who the caller is. This is typically the case with signal handlers and start-up routines that are called directly by the kernel and do not go through the normal function call sequence. Because these functions are used very infrequently, they can typically be ignored.

The numbers in brackets are simply indices to help in locating a function in the listing. An alphabetized listing of all the functions and their relative index numbers are included at the end of the output. This can be a great time saver when instrumenting large applications.

The order and percentage of time shown for each main entry may seem incorrect at first. This is because gprof includes the time accumulated by all the descendents of a function in figuring out its ranking. Therefore, functions such as main that are the source of all the follow-on function calls always appear at the top of the list. The idea here is to bring attention to the top routine that has created the most expensive thread of execution.

As a summary, gprof shows a more conventional listing of percentage of time used by each function in a manner similar to prof. You may want to start with the function ranking in this table instead of the detailed listings shown first.

The additional code generated for call graph profiling significantly increases the execution time of the program. You can see this by timing the profiled executable:

```
SunOS4.1% /bin/time cpu_hog.p
        31.5 real        31.2 user        0.0 sys
```

Fortunately, the added CPU time is of little concern because all the functions are penalized equally.

13.5 Opportunities for Optimization

We start our analysis by looking at the sorted function call times. You should start from the top function and work your way down as the payoff decreases sharply. In our case, the sort and swap routines are the highest consumers.

Looking at call counts for the swap routine, we notice that is extremely large—well over 12 million function calls! Because the swap routine itself is very small, this sort of code sequence lends itself nicely to inlining. By embedding the code for swap directly inside the sort routine, we can eliminate the overhead of the function call.

To keep the code readable, we use the C language macro facility to replace swap with the equivalent functionality. (If you are using C++, simply use the inline keyword and include the function code in a header file to accomplish the same thing). The resulting code follows:

```
1   #define swap(first, second)  \
2       { \
3             register short temp; \
4             temp = *first; \
5             *first = *second; \
6             *second = temp; \
7       }
8
9   #define COUNT 5000
10  short array[COUNT];
11
12  main()
13  {
14      register i;
15      int intcmp();
16
17      for(i = 0; i < COUNT; ++i) /* initialize the array in rev. order */
18          array[i] = (short)COUNT-i;
19
20      sort(array, COUNT);
21
22      if(array [0] != 1 || array [COUNT-1] != COUNT)
23          printf("Sort failed!\n");
24  }
25
26  sort(array, nel)
27  short array[];
28  int nel;
29  {
30      register i, j;
31      --nel;
32      for (i = 0; i < nel ; ++i)
33          for( j = 0; j < nel; ++j)
34          {
35              if(array[j] > array[j+1])
36              {
37                  swap(&array[j], &array[ j+1]);
38              }
39          }
40  }
```

Now, let's time the new program (without profiling) to see the reduction in the CPU usage:

```
SunOS4.1% /bin/time cpu_hog.inline
        10.4 real        10.4 user         0.0 sys
```

The user time with inlining is reduced to 10.4 seconds from 12.0 for a total improvement of 13%.

Of course, this sort of improvement is possible only when the number of calls is very high and the work actually performed inside the function is small relative to the call overhead.

In addition, the speed-up is a function of the processor architecture and compiler function call/return protocol.

After inlining, we are down to the `sort` routine, which is now responsible for almost all the time used by the program. Further changes to the program are unlikely to generate much of an improvement because most compilers can generate fairly optimal code for what is left.

All is not lost, however. Algorithm savvy readers would be quick to point out that the bubble sort algorithm used in the example is one of the most inefficient sort methods. A much preferred algorithm is Quick Sort, which substantially reduces the number of swaps required. Fortunately for UNIX users, Quick Sort is a standard library routine, which ships with every system. Using it is a matter of calling the `qsort` routine with the right arguments. The following revision of our sample program does exactly that:

```
1   #define COUNT   5000
2   short array[COUNT];
3
4   main()
5   {
6       register i;
7       int shortcmp();
8
9       for(i = 0; i < COUNT; ++i) /* initialize the array in rev. order */
10          array[i] = (short)COUNT - i;
11
12      qsort((short *)array, COUNT, sizeof(array[0]), shortcmp);
13
14      if(array [0] != 1 || array [COUNT-1] != COUNT)
15          printf("Sort failed!\n");
16  }
17
18  int shortcmp(i,j)
19  short *i, *j;
20  {
21      return(*i - *j);
22  }
```

Now let's time the new program:

```
SunOS4.1% /bin/time cpu_hog.qsort
        0.1 real         0.0 user          0.0 sys
```

The results are hard to believe. The user time has practically dropped to zero. We let you compute the percentage improvement (see Table 13.2 to put things in perspective).

Of course, we picked our example program carefully to make a point. That is, despite some gains achieved from fine-tuning the code, it is always best to think of new ways to solve a problem than to optimize an inefficient algorithm. As a general rule, speeding a program by a factor larger than two or three by just modifying the code is difficult. On the other hand, new algorithms (as seen in our example) have the potential for substantial

Table 13.2 Time for the Three Versions of the Program

Program	DEC Alpha	Sun cc on SS2
cpu_hog	4.2	12.0
cpu_hog.inline	3.4	10.4
cpu_hog.qsort	0.0	0.0

speed-ups. Of course, nothing is stopping you from applying both methods. Start with an efficient algorithm and follow it up with profiling and fine-tuning the code.

Now that we have wetted your appetite for improving program execution time, let's look at some generic techniques for optimizing programs.

13.6 The Optimizer

As you have seen in our examples, we have been careful to always use the compiler optimizer flag, -o. This tells the compiler to generate the most optimal code it can. How much optimization actually gets performed is highly compiler-specific. Some optimizers are very aggressive in nature, whereas others settle for very simple and localized techniques. Evaluating the efficiency of the optimizer is a fairly complex job and beyond the scope of this book. But, in general, optimizers work by analyzing the program and removing redundant code or relocating code sequences to better optimize the instruction sequence for the CPU. As an example, let's take a look at a simple C program:

```
main()
{
    register i;
    double x = 12, y;

    for(i = 0; i <2000000; ++i)
        y = (x + 1) * (x + 1) / ((x -1) * (x -1));
}
```

Compiling the program unoptimized shows an execution time of 4.7 seconds versus only 0.1 second when optimized. A huge difference! Some things look obvious though. Why compute (x + 1) and (x - 1) twice in each iteration? We could precompute these once (outside the loop because x does not change inside the loop) and then just use the results. We could go one step farther and simply square (x + 1) and (x - 1) outside the loop. While we are at it, we could move the entire computation for y above the loop because its value does not change inside the loop! This is indeed what the optimizer detected, which resulted in the huge improvement in CPU usage. This sort of optimization is referred to as code motion with the computation of y being loop-invariant.

Aside from the -o option, some compilers have other optimizer levels such as -o2, -o3, and -o4. The higher levels sometimes lead to unsafe optimizations that change the operation of a program. The C language allows variables to be accessed both by name and pointers. This makes it hard for the optimizer to track changes to program variables because the value of a pointer is not usually known at compile time. The higher optimizer levels, for example, tell the compiler that it is safe to assume that the only time a variable is changed is when it is referenced by name. This allows the optimizer to find more opportunities for optimization.

Of course, higher-level optimizations should be used only if they do not change the program behavior. So, you need to be careful and truly understand the usage of variables in your program before resorting to these unsafe optimization levels. This brings us to another point. If you notice, we have included some simple consistency checks in our first example (line 14 in the original listing). This sort of practice becomes very important if an optimization (performed by you or the compiler) breaks the program.

13.7 Other Optimization Techniques

Now that we have convinced you that the optimizer is very smart and can do a lot to speed up your program, the question as to why bother with profiling and optimization by hand may come up. This has to do with the fact that even the best optimizers are limited in scope of what they can do. In our sample program, no optimizer would have known to replace the call to our sort routine with qsort. In other words, the optimizer is unable to make algorithmic changes to the program even though this is usually your most effective tool in speeding up a program.

Another major limitation is that, with a few minor exceptions, optimizers work only in one function or source file at a time. To see the effects of this limitation, let's modify our last example and move the computation for y to a separate function to see what happens. The new program looks like this:

```
main()
{
        register i;
        double x = 12, y;

        for(i = 0; i <2000000; ++i)
                y = compute_y(x);
}
compute_y(x)
double x;
{
                return( (x + 1) * (x + 1) / ((x -1) * (x -1)));
}
```

This time, the unoptimized program takes 6.9 seconds to run. The increased time (from 4.3 seconds) is due to addition function calls for the compute_y routine, which is not surprising. What is surprising is that the optimized version takes 5.3 seconds to run instead of

0.1 in our former example. In other words, the optimizer was not able to improve program execution by much. The reason is that when the main loop is being compiled, the compiler has no idea what `compute_y` is doing. Without this information, it would be unsafe to simply move `compute_y` above the loop. So, the compiler left it alone. Although smarter compilers can solve this problem (by inlining `compute_y` and then optimizing the code), very few can do anything if `compute_y` is moved to another file.

A sometimes useful optimization technique is to concatenate all the source files and compile them as one file. Assuming that your optimizer looks beyond function calls, this would generate more optimal code, assuming that the compiler can handle optimizing very large files (some cannot).

13.7.1 Using System Libraries

Vendors usually ship a set of highly tuned libraries to use with your programs. The most common ones are listed in Table 13.3. Unfortunately, many of these routines sit unused because users do not know about them. This is a shame because these routines are written in assembly language and are highly tuned for the architecture that they run on. The memory move routines, for example, take into account such things as reducing the loop count (by moving the largest amount of data possible in each iteration even if the array arguments are byte oriented) and processor pipeline scheduling. These routines run up to twice as fast as the best code generated by the compiler. So, use them whenever possible.

13.7.2 Inlining

You have already seen how function inlining can benefit your programs. Inlining is useful only if a function is being called very frequently and the actual code contained in the function is trivial (i.e., does not use much CPU time of its own). Functions with loops or many conditional statements rarely benefit from inlining because the overhead of the function call is small compared to the work done in the routine.

To get a better feel for how expensive an actual function call is, run the following benchmark:

Table 13.3 Built-In Library Routines

Name	OS	Usage
bcopy	BSD	Copies source array to target
bzero	BSD	Sets array to zero
memcpy	SysV	Copies source array to target
memset	SysV	Sets array to any value including zero
strxxx	All	Collection of strings routines (see manual page for string(3)) for copying and manipulating null-terminated strings
qsort	All	Sorts an array of arbitrary (but fixed size) elements

```
main()
{
    register i;

    for(i = 0; i < 10 * 1000 * 1000; ++i)
            func();
}
func()
{
}
```

To get the overhead for each call, simply divide the time by the number of calls and express it in microseconds (i.e., multiply it by 1 million). For example,

```
% /bin/time func_overhead
          2.1 real        2.0 user        0.0 sys
```

Because the program performs 10 million function calls in 2.1 seconds, the overhead is approximately 0.2 microseconds per call. We say *approximately* because the loop over-head needs to be subtracted (which you could do by timing the program without the func-tion call). Also keep in mind that functions with one or more arguments run slower.

Once you have the function call overhead, you can quickly determine how much time inlining is going to save. For example, if profiling showed that a function was being called 1 million times, the savings would be only 0.2 seconds in our sample system.

Alas, nothing is free. The problem with inlining is that it can make the code less readable. Our technique of using macros solves this problem although, as with all macros, you must be careful about their definition. Poorly written macros can get interpreted incorrectly due to operator precedence. The common solution is to use large numbers of parentheses to isolate the argument, which further detracts from the readability of the code.[3] A better solution is to ask the compiler to do the inlining for you. This is typically done by listing the functions to be inlined in a file and then passing its name to the compiler. Refer to the documentation for your C compiler for more information.

Another problem with inlining is that it makes the code bigger. If you inline 100 invoca-tions of a 100-byte function, you increase your code size by 10 Kbytes. Whether this is significant or not depends on your situation. In most cases, the higher memory usage is worth the reduction in the CPU usage.

13.7.3 Data Alignment

In declaring variables or allocating memory dynamically (by calling `malloc`, for example), few programmers worry about what address the linker assigns to their data. The default

---

3. The C++ advocates are quick to brag about the inline feature of the compiler that lets you easily tag functions to be inlined.

placement, however, can be suboptimal in some cases. The issue is not the memory address itself but what boundary it lands on. For example, although CISC processors are able to access 32-bit data that are not on 32-bit boundaries, they do so at a high performance penalty (they must access two consecutive words to extract one). RISC processors generally do not tolerate this and force you to place items on at least word boundary. Some, such as MIPS, allow byte boundary placement, but every access causes a trap into the kernel, which goes through long code sequences to emulate the CISC behavior. Needless to say, access to the elements of such arrays results in huge overheads. If you ever see high trap count (shown in BSD's `vmstat`) when running a CPU-bound process, this could be the cause.

There are other reasons to place things on nice boundaries. The previously mentioned memory movement routines work best when their target and source arrays are both aligned on double-word (64-bit) or larger boundaries. This lets them use the CPU instructions that can handle 64-bit quantities (if available), which increases the efficiency of the operation tremendously by minimizing the loop count.

The compiler on most systems already instructs the linker to place variables and structures on single-word (32-bit) or double-word (64-bit) boundaries. You run into a problem when character array elements are arbitrarily cast into word or double-word entities (a practice that is very prevalent in the old, "dusty deck" FORTRAN programs).

13.7.4 Data Access Pattern

Beyond data alignment, you also need to be careful about how you access your data. Due to the way the cache fill logic works (i.e., reloads are done in units of lines or 4 to 16 bytes) and faster row or page mode access time of paged mode DRAMs, you should organize your array access to occur on a sequential basis. A common mistake is to access an array in the wrong order. Take the following program, for example:

```
1   #define ROWS    3000
2   #define COLUMNS 3000
3   char array[ROWS][COLUMNS];
4
5   main()
6   {
7           register i, j;
8
9           for(i = 0; i < ROWS; ++i)
10                  for(j = 0; j < COLUMNS; ++j)
11                          array[i][j] = 0;
12  }
```

This program runs in 2.3 seconds (user time). Now, if you change line 11 to

```
11                  array[j][i] = 0;
```

the runtime goes up to 2.6 seconds or roughly 15% higher. The difference can be much more dramatic on some other processors. The reason has to do with the way C generates code for accessing multidimensional arrays. Two-dimensional arrays like the one in our example are created row after row. That is, the second row follows the first one in memory and so forth. So when you access the array with the right element "changing the fastest," you are accessing sequential memory elements. In the unmodified version, the program is touching 1 byte in each row and then jumping to a new row. This causes the cache to thrash as only part of a cache line used each time. The same goes for the row cache in page mode memories, although because of much larger line size (an entire row) the problem is not as severe.

13.7.5 Other Optimization Techniques

Besides using the methods already described, there a few other things that you can do to speed your application.

- **Use memory to save CPU cycles.** Avoid using slow operations such as bit fields to keep track of data. Instead, store each bit as a byte (or even a word) so that you can quickly determine its value. It is much faster to check to see if an entire byte is nonzero than trying to test a specific bit in an integer.

- **Use register variables.** Keeping integer, short, and byte values in CPU registers (by declaring them as `register`) you tell the compiler/optimizer that the variable is frequently accessed and should have its own dedicated CPU register. This technique is especially effective in faster CPUs because it not only makes the data quickly accessible to the CPU but also avoids slow reads and writes to memory or caches. Although some compilers ignore the `register` declarations and other architectural restrictions may limit how many `register` variables really wind up in the CPU register set, there is still no harm in declaring them that way.

- **Use multiply instead of divide.** Few FPUs have divide instructions, and those that do, run slower than multiply. So, instead of dividing a number by a value, multiply it by its reciprocal. Take the following program, for example:

```
 1   double a, b;
 2   main()
 3   {
 4       register i;
 5
 6       for(i=0; i < 10000000; ++i)
 7       {
 8           b = a / 4 ;
 9       }
10   }
```

This program takes 13.3 seconds to run on SPARCstation 2. Now, if you change line 8 to

```
 8           b = a * 0.25 ;
```

the execution time drops to 4.7 seconds or almost three times faster! The difference may be more or less dramatic depending on your FPU architecture.

The only drawback to this technique is the potential lack of accuracy produced by inversion of small numbers.

- **Use shift instead of integer divide or multiply.** This is an old assembly language trick that takes advantage of the fact that instead of multiplying a number by two, you can simply shift it to the left once. Likewise, for divide by two, simply shift to the right once. The same goes for any power of 2. For example, to multiply by eight, simply shift to the left three times.

  The speed-up comes from the fact that shift operations are often many times faster than divides and even beat integer multiplies. Note that some compilers are smart enough to do this optimization for you automatically

- **Pass structures using pointers only.** If you pass a structure by name (really by value) to a function, the compiler makes a complete copy of it on stack. This is not too bad if the structure is only a few bytes, but it quickly becomes a problem if it is hundreds of bytes long. So, pass a pointer to it assuming that the function does not think it has a private copy of it passed to it.

13.8 Dynamic Shared Libraries

As we mentioned in Chapter 2, the kernel shares the text segment among multiple copies of a program. But it does so only if all the executables are loaded from identical images (i.e., all have to have the same inode). This level of granularity is too coarse for efficient usage of memory. Take the standard `libc` library used in many UNIX utilities and applications. Ideally, the system should load one copy of `libc` in memory and let all user processes share it. But, because traditional implementations of UNIX link `libc` directly into the application image, this is not possible.

Shared libraries are a potential answer to this problem. By keeping the library separate from an application, the text segment of the library can be shared among multiple applications. Programs would then attach to the shared library at runtime.

The first implementation of shared libraries required that routines in the library be located at fixed addresses in the user address space (which had to be reserved) and hence the term *Static* Shared Libraries. They did not catch on because this restriction was too limiting. All current implementations use Dynamic Shared Objects (DSOs), which allow library routines to be attached (linked) at arbitrary locations in user programs.

The flexibility of dynamic shared libraries comes at the price of longer start-up time. Because the application is not fully linked before execution (it is left as Position Independent Code or PIC form), it needs to be "linked on the fly" as it is being loaded into memory. A runtime linker generates a final executable before the process starts to run. This results in slower program load time in addition to higher CPU usage. In essence, the linking step needs to be repeated every time a program is executed rather than once at compile time.

Dynamic linking is fine in environments where a program is started once and used for a long time (e.g., a CAD application). But in cases where many small programs are executed frequently (e.g., in general time-sharing use), shared libraries cause significant performance degradation. The overhead of linking such programs on every invocation can double or triple their total execution time.

Another unexpected overhead is the performance degradation in functional call sequences. Due to the requirement for PIC generation, function calls must be performed through a jump table instead of a direct jump instruction. The slowdown is especially noticeable on functions with two or fewer arguments, which unfortunately are the most common.

Last but not least, you should keep in mind that *dynamic shared libraries do not necessarily save any memory.* In some cases, they can actually cause the memory usage of your application to increase! This occurs if you try to use just a few small functions out of a large library. When you link an application statically (i.e., at compile/link time), the only functions included in your executable are the ones that you call. In contrast, when you use dynamic shared libraries, the entire data segment of the shared library would be attached to your application regardless of whether you use one function or a hundred out of the library. This can add considerably to the size of your process. To see this problem in action, let's look at a sample program:

```
% cat lib.c
main()
{
        sleep(60);
}
```

Now, let's compile this both as a dynamic shared object (the default on SunOS 4.1) and static (by using the compiler option, -Bstatic):

```
% cc -Bstatic lib.c -o static_lib
% cc lib.c -o dynamic_lib
```

Before running these programs, let's look at their static size:

```
den[17]% size *lib
text     data    bss     dec      hex
8192     8192    0       16384    4000      dynamic_lib
16384    8192    0       24576    6000      static_lib
```

On the surface, it seems that the static version is larger due to inclusion of the libc function, sleep, in the executable (the text size doubled to 16384 from 8192). But when you run the two versions and look at the dynamic memory usage, quite a different picture appears:

```
den[14]% ps -l
        F UID    PID   PPID CP PRI NI  SZ  RSS WCHAN      STAT TT  TIME COMMAND
20008201 403   5298   5268  0  15  0  16  172 kernelma S   p6  0:00 dynamic_lib
20008201 403   5299   5268  0  15  0  16   28 kernelma S   p6  0:00 static_lib
```

The resident set size or the actual memory usage of the dynamic version is 178 Kbytes versus only 28 Kbytes for the static version. Shared libraries in this case increased the

292 Chap. 13 Optimizing User Programs

memory required by almost sixfold instead of reducing it! Of course, our test is an exaggerated example of what could happen. So, the best advice is to link your application both ways and see whether any benefit is gained from shared libraries.

13.9 Process Timing Mechanism

Because much of the information in this chapter relies on profiling and timing user programs, it is very important to understand how they really work and their limitations. Otherwise, you may wind up chasing nonproblems.

The kernel keeps track of the amount of CPU time a process is using as it runs whether it is being timed or not. The various versions of `time` simply query this information from the kernel.

The elapsed time is simply computed by finding the difference in the current date/time before and after a process runs. Again, this is done by asking the kernel for the current data and time.

The main mechanism in the kernel for time keeping is the clock ticks. These are hardware interrupts that occur 50 to 100 times a second. On every interrupt, the kernel simply increments an internal counter, which represents the total number of ticks since January 1, 1970. (This value can readily be converted to a standard date and time format using library functions.)

On every clock tick, the kernel also checks to see if it is running a process. If so, it increments one of two counters (user and system time), depending on whether the process was interrupted while executing its user code or while in the kernel (presumably because of a system call).

13.9.1 Basic Timing Inaccuracies

The kernel measurement of system time (for each process) is inherently flawed and should not be trusted to a great degree. The reason is that the kernel does not really try to determine on whose behalf it is executing its code when a clock interrupt arrives. Let's look at what happens when a disk interrupt occurs on behalf of sleeping process A (which has issued a disk I/O request) when process B is running user code. The CPU stops executing process B and branches to the disk interrupt handler in the kernel. Now, if a clock interrupt arrives in the middle of the disk interrupt, *the kernel incorrectly increments the system time for process B because it is the currently executing process.* The system time for process A should have been incremented instead because the disk interrupt is being processed on its behalf.

A related problem occurs when a process is being timed that itself is doing a lot of I/O requests. In this case, the process may get undercharged for its CPU usage. The reason is that when a process issues an I/O request, the kernel puts it to sleep and branches to the idle loop and waits there if it has nothing else to do. If a clock interrupt arrives later when the kernel is executing the disk interrupt code, the kernel does not charge the process since it thinks it was not running anyone (it was interrupted in the middle of the idle loop). *The bottom line is that it is best not to trust the per-process system time if there are a lot of I/O activities in the system.*

Even though the elapsed time computation is fairly accurate, the timing can be greatly affected by other activities in the system. For example, if you run two copies of a CPU-bound program, the real time for each copy doubles while the user and system times remain relatively constant. This is because the CPU has twice as much to do and, naturally, takes twice as long to run both jobs. (The user and system times are not affected because they are computed on a per-process basis.) *Therefore, it is critical to make sure that the system is completely idle before trusting the real time.*

A common mistake is to equate the elapsed time with the CPU usage of the program. Although this is true of some highly CPU-bound programs, it is not the case for a large percentage of applications you are likely to run. The reason is that the elapsed time not only includes the amount of time a program was running on the CPU, but also how long it was waiting in the system. The components that make up the elapsed time are

$$Real\_Time = User\_Time + System\_Time + I/O\_Wait\_Time +$$
$$CPU\_Wait\_Time + User\_Sleep\_Time \qquad (13.1)$$

I/O_Wait_Time is how long a process has spent waiting for its I/O request (e.g., a disk or terminal `read`) to finish. CPU_Wait_Time is the amount of time a process was waiting in the run queue before it was run by the CPU. User_Sleep_Time is any idle time due to the process calling any system calls (e.g., `sleep`) that resulted in the process being put to sleep.

On an otherwise idle system, CPU_Wait_Time is negligible and can be ignored. Also, user processes rarely give up the CPU on their own; therefore, User_Sleep_Time is also typically zero. Using these assumptions, we can arrive at a useful metric for measuring the I/O wait time of a process:

$$I/O\_Wait\_Time = Real\_Time - User\_Time - System\_Time \qquad (13.2)$$

As an example, if a program takes 50 seconds to run and the sum of its user and system times were 5 seconds, the I/O wait time would be 45 seconds. This immediately tells you that the performance of the program has little to do with the speed of the CPU, which is an important observation.

13.9.2 Profiling Mechanism and Limitations

As you have already seen, profiling programs involve counting the number of times each function is called along with time spent in each. Counting each time a function is called requires that additional code be added to the entry point of every function in the program. This new code simply increments a counter corresponding to the specific function that is being called. The code is automatically generated by the compiler when you specify the -p option. Therefore, by its nature, profiling code increases the function call overhead and is the main reason for the increased execution time of profiled programs.

Timing the amount of time spent in each function is done with the help of the kernel. The profiling library routines that get attached to your program notify the kernel upon program start-up that the application is being profiled. From then on, anytime the kernel receives a clock interrupt, it checks to see if it interrupted the user code of a profiled program. If so, it increments a counter in a user array corresponding to the interrupted *program counter value*. It is the job of the profiling programs (prof and gprof) to accumulate all the program counter samples that are within the boundaries of a function to arrive at the total time spent in that function.

> *Because the kernel requires a separate counter for each possible program counter value, the timing buffer and hence the size of a profiled program can grow substantially.*

The size of the profiling array is directly proportional to the text size of the process divided by the minimum instruction size. For example, if you are profiling a program that has a 1-Mbyte text segment and instructions always start on 32-bit boundaries, then the profiling buffer needs to have at least 256,000 counters. Assuming a counter size of 2 bytes, the program size grows by 0.5 Mbyte when you profile it. The increased data size sometimes causes profiled programs to fail due to lack of adequate swap space or too low of a soft limit imposed on the data segment size (see the limit section of the C shell manual page).

Although call counting is mostly reliable, the same can not be said of the function timing. Because the CPU can execute thousands of instructions in a single clock tick, it is possible for the profiling tools to completely miss how much time certain routines are using. Luckily, this is not much of a hindrance because, if a routine gets called frequently enough, chances are good that the clock ticks will eventually catch some invocations of it. If a function gets called infrequently with very short execution, the profiled time incorrectly shows as zero. Fortunately, these functions do not need optimization, so this is not much of a problem in real life.

As we mentioned, profiling tools save the profiling data in special buffers (sometimes called buckets) inside the user program. Once a profiled program exits, a special library routine (that is automatically linked with your program when you specify profiling) saves this data to a disk file. If the program exits abnormally (or never at all), the data never get saved, and you will not be able to see the profiling data. For example, a network daemon process that runs forever cannot be profiled. One commonly used solution is to add a special mechanism to the program to force it to exit on demand (for example, a SIGUSR signal that can be sent to it with the kill program).

13.10 Profiling in Languages Other Than C

Although a C program was used in this chapter as an example, profiling is not limited to the C language alone. Depending on the diligence of your UNIX vendor, you may also be able to use the profiling tools on programs written in FORTRAN and other languages. On the other hand, assembly language support is generally limited to measurement of time spent in each routine and not the call count statistics. Although it is possible to modify assembly programs and add the necessary code to entry point of each function to perform the call counting, it requires extensive knowledge of the function call protocol and how profiling routines work—both of which are somewhat involved. Because assembly language usage is rare in UNIX programs, this should not be much of a hindrance.

If you really need the call counting information and do not mind the timing result to be skewed a bit, you can modify your program to call a C wrapper function that simply calls the assembly language routine. Then, the number of calls to this C routine is the same as the ones to the assembly language. C language macros and conditional compilation with `ifdefs` can be used to turn this "kludge" on and off quickly.

13.11 Results and Conclusions

UNIX profiling tools provide most of the information necessary for optimization of UNIX programs. Call graph profilers such as `gprof` are especially powerful tools, useful not only for optimization purposes but also as tools for analyzing the dynamic behavior of programs. Given some knowledge of common optimization techniques, programs can be sped up with little effort.

Bibliography

Listed below are the books I consulted in preparation for writing this text. While some are more useful than others, they all make valuable companions to this text.

Bregman, Phyllis Eve and Sally A. Browning [1993]. *UNIX System V Performance Management*, PTR Prentice Hall, Englewood Cliffs, NJ.

Cockcroft, Adrian [1995]. *Solaris Performance Tuning*, PTR Prentice Hall, Englewood Cliffs, NJ.

DEC [1994]. *DEC OSF/1 System Tuning and Performance Management*, Digital Equipment Corporation, Maynard, MA.

Dowd, Kevin [1993]. *High Performance Computing*, O'Reilly & Associates, Inc., Sebastopol, CA.

Gray, Jim [1993]. *The Benchmark Handbook for Database and Transaction Processing Systems*, Morgan Kaufmann Publishers, Inc., San Mateo, CA.

IBM [1994]. *AIX Versions 3.2 and 4.1 Performance Tuning Guide*, International Business Machine Corporation. Part number SC23-2365-03.

Loukides, Mike [1990]. *System Performance Tuning*, O'Reilly & Associates, Inc., Sebastopol, CA.

Mason, Susan A. [1994]. *SBus Handbook*, PTR Prentice Hall, Englewood Cliffs, NJ.

Miscovich, Gina and David Simon [1994]. *The SCO Performance Tuning Handbook*, PTR Prentice Hall, Englewood Cliffs, NJ.

Patterson, D. A. and J. L. Hennessy, [1990]. *Computer Architecture: A Quantitative Approach*, Morgan Kaufmann Publishers, San Mateo, CA.

Santifaller, Michael [1991]. *TCP/IP and NFS Internetworking in a UNIX Environment*, Addison-Wesley (Deutschland), Gmbh.

SCO [1992]. *System Administrator's Guide, Operating System, Networking, and DOS Services*, The Santa Cruz Operations, Inc., Santa Cruz, CA.

Spuler, David [1992]. *C++ and C Efficiency*, PTR Prentice Hall, Englewood Cliffs, NJ.

SunSoft [1993]. *Solaris 2.3 Administering Security, Performance, and Accounting*, Sun Microsystems Inc., Mountain View, CA. Part number 801-5282-10.

Index